THE POETRY OF PHILIP LARKIN
A STUDY IN LONG PERSPECTIVES

S. N. PRASAD

RoseDog Books
PITTSBURGH, PENNSYLVANIA 15238

RoseDog Books
585 Alpha Drive
Suite 103
Pittsburgh, PA 15238
Visit our website at www.rosedogbookstore.com

ISBN: 978-1-63867-798-7
eISBN: 978-1-63867-872-4

THE POETRY OF PHILIP LARKIN
A STUDY IN LONG PERSPECTIVES

In the loving memory of my second son,
[Er.] ASHUTOSH KUMAR (1971 – 1999)
S. N. Prasad

Listen to presences inside poems,
Let them take you where they will.

Follow those private hints,
And never leave the premises.

Rumi

Table of Contents

    "Church Going"
    "Toads"*
    (*This poem has been analysed together with
    "Toads Revisited" in the next chapter.)
    "Deceptions"
    "I Remember, I Remember"

    "Here"
    "Mr Bleaney"
    "Nothing to be Said"
    "Naturally the Foundation will Bear Your Expenses"
    "Home is so Sad"
    "Toads Revisited"
    "Water"
    "The Whitsun Weddings"

Preface

A poet who writes that "Nothing, like something, happens anywhere" and that whole "nations" live life as vague "as [that of] weeds," and also that all our ways are "Ways of slow dying," has to be taken very seriously. Philip Larkin is not the only post-modern writer to hold these and similar views in his creative writing. All major writers of his age , and many even of earlier ages, hold/ have held a grim view of the human situation. And the mainstream scientists of the highest rank have been warning us that if we do not mend our "days and ways," disaster will overwhelm us. Larkin's major poems have to be placed in very wide contexts to understand the message they convey, which is to tell us truth about everything, from "celestial recurrences,/ The day the flowers come,/ And when the birds go" to the mores of our psycho-social-cultural life. This is all the more necessary in view of what he says in these lines: "In a humanist society, art – and especially modern, or current art – assumes great importance, and to lose touch with it is parallel to losing one's faith in a religious age." Ours is not a religious age; that is an age long gone by. We live in a humanist society. A humanist society has its foundations in a rationalist outlook or system of thought which attaches prime importance to human rather than divine or supernatural matters. In such a society art is not only the mainstay of man's spiritual life but also a means of his cultural rejuvenation. And this mainstay or means must have the strength of truth. In his poetry, at least in his major poems, and their number is large enough to earn him the status of a major poet in the English language, Philip Larkin aims at bringing about a spiritual regeneration in us, lest we should come to a dead end in our evolutionary progress.

In the present work, I have analysed thirty of Larkin's major poems which, as I feel, convey the poet's message as clearly as works of art can. The selection is a purely personal choice and is without prejudice to the merit of some of Larkin's other equally major poems.

S. N. Prasad

CHAPTER ONE
Introduction: "Long Perspectives"

The world is my country...science my religion:
Christiaan Huygens

Saul Bellow, in his novel *Humboldt's Gift* (1973), wrote these great lines regarding the sorry existential condition of man's life: "But now our daily moonshines are such, our preoccupations are so low, language has become so debased, the words so blunted and damaged, we've said such stupid and dull things, that the higher beings hear only babbling and grunting and TV commercials– the dog-food level of things."[1]

Earlier, Graham Greene, in his novel *The Comedians* (1966), wrote these lines which make us feel ashamed of complete lack of dignity in human existence: "If the spirit hovers, as some believe, for an hour or two over the cadaver it has abandoned, what banalities it is doomed to hear, while it waits in a despairing hope that some serious thought will be uttered, some expression which will lend dignity to the life it has left."[2]

William Golding, in his very first novel, *Lord of the Flies*, wrote that human civilization was "in ruins"[3] and the title of one of his later novels, *Darkness Visible*, tells us bluntly that our world is now no better than the hell in Milton's *Paradise Lost*. And in a prose piece entitled "Fable," he wrote: "man produces evil as the bee produces honey."[4] Albert Camus, in his Nobel Prize acceptance speech in 1954, spoke thus of the debased kind of life the people of his generation lived: "Heir to a corrupt history, in which are mingled fallen revolutions, technology gone mad, dead gods and worn-out ideologies, where mediocre powers can destroy all yet no longer know how to convince, where intelligence has debased itself to become the servant of hatred and oppression…"[5]

Samuel Beckett, in his play *Waiting for Godot*, says that "People are bloody ignorant apes"[6] and with a unique creative power shows that human civilization has gone rancid/putrid and man's essential being is decaying. Vladimir in that play sounds right when he says that he and Estragon – the two tramps in the play – belong to "the foul brood to which a cruel fate" has consigned them. Even so, he claims that "at this place, at this moment of time all mankind is us."[7] This is indeed tragic. And Albert Camus, in his comment on Kafka's novel *The Trial*, writes:

> In *The Trial*, Joseph K is accused. But he doesn't know of what. He is doubtless eager to defend himself, but doesn't know why. The lawyers find his case difficult. Meanwhile he does not neglect to love, to eat, or to read his paper. Then he is judged. But the courtroom is very dark. He doesn't understand much. He merely assumes that he is condemned, but to what, he barely wonders. At times he suspects the same and he continues living. Some time later, two well-dressed and polite gentlemen come to get him and invite him to follow them. Most courteously they lead him into a wretched suburb, put his head on a stone and slit his throat. Before dying, the condemned man says merely: 'like a dog.'[8]

(In my edition of the novel, they do not slit his throat. One of the two takes out a "butcher's knife" from its sheath, then they pass it to each other several times across K's face and then, while one of them firmly catches hold of K's throat, the other "thrust(s) his knife into his heart and… [turns] it there twice"). Camus also omits the last words Kafka wrote as a comment on the utterance of Joseph K while dying like a dog: "it was as if he meant the shame of it to outlive him."[9] But speaking of people's opinion as to what *The Trial* means, Camus says, "People have spoken of an image of the human condition," and adds, "to be sure." The human condition is shameful.

We will now go to three scientists to listen to what they have to say about man and his "days and ways."[10] On the very first page of his book *Plant and Planet*, Anthony Huxley writes:

This book takes what one might call 'the plant's-eye-view.' But the eye is also squinting at the human race. Plants do many things that we can and many things that we cannot. Man is as the blink of an eye in evolutionary terms, while plants are the earliest form of life; it is a great pity that in this blink man has turned into such a scourge of nature.[11]

And J.B.S. Haldane writes these grim lines regarding the future of man in the context of evolution of life on our planet:

And the usual course taken by an evolving line has been one of degeneration. It seems to me altogether possible that man will take this course unless he takes conscious control of his evolution within the next few thousand years. It may very well be that mind, at our level, is not adequate for such a task…If that is the case we are perhaps the rather sorry climax of evolution, and less can be said in favour of existence than many of us suppose.[12]

And Sigmund Freud says this about the poor civilizational achievement of man, so poor that it is not worth defending at all:

While mankind has made continual advances in its control over nature and may expect to make still greater ones, it is not possible to establish with certainty that a similar advance has been made in the management of human affairs, and probably at all periods, just as now once again, many people have asked themselves whether what little civilization has thus acquired is indeed worth defending at all.[13]

We shall also go to a historian and listen to what he has to say about the origins, nature and achievement of the Sapiens. Quite early in his book, *Sapiens: A Brief History of Humankind*, Yuval Noah Harari writes, "Just 6 million years ago, a single female ape had two daughters. One became the ancestor of all chimpanzees, the other is our own grandmother (p.5)." Later on in his book he says many unflattering things about man. On page 69 he writes, "The wandering bands of story-telling Sapiens were the most important and most destructive force the animal kingdom had ever produced." On page74 he says, "the historical record makes *Homo sapiens* look like an ecological serial killer." On page 82 he writes, "We have the dubious distinction of being the deadliest species in the annals of biology." On page 465 he says, "Unfortunately, the Sappiens regime on earth has so far produced little that we can be proud of." And so on. The very first chapter of his book is entitled "An Animal of no Significance."

And the last passage of the book(p.466) makes a grim reading.

And now we will listen to the beloved Bard when he speaks thus of the tragic condition of human existence: "there is so great a fever on goodness that the dissolution of it must cure it" (*Measure for Measure*, Act III. sc.ii, ll 216-217).

We shall once again go to Saul Bellow, this time to his novel *Herzog*. In a passage in this novel, he says that while ordinary people are "dying" for want of even an atom of "good sense, clarity, truth," those privileged to have had social, economic, educational, intellectual advantages have not only failed the people, but their life-style has also been causing greater and greater harm to human existence, qualitatively speaking:

> The people who come to evening classes are only ostensibly after culture. Their great need, their hunger, is for good sense, clarity, truth – even an atom of it. People are dying – it is no metaphor – for lack of something real to carry home when day is done. See how willing they are to accept the wildest nonsense. O Smithers, my whiskered brother! What responsibility we bear, in this fat country of ours! Think what America could mean to the world. Then see what it is. What a breed it might have produced. But look at us – at you, at me. Read the paper, if you can bear to.[14]

One can go on quoting similar views expressed by great scientists, philosophers, creative writers and thinkers regarding the sorry, shameful condition of human existence which man has landed himself in with his own folly and criminality. Sir James Frazer is right when he observes: "If mankind had always been logical and wise, history would not be a long chronicle of folly and crime."[15] Our present existential situation is so sorry that William Golding asks us this question in *The Scorpion God:* "Do you suppose any God who keeps his eyes open can do other than weep for what he sees?"[16] The French novelist J. K. Huysmans, in his novel *Against Nature*, speaks of the "pestilential filth" that has infected the very life-breath of human civilization:

It was all over; the bourgeois were guzzling like picknickers from paper bags among the imposing ruins of the Church – ruins which had become a place of assignation, a pile of debris defiled by unspeakable jokes and scandalous jests. Could it be that the terrible God of Genesis and the pale martyr of Golgotha would not prove their existence once for all by renewing the cataclysms of old by rekindling the rain of fire that once consumed those accursed towns, the cities of the plain? Could it be that this slime would go on spreading until it covered with its pestilential filth this old world where now only seeds of inequity sprang up and only harvests of shame were gathered.[17]

Scott Fitzerald expresses his anger at the trivial and downright bad existence that his generation of men lived in these words in his novel *This Side of Paradise*: "For the first time in his life he rather longed for death to roll over his generation, obliterating their petty fevers and struggles and exultations."[18] And in his novel *Darkness Visible*, William Golding wrote, "We're damned with our own triviality."[19]

The question that now stares us in the face is whether man will meet with an ignominious death as millions of other species met with in the past or he will pull himself by his bootstraps as no God will come to his rescue. The anthropologist Richard Carrington is absolutely right when he says in his book *A Million Years of Man*: "It is not…any longer possible for rational people to regard man as the spoiled child of the cosmos, eternally protected by a benevolent personal Creator, and occupying in the earth a favourable ante-chamber to Heaven"[20] (AMYoM, p.288). And Saul Bellow expresses a similar view when he says to us in his novel *Herzog*: "This is a bourgeois civilization. I am not using this term in its Marxian sense. In the vocabulary of modern art and religion it is bourgeois to consider that the universe was made for our safe use and to give us comfort and support."[21] And on page 320 of the same novel, he tells us something regarding the descent of Man that horrifies us:

Latest intelligence from the Olduvai Gorge in East Africa gives ground to suppose that man did not descend from a peaceful arboreal ape, but from a carnivorous, terrestrial type, bad news...for the optimists, for the lenient hopeful view of human nature.22

And the philosopher John H. Hick, in his book *Philosophy of Religion(p.95)*, writes, "human life is essentially a form of animal life and human civilization a refined jungle in which self-concern operates more subtly, but not less surely, than the animal tooth snd claw."

It is not that man's fate is sealed for ever. But human nature being what it is – Joseph Conrad says in his novella *The Shadow-Line*: "Human nature is, I fear, not very nice right through. There are ugly spots in it."[23] And Anton Chekhov, in his short story "An Artist's Story," writes:

We are higher beings, and if we were really to recognize the whole force of human genius and lived only for higher ends, we should in the end become like gods. But that will never be – mankind will degenerate till no traces of genius remain."

One cannot, therefore, be very optimistic about man's future. Even so, if man does not want his throat slit by an inexorable fate and die an ignoble death, inevitable if he persists in his perverse ways, he will have to make a Herculean efforts to ensure his survival. There are some among us, although they constitute a microscopic minority among seven billion or more human beings living now on this planet, who are, in Steven Weinberg's words, not content to comfort themselves with tales of gods and giants, or to confine their thoughts to the daily affairs of life, they also build telescopes and satellites and accelerators and sit on their desks for endless hours working out the meaning of the data they gather. The effort to understand the universe is one of the very few things that lifts human life a little above the level of farce, and gives it some of the grace of tragedy.[24]

Man can understand the universe because of him having had "some special relation" to it and because "human life is not just a more-or-less farcical outcome of a chain of accidents reaching back to the first three minutes of the universe coming into existence, but we are somehow built in from the beginning."[25]

As we are built in from the beginning, it is necessary for us to trace back our origin to the origin of the universe itself. The imperative need of such a task has been emphasized by many thinkers. M. R. Cohen, in his book *The Faith of a Liberal*, writes thus about the significance of our "cosmic roots and surroundings:" "And our view of the human scene becomes narrow, unillumined, and passionate if we do not rise above its immediate urgency and see it in its cosmic roots and surroundings."[26] Carl Sagan asserts in his book *Cosmos* that man's future depends on how well he understands his relationship with, or his place and status in, cosmos: "I believe our future depends on how well we know this Cosmos in which we float like a moat of dust in the morning sky."[27] And Richard Carrington tells us that "man and his planetary home are ultimately the products of cosmic forces" and that "The earth's climates are related to the action of cosmic forces, such as the intensified or reduced sunspot activity and the filtering effect of dust particles or clouds of gas far out in space" (AMYoM, p.8). He asks us to "realize that the whole of man's existence, from the most misguided machinations of his politicians to the highest achievements of his greatest artists and thinkers, is indissolubly bound up with the slightest physical change in the sun and the movements of the stars in their courses" (Ibid. pp.6-7), and so he writes in the last chapter of his book: "The nature of man can be understood only by relating him so far as our limited vision will allow to his context in space and time. It is impossible to understand the human phenomenon except by considering it as an aspect of the universe as a whole" (Ibid. p.300).

It is obvious that it is of utmost importance for us to know the whole truth about our existence, which for the most part, if not entirely, at present lies buried in the debris of man's superstitions, irresponsibilities, follies, and crimes accumulated over the millennia. To resurrect this truth and thereby make man see his essential nature, we will have to go to sciences because, as Martin Heidegger writes in his *Existence and Being*, "What the sciences accomplish, ideally speaking, is an approximation to the essential nature of all things."[28] Julian Huxley says that science performs two very important functions: "control and comprehension." With regard to comprehension, he writes, "The comprehension may be of the universe in which we live, or of ourselves, or of the relations between ourselves and our world."[29] Henri Bergson says that even philosophy must now be scientific, "Nowhere is it clearer that philosophers cannot today content themselves with vague generalities but must follow the scientists in experimental detail and discuss the results with them."[30] No wonder, the Egyptian novelist Naguib Mahfouz says, "If the prophets were sent back today, they would surely choose science as their divine message."[31] And Sir Charles Sherrington, in his great book *Man on his Nature* (MohN p.118), tells us that John Keats thought that the highest material for poetic creation could be found in scientific view of the world. Sherrington writes, "We can understand Keats' sighing against science, 'there was an awful rainbow once in heaven!'" However, Sherrington says, "he[Keats] was 'to find,' as has been written of him, 'material in the scientific view of the world for the highest achievement of poetry.'"

We cannot but agree with Julian Huxley that man's comprehension should, first, be of the universe in which he exists, howsoever insignificantly. We shall begin our effort to comprehend the universe in a very modest way with a look at the following passage in Steven Weinberg's book already referred to above – the passage in which he tells us how our universe (there are perhaps more than one universe) came into existence:

> In the beginning there was an explosion. Not an explosion like those familiar on earth starting from a definite center and spreading out to engulf more and more of the circum-ambient air, but an explosion which occurred simultaneously everywhere, filling all space from the beginning, with every particle of matter rushing apart from every other particle.[32]

This explosion, also known as the Big Bang and responsible for bringing into existence space-time continuum, took place about 14 billion years ago. Weinberg writes, "At about one hundredth of a second, the earliest time about which we can speak with any confidence, the temperature of the universe was about a hundred thousand million (10^{11}) degrees centigrade." At such a high temperature, "none of the components of ordinary matter, molecules or atoms, or even the nuclei of atoms, could have held together."[33] Further, Weinberg writes: "rushing apart in this explosion consisted various so-called elementary particles....These particles – electrons, positrons, neutrinos, photons – were continually being created out of pure energy, and then after short lives being annihilated again."[34]

But the temperature of the universe kept dropping fast and at the end of three minutes after the explosion it came down to one thousand million degrees. As regards "the contents of the universe" at this point of time, Weinberg writes:

> At the end of first three minutes the contents of the universe were mostly in the form of light, neutrinos, and anti-neutrinos. There was still a small amount of nuclear material, now consisting of about 73 percent hydrogen and 27 percent helium, and an equally small number of electrons left over from the era of electron-positron annihilation.[35]

Weinberg says that this cosmic matter kept cooling down and getting less and less dense. About the density of the "cosmic soup," as he calls it, at one hundredth of a second after the Big Bang, it was "about four thousand million (4×10^9) times that of water."[36] But this matter kept rushing apart, "becoming steadily cooler and less dense." Continuing, Weinberg tells us how, after a few hundred thousand years, galaxies came to be formed:

> Much later, after a few hundred thousand years, it could become cool enough for electrons to join with nuclei to form atoms of hydrogen and helium. The resulting gas would begin under the influence of gravitation to form clamps, which would ultimately condense to form the galaxies and stars of the present universe. However, the ingredients with which the stars would begin their life would be just those prepared in the first three minutes.[37]

At this point it is necessary to know a few facts about the galaxies and the stars. First of all we should know that these galaxies have been rushing apart from one another ever since their coming into existence. Fred Hoyle writes thus: "the galaxies are rushing away from each other at enormous speeds, which for the most distant galaxies that we can see with the biggest telescopes become comparable with the speed of light itself" (TNotU, pp. 104-105). The next important thing to know about these heavenly bodies is that there are vast empty spaces between any two galaxies or any two stars. Fred Hoyle call them "background material" and writes: "the galaxies occupy only a very small fraction of the whole space….the background material outweighs by a large margin all the galaxies put together….it is the background material that controls the universe as a whole" (TNotU, p.102).

Carl Sagan gives a more thrilling description of the inter-galactic dark spaces. He writes:

> No planet or star or galaxy can be typical, because the Cosmos is mostly empty. The only typical place is within the vast, cold, universal vacuum, the everlasting night of intergalactic space so strange and desolate that, by comparison, planets and stars and galaxies seem achingly rare and lovely.[38]

He writes further on the same point in a more beautiful and figurative language:

> From an intergalactic vantage point we would see, strewn like sea froth on the waves of space, innumerable faint, wispy tendrils of light. These are the galaxies. Some are solitary wanderers, most inhabit communal clusters, huddling together, drifting endlessly, in the great cosmic dark.[39]

This "cosmic dark," known as "dark matter," Weinberg says, not only "does not consist of luminous stars…it is not even present in the form of atomic particles – protons, neutrons and electrons – that make ordinary atoms."[40] Even the individual star systems in a galaxy are not next-door neighbours. Instead, "each is an island in space, quarantined from its neighbours by the light years."[41] And Richard Carrington tells us, "the size of even the largest stars is as nothing compared to the vast distances that separate them." And as far as the galaxies are concerned – Carrington calls them "star cities" – they are "spread out in space at distances of between $4^{1/2}$ and 2 million light years from one another to the observable horizon of the universe" (AMYoM, pp.3-4).

And now it is necessary to know something about the size of the universe. Stephen Hawking says that at the time of the Big Bang singularity "the universe is thought to have zero size" and its density was infinite. But now the observable size, observable with the most powerful telescopes, of the universe is "a million million million million (1 with 24 zeros after it) miles."[42] And in this observable universe there are some hundred thousand million galaxies and in each galaxy there are some hundred thousand million stars. Our galaxy, known as the Milky Way, is just one among the hundred thousand million galaxies. Steven Weinberg writes thus about our galaxy:

> It is now thought that the Milky Way consists of a flat disk of stars, with a diameter of 80,000 light years and a thickness of 6,000 light years. It also possesses a spherical halo of stars, with a diameter of about 100,000 light years. The total mass is usually estimated at about 100 thousand million solar masses. The solar system is about 30,000 light years from the centre of the disk... The disk rotates, with speeds ranging up to about 250 kilometer per second, and exhibits giant spiral arms.[43]

Stephen Hawking says that "the stars in the spiral arms orbit around its [Milky Way's] centre about every several hundred million years. Our sun is just an ordinary average-sized yellow star near the inner edge of one of the spiral arms."[44]

What is the status of our Earth in the mind-boggling vastness of the universe? Richard Carrington says that in comparison with the "spatial environment" of the universe "our earth is thus seen to be far smaller and less noticeable than a speck of dust floating in the Pacific Ocean" (AMYoM, p.4). Carl Sagan calls the Earrth "a mere mote of dust circling a humdrum star in the remotest corner of an obscure galaxy."[45] And Fred Hoyle writes with very humour: "if some cosmic jester were to grab hold of the Earth and were to put us near such a body [catastrophic outburst of a supernova] the whole of the Earth would be entirely crushed and would be spread as thin scum over the surface of the body" (TNotU, p.79), that is, the supernova.

This entire cosmic show – and our earth, though no more than a mote of dust floating in the cosmic space, is contained in the cosmos – is created from energy. Werner Heisenberg, in his book *Physics and Philosophy*, refers to the views of several ancient Greek philosophers regarding the nature of the "fundamental substance" or "the ultimate building blocks of matter." When he comes to Heraclitus, he finds that Heraclitus regarded fire as "the basic element."[46] Commenting on Heraclitus' concept, he writes:

We may remark at this point that modern physics is in some ways extremely near to the doctrines of Heraclitus. If we replace the word 'fire' by the word 'energy' we can almost repeat his statements word for word from the modern point of view. Energy is in fact the substance from which all elementary particles, all atoms and therefore all things are made, and energy is that which moves. Energy is a substance, since its total amount does not change, and the elementary particles can actually be made from this substance as is seen in many experiments on the creation of elementary particles. Energy may be called the fundamental cause for all change in the world.[47]

A few pages on, Heisenberg repeats what he says here about energy. On page 35 of his book he writes:

Since mass and energy are, according to the theory of relativity, essentially the same concepts, we may say that all elementary particles consist of energy. This could be interpreted as the primary substance of the world....Energy is in fact that which moves; it may be called the primary cause of all change, and energy can be transferred into matter or heat or light.[48]

Heisenberg reveals to us in a very lucid manner how scientists and engineers have discovered the elementary particles – their number, according to him, is at present 21 – which are direct manifestations of energy and the ultimate building blocks of all phenomena, cosmic as well as terrestrial. Atoms, as we know, has three "building stones of matter"[49] – Heisenberg's phrase – electron, neutron and proton. But Heisenberg writes, "the experiments carried out by cosmic radiation or of the big accelerators have revealed new elementary particles."[50] These particles are "created in these processes of highest energies and disappear again after a short time" – in "roughly only a millionth part of a second." These experiments "have shown the complete mutability of matter." These particles are created "from kinetic energy and annihilated into energy." So Heisenberg writes: "All the elementary particles are made of the same substance, which we may call energy or universal matter; they are just different forms in which matter can appear."[51]

So we see that on the one hand, as Julian Huxley tells us, the diameter of that part of the universe which is "visible with the new 200-inch telescope is nearly a thousand million light years"[52] across and, on the other, this vast show is constituted of elementary particles as small as "a millionth of a millionth of an inch,"[53] as Stephen Hawking puts it.

This perception of the universe in all its vastness and minuteness with all its implications – philosophical, spiritual, moral (also religious) as well as political, social, economic – must be the vital part of the living, everyday consciousness of the educated class of people, if not of the masses. Of course man has to have many more perceptions or cognitions of this kind in order to be the winner in the race for survival of the fittest. Winning the race does not mean winning at the cost of other creatures on our planet or degrading the geological structure of the earth or disturbing the ecological balance of the biosphere. But these things in some detail will form part of this Chapter later. At the moment we will try to see and comprehend how the stars are born and how in that process our earth itself came into existence. Fred Hoyle gives graphic descriptions of how galaxies, stars and planets come into existence. First of all he tells us how galaxies are formed: "Astronomers are generally agreed that the Galaxy started its life as a rotating disk of gas with no stars in it. There would everywhere be small disturbances in the detailed motions of the various bits of gas, especially near the edge of the disk" (TNotU, p. 55).

It was this disk of interstellar gas that gave birth to the hundred thousand million stars through the process of condensation. This disk was, Fred Hoyle tells us, "gravitationally unstable." So it broke up "into a large number of separate irregular clouds." He also tells us that the distance across "an individual cloud lies between ten and a hundred light years."(TNotU, p.56). A star is nothing but a very condensed cloud of interstellar gas. It is so condensed that whereas "a large matchbox" full of interstellar gas would contain, on an average, only about 10,000 atoms, the same matchbox full of the condensed gas in a star like the sun "would contain about a hundred million million million million atoms."(TNotU, p. 54). And yet, he writes, "the total quantity of material comprising the whole interstellar gas seems to be appreciably greater than the material in all the stars [100billionx100 billion] put together" (TNotU, pp. 54-55). And it is this gas, and not the stars, that rules the galaxies. It controls the birth and motions of the stars "and the way in which they are allowed to grow" (TNotU, p.55). Fred Hoyle sums up the whole process of star- formation in these words: "first a whirling disk of gas, then eddies, clouds, condensations and finally stars" (TNotU, p. 57). Then he tells us how planets are formed. He says that there is an "exceptional class of stars – supergiants." A supergiant contains at least ten times as much material as the Sun" and is "at least a thousand times brighter than the Sun." These are massive stars but they "are extremely prodigal at the rate at which they consume hydrogen." So their lifetime is short, "shorter than the age of the Earth" (TNotU, p. 75).) When a supergiant consumes its supply of hydrogen it collapses. Fred Hoyle discusses in fine detail the process of this collapse:

> What happens is that the star breaks up not in one enormous explosion, but through the steady showering off material, rather like a gigantic Catherine wheel. The steadiness of this process is occasionally punctuated by a sort of spluttering in which a cloud of material, roughly comparable with the Earth in total mass, gets ejected into space with a speed of about 10,000,000 miles an hour. When this happens the hot inner regions   of the star become exposed for a while and this leads to a temporary increase in its brightness. Such occurrences are familiar to the astronomer, who refers to them as ordinary novae. But explosions on a far grander scale than this are also observed, and are called supernovae(TNotU, p. 77).

He writes that a supergiant

> collapses catastrophically because of a rapid absorption of energy by the nuclear processes and not because of a slow loss of energy at its surface. Instead of being slow and steady, taking hundreds of thousands of years, the collapse becomes swift and catastrophic. The rotary forces grow rapidly until they become so large that the collapse of most of the star is halted and a large part of it gets flung out into space in a supernova explosion. Such an explosion is the most violent outburst occurring in Nature (TNotU, p. 78).

He compares this outburst with the explosion of a hydrogen bomb and says that compared "with a supernova a hydrogen bomb is a mere trifle" and says that while "a hydrogen bomb would be sufficient to wipe out the whole of London….a supernova is equal in violence to about a million million million million bombs all going off at the same time (TNotU, p. 77). He says that "the Earth actually was at one time a part of a supernova" (TNotU, p.79). And then he says how the planets in the solar system came into existence as a result of this supernova. He says that our Sun had a companion star. This companion star exploded with an extreme violence, that is, a supernova occurred. Fred Hoyle says that when a supernova occurs

> most of the material – that is to say, considerably more material than there is inside the whole of the Sun gets blown out into space as a tremendous cloud of fiercely incandescent gas moving at a speed of several million miles an hour. For a few days the accompanying blaze of light is as great as the total radiation of all the 10,000,000,000 or so stars in the galaxy. It was out of such a holocaust that the Earth and planets were born (TNotU, p. 88).

After the supernova, "a dense stellar nucleus'" of what was our Sun's companion star was left over. The nucleus did not stay with the sun; "it moved off and is now some unrecognized star living in some distant part of the Galaxy" (Ibid. p.88).

Then, Fred Hoyle tells us, this tremendous cloud of incandescent gas "settled down into a flat circular disk that rotated round the Sun – that is to say, it spread out around the Sun and then it settled down into a disk." He says that "the main part" of this gas was "distributed in the regions where the orbits of the great planets, Jupiter, Saturn, Uranus and Neptune lie" (TNotU, p. 90).

Then the process of condensation of this gas began. Fred Hoyle says that "if any particular condensation should ever happen to grow to a certain critical size, which is about 100 miles across, the gravitational pull of the condensation itself would begin to play a dominant role" (TNotU, p. 91) . Its pull reaches out "into the surrounding gas and drags it into the condensation." So a few large bodies – Fred Hoyle calls them "primordial" planets – were formed. The Earth and other small planets – Mercury, Venus, Mars, Pluto – were not formed as a result of primordial condensation. Not even the great planets – Jupiter, Saturn ,Uranus and Neptune – are primordial planets. The primordial planets were very large and rotated on their polar axes in addition to orbiting around the Sun. Fred Hoyle writes:

Once the primordial planets had formed into a compact state, their times of rotation must have become less than about seven hours, and as Lyttleton showed it in 1938, a solid planet rotating as rapidly as this must break up under the power of its own rotation. The great planets must be the main chunks arising from these processes of break-up (TNotU, p.92).

Comparatively "small blobs" broke loose from the primordial planets and started circling round the planets. They are the satellites or moons of the planets. But a few larger blobs "escaped, and these are the five small planets – Venus, Mercury, Mars, Pluto and the Earth." Fred Hoyle sums up his discussion of the origin of the Earth and other planets thus: "there were a number of big primordial planets that broke up about 2,500,000,000 years ago, and one of the bits of the debris was our Earth and another the Moon" (TNotU, p.93).

A. I. Oparin, however, refers to the theory developed by Fresenkov who, "after thoroughly investigating the isotopic composition of meteorite matter" concluded "that the sun and its surrounding planets were formed in a single process associated with the explosion of a supernova in the corresponding region of the galaxy."[54]

Now that our Earth has been created we will try to see and comprehend what happened on its surface – land as well as water – in the course of its 4.6 billion year long history. But before doing that, we will quote a very significant passage from Oparin's book referred to above. It can serve as a good summing up of the whole discussion of the cosmic or inorganic evolution beginning with the Big Bang singularity, which happened 12-20 billion years ago (Oparin's figure), and the successive steps by which galaxies, stars, planets, etc. came into existence down to the creation of our own earth:

> Modern astronomical data show the amazing integration of the entire galactic system into a single entity. The evolution of the universe is represented to us now as a single process of development, where each successive stage is inseparably connected with the previous one and can be understood only by studying this previous stage. Until recently, in discussing the question of the origin of life, the existence of planets like the Earth with specific dimensions and a specific composition

of matter has been somewhat taken for granted. However, now we know that the existence, not only of the Earth, but even many elements necessary for its formation had their source and their history of development in the stellar Universe and can be understood only in the light of a perception of history of the Universe.[55]

Now that we have seen how, through a process of evolution of cosmic matter, our Earth came into existence and how, in the ultimate analysis, the Earth is made from the same cosmic matter as the stars are, our next step in the quest for self-knowledge should be to see how life first originated on the Earth and how this life, through a process of trial and error in which many forms of life were rejected and became extinct, more and more complex forms culminating in the evolution of Man took place. But here we will have a look at the following passage in Stephen Hawking's book *A Brief History of Time*:

> The first one or two thousand million years of the earth's existence were too hot for the development of anything complicated. The remaining three thousand million years or so have been taken up by the slow process of biological evolution, which has led from simplest organisms to beings who are capable of measuring time back to the big bang.[56]

In a table on page 58 of his book, Oparin shows the origin of the Earth "with its present-day mass and composition" as ">4.5" billion years "before our time"; "Differentiation of Earth's material, formation of the Earth's crust" as >4 billion years ago and formation of the oceans as more than three billion years ago.[57] G. Brent Dalrymple says that it is not certain when the Earth's "primordial crust, if such ever existed," was formed. But he says, "Rocks exceeding 3.5 Ga in age are found on all the continents." It is, however, "intriguing," he writes, "that most of the earliest rocks found to date are metamorphosed sedimentary rocks and lava flows rather than igneous crust." But he says that since "the earth has been a tectonically active planet since birth" it is possible that its earliest crust has "long since been destroyed by recycling."[58]

In his book *Evolution in Action*, already referred to above, Julian Huxley speaks of "the comprehensive evolution in all its aspects," by which he means evolution "comprising three main phases." These phases are "the inorganic or, if you like, cosmological; the organic or biological; and the human or psycho-social." He says that these three phases differ "radically" from each other "in their extent, both in space and time, in the methods and mechanisms, by which their self-transformations operate, in their rates of change, in the results which they produce and in the levels of organization which they attain."[59]

These three sectors of the universal process also differ in their time-relations. But, Huxley writes: "The second phase is only possible on the basis of the first, the third on the basis of the second; so that, although all three are in operation today, their origins succeeded each other in time. There was a critical point to be surmounted before the second could arise out of the first, or the third out of the second."[60]

For a detailed study of the evolutionary process in the first sector Huxley refers his readers to "standard works like those of Sir James Jeans or Sir Arthur Eddington, or the more recent picture so vividly sketched by Fred Hoyle in his little book *The Nature of the Universe*." We have already had a look at Fred Hoyle's book as well as some other books regarding the evolutionary process during the first phase. But Huxley himself says some remarkable things about this sector which we will do well to have a look at:

> This sector of reality comprises all the purely physico-chemical aspects of the universe throughout the whole of space, inter-galactic as well as interstellar, all the galaxies, all the stars and stellar nebulae. The diameter of that part of it visible with the new 200-inch telescope is nearly a thousand million light years; and there is a celestial region of unknown size beyond the range of any telescope that we may ever be able to construct.[61]

Regarding the "mechanism" of the "transformations" incessantly going on in this sector, Huxley says that they are due to "physical and very occasionally chemical interaction." He writes further:

> The degree of organization to be found in it is correspondingly simple: most of this vast sector consists of nothing but radiations, subatomic particles, and atoms; only here and there in it is matter able to attain the molecular level, and

nowhere are its molecules at all large or complicated. Very few of them contain more than half a dozen atoms, as opposed to the many thousands of atoms in the more complex organic molecules found in living substance.[62]

As regards the view held by people over the centuries that the universe was created to serve some purpose, Huxley's considered opinion is expressed in these words:

Nowhere in all its vast extent is there any trace of purpose, or even of prospective significance. It is impelled from behind by blind physical forces, a gigantic and chaotic jazz dance of particles and radiations, in which the only overall tendency we have so far been able to detect is that summarized in the Second Law of Thermodynamics – the tendency to run down.[63]

Now it is time for us to come to what Huxley calls organic or biological sector. In respect of both "spatial extension" and temporal length this sector is "very much" restricted. Huxley refers to the views of some astronomers who maintain that some stars in our galaxy have planets like our earth. According to some of them, there are a hundred thousand planets in our galaxy on which life exists, while according to others there are "only a few thousand or even a few hundred." But, he writes: "Whatever the truth turns out to be, the biological sector, considered spatially as the area occupied by life, cannot at the very outside constitute more than a million-million-millionth part of the extent of the visible universe, and probably much less."[64]

As regards "the extension of the biological sector in time" on the earth, it "appears to be about two thousand million years old." But "the level of organization reached in this sector is almost infinitely greater than in the preceding sector."[65]

And now we shall consider in some detail the evolution of life in the biological sector during the two thousand million years. In this task we shall take the help mainly of one of the most prestigious books in this field, namely, *The Meaning of Evolution* by G. G. Simpson. Simpson discusses the origin and evolution of life on the earth with the authority of a master in his field. But first we shall have a look at two excerpts from his book *Biology and Man*. On page

45 of this book he writes, "...man has slowly evolved from ape, reptile, fish, invertebrate, protist, and ultimately from simple matter."[66] And earlier in this book (p.7), he wrote the following significant lines:

> The very simplest living organism (I exclude viruses from that category) are enormously more complex than any inorganic system. Organisms do in fact have characteristics and processes that do not occur in conjunction in nonorganic materials and reactions. Those who believed in a vital, non-material element peculiar to organisms were quite right to this extent. But they were wrong as to the nature of the element. It is organization. It is the complexity and the kind of structural and functional assembly in living organisms that differentiate them from non-living system.[67]

And in the beginning of *The Meaning of Evolution*, Simpson writes that "There is no reason to postulate a miracle" regarding the origin of life on earth, "Nor is it necessary to suppose that the origin of the new processes of reproduction and mutation was anything but materialistic." Then he says that it is not known when life first appeared on our planet. But scientists believe that the original form of organic life must have come into existence by a "chance organization of a complex carbon-containing molecule capable of influencing or directing the synthesis of other units like itself." Such an organization, Simpson says, "would be, in barest essentials, alive" and "would be similar or analogous to a virus." Then there are scientists who believe that the "first form of life was a 'protogene' which, after the chance basic chemical combination into an organization capable of reproduction and mutation, was slowly developed by mutation into the gene combinations of organisms more indisputably alive in the full sense." Simpson says that "above the level of the virus," if the virus is granted the status of an organism, "the simplest living unit is almost incredibly complex" (TMoE, p.15). And from the "living molecule or protogene" to the amoeba the distance covered by the evolutionary force was as astoundingly vast as that from the amoeba to the evolution of man. He also says: "All the essential problems of living organism are already solved in the one-celled (or, as many now prefer to say, noncellular) protozoan and these are only elaborated in man or the other multicellular organisms" (TMoE,p.16).

And in a great passage in his book, *Man on his Nature* (MohN,p.80), to which we shall come again and again in this work, Sir Charles Sherrington writes thus about the origin of life on earth:

> A great American physiologist, Lawrence Henderson, has set forth the particularity of the physical and chemical conditions whose occurrence on Earth's side render possible the existence of the systems we call 'living.' Certain anomalous properties of water, in conjunction with unusual powers and space-relations of the carbon-atom, along with exceptional conditions of radiation and temperature, are shown to form a sort of conspiracy of circumstance allowing life to be, and here and now. There was a stage 'in the dark backward abysm of Time' when our planet's side was not yet a place possible for the life now around us. A stage ensued, however, when things would by a bare margin just permit the type of energy-system we speak of as living. Slender though that chance, it was, so to say, seized. Life appeared. Perhaps in some warm runnel of tidal mud or frothy ooze. It would, we must think, be a tiny thing, perhaps clustered and numerous; to all outward appearance impossibly fraught with what it has become today. It was, we may think perhaps numerous, but in microscopic specks. Yet its destiny was to invade the land and clothe continents with its growth. To venture ocean and in time to populate it. To populate it with countless millions of feeding mouths, and to feed them, while their fins oared them about, fins prophetic of the birds' wing, and of the human hand. Millions of feeding mouths voiceless but yet potential of birds' song and human speech. Mere mechanism and yet charged with germinating reason (MohN,p.80).

Simpson says that rocks two thousand million years old are available for our inspection but fossil records of life are available only for the last quarter of this long period. For the three-fourths of this period, known as the pre-Cambrian, covering 1500,000,000, years, no reliable evidence of life has been established although, he says, "the earth has been more or less, as we know it, a fit abode for life for a period of the order of 2000,000,000 yours" (TMoE, p.11). However, he says, we find definite evidence of the existence of "algae – simple and lowly plants but not the lowliest...from at least the middle part of the long pre-Cambrian span onward" (TMoE,p.17). We shall ignore the pre-Cambrian and go along the path of organic-biological evolution from the beginning of the Cambrian to the present geological era. The last quarter of the two thousand million years covers 505 million years. This period is divided into three geological eras – Paleozoic (Ancient Life), covering a period of 300 million years from the end of the pre-Cambrian; Mesozoic (Intermediate Life), comprising 130 million years in the middle; and Cenozoic (Recent Life), covering a period of 75 million years from the end of the Mesozoic to the present time. The three eras are divided into epochs covering different spans of time.

The Paleozoic era comprises the following periods from the beginning:

Cambrian (80), Ordovician (65), Silurian (35), Devonian (45), Mississipian (25), Pennsylvanian (25), and Permian (25).

The Mesozoic era is divided into the following periods from the beginning:

Triassic (40), Jurassic (30), and Cretaceous (60).

And the Cenozoic is divided into two periods: Tertiary (74) and Quaternary (1). The Tertiary is subdivided into the following epochs from the beginning: Paleocene (17), Eocene (19), Oligocene (11), Miocene (16), and Pliocene (11).

The Quaternary, covering a period of 1 million years, is divided into two epochs: Pleistocene and Recent.

[The figures within brackets indicate millions of years.]

The total span of Man's existence so far on the earth covers a period of the last one million years known as the Quaternary.

Simpson says that some of the early Cambrian rocks "laid down about 500,000,000 years ago, are crowded with fossils" (TMoE, p.16). According to him, "seven or eight major grades of animal organization originated during this period but not instantaneously or simultaneously"(TMoE, p.18). The Cambrian is the longest geological era whose "length is variously estimated at from 60,000,000 to 90,000,000 years" (TMoE, p,19). The animal organizations whose fossils are available arose during different periods of this long era. It is also likely that some of them originated in the later part of the pre-Cambrian and slowly acquired parts because of which their fossils are found in the Cambrian rocks in different parts of the world.

Simpson says that there are some one million "species of animals in the world today" and "About three-fourths of these are insects." As regards the seas, the present number of species in them is "approximately 150,000." He also says that whereas "the seas have been continuously inhabited since Cambrian (by inference also pre-Cambrian) times" TMoE, p.22), land animals appeared in a modest way in the Devonian. These land and aquatic organisms have been put in different general categories by zoologists and these broad categories are technically known as phyla. Regarding the records of their origin, evolution and extinction over the ages, he writes:

> Their records fluctuate and differ in remarkable and instructive ways. Some types have risen rapidly and then dwindled slowly to extinction. Others have slowly attained importance, then quickly dwindled. Still others have continued from ancient times with relatively little fluctuation (TMoE, p.23).

Then, a student of organic evolution finds a "bewildering array of tens of millions of minor species of animals, ancient and recent," tending "to obscure the pattern of life's history." But he writes: "Endlessly diverse as these groups seem to be, they represent variations on a relatively small number of basic themes, general types of organization"(TMoE,p.23). These general types, as stated above, are called phyla.

Simpson says that zoologists differ in their opinion as to the number of phyla, although most of them fix the number at twenty. He discusses only fifteen phyla, of which eleven are "the most important basic types" and adds, "All the phyla include large numbers of extremely diverse animals many of which look extremely different from these examples" (TMoE, p.26). Of all the phyla, four, namely, Protozoa. Mollusca, Arthropoda, and Chordata are of interest to us. A few lines from Simpson's description of each of them are quoted below.

> "Protozoa. These animals had no differentiation of their substance into separate cells. They carry on the life processes with relatively simple, although already very complex, organization within an undivided mass of protoplasm analogous to a single cell of the animals of other" phyla, all of which are multicelled or metazoan" (TMoE, p.24).

"Mollusca. This is the most varied, dominant, successful of the primarily aquatic phyla, both at the present time and throughout most of the fossil record. Representatives are very familiar: Clams, snails, octopuses, and others. The success and variety of this group is shown by the fact that it not only dominates in the sea but is also abundant in fresh waters and has developed successful non-aquatic types, such as the garden snail" (TMoE,pp.27-28).

"Arthropoda. If sheer weight of numbers is the deciding factor, this is the most spectacularly successful of all the phyla, for it includes the insects. Its basic plan involves the advanced tissue differentiation and jointed structure also seen in the annelid worms, plus the development of legs and of a hard coat or external skeleton. The potentialities are enormous and orthropods occur exuberantly from the depths of the sea to the upper reaches of the air. Besides the insects, familiar examples are crabs and other crustaceans and the scorpions, spiders and their allies. There are many known fossil arthropods and the record is good for several groups, although it is deficient for the insects, in proportion to their probable abundance and importance in later geologic times" (TMoE, p 28).

"Chordata. This phylum shares complex tissue and organ differentiation, bilateral symmetry. and some other features with several preceding phyla, but as its most general distinctions are internal supporting structure consisting of a longitudinal rod along the back, jointed in all but a few of the relatively simplest types. The jointed forms, which thus comprise most of the phylum, are the Vertebrata. In evolutionary success, this plan vies with that of the arthropods – we humans readily assign it first place, for we are chordate ourselves. The record is generally good and is, to us, the most interesting of all" (TMoE, .p.28).

Most of these phyla came into existence in the Cambrian. But Chordata appeared during the Ordovician, which covered a period of 65 million years between 425 and 360 million years from now. Of the 15 phyla discussed by Simpson, 14 are invertebrate and Chordata alone comprises the vertebrata.

Simpson then points to an important aspect of evolution, which is that different phyla undergo fluctuations in the course of their evolution. He says that some of them – arthropods, chordates, protozoans, coelenterates, bryo-zoans and mollusks – despite fluctuations are at present more varied than at any other time. "On the other hand," he says, "the brachiopods are certainly far less numerous now than they had been during most of their long previous history" (TMoE, p.32). Then he refers to crises, that is, restrictions in the evo-lutionary history of certain phyla. He says that "in the Permian (last period of the Paleozoic) or Triassic (first of the following era)" there was "a crisis in the life of the seas" because of which the aquatic phyla bryozoans and echinoderms suffered restriction. It was, however, "followed by another expansion in the Jurassic or Cretaceous." The amphibians suffered a great decline towards the end of the Triassic, say between 170 and 165 million years from now, "while the reptiles held their own through this time of crisis only to decline rapidly at a much later date, in the late Cretaceous", that is, between 80 and 75 million years from now. This crisis, Simpson says, was a major one and "suggests a radical and widespread alteration of living conditions on the earth..." (TMoE, p.33). Stressing this point, he writes: "This apparent correlation between phys-ical conditions on the earth and the history of life is a striking example of the unquestionable fact that life and its environment are interdependent and evolve together" (TMoE, p.34).

In chapter IV of his book, Simpson traces the history of the Vertebrates. We have seen above that Chordates comprise the Vertebrates, that is, organ-isms which originally had jointed dorsal stiffening rod which gradually got modified into jointed backbone.

There are eight classes of the vertebrates. Simpson writes: "Four of these [classes] characteristically have fins and are primarily adapted to swimming in the water, while four characteristically have legs and are primarily adapted to walking on a solid surface" (TMoE, p.38).

The four aquatic classes are: Jawless Fishes (Lampreys), Placodermi, Car-tilage Fishes and Bony Fishes. Placodermi is the least familiar of the aquatic classes because it went extinct long ago – sometime soon after the Permian. Simpson writes: "It is probably no coincidence that this extinction falls in the time of crisis for marine invertebrates mentioned above" (TMoE, p42). The jawless fishes, Agnatha, are "exemplified today by lampreys." Continuing, he says "Their most striking peculiarity is that they lack a separately movable lower jaw jointed to the skull, so obvious a feature of all the other vertebrates, be they sharks, trout, frogs, lizards, sparrows, or men." In the cartilage fishes "the evolution of the jaws becomes well advanced." But "the outstanding peculiarity of these animals is that bone, present in placoderms and doubtless also in the ancestors of the cartilage fishes...is lost and the skeleton comes to consist of cartilage only, a substance somewhat weaker than bone although tough and resilient" (TMoE, pp.39-40). Simpson mentions "sharks, rays, and the less familiar chimaeras" as the "living representatives" of cartilage fishes.

Bony fishes have been the most successful of the four aquatic vertebrates. They have, Simpson says, "an advanced type of jaw structure" and "a bony skeleton...developed further than in the bony placoderms." The most surprising thing about these fishes is that they possess lungs as well as gills. He writes, "almost all the familiar fishes of today are bony fishes...except the relatively few lampreys, sharks, and their relatives." (TMoE, p.40)

As regard the origin of these aquatic classes, Simpson says that first appeared the jawless fishes in the Ordovician (between 425 and 360 million years from now); "then Placodermi in the Silurian" (between 360 and 325 million years from now); and finally the cartilage and bony fishes "at about the same time, in the Devonian" (between 325 and 280 million years from now.

The "four classes of walking vertebrates" are Amphibia, Reptilia, Aves and Mammalia. Simpson says that there are some interesting parallels between the four classes of aquatic and land vertebrates. He writes:

> In each case there are two successive grades of early forms, the second of which soon overshadows or largely replaces the first: Agnatha and Placodermi among swimmers, Amphibia and Reptilia among walkers. In each case, too, the second of these early classes gives origin, more or less simultaneously but independently, to two others, which rise jointly to dominance and which include the great bulk of the Tertiary and Recent faunas: Chondrichthyes [cartilage fishes] and Osteichthyes [bony fishes] among the aquatic, Aves [birds] and Mammalia among the land forms" (TMoE, p.43).

But there are radical differences also among these aquatic and land classes. Simpson writes:

> Among the aquatic classes the two earliest dwindled to insignificance and extinction, respectively. The Amphibia and

Reptilia dwindled also, but each found special niches where there was no competition from other classes and in which they retained considerable importance. The Condrichthyes and Osteichthyes, although different in original   habitat, were to some extent parallel and came into competition at various points so that the success of one (Osteichthyes) has probably had an inhibiting influence on the other. The birds and mammals, on the other hand, arose with basically different adaptive characters and as a rule retained them, so that they have not seriously competed....Neither inhibited the other and both expanded greatly at about the same time (TMoE, pp.43-44).

Then Simpson says that the Amphibia arose in the late Devonian (325-280 million years from now) from bony fishes, Reptilia arose in the Pennsylvanian (255-230 million years from now) from Amphibia, and "both Mammalia (late Triassic or early Jurassic – Triassic, a period of 40 million years from 205 to 165 million years from now and Jurassic, a period of 30 million years from 165 to 135 years from now) and Aves (Jurassic) from Reptilia."

From the Permian (230-205 million years from now) onwards the Amphibians were "overshadowed by the far more numerous and varied Reptilia" and after the Triassic they declined almost to extinction, but not quite." Two of their main lines – "that of the frogs and of the salamanders survived." The line of the frogs underwent a modest expansion during the Tertiary and "have won... a rather small but significant place in the present life of the continents" . But these later amphibians did not replace the earlier ones. Simpson says, "The most abundant types of earlier amphibians were replaced by reptiles – and perhaps to some extent also by fishes of the successful Mesozoic groups."(TMoE, p.45).

During their early phase the reptiles expanded rapidly and this expansion "continued abundant throughout the Mesozoic, with some slight diminution in the earlier Jurassic" (TMoE, p.46). But "the Cretaceous [a period of 60 million years between 135 and 75 million years from now] was apparently their greatest period in absolute abundance and in variety of lesser types." But in the late Cretaceous and early Tertiary the reptilian history met with a great crisis . Simpson says, "Like the Jurassic crisis in amphibian history, this was a phenomenon of restriction without replacement." Out of the ten orders present during the Cretaceous only four survived this crisis. Even these "declined from their high points." However, "three of them, those of the turtles (Chelonia), the snakes and lizards (Squamata), and the crocodiles (Crocodilia), retained considerable importance through the Tertiary and into the Recent" (TMoE, p.47).

Then Simpson comes to mammals and birds and says that both appeared in the Jurassic, that is , between 165 and 135 million years from now. Both groups had originated much earlier but had remained obscure and did not have any appreciable expansion for a long period of some seventy-five million years, that is, until early Tertiary era that began some 75 million years from now. He writes thus about the expansion and diversity of these two orders:

> The record for birds...suggest rapid basic expansion in the early Tertiary, into the Miocene[a period of 16 million years, twelve million years from now], followed by Increasing minor diversity within the groups thus established, down to the present day with its total of 8,600 bird species. Mammals reached their high point in the Pliocene [a period of 11 million years, one million years ago from now], but have since declined somewhat to a total of species conservatively estimated at 3,500 – although some authorities would give a much higher figure(TMoE,p.49).

In Chapter V of his book, Simpson discusses the records and radiations of Reptiles. The class of reptiles is divided into sixteen orders, of which twelve went extinct during different geologic eras. One order Rhynchocephalia, "never a very large or dominant group, was reduced almost to extinction or survives only in a single relic form on islands off New Zealand, the lizardlike Sphenedon or Hotterio (TMoE, P.47). So this order of reptiles can be ignored. The three surviving orders are mentioned above.

Simpson refers to an important evolutionary phenomenon known as "adaptive radiation." He explains this phenomenon as follows:

> Hitherto in this discussion the stress has been on the fact that there are major structural and functional grades and types, which have run their courses and waxed and waned in the course of geologic time as their various potentialities arose, were developed in different lines of descent, or were taken

over by one group from another. Now it is time to exemplify the remarkable variety of such potentialities even within a group arising from one basic structural type, to suggest the way in which these potentialities can expand in the course of evolution and can enable their possessors to push into environments and to follow ways of life radically different within the group and radically different from those of its ancestral and basic type. Adaptive radiation is, descriptively, this often extreme diversification of a group as it evolves in all the different directions permitted by its own potentialities and by the environments it encounters (TMoE, p.53).

The two oldest and most primitive orders – Cotylosauria and Pelycosauria – of the reptiles had this pattern of evolution: "origin, gradual rise to a climax, and gradual decline to extinction" (TMoE, p.51). Several others reached the maximum near the time of their first occurrence and then declined "slowly (Ecosuchia), moderately (Ichthyosauria, Rhynchocephalia, Pterosauria), or relatively rapidly (Therapsida) to extinction." Only one order, the dinosaurian (Ornithischia) expanded "rather slowly to a climax almost immediately following extinction." The three orders of reptiles – Chelonia, Squamata and Crocodilia – have had closely similar patterns of evolution: "They originate rather obscurely, expand in a gradual way to strongly marked maxima in the Cretaceous, and then they continue with fluctuations to the present day"(TMoE, p.52).

Simpson describes the basic type of reptile thus:

> The basic type of reptile is a vertebrate living on land throughout its life, including the time when it is developing as an embryo, laying eggs and taking little or no care of its young, equipped with four stout legs on which it can walk or run rather clumsily, long and low in body, with a large number of little differentiated conical or peglike teeth, and with a complex brain adequate to control this bodily apparatus but relatively poor in the higher (or, at least, later development) associated centers of the cerebrum. (TMoE, pp 53-54).

There were many adaptive radiations in reptiles in which "almost every one of ...the features of the basic reptile" (TMoE, p.54) was lost or greatly modified. We may refer to some of these adaptations. Two very radical departures were aquatic and aerial reptiles. The two such aquatic reptiles were ichthyosaurs and plesiosaurs. Simpson says that ichthyosaurs "developed a fishlike tail and a dorsal fin. Their legs were reduced and modified to paddles, steering instruments quite incapable of supporting the body. Thoroughly aquatic, they became amazingly fishlike in external form and passed their whole lives in the sea" yet "every bone in their bodies was different from that of any fish, although adapted to thoroughly fishlike activities."

The other "thoroughly aquatic but less fishlike type of reptile is seen in plesiosaurs…they had large, rather flattened bodies, more or less turtlelike though usually not armored. The legs became large flippers with which the animals sculled their way along. The tail was tapering and the neck was extraordinarily long" (TMoE, p.54).

Another kind of adaptive radiation in reptiles brought into existence flying reptiles, "a group birdlike in some respects, still more batlike, but with reptilian peculiarities of their own." These creatures "flew by means of a leathery membrane supported and extended by an enormously elongated finger; not by several long fingers on each hand as in the bats" (TMoE, p.56).

Then there were a number of new radiations of "medium-sized to large land dwellers" collectively known as dinosaurs. They were "all derived from ancestors closely similar to each other and little removed from the basic reptilian type in the Triassic" (TMoE, p.57). This group included a number of creatures of which Brontosaurus, "the popular image of 'the dinosaur,' thanks to excellent publicity, [was]a hulk of thirty tons in weight, more or less, some seventy feet in length, with four post-like legs, a whiplash tail, and a long neck carrying a ridiculously small head for so big a beast, with teeth fitted only for gathering soft, aquatic vegetation as food" (TMoE, p.57).

Finally, Simpson mentions "the mammal-like reptiles." He says that this radiation also included "a large number of divergent subtypes; but as a unit of the broader reptilian radiation their special interest lies in the fact that their adaptive trends were mainly in the direction of the mammals and the mammals did, in fact, arise from them" (TMoE, p.59). But towards the end of the Mesozoic and in the beginning of the Tertiary "most of the divergently specialized sorts of reptiles" suffered "total and irrevocable" elimination. And, Simpson writes, "The survivors were types that had occupied niches in the ecology of the earth not successfully occupied by any earlier forms and not, as it happened, closely approached by any of those that came later" (TMoE,p.61).

In Chapter VI of his book, Simpson discusses the rise of mammals which involved, he says, "the development of numerous interrelated anatomical and physiological characters that proved in the long run to be more effective in many (not all) of the spheres of life occupied by the reptiles." He says that "the evolution of these new and, as the outcome proved, potent features began among certain of the reptiles, and very early in the reptilian history." And then he writes these interesting lines which throw a floodlight on the passage of life from the protogene or protovirus right up to the mammal from which man has descended:

> In a sense the mammals, and the birds too, are simply glorified reptiles. But in a similar sense the reptiles are glorified amphibians, the amphibians glorified fishes, and so on back until all forms of life might be called glorified amoebas, and the very amoebas could be considered glorified protogenes or protoviruses (TMoE, p.62).

These are words of great wisdom and truth and every man should have them etched in his mind as well as in his inmost being. Man should know his place in the great chain of being which had its beginning on the earth more than 1,000,000,000 years ago. This will give him the right kind of humility which, in turn, will give him the right kind of wisdom to remain in the mainstream of organic evolution so essential for him to discharge his functions in this mainstream.

Then Simpson discusses the features of the mammalian order that were of a superior kind to those of the reptilian order. We may refer to some of the important features:

> Mammals "came to be adapted for a higher or more sustained level of activity and for a more constant level of metabolism." Most of the mammals "maintain a body temperature relatively independent of temporary activity or of external heat and cold. (This is what is meant by being 'warm-blooded;' a 'cold-blooded' animal may have warmer blood than a mammal if it has been exercising violently or is exposed to the hot sun, but its blood cools down again when it stops muscular action or when it moves out of the sun.)" The bones of the skeleton grow in a way that maintain firm, bony joints even

while they are growing. Growth ceases and the bones knit firmly at an appropriate size characteristic for each kind of mammal. These arrangements are mechanically stronger than in animals, like the typical reptiles, in which the joints are more cartilaginous and continue to grow at decreasing rates through most or all of the animal's life. In connection with these features, the basic type of mammal which was quadrupedal, came to have legs drawn in directly under the body and to hold the body well up off the ground. This stance led to characteristic modifications of almost every muscle and bone in the body in comparison with those of the typically sprawling basic reptiles (TMoE, pp63-65).

Simpson says that all the physiological and anatomical changes that took place in the reptilian order leading to the evolution of mammals "had been... established in the Jurassic, in which four quite distinct sorts (orders) of mammals are known from unfortunately scanty remains" (TMoE, p.66). Then he says that "the mammalian orders have much the same variety of histories of expansion and contraction as do the reptilian orders."(TMoE, p.69). Only rodents, he says, "seem to demonstrate a pattern which might be expected as the usual one but which is, in fact, exceptional: fairly steady increase throughout their history" (TMoE, p.70).

Then Simpson discusses the histories of some of the important mammalian orders. But because primates are of special interest to us – we humans belong to the order primate – the history of the Primates will receive our special attention. Simpson starts the discussion with the observation that we humans are the most intelligent creatures so far because "superior intelligence" is the "distinctive feature" of "the basic primate plan, or to the basic plan of the mammals in general" (TMoE, p.78). But he also says that "the first primates were not characterized by advanced intelligence" and the level of their intelligence was more or less the same as that of the mammals. He says, "Intelligence developed among primates in the course of their later evolution" (TMoE, p.80).

Simpson says that "Primates arose in the Paleocene [a period of 17 million years between 75 and 58 million years from now]." But fossils of the primate brain that have been found are "from some time along in the Eocene [a period of 19 years between 58 and 39 million years from now], when considerable evolution beyond the Paleocene forbear is likely" (TMoE, pp. 79-80).

Regarding classification of primates there are differences of opinion among scholars, and so it is "a mess." But, Simpson says, "Broadly speaking, four general levels and types of structure can be distinguished among the primates" (TMoE, p.81). These four primate groups are: "the prosimians; the capuchin monkey, the South American monkeys or ceboids; the macaque, the Old World monkeys or ceropithecoids; and "the chimpanzee, an ape, and... man both represent the broadly manlike or hominoid group." And "Each group includes a variety of different forms" (TMoE, p.82). Then he dwells on in some detail he history of each of these four groups.

The oldest group of "the known primates" are "called the prosimians" and "they do not lead directly into any of the other three groups;" also they have been "unprogressive in brain evolution." They "include, among now living animals, the lemurs, indris, aye-ayes, lorises, pottos, galagos, tarsiers, and, with some reservations, the tree shrews" (TMoE, pp.82-83).

The second group, known as ceboids, includes such monkeys as "marmosets, howling monkeys, capuchins, spider monkeys and others." These primate groups have always lived in South America. In recent times they have, passing "through Central America", extended their habitat to "tropical Mexico." These monkeys can hang from trees by their tails (TMoE, p.83).

The Old World monkeys known as *Cercopithecus* are the third group of primates. They are common African monkeys. Their brains are more evolved than those of the prosimians and their faces are closer to human faces than those of the South American monkeys. Simpson says that "they have tails but they cannot hang by them" (TMoE,p.83).Macaques, rhesus monkeys, baboons, mandrills, langurs and other monkeys belong to this group and they are found "throughout Africa and southern Asia and barely into Europe at Gibraltar" (TMoE, p.83).

About the fourth group of the primates, to which man belongs, Simpson writes as follows:

> The fourth group, automatically highest in our view, is that of the apes and men or hominoides (named by *Homo* after himself). They have no tails, are relatively large in size, and exhibit in various degrees the highest development of intelligence yet attained. The living forms are the gibbons, orangutans, chimpanzees, gorillas and man (TMoE, pp.83-84).

Simpson says that there is something interesting about the origin of the four groups of the primates. They "do not… represent four successive steps, each leading to the other, like, on a larger scale, Osteichthyes to Amphibia, Amphibia to Reptilia, and Reptilia to Mammalia" (TMoE, p.90). The Prosimians arose first and then the other three groups "arose at about the same time and not from one another" (TMoE ,p.90).

Then Simpson discusses in some detail the radiations the four groups of primates underwent in different geological eras. We will leave out the first three groups and only see how out of the many hominoid radiations the surviving lines of the apes and man came into existence. He writes thus:

> Hominoid radiation reached an early climax in the Miocene; since then there has been a weeding out of the lines, many of which became extinct, with increasing specialization and divergence of the relatively few surviving lines. Recent discoveries increasingly emphasize the diversity of this radiation and show how baseless were the old arguments as to whether man is nearer or more closely related to one or another of the recent apes. The argument rested on false premises, a misconception of the sort of evolutionary pattern here exemplified, similar to the misconception of a ceboid cercopithecoid- hominoid evolutionary line. It now seems reasonably certain that the four (main) types of apes and man are independent surviving lines, divergently specialized, all deriving separately from the Miocene radiation. The characters shared by any two or more of them may assist in inference as to the basic type from which the radiation arose, but are irrelevant as to nearness or distance of special blood affinity between particular survivors (TMoE, p.92).

Now that man has appeared on the earth we will have to go to Anthropology to understand how, in the course of one million years of his existence here, he has evolved from a manlike ape to the modern man, who prides himself on being the crown of Creation. But we will stay with Simpson for a little while more to understand certain very important things about Evolution and man's place in the scheme of things here. The rest of Simpson's book, which covers more than two-thirds of it, is devoted to discussions of very important matters relating to Evolution, such as Oriented Evolution, Opportunism in Evolution, Forces of Evolution, Progress in Evolution, Man's place in Nature, Search for an Ethic, Knowledge and Responsibility, Natural Selection and Mutation – all very important issues, important because man's further evolution and survival depends on a clear perception of them and, in the light of that perception, continually re-orienting his social, religious, intellectual life and ethical values. We quote below a famous passage from his book, in which he gives his considered evaluation of man's evolution, his place in the scheme of things and the significance of his being as an organism:

> Man was certainly not the goal of evolution, which evidently had no goal. He was not planned, in an operation wholly planless. He is not the ultimate in a single constant toward higher things, in a history of life with innumerable trends, none of them constant, and some toward the lower rather than the higher. Is his place in nature, then, that of a mere accident, without significance? The affirmative answer that some have felt constrained to give is another example of the "nothing but" fallacy. The situation is as badly misrepresented and the lesson as poorly learned when man is considered nothing but an accident as when he is considered the destined course of creation. His rise was neither insignificant nor inevitable. Man *did* originate after a tremendously long sequence of events in which both chance and orientation played a part. Not all the chance favored his appearance, none *might* have, but enough did. Not all the orientation was in his direction, it did not lead unerringly human-ward, but some of it came this way. The result is the most highly endowed organization of matter that has yet appeared on the earth – and we have certainly no reason to believe there is any higher in the universe. To think that this result is insignificant would be unworthy of that high endowment, which includes among its riches a sense of values (TMoE, pp.292-293).

And in another very powerful passage towards the end of his book, Simpson speaks of man's kinship with other forms of organic life thrown up by the forces of Evolution as well as of his uniqueness as an organism in whom a new kind of evolutionary power has been striving to shape a being who can, if only he lives a good and responsible life, really become the crown of creation. The passage in question is quoted below:

Man is the result of a purposeless and materialistic process that did not have him in mind. He was not planned. He is a state of matter, a form of life, a sort of animal, and a species of the Order Primates, akin nearly or remotely to all of life and indeed to all that is material. It is, however, a gross misrepresentation to say that he is just an accident or *nothing but* an animal. Among all the myriad forms of matter and of life on the earth, or as far as we know in the universe, man is unique. He happens to represent the highest form of organization of matter and energy that has ever appeared. Recognition of this kinship with the rest of the universe is necessary for understanding him, but his essential nature is defined by qualities found nowhere else, not by those he has in common with apes, fishes, trees, fire or anything other than himself (TMoE,p.344).

And now we will go the anthropologist Richard Carrington, who we have already referred to above, to know about the evolution of Man from the Order Primate to *Homo sapiens*, the species to which all men and women of the world now belong. But first we will refer to some lines and a passage in his book *A Million Years of Man* (AMYoM). On page 8 of his book he writes that "both man and his planetary home are ultimately the product of cosmic forces" and that "Man is a member of the whole vast family of living things, and his present state is the direct result of the evolutionary process that has operated over the last two thousand million years." And in the following passage he tells man about his status in the 45000 million year long history of the earth:

Let us imagine that the 45000 million years of earth history are represented by the distance of a hundred miles, and that we are walking from the time of the earth's origin towards the present. On the first half of our journey we should come across no life at all, and would have to continue for no less than eighty-eight miles before even such simple invertebrates as worms and jellyfish began to appear in any numbers. At ninety-three miles certain organisms would be leaving the water to invade the land, but our own parent group, the mammals, would not appear until we are already within two miles of our goal. The whole of man's physical evolution since the beginning of the Pleistocene would occupy only the last twenty yards of our journey, and the age of written history, with all its panoply of civilization, could be contained twice over in our very last stride (AMYoM, pp.115-116).

And in a very interesting passage in his book *The* Web *of Life*, Fritjof Capra tells us how "the Californian environmentalist David Bower has devised a very ingenious narrative by compressing the age of the Earth into the six days of the Biblical creation story." Capra writes:

In Bower's scenario, the Earth is created on Sunday at midnight. Life in the form of the first bacterial cells appears on Tuesday morning around 8:00 A.M. For the next two and a half days, the microcosm evolves, and by Thursday at midnight it is fully established, regulating the entire planetary system. On Friday around 4:00 P.M., the micro-organisms invent sexual reproduction, and on Saturday, the last day of creation, all the visible forms of life evolve. Around 1:30 A.M. on Saturday, the first marine animals are formed, and by 9:30 a.m the first plants come ashore, followed two hours later by amphibians and insects. At ten minutes before five in the afternoon, the great reptiles appear, roam the Earth in lush tropical forests for five hours, and then suddenly die out around 9:45 P.M. in the meantime, the mammals have arrived on the Earth in the late afternoon, around 5:30 , and the birds in the evening, around 7:15. Shortly before 10:00 P.M., some tree- dwelling mammals in the tropics evolve into the first primates; an hour later some of those evolve into monkeys, and around 11:40 P.M., the great apes appear. Eight minutes before midnight, the first Southern apes stand up and walk on two legs. Five minutes later, they disappear again. The first human species, *Homo habilis*, appear four minutes before midnight, evolves into *Homo erectus* half a minute later, and into the archaic forms of *Homo sapiens* thirty seconds before midnight. The Neanderthals command Europe and Asia from 15 to 4 second before midnight. The modern human species, finally, appears in Africa and Asia 11 seconds before midnight and in Europe 5 seconds before midnight. Written human history begins around two thirds of a second before midnight.[68]

Man, as we have seen above, has descended from the class Mammalia and belongs to the order Primate. The order Primate contains two suborders "Prosimii (the prosimians or lower primates)" and "Anthropoidea (the higher primates)." Prosimii contained about 12 families, six of which – "tree-shrews; lemurs, indris and woolly lemurs; aye-aye; lorises and galagos; and Tarsius" – are living, while the others "are represented only by extinct forms, mainly from the early Tertiary (AMYoM, p.17). The other suborder of the primate, that is, Anthropoidea, contains three Superfamilies. The first of these is known as Ceboidea to which belong New World monkeys, such as marmosets and tamarins. The second Superfamily is known as Cercopithe coidea. Old World monkeys, such as macaques, baboons, langurs, colobus monkeys, etc. belong to this Superfamily. The third Superfamily is called Hominoidea, which contains two Families known as Pongidae and Hominidae. To Pongidae belong the gibbons; "about seven genera of extinct apes from the Miocene and Pliocene;" Proconsul; Oreopethicus; "Ponginae (the living great apes and at least one extinct form)." The second Family consists of two Subfamilies, Australopithecinae and Hominae. The first of these Subfamilies contains the genera Australopithecus, Paranthropus and Zinjanthropus. The second Subfamily contains two genera, namely, Pithecanthropus and Homo. The genus Homo contains two species, namely, homo neanderthalenesis and homo sapiens. Men and women of all races and all nations living on the earth now are homo sapiens.

Carrington writes that "the Hominoidae, the group which most closely concerns our present story, is divided into two 'families,' Pongidae, or apes, and Hominidae, or 'men,' both represented during the last million years by several different genera and species." He also points to the "close relationship of all these animals to one another ...proved mainly by studies of their skeletal anatomy and embryonic development." He says that the similarities are so striking that we can have no doubt that "all these creatures shared a common ancestor a few million years back in the geological past." As regards the striking "likenesses between the embryonic young of primates," Carrington says, "laymen, and even some professional biologists, would find it very difficult to distinguish the embryo of a man from that of, say, a gorilla or a chimpanzee," and adds, "Even without technical studies, however, the fact that monkeys and men are closely related could scarcely be doubted by an unprejudiced mind. The chimpanzee and other pongids especially are so reminiscent of ourselves in appearance and behavior that we must immediately recognize them as our kin (AMYoM, p.18)."

A chart (pp.32-33) in Carrington's book shows the sequence of events in the history of the primates. During the Jurassic (between 180-125 million years from now) reptiles ruled the earth – "dinosaurs on land, pterosaurs in the air and ichthyosaurs, plesiosaurs and mosasaurs in the seas." Mammals began to evolve from reptiles. During the Cretaceous (125-59 million years from now) "Apotheosis of the ruling reptiles" was "followed by their total extinction" and "Fossil remains of small insectivores foreshadow the evolution of the primates." During the Eocene ('dawn of the recent' – 58-35 million years from now) "first definite fossil evidence for primate evolution" has been found. "Tree-shrews, lemurs and tarsoids were well-established....The tarsoids Necrolemur and Microchoerus may have been close to the human stem." Then followed the Oligocene, covering the period 34-27 million years from now. Carrington says that during this period "Division of the lines leading to monkeys on the one hand great apes, sub-men and man on the other" occurred. He says that "Parapithecus of Egypt may be near the dividing point. During the Miocene (26-13 million years from now) "Division of the lines leading to the great apes, sub-men and man" took place. "Proconsul of Africa may be ancestral to the living gorillas and chimpanzees and near the ancestry of man." Then followed the Pliocene, which covered a period of 11 million years from 12 to 2 million years from now. Finally followed the Pleistocene – a period of one million years touching the shores of the present time. During this period the evolution of man took place. The last 10,000 years of this period is called Holocene ('wholly recent') and is the period of "recent human history" (AMYoM, pp.32-33).

We shall now make a survey of one million years of the evolution of man. But before that we will take note of some points that Carrington makes. The first is that "biological science alone does not provide any evidence whatever that evolution has a discoverable purpose or goal" and that "the meaning of the whole process, if it exists at all, must therefore probably be sought in a synthesis of all the sciences, with the evidence derived from such higher products of evolution as religious and artistic experience" (AMYoM,p.13). Another important point to note is that the Hominoidea, of Old World origin, "consists of four man-like apes – gibbons, orangutans, chimpanzees, and gorillas – and man himself." Of these the gibbons are "the smallest and most primitive of all hominoids." It is , however, the other three genera of man-like apes" – oran-gutan, chimpanzee and gorilla – that "are our nearest living relations in the animal world, sharing with us many common characters not only in structure but in intelligence, behaviour, and even in such details as similarity of blood groups" (AMYoM,p.26). This does not mean that we are the descendants of these apes. These hominoids "represent a fairly early divergence from the de-velopment of other primates." Carrington writes:

> The popular superstition about Darwinism, that 'man is de-scended from monkeys,' is therefore seen to be based on a misconception. Man certainly shares a common ancestor with all living members of the primate order, but the idea that he is the descendant of any existing species of monkey is quite untrue (AMYoM,pp.25-26).

Another very important thing to keep in mind while surveying the evo-lution of man is the evolution of the brain in man. Tree-dwelling life of pri-mates was conducive to the evolution of the brain in them. Such a life requires a better co-ordination of the senses than in the ground-dwelling mammals. In an illuminating passage in his book, Carrington tells us how this advantage ac-crued to the Primate:

> The new balance of sensory mechanisms is reflected in evo-lution in important changes in the organization of the brain. The primitive vertebrate brain simply consists of three hol-low expansions of the organ known as the 'neural tube', each specialized for different activities and referred to respectively as the fore-brain, the mid-brain and the hind-brain. Over-lying these, like the skin of an orange, is the 'cerebral cortex,' which is the seat of the coordinating mechanisms which de-termine the total effectiveness of the organism in relation to its environment. The development of higher types of brains from lower types consists very largely in an increase in elab-oration of the cerebral cortex, which sorts out impressions from the various sense organs and weighs them one against the other before the motor nerves set in train the appropriate response. Tree-dwelling life obviously demands a response based on a greater degree of co-ordination between impres-sions from different senses than one which is mainly based

on the reports from a single sense, such as that of smell. The coordinating mechanism, or cortex, of the brain therefore normally shows a progressive increase in size in primates at the expense of the areas limited to receiving sensory impressions alone (AMYoM, pp35-36).

Now we shall see what Carrington has to say about the Great Ice Age during the Pleistocene. He says that it was not a continuous Ice Age but four ice ages that covered varying periods of time, with gaps between them between 600,000 and 10,000 years from now. For 400,000 years from the beginning of the Pleistocene the climatic conditions on the earth were more or less the same as we have them now. There were Ice Ages even before the Pleistocene. Carrington writes: "The Pleistocene glaciations are by no means unique in the history of the earth. Equally severe episodes of glaciation occurred at several other periods in the geological past, and have left evidence in the rocks of more than 500 million years ago" (AMYoM, p.52).

The period of 400,000 years before the Great Ice Age is known as the Age of the Southern Elephant. The typical mammal of the period was the southern elephant, "which had short tusks, a peculiarly flattened forehead, and a peaked cranium." A particular kind of rhinoceros was also common. The "young of both these species were preyed on by the last of the great sabre-toothed cats." There were forests in which there were plenty of deer. The plains "covered with lush carpets of grass" (AMYoM, p.54) had horses, bisons and many other cattle. Many trees still found in many parts of Europe flourished during this period. The flora of this period was, Carrington says, "characteristic of a temperate and fairly equable climate" (AMYoM, p.53).

Then followed the Great Ice Age with three of the four glaciations with gaps (interglacial periods) between them. The whole of this Age covered a period of about 520,000 years (from 600,000 years to 80,000 years from now.) This period is known as the Age of the Ancient Elephant. This period "fluctuated with the alternating phases of heat and cold" and so "the flora and the fauna were constantly migrating north and south with the changes in climate, and nowhere did the pattern of life remain stable throughout the period." Even so, Carrington says, "a number of forms can be singled out as typical." The best-known mammal of this period was "the ancient, or single-tusked elephant." He writes: "It was among the giants of its order, some specimens standing over 14 feet at the shoulder." "Yet," he says, " in spite of its size and formidable tusks it was almost certainly one of the animals hunted by the early man " (AMYoM, p.54). Another typical animal of the period was Merck's rhinoceros. Carrington says that the fauna of this period also included "the giant deer, or so-called 'Irish elk,'...a primitive species of wild boar,...the spotted hyena, the hippopotamus, an early form of lion, and monkeys very similar to the living macaques," all of which "are now extinct or restricted entirely to the exotic environment of Africa or southern Asia." But, he says, there were also other animals as "the brown bear, the wolf, the hamster, and the red and roe deer" (AMYoM, 55).

After this phase of glaciations came "two faunal periods." The first of these covered a period of 65000 years from 80000 years until 15000 years ago from now. The second period started 15000 years ago and continues even now. Carrington writes that these two periods are "often named the Age of the Woolly Mammoth [which] coincides with the peak of the Fourth...Glacial Phase." The second period is known as the Reindeer Age and "covers the gradual decline of glacial conditions in northern Europe and the dawn of the modern world." This period "saw the first consolidation of human society and culture."

In the concluding paragraph in the chapter "The Pleistocene World," Carrington writes: "This, then, was the environment in which the human adventure took place, and these were the animals with whom early man shared the world" (AMYoM,p.57). What is implied here is that man was one of the Pleistocene animals, that is, his origins are low. The only thing that distinguished him from the other animals of the period was that he had brain enough and tricks enough up his sleeves to drive away cave bears and occupy their dwellings, decoy and kill even big animals like the rhinoceros and bison and eat their flesh. Carrington writes: "rhinoceros steak probably figured largely on the menu of the cave kitchens of the time" (AMYoM p.56).

Carrington says that "the shape of human history reveals itself" in a distinct form "in the first half of the Pleistocene" because for the first time were found fossils of bones of "a group of pre-human or near-human primates, known as the australopithecines which seem to have been widely distributed in south and east Africa some 600,000 years ago." In 1924 "the cranium of an animal unlike any that had been discovered before" was discovered at a place called Taungs in Africa by a quarryman "after the detonation of a blast charge." In this region "commercial quarrying had been going on since 1910 and remains of different types of animal had come up from time to time. The cranium was submitted to Professor Raymond Dart of Johannesburg, who, with a remarkable insight "claimed that it belonged to a previously unknown species of hominid" and "named [it] *Australopithecus africanus*" – literally, 'southern apes.' (AMYoM,p73). Carrington rightly holds the view that this discovery was "of the highest importance in tracing the course of human ancestry."

Carrington says that since "the discovery of the Taungs skull many other remains of australopithecines have been extracted from south African formations and scientists have been able to re-construct the physical features as well as the life-style of this sub-human ape." He says, "we now have a sufficiently large collection of australopithecine remains to draw a remarkably clear picture of the creatures" (AMYoM,p.74). He says, "they were a race of erect-walking primates about the size of modern pygmies with moderately large brains, who may have made simple tools from wood, horn and bone and possibly also possessed the power of speech' (AMYoM, p.75). The comparatively large size of their brain and the many similarities scientists have found between their bone structure and that of *Homo sapiens* make it clear that "the australopithecines may be cousins, or even ancestors, of *Homo sapiens*" (AMToM, p.76).

Australopithecines lived more than half a million years ago and the region in which they lived had "arid climate very similar to that found in the region today" (AMYoM,p.80). They had their homes "in caves in low hills rising from the plain," where, Carrington says, "they probably lived by a mixture of hunting and food-gathering." Continuing, he writes:

> Although nuts, berries and eggs must have formed an important part of their diet, it seems certain that their favourite food was meat. Bones of baboons, antelopes, tortoises, rodents, bats and birds have been found mixed with the fossil remains of the australopithecines themselves, and these creatures probably formed their main prey (AMYoM,p.80).

But a very important question, whether the australopithecines are "directly ancestral to modern man" or they are "an aberrant side-branch lying somewhere between the main human stem and the line leading to the modern great apes," remains to be answered conclusively. However, Carrington says, "although perhaps not directly ancestral to ourselves, [they] were so close to the human line of descent that they certainly represent an evolutionary phase through which our species must have passed" (AMYoM, p.81).

Then Carrington discusses the evolution of another group of hominids "whose close connection with ourselves is much less in doubt." This group is known as pithecanthropoids and it evolved in south- eastern Asia. In 1891 remains of early man were found in Java. The scientist who found them gave the creature the name *Pithecanthropus erectus*, 'the erect ape-man.' Carrington says that "a parallel operation…was going forward in China" at a place "some forty miles from Pekin" (AMYoM, p.84). A molar tooth was discovered here. Based on its study a new genus of hominid was identified and named *Sinanthropus* pekinensis, or 'China-man of Pekin.' From 1929 onwards, intensive study of the region was carried on and "by 1938 the fossil bones of nearly forty individual specimens of *Sinanthropus* had been brought to light" (AMYoM,p.85).

Later comparison of the fossil remains of the Java man and Pekin man showed that they most "certainly belonged to the same genus of hominid" and so the "two creatures are now almost invariably referred to by the generic name of *Pithecanthropus*" (AMYoM, p.85). Carrington then dwells on some of the physical features of *Pithecanthropus*. He writes: "*Pithecanthropus* was rather short by modern standards, a typical full-grown male being little over five feet tall. The Java femur shows that he stood completely erect….The aspect of the pithecanthropus was nevertheless very brutish compared with our own." As regards their brain size, Carrington says that the average size of the brain of the Chinaman of Pekin was larger than that of the Java man:

> Five of the Chinese skulls were found to range in capacity from 850 c.c. to 1300 c.c. with an average of 1075 c.c., while the corresponding figures for three of Javan skulls were 755 c.c. to 900c.c. with an average of 860 c.c. Thus even after the brain-body ratio has been taken into account it seems that China man had by far the higher mental endowment (AMYoM, p.87).

As regards the age of the pithecanthropus, Carrington says that it "is now more or less universally accepted as late Lower and Middle Pleistocene, that is to say, between half a million and 200,000 years ago." He also says that "the pithecanthropoids began to flourish at about the same time that australopithe-cines of Africa were beginning to decline" (AMYoM,p.89). The two groups ex-isted at the same time for a certain period in their respective habitats. So "this makes it unlikely that the pithecanthropoids were direct descendants of the known australopithecines" (AMYoM, p.85). Carrington sums up the status of this hominid in the history of the evolution of man as follows, "we can at best say that *Pithecanthropus* was a member of the human family who represented a phase of evolution between the australopithecines on the one hand and Nean-derthal man and modern man on the other, even though his direct descent from the former is doubtful and his ancestral connection with latter cannot yet be proved" (AMYoM,p.89-90). He says that no remains of "the cultural achieve-ments" of Java man have yet been found, but that "does not mean …that Java man had no cultural tradition, for he almost certainly did, but simply that its nature is still unknown." Regarding the cultural tradition of the Pekin man, we know that he "not only made fire but also possessed a tool-making tradition far in advance of the pebble-tool culture of the australopithecines" (AMYoM, p.91). Also, Pekin men were hunters. Large numbers of bones of animals, especially those of deer, have been found with their remains. They were also as violent to their own kind "as modern man is to his" (AMYoM, p.93). Carrington says that "charred human bones are found among those of [their] animal prey." They often killed the weaker men of their kind, broke open their skulls and ate the contents thereof. Carrington writes: "It may well be that the fried brains of Pekin man's weaker neighbours, garnished with nuts and berries…formed the main course of many a primitive feast on the Chili plain" (AMYoM,p.93).

Carrington holds the view that "beyond any reasonable doubt…all the pithecanthropoids had speech." Then he draws our attention to two very im-portant aspects of their cultural life. One, they had some kind of religion which taught them "the earliest reverence for the dead in human history," which was expressed in "some kind of ritual burial." Fossils of seven Pekin men lying to-gether and red ochre or haematite spread over them have been found. The second important aspect of their cultural life was "the dawn of the decorative sense which is so characteristic of man." Carrington writes: "For the first time in the record of human evolution ornaments such as beads and perforated teeth and shells are found in association with these fossils." And so he writes: "Both these developments are evidence of higher social activities than the basic co-operative interactions of a hunting group" (AMYoM, p.93).

Carrington sums up his discussion of the importance of *Pithecanthropus* in the evolutionary process which finally brought into existence *Homo* sapiens:

> To sum up, *Pithecanthropus* is of exceptional importance as representing the second main phase through which human evolution probably passed (the australopithecines being, of course, the representatives of the first). The fossil and archaeological evidence shows that between quarter and half a million years ago an erect-walking proto-human creature existed on the earth with a tool-making tradition, almost certainly the power of speech, and a social organization based on food-gathering and hunting (AMYoM, p.94).

The third phase in the evolution of man was the advent of the Neanderthalers, who inhabited the earth "between some 160,000 and 40,000 years ago." Carrington says that "the Neanderthalers were the dominant species of man on earth from the end of the Middle Pleistocene until they were superseded by our own species some 40,000 years ago" (AMYoM, p.101).

Although pithecanthropus succeeded australopithecines as inheritors of the earth, the latter were not the physical ancestors of the former. But, Carrington says, "the Neanderthalers and modern man represent two divergent lines of descent from pithecanthropoid ancestors, the former having the earlier cultural flowering and then being superseded by the latter some 40,000 years ago" (AMYoM, p.95). In 1856 for the first time fossil remains of the Neanderthal man were found in a valley in Germany after which this hominid is named. Since then up to now "fossil remains of some sixty individuals" (AMYoM, p.96) have been discovered. Carrington says that Neanderthaloids lived "not only in Western Europe, where the fossils are most common, but in the Middle East, north and south Africa, and central and south-eastern Asia" (AMYoM, p.97).

The fossils of Neanderthaloids are not all alike. They are of several kinds. Some of them look very much like those of *Homo sapiens*, while some seem to have belonged to "a more brutish creature which in life may have closely resembled the shambling ape-man of popular imagination." There are also fossils that seem to have belonged to creatures "representing transitional phases between pithecanthropoids and Neanderthalers," Carrington discusses the two main types: "the conservative or so-called 'classical type,' and the more progressive type with an anatomy approaching that of *Homo sapiens*" (AMYoM, P.97).

Carrington presents this picture of the classic Neanderthaler: "Brutish in aspect…a stocky, erect-walking creature, broad-shouldered and barrel-chested, with short, thickset legs, powerful arms, and a head with receding brow and chin which by our standards would appear considerably too large for the body." As regards "the progressive members of the species," he says that "the Ehringsdorf and Steinheim skulls from Germany, and the Mount Carmel and other skeletons from Israel" indicate that they were "much more like ourselves" (AMYoM, p.98). But their life had a disturbing aspect, that is, they also sometimes killed weaker members of their own kind, broke open their skulls and feasted on their brains just as their *Pithecanthropus* forbears used to do. Then Carrington says something interesting about the fossils of the two types of Neanderthal man. He writes: "Contrary to what one might expect, the progressive Neanderthal fossils can generally be dated to an earlier period than those of the classic or conservative type" and adds:

> This shows that they cannot be lineally transitional between the classic Neanderthalers and modern man, but probably represent a parallel line of Neanderthaloid evolution with less extreme specializations than the classic type. Another possibility is that the progressives are hybrids between the classic Neanderthalers and some variety of *Homosapiens* (AMYoM, p.102).

Carrington says that "the Neanderthalers knew the art of making fire and fashioning tools." The tools they made are called Mousterian tools named after the place known as La Moustier. These tools are "of the so-called 'flake' type." He writes: "Two main kinds of flakes are recognizable at Mousterian sites. The first are 'points', tools of roughly triangular shape with a heavy butt and two carefully trimmed convex edges meeting at a sharp, pointed tip. The second are 'side-scrapers,' with a trimmed working edge, usually parallel with the long axis of the flake and opposite the butt" (AMYoM, p.102). The Neanderthalers used "animal skins as clothing" because "their homelands were subjected to the icy conditions of the Wurm glaciations." Carrington says that in the latter part of the Third Interglaciation these people lived in rough tents clustered around central hearths across the countryside. But with the onset of icy conditions they would take shelter in caves and for that they would fight tough battles with giant cave bears and cave lions that lived in those caves.

The Neanderthalers were "fearless hunters" (AMYoM, p.104) and even with their primitive tools they used to kill woolly rhinoceros and woolly mammoths and eat their flesh and "smaller creatures were probably run down with throwing stones, trapped in pits, or ambushed by spearmen" (AMYoM,p.104).

Then Carrington talks about what he calls the "metaphysical beliefs" of the Neanderthalers and says that these beliefs were expressed in "hunting magic, animal worship and ritual burials" practised by them. In many caves of Mousterian times in Germany, Switzerland and France scientists have found skulls of bears arranged in certain ways that suggest "a ritual significance" (AMYoM, p.105). Carrington gives examples of the long tradition of bear rituals performed by several primitive peoples "in the outlying regions of northern Europe." He says that "it would be rash to draw any definite conclusions about the hunting customs of the Neanderthalers from these modern instances, but when they are considered in conjunction with the cave bear finds of the Mousterian period the likelihood surely is that some kind of similar magic rites must have been practised" (AMYoM, p.106).

Carrington says that the Neanderthalers "had a profound respect for the dead of their own kind" and so we find evidence of "ritual burials." Ritual burials were practiced "to some extent by the pithecanthropoids" but they became a characteristic feature of the Neanderthalers' life.

All examples of burials occurred in caves and they "date from the end of the Last Interglacial phase" (AMYoM, 107). These burials, he says, were of "magico-religious" kind and asks the question: "What may the meaning of such rituals have been"? He provides the answer in the words quoted below:

> Modern anthropological literature is full of instances of special veneration or fear of the dead among primitive peoples, while the records of ancient civilizations, such as that of ancient Egypt show how deeply the dead were revered and how every effort was made to provide goods for their use in the afterlife. Even in the comparatively advanced civilizations of today the ritual of the of the funeral service, the burial of the dead and the erection of tombstones (or the ceremonial

burning of the body and the scattering of its ashes) are evidence of a similar attitude.

Carrington says that "the burials of the Neanderthalers were conducted
in the same spirit" (AMYoM, p.109). In his concluding remarks on the life of
the Neanderthalers he says they were not always "brutal, soulless savages." Because of the "rigours of their life" they had to be tough and often ruthless;
"but alongside these qualities we see the dawn of wonder at the world, and
perhaps also even of that reverence for life, which was one day to produce the
highest achievements of human spirit" (AMYoM, p.111).

And then Carrington discusses the somewhat mysterious appearance of
Homo sapiens between 40,000 and 35,000 years from now and how they
grabbed the earth by physically destroying the Neanderthalers, who, though
physically stronger than them, were less brainy. After briefly covering Carrington's discussion of the evolution of *Homo sapiens*, we will have a look at
William Golding's novel *The Inheritors*, in which the novelist presents an artist's
perception of the nature and character of this hominid at a crucial point of
time in the evolutionary history of man, that is, when, after destroying the last
surviving group of the Neanderthalers, they take control of earth.

Before discussing the fossil remains of this hominid found at several sites and
some relevant facts about their evolution, Carrington tells us to keep in mind
certain things about our position in the universe. He says, " the period of our oc-
cupation of the earth has been incredibly short." He also advises us not to cherish
any illusions about our "significance in the cosmic scene" (AMYoM, P.115). We
have seen above what Anthony Huxley, Fritjof Capra and Carrington himself
have said about the period of man's occupancy of the earth during the 4.6 billion
years of its existence. And of the 40,000 years or so of his existence here the history of his civilized life covers only the last seven or eight thousand years. So,
keeping in mind these humbling truths about ourselves, Carrington says, "Only
by bearing the facts about our origins and understanding the way we have developed can we hope to speculate with any responsibility on the meaning of our individual lives and our relation to the universe around us" (AMYoM, p.115).

And it was time man did so.

Then Carrington tells us about the fossil remains of *Homo sapiens* found
at different sites, their physical features, their origins, their way of life and, finally, how they came to take possession of the earth.

The first fossil remains – "the skull and some other bones of an old man and parts of the skeletons of four other individuals" (AMYoM, p.116) – were found in 1868 "in a rock shelter under an overhanging cliff" in a French village. Near these were hearths and also a number of flint instruments. The rock shelter is called Cro-Magnon and so, Carrington says, " 'Cro-Magnon man' is the name still popular to this early physical type of *Homo sapiens*. Then he describes the physical features of the Cro-Magnon man. These men were taller than the Neanderthalers, "with long limbs, straight thigh-bones, and a *foramen magnum* in the centre of the skull-base, showing that they stood completely erect" (AMYoM, p.116).Their forehead was "high and domed" which gave them "an exceptionally 'intellectual look,'" The brain volume of the Cro-Magnon man was "some 1600 c.c., which is considerably greater than that of most modern adults" (AMYoM, 117).

But the story of the evolution of modern man is a complicated one. In 1900, some fossil remains were found "near Menton on the French Riviera." In a cave at Grimaldi "the scientists found the well-preserved skeletons of an old woman and a youth between fifteen and sixteen years of age" (AMYoM, p.117). Several eminent authorities regard these Grimaldi skeletons "as being of Negroid type." Scientists faced another problem when another skeleton was found in a rock-shelter at another place in France. This skeleton "recalled to many anthropologists the physical traits of modern Eskimos" (AMYoM, p118). The name of the village where this rock-shelter is located is Chancedale. But, Carrington writes, "Whatever the status of the men of Grimaldi and Chancedale, there is no doubt that the Cro-Magnons are the foundation stock of *Homo sapien*" (AMYoM, p.118). Then he tells us in the following passage how these ancestors of ours destroyed the dwindling species of the Neanderthalers and grabbed the earth:

> Between 40000 and 35000 year ago they were rising to complete ascendency in Europe, and Neanderthal man dwindled in numbers and soon became extinct. The triumph of the new species is particularly significant in that, physically speaking, the Neanderthalers were by far the more powerful of the two. The Cro-Magnon succeeded mainly by the power of their brains. Their superior intelligence enabled them to devise more efficient methods of capturing game, and the

Neanderthalers found themselves constantly losing in the battle for food. When, as seems likely, this competition led to warfare between the two species, the physically weaker Cro-Magnon nevertheless showed greater cunning, and annihilated their brawny rivals by use of superior tactics and more efficient weapons. Superiority of brain, the legacy of arborial life which nearly sixty million years previously had swept the primates to the top of the evolutionary ladder, was now beginning to play its part in the direct rivalries between man and man. This process has gone on through the whole of human history and is as apparent today as it was 35000 years ago (AMYoM, p.119).

Carrington says that we have to know from where this species of man came and "what are its relationships with the other species of the genus Homo." This is a very difficult problem in physical anthropology because the fossil remains available are not enough to establish with certainty their descent. Also, the place of origin of this species that "advanced into Europe and replaced the Neanderthalers" (AMYoM, p.119) remains unknown. But this much appears to be certain: that "men of *sapiens* type were evolving along a different line from the Neanderthalers well before the Upper Palaeolithic dawned" (AMYoM, p.122). Then in one paragraph, quoted below, Carrington succinctly describes the direct line of the evolution of the primates until *Homo sapiens* took control of the earth:

The rise of the primates began…at the end of the Age of Reptiles. Its course through the Tertiary period was fairly obscure, but in the first half of the Pleistocene the race of advanced ground-dwelling hominids known as australopithecines was established in South Africa. Somewhat later the distinctly manlike pithecanthropoids appeared in south-east Asia and elsewhere, and showed the beginnings of characteristic human activities as cooking, tool-making and killing each other for material gain. These were followed in turn by the Neanderthalers of Europe and the Middle East, and by a race of long-limbed, thin-skinned upright hominids essentially similar to ourselves. The last two types of man seem to have existed side by side in several regions, but whether they can both trace their origins on roughly parallel lines to a pithecanthropoid ancestor, or whether *Homo sapiens* diverged from a proto-Neanderthaler some 200,000 years ago is still unknown. All that seems certain is that Neanderthal and *sapiens* lines split at a fairly remote period (even though some interbreeding may have occurred later) and that our own species eventually grew so much in intelligence that, in spite of physical inferiority, it swept the Neanderthaloids from the face of the earth (AMYoM, p.123).

And now we will make a brief reference to William Golding's classic *The Inheritors*. We know that Jesus Christ said that the meek shall inherit the earth. But *Homo sapiens*, who inherited the earth some thirty-five millennia ago, were not meek then nor are they any meeker now although we cannot afford to be completely pessimistic about their future.

Golding's novel opens with the central characters appearing one by one in quick succession in a dramatic manner at a point in their journey from the place of their winter sojourn in caves to their summer abode, which they are now approaching. These characters are Lok, Liku, Fa, the new one, Ha, Nil, the old woman and Mal in order of their appearance. Mal is an old patriarch and the old woman is his wife although family as an institution in the modern sense does not exist among them. Lok and Ha are young men, presumably the sons of Mal and the old woman. Fa and Nil are young women. Fa is Lok's mate and Nil is Ha's. Liku, a little girl, seems to be Lok and Fa's daughter and the new one, a baby boy, is Nil's son, presumably by Ha. The baby still sucks mother's milk and the novelist tells us that "though the skin was slack" in Nil's "heavy body her breasts were stretched and full and the white milk stood in the nipples" (TI, p.25). And though the baby is Nil's, he is sleeping on Fa's back with his "hands gripping her hair at the neck and his feet holding the hair farther down her back" (TI, p.12). Family relationships as they are known as father, mother, husband, wife, son, daughter, brother, sister are not known to them, and yet this group of eight is a close-knit family, with Mal as a loving father figure and the old woman is very gentle and is looked upon with awe by all the young members. All of them are knit together with deep feelings of love and affection for each other.

These people are hungry and tired. In their winter habitat they have had a lean period, and they are tired because of the long trek from their winter

abode to summer quarters. Still, they are cheerful and look forward to a pleasant stay here. These simians or, to be more accurate, Neanderthalers, are for
the most part vegetarians. They eat grubs, fungi, tender shoots, berries and
honey. Meat they eat but although they call it "sweet" they call it "wicked"
also. They eat it when it is what they call "without blemish." What it means is
that they do not kill animals for meat, but they eat it when they are killed by
cats by which they mean tigers, leopards, etc. While the group is approaching
the place of its stay in the mountains, Lok looks forward to a nice time as follows: "The food reminded Lok of his own hunger. Now they had left the dank
winter cave by the sea and the unnatural tasting food of beach and salt marsh
he had a sudden picture of good things, of honey and young shoots, of bulbs
and grubs, of sweet and wicked meat" (TI, p.24).

Conceptual thinking has not evolved in the brain of these people. They
think in terms of pictures. They have their own religion and their own simple
but remarkable theology. Their belief in this regard, as explained by Mal to
his family, is as follows: ' "There was the great Oa. She brought forth the earth
from her belly. She gave suck. The earth brought forth woman and the woman
brought forth the first man out of her belly" ' (TI, p.35). Later in the novel,
we come to know something about the religion – magic – practised by *Homo
sapiens*. This religion is purveyed by a witch-doctor named Marlan , who ruth-
lessly butchers Liku and serves her meat to the cannibal *sapiens*. The scene in
which this butchering of Liku, a very lovable girl and the joy and pride of her
parents, Lok and Fa, takes place is of blood-curdling horror. But these things
happen later in the novel.

The family arrive at their summer abode on a terrace with a roof of rock
overhanging it. The old woman has carried fire in a ball of clay. She opens the
ball, breathes into it, and the dry twigs and branches of trees left here last year
by them are heaped on it. Soon there is a brilliant fire. Mal finds his usual seat
and although he is going to die soon, he is happy and says, ' "We are home!"
' (TI, p.32). There is tragic irony of the most horrific kind in these words because, within days, this home will be a place of utter desolation as all members
of this family, except "the new one," will be destroyed one by one by the *sapiens*,
who have been present on the scene from before the arrival of the Neanderthal
family. Each killing strikes our inmost heart with horror; the horror reaches
its climax when poor Liku is butchered in our very sight and her roast meat is

eaten by the cannibalistic *sapiens* with relish. We shall end our brief and incomplete discussion of the novel with a quotation from an essay by John Peter published in *Kenyon Review*:

> *The Inheritors*, published in 1955, is again an indictment of natural human depravity…This time the central characters are a group of hairy simian pre-humans, much like Yahoos in appearance but in other respects very different; the people, as they call themselves, are as intelligent as their experience permits them to be, are warm-hearted and reverent – quite simply, good – and Golding invests them with a quite extraordinary charm. The group is only a remnant, those who have survived a forest fire, and the story tells of their encounter with other creatures whose existence hitherto had been unknown to them, men and women. Their instinctive reaction to the strangers is one of admiration and affection (It is typical that they should first regard the poisoned arrows shot at them as gifts), but for their part the humans hate and fear them, killing them at sight. Inevitably they are destroyed. The narrative closes with a last survivor, Lok, in his death-throes, howling his grief for the companions he has lost, for the inexplicable misery that has possessed him; while the humans row away in their dugout down the lake.[86]

We have now seen how our ancestors came into existence and how they took control of the earth. And we, their descendants for better or for worse, have now a firm grip not only of the biosphere and stratosphere of the planet but are also trying to make our presence felt in the outer space. But how about our organic structure, that is, our body and the various elements or constituents that go into its making? To know this we will go to a great book, *Man on his Nature*, already referred to above, by Sir Charles Sherrington. This book has won universal acclaim. Erwin Schrodinger, a Nobel laureate in Physics, quotes a number of passages from Sherrington's book in his *What is Life?* with *Mind and Matter* and says that Sherrington was "at the same time (rare event!) a man of highest genius and a sober scientist."[87] He calls *Man on his Nature* a "momentous" work and writes further: "I cannot convey the grandeur of Sherrington's immortal book by quoting sentences; one has to read it oneself."[88]

But before going to Sherrington's book we will pause a moment and think about our essential nature. From what has been said above by great creative writers, scientists and thinkers it should be clear that man's origins are not divine, as it was traditionally believed to be, and his nature as a species is anything but meek. Also man should now jettison his unsustainable belief in his divine origin and radically re-orient his world-view and his affairs. Carrington gives us some sane and sober advice in his very Preface. He says that until the middle of the nineteenth century it was believed that

> Man... was the creation of a personal and supernatural deity who would watch over his chosen protege like a benevolent father watching over a son. If this privileged creature conducted himself according to some authoritarian tenets, or duly repented of any failure to observe them, he would be rewarded by an indefinitely prolonged happiness n Heaven. According to this view, the so-called 'brute creation' had been summoned into existence by God especially for the benefit of man.

But, Carrington rightly observes,

> Darwin and his immediate successors proved conclusively that we have evolved by the same basic laws of nature which govern the growth of all other organisms. More recently it has come to be understood that even the physical universe is part of the same process, and that life developed as logically and naturally from inorganic matter as man has developed from the ranks of the Mammalia to become the dominant species on earth.

Continuing, he writes, "The implications of this new world-view offer an extraordinarily exciting challenge to the human mind. Man must now cut away the dead wood of traditional beliefs and approach the whole problem of his role in nature with a new humility" (AMYoM, pp.xiii-xiv).

Before we begin our discussion of the physiology of man, as described in authentic and magnificent detail by Sherrington, we should agree with him that there is in man's body no supra-material entity commonly known as the soul. Sherrington again and again refers to the views of a sixteenth-century French physician-philosopher named Fernel who believed that this soul, perhaps drawn from some star or even from some more celestial source, entered a man's body and lived in it so long as the man was alive, in fact it was a man's life, and went back to its original home the moment the man died or, to be more precise, its departure from the man's body resulted in his death. We quote below the following passage from Sherrington's book in this regard:

> Life was for Fernel a principle which was resident in the body. That principle was not of a piece with the body. What the body did was the result of its activation by this principle inside it, 'its life.' This settled, certain other things flowed thence. Consequences without indeed observational proof. The human principle of life entered the body at its due time from without , all in a moment, and that at that moment the individual became a separate existence from the material existence. This principle ,or soul, came to the body from the stars or perhaps from the 'primum mobile' beyond the stars. At death this living principle, or at least that part identified with rational mind, returned from the body to the celestial region from which it came (MohN, pp.62-63).

> And much earlier, Anton Chekhov, in his play The Seagull(Act 1) wrote: "No one has grounds for separating spirit from matter since it is possible that spirit itself is the combination of atoms of matter."

Now no mainstream scientists, philosophers, creative artists or thinkers believe in such a fairy tale.

Sherrington says that the smallest building blocks of organic life are cells. The cell was discovered in the 17th century by Robert Hooke of the Royal Society. He says this about the breathtaking discovery of the cell: "In the seventeenth century they [cells] came as a revelation comparable with the expansion of the nine Ptolemaic spheres to the immensities of the Galileo-Newton universe" (MohN, p.64). And now we know that "the whole of that part of the animate world which is individually visible to the unaided eye is built up of cells" (MohN, p.53). Carl Sagan in a beautiful passage in his book *Cosmos* says that "The living cell is a regime as complex and beautiful as the realms of the galaxies and the stars" and that "The elaborate machinery of the cell has been painstakingly evolved over four billion years."[89]

Sherrington says that cells in an organism live a double life. He explains this duality as follows:

> The human individual is an organized single family of cells, a family so integrated as to have not merely corporate unity but a corporate personality. The doings of this cell-assembly are – itself supposes, society allows, and the Law decrees – those of a being which is one, a unity. Yet each of its constituent cells is a life centred in itself, managing itself, feeding and breathing for itself, separately born and separately destined to die. Further, it is a life helped by and in its turn helping the whole assembly, which latter is the corporate; co-operation is the one key to the integration of the individual cells. (MohN, pp.65-66).

Sherrington repeats this point in these words, "Each cell is an organized life-system centred upon itself" and "our life which in its turn is a unitary life consists utterly of cell-lives" (MohN, p.66). It is these cells as living units in themselves and organizing themselves in strange ways that give us our particular organic structures with our life – a life that begins with animal impulses or instincts and is capable of rising, by slow degrees, to a transcendent outlook of life. Sherrington says that "the life of the constituent cell" and "the life of the total constituted organism" are called "general physiology" and "special physiology" respectively.

Sherrington first discusses general physiology, that is, life of individual cells. He says that a cell is "a tiny droplet of granular jelly" and adds: "That is, it is not material in any single pure phase, solid, fluid, or gaseous; it is a mixture of all these. That is partly phrased by calling it colloid" (MohN, p.69). He says that the cell is microscopic, but it is larger than "bacterial spore, and the 'virus' is smaller still." Also, it is "vastly larger than any molecule." On the surface of one cell there is room enough "for some hundreds of millions of the great rod-shaped or skein-shaped protein molecules, bristling with chemical receivers. Its content of these rushing whirling electrical charges, some of them spinning many millions of times a second, is beyond practical enumeration." Also, a cell has no parts, it is "structureless" and so "unable to come to pieces" (MohN, p.70). Then Sherrington gives us some more amazing facts about the nature of the cell. He says that although the cell "is fluid and watery, most of...[it is]

not a true solution" and that there are "great molecules of protein and aggre-gated particles...suspended, not dissolved." Then he says that the cell is not a "static system." Continuing, he writes:

> It is energy-cycles, suites of oxidation and reduction, concat-enated ferment-actions. It is like a magic hive the walls of whose chambered spongework are shifting veils of ordered molecules, and rend and renew as operations rise and cease. A world of surfaces and streams. We seem to watch battalions of specific catalysts...lined up, each waiting, stop-watch in hand, for its moment to play the part assigned to it. Yet each step is understandable chemistry (MohN, p.70).

Then Sherrington speaks of the foci in the cell. These "cell foci," he tells us, "co-exist for different operations, so that a different thousand processes go forward at the same time within it." He elaborates further on the function of the foci: "The foci wax and wane as they are wanted. That the cell's field is a colloidal field makes much explicable. The total system is organized. The various catalysts work as co-ordinately as though each had its own compartment in the honeycomb and its own turn and time" (MohN, p.71). Then he says that a cell has a "kernel," that is, a nucleus. The nucleus is "directive; a nest of ferments." The cell has an "outer surface" too. About this outer surface he has to say this:

> It would seem the proteins there connect with those of the nucleus by protein threads. Proteins, which are the very basis of the cell, provide it with a sort of quasi-skeleton. They can make semi-rigid rods; they can spread film-like, in touch with the fatty films of the cell's outward skin. The cell thus gets a subvisible skeleton in accord with the scheme of its internal directive organization. It is of course in constant commerce with the chemical world around it. In the case of a cell inside the body packed in among the others this chemical world around it is a very special chemical world. We can regard the cell's outward surface as a mosaic of a million chemical poles attracting to it and retaining what can dovetail with their pat-tern and enter the electrical construction (MohN, p.71).

Sherrington says that life is "an energy-system" and it "is so woven into the fabric of Earth's surface that to suppose a life isolated from the rest of that terrestrial world even briefly gives an image too distorted to resemble life" (MohN, p.79). And in very lucid language he tells us about the process through which this energy-system gets organized into units of organic life, that is, cells:

Matter almost resolves itself into the electrical. Electrical charges move from or toward one another. They group themselves into certain types of systems, groups called atoms. These groups can be broken up into their components and can be reassembled. Again sets of groups are formed by the so-called atoms arranging themselves into further systems, as are the atoms gathered together in them. It is in accord with certain aspects of this behaviour that some mixtures of molecules arrange themselves as a complex of phases, the colloid state, with molecular aggregates often of molecules of great complexity. The colloidal state plays a great part in the living cell. As compared with some particles of the colloidal state, the smallest unit-lives themselves are but little larger. They are, however, all of them large enough to contain a number of molecules of the chemical classes, protein, fat and carbohydrate. These are commonly associated together in the organization of a complex which is said to live (MohN, p.86).

Then Sherrington raises a very interesting question: Do cells have mind? He says that this question "is not decisively answerable." But some scientists have shown that "the free single cell, for example paramaecium, can be trained to some extent. That is, that it can learn" (MohN, p.88).

After describing in fascinating detail the nature of the cell, Sherrington discusses the "Odyssey," the journey of the single cell, the journey of "a pinhead's egg to a grown man," that is, he enters the field of special physiology. He writes: "The body is made up of cells, thousands of millions of them, in our own instance about 1000 billion. It is a unity which has become a multiplicity while keeping its unity. At its beginning it is just one cell and the whole body is the progeny of that one" (MohN, p.92).

When a man and a woman have sex the spermatozoon and ovum may blend together and produce a new cell in the womb of the woman. This new cell is, Sherrington tells us, "a speck of granular jelly, bearing no likeness to either parent or to man at all" (MohN, p.93). This one cell tears itself into two cells. Then through a process of multiplication there are "4,8,16,32 and so on; only to slow down after reaching millions upon millions. Not to stop altogether until by misadventure or, after years, by natural term, there falls upon the whole assembly that subversive change called 'death' " (MohN, p.93).

Sherrington tells us that when, through multiplication, there are thirty-two cells, they form a little ball. The cells in this ball, he says, "can be likened, crudely enough, to a set of magic bricks." Continuing, he writes: "The one cell, the original fertilized cell, grows into two and two each in two, and so forth. When that has gone on in the aggregate some 45 times there are some 26 million million magic bricks all of a family. That is about the number in the human child at birth" (MohN, pp93-94).

Though the cells are of one family and are blind and without senses, yet they perform, as if by design, different functions in forming different parts of the body in the dark womb. Sherrington writes:

> The cells of the various parts of the systematized assembly assume special shapes, octagonal, stellate, threadlike, or what not. They, as the case may require, pour out cement which binds, or fluid in which they shall move free. Some will have changed their stuff and become rigid bone or, harder still, the enamel of a tooth; some become. fluid, so to flow along tubes too fine for the eye to see. Some become clear as glass, some opaque as stone, some colourless, some red, some black. Some become engines of mechanical pull, some scaffoldings of static support. Some a system transmitting electrical signs. It might serve as a text for democracy…The whole astonishing process achieving the making of a new individual is thus an organized adventure in specialization on the part of countless co-operating units. It does more than complete the new individual, it provides for the future production of further individuals from that one (MohN, pp94-95).

But, Sherrington says, there is an exception. The original fertilized cell which produced two cells which, in turn, produced four and so on, does not change. He writes, "It retains the old original nature of the ancestral cell." And this is necessary, otherwise there will be no procreation. This cell "retains its original germinal and general nature; and even this has to ripen. It gets "specialized for reproduction" in due course (MohN, p.95).

Then Sherrington says that "Water is the very menstruum and habitat of each and every cell." The little ball of the first thirty-two cells is "filled with water." He writes: "The growing membrane, half floating, can fold. It shapes itself, it feeds, water is a generous solvent; and it admits electrical activities, chemical compounds separating with opposite charge....Water, within and without allows the cell free scope for action" (MohN, p.96). Then he describes in vivid detail how different limbs including nerves, muscles, bones etc. are made in the foetus:

> Nerves seem *for* their purpose, constructed in view of what *will* be 'wanted' of them. Before ever they function they grow where they *will* be wanted, they make the 'right' connec- tions....In the particular prodigy before us now, that of mi- croscopic cell becoming a man, we incline to read the whole story in that way. We say 'it grows into' a child. Grows? Levers laid down in gristle, becoming bone when wanted for the heavier pull of muscle which *will* clothe them? Lungs, solid glands, yet arranged to hollow out at a few minutes' no- tice when the necessary air will enter. Limb-buds, futile at their appearing and yet deliberately appearing, in order to become limbs in readiness for an existence where they will be all-important. A pseudo-aquatic parasite, voiceless as a fish, yet constructing within itself an instrument of voice against the time when it *will* talk. Organs of skin, ear, eye, nose, tongue, superfluous all of them in the watery dark where formed, yet each unhaltingly preparing to enter a day- lit, airy, object-full manifold world which they will be wanted to report on. A great excrescence at one end of a nerve-tube, an outrageously outsized brain, of no avail at the moment but where the learning of a world which is *to be* experienced will go forward (MohN, p.98).

It is a miracle; we do not know why the various kinds or groups of cells build various organs and limbs of our body in the dark womb. Sherrington quotes a scientist as saying that " 'we can only understand an organism if we regard it as *though* produced under the guidance of thought for an end,' as a final cause at work" (MohN, p.99). As to the how and why of the process through which millions upon millions of cells in the growing embryo form its different parts and their constituents, Sherrington writes:

Suppose tentatively, at pause before this riddle, we allow the premiss that in this developing embryo there resides some form of mind or psyche, and even in each of its constituent cells, and not inferior to what as human individual it will ever have. Mind so present and intent on producing the child to be, would still be faced at every step with 'how.' (MohN, p.99).

Sherrington writes further on this mystery: "The microscope merely resolves the mystery into some millions of separate microscopic growing points, each still a mystery. We ask what is the process going on at each of these?" (MohN, p.99).

Sherrington asks how does "a pin's-head ball of cells in the course of so many weeks" becomes a child? He says that "A highly competent observer, after watching a motion-film photo-record taken with the microscope of a cell-mass in the process of making bone, writes: 'Team-work by the cell-masses. Chalky spicules of bone-in-the-making shot across the screen, as if labourers were raising scaffold-poles. The scene suggested purposive behavior by individual cells, and still more by colonies of cells arranged as tissues and organs'" (MohN, p.104).

Sherrington describes the amazing nature and function of muscle. He writes:

The essential service of muscle to life is, quickly and reversibly, to shorten so as to pull. Its shortening is called 'contraction.' The importance of muscular contraction to us can be stated by saying is that all man can do is to move things, and his muscular contraction is his sole means thereto. Each muscle- fibre is a simplified miniature of muscle, in size just visible to the naked eye...A muscle is composed of bundles upon bundles of its fibres set lengthwise so as to pull on the muscle's tendon. Each fibre is seen by the microscope to consist of strands of lengthwise running fibrils arranged in packets and bathed liberally in nutritive juice within the fibre. Beyond that, to further degrees of minute structure, the microscope can hardly carry. X-ray examination then continues the analysis. The unit of measurement is the millionth of a millimeter. The ultimate filament then revolves itself in countless lengthwise lines of giant molecules...Such a molecule is, as molecules go, immensely large; it weighs about 500,000 times the hydrogen-gas molecule. It is a protein (myosinogen), and it is one of the folding molecules which by buckling back on itself becomes shorter. A cross-section of our sample muscle-fibre would cut 150 millions of them. It is as if for each square millimeter of a muscle's cross-section a set of pullers five times more numerous than earth's entire human population were aligned to pull co-ordinately in one and the same direction (MohN, p.102).

Then Sherrington describes the structure of our eye. The eyes are man's precious possessions and their creation is something which fills us with wonder. The embryo begins constructing them – two perfectly identical eyes – when it is itself smaller than them. Sherrington calls the embryo at that stage "that little pin's-head bud of multiplying cells...feeding itself on the juices from its mother." And it is precisely from these juices that the eyes are made. And what are these juices made from? Sherrington writes: "The magic of these juices goes by the chemical names, protein, sugar, fat, salts, water. Of them 80% is water." He says that "The eye-ball is a little...spheroid camera" and its "small-ness is part of its perfection" (MohN, p.105). The eyes are formed when the embryo has still a few weeks more to live in the dark womb of the mother. He describes how they are formed:

The little hollow bladder of the embryo-brain, narrowing it-self on two points so as to be triple, thrusts from its foremost chamber to either side a hollow bud. This bud pushes toward the overlying skin. That skin, as though it knew and sympa-thized, then dips down forming a cuplike hollow to meet the hollow brain-stalk growing outward. They meet. The round end of the hollow brain-bud dimples inward and becomes a cup. Concurrently, the ingrowth from the skin nips itself free from its original skin. It rounds itself into a hollow ball, lying in the mouth of the brain-cup. Of this stalked cup, the optic cup, the stalk becomes in a few weeks a cable of a million nerve-fibres connecting the eye-ball itself with the brain. The optic cup, at first just a two-deep layer of somewhat simple-looking cells , multiplies its layers at the bottom of the cup where, when light enters the eye – which will not be for some weeks yet – the photo-image will in due course lie. There the layer becomes a fourfold layer of great complexity. It is strictly speaking a piece of the brain lying within the eye-ball (MohN, p.107).

Then Sherrington says that "The deepest cells at the bottom of the cup become a photo-sensitive layer – the sensitive film of the camera." When light acts on the retina – "and it is from the retina that light's visual effect is known to start" – it is "absorbed" there (MohN, p.107). Then there are "nerve-lines connecting the photo-sensitive layer of the brain." Sherrington says "They are in series of relays" and adds:

> It is the primitive cells of the optic cup, they and their progeny, which become in a few weeks these relays resembling a little brain, and each and all so shaped and connected as to transmit duly to the right points of the brain itself each light-picture momentarily formed and 'taken.' On the sense-cell layer the 'image' has, picture-like, two dimensions. These space-relations 'reappear' in the mind (MohN, p.108).

But in the mind this two-dimensional pictures become, as if by some magic, three-dimensional. Sherrington writes: "...the mind adds the third dimension when interpreting the two dimensional picture! Also it adds colour, in short, it makes a three-dimensional visual out of an electrical disturbance."

As regard the nerve-lines of the retina to the brain, Sherrington refers to the findings of "Cajal, the gifted Spanish Neurologist," who studied an insect's eye for two years. He quotes Cajal's own words regarding his findings:

> "'The complexity of the nerve-structures for vision is even in the insect something incredibly stupendous. From the insect's faceted eye proceeds an inextricable criss-cross of excessively slender nerve-fibres. These then plunge into a cell-labyrinth which doubtless serves to integrate what comes from the retinal layers. Next follow a countless host of amacrine cells and with them again numberless centrifugal fibres. All these elements are moreover so small the highest powers of the modern microscope hardly avail for following them. The intricacy of the connexions defies description" (MohN, p.108).

There are some more amazing facts regarding constitution of the human eye. Sherrington says that there are "about 137 million separate 'seeing' elements spread out in the sheet of the retina." Continuing, he writes:

> The number of nerve-lines leading from them to the brain gradually condenses down to little over a million. Each of these has in the brain, we must think, to find its right nerve-exchanges. These nerve-exchanges lie far apart, and are but stations on the way to further stations. The whole crust of the brain is one thick tangled jungle of exchanges and of branching lines going thither and coming thence. As the eye's cup develops into the nervous retina all this intricate orientation to locality is provided for by corresponding growth in the brain. To compass what is needed adjacent cells, although sister and sister, have to shape themselves quite differently the one from the other. Most become patterned filaments, set lengthwise in the general direction of the current of travel. But some thrust out arms laterally as if to embrace together whole cables of the conducting system (MohN, 110).

Another amazing thing about the eye and brain relationship is that the eye sends "individually evanescent, electrical potentials" to "the cell-and-fibre of the brain throughout the waking day." Sherrington says that these "streams" of "electrical potentials," which are "tiny" and "evanescent," are conjured up by the mind into a kind of power that sees concrete objects in all their varieties, colours and dimensions including their distance, nearness and direction from each other. He writes how this miracle – miracle because physics and chemistry have not been able to explain this process – happens:

> Electrical charges having in themselves not the faintest elements of the visual – having, for instance, nothing of 'distance,' 'right-side-upness,' nor 'vertical,' nor 'horizontal,' nor 'colour,' nor 'brightness,' nor 'shadow,' nor 'roundness,' nor 'squareness,' nor 'contour,' nor 'transparency,' nor 'opacity,' nor 'near,' nor 'far,' nor visual anything – yet conjure up all these. A shower of little electrical leaks conjures up for me, when I look, the landscape; the castle on the height, or, when I look at him, my friend's face, and how distant he is from me they tell me…

It is a case of 'the world is too much with us;' too banal to wonder at . Those other things we paused over, the building and shaping of the eye-ball, and the establishing of its nerve connections with the right points of the brain, all those other things and the rest pertaining to them we called in chemistry and physics and final cause to explain to us. And they did so, with promise of more help to come. But this last, not the eye, but the 'seeing' by the brain behind the eye? Physics and chemistry there are silent to our every question. All they say to us is that the brain is theirs, that without the brain which is theirs the seeing is not. But as to how? They vouchsafe us not a word. Their negation goes further – they assure us it is no concern of theirs at all (MohN, p113).

One thing that Sherrington once again makes clear is that man's mind is as terrestrial as his body and he rejects Fernel's belief "that our mind is no terrestrial product but derives its nature from the stars (MohN, p.139)." He expresses his view very cogently in these words:

our bodily life carries with it its own evidence that its origin is terrestrial. If we employ exotic to mean a non-terrestrial provenance, there is no ingredient in bodily life which is exotic. Its chemical elements are among those commonest on our planet. Its whole is redolent of Earth, whence it was dug. Even likewise with finite mind. Its ways affirm it to be so. Its history proclaims it to be so. Our stock is the vertebrate stock; our body is the vertebrate body; our mind is the vertebrate mind. If the vertebrates be a product of the planet, our mind is a product of the planet (MohN,p.137).

Sherrington, referring to Dante's "noble imagination" travelling "Inferno, Purgatory and Paradise" says that "it still walked Italy, the Italy he loved and grieved for." And as regards Plato's *anima mundi*, he says "it is wholly terrestrial fancy" (MohN, p.138). Then he refers to the observation of a character in Shakespeare that "mind is the slave of life" and writes: "Mind's errand to life does bear that guise. Is one 'slave of life' the more. It was a further contribution to life's exploitation of the planet's side. Mind became one more tool for life and one more condition amid which life worked" (MohN, p.139).

In a very important section of his book, Sherrington describes the construction and function of the brain and its relationship with the mind. He says that in a newborn baby there is no mind. He writes:

> Chemistry builds. All of that imperative growth and development which produces a child from an egg-shell is in the main chemical building, operated, regulated, coordinated and unified chemically. The new-born infant may indeed be said to be a product of chemical integration. Our sixteenth-century Fernel would say it constructs a tenement for mind but – and that he would have found natural enough – it does not produce the tenant (MohN, p.167).

Instead, Sherrington says, "the integration of the body in virtue of one of its features brings with it mind – recognizable mind" (MohN,p.168). He also says something which is very revealing – revealing of the nature of cells in our body and how the integration of these billions of cells in it appears, as can be seen as urge-to-live and zest- to- live. He writes: " 'Life has an itch to live.' This itch is universal with it. Under the microscope it gives us tiny lives hurrying hither, thither, feeding. Driven, each says almost as clearly as if it spoke, by 'urge-to-live.' The one key-phrase to the whole bustling scene seems 'urge-to-live' " (MohN, p.170).

This 'urge-to-live' that can be seen in the hurrying-hither-and-thither-and-feeding cells under the microscope can be seen as 'zeal-to-live/zest-to-live' in life's activities in men and women – "individuals hurrying hither and thither, hastening to earn, entering restaurants…" (MohN, p.170). Sherrington, therefore, asks, "if a form of mind there can be in that microscopic population, though as a germ so remote that no word of ours can duly fit it, is it not probable that that mind is 'zest-to-live' in germ?" (MohN, p.170).

Then Sherrington talks about two very important things – (a) man's place on this planet vis-à-vis other organisms and (b) the evolution of the mind. Regarding (a), he refers to Fernel's view that "man has a soul which nothing else earthly has" (Ibid.p. 170) and that "Animals bring no message to him about himself except that they are for his use." Sherrington says that even as late as in the late eighteenth century the philosopher Kant held the view similar to that of Fernel – that "animal kind was simply food for man's body, draught for his plough, furr for his warmth, remedies for his ailments" (MohN, p.171). He says that "New knowledge has put us in a new perspective" and that "Other life …is not now another order of being, but our kith and kin." Continuing, he writes:

> Their nature and ours are one. They are each and all impelled as are we by the same 'urge- to- live.' We and they are all comrades in one same great adventure – life. They and we are striving toward the same goal. All of us were launched and are steered by one same 'urge-to-live.' For me to know that is for me to see the animal for the same   end as I am. It gives me a basis for understanding other life along with mine (MohN, p.171).

Then Sherrington discusses the evolution and nature of the mind. Again he rejects Fernel's view of man's mind as something "created by heaven" and says this: "For us man's mind is a recent product of our planet's side, produced from mind already there long previously, yielding man's mind by gradual change of previous mind" (MohN, p.173).

Now that it is evident that all organisms including plants share the same life and thus the barrier between man as endowed with divine life and other creatures as having been deprived of this blessing has disappeared, it follows that mind that has reached the level of conceptual thinking in man came to exist in lower creatures much earlier. Sherrington says that today we know that "even our poor relations, the fish and amphibian, can 'learn' " and that "The man-like ape clearly has symbolic thinking" (MohN, p.172). And he asks: "When [our pet dog] sidles to us with half-averted face and asks a word of praise or notice from us, is he not self-conscious" (MohN,p.173)?

The most marvellous section in Sherrington's book is the passage in which he describes the human mind both in its waking and sleeping states. We cannot help quoting the entire passage:

> A scheme of lines and nodal points, gathered together at one end into a great ravelled knot, the brain, and at the other trailing off to a sort of stalk, the spinal cord. Imagine activity in this shown by little points of light. Of these some stationary flash rhythmically, faster or slower. Others are travelling points, streaming in serial trains at various speeds. The rhythmic stationary lights lie at the nodes. The nodes are both goals whither converge, and junctions whence diverge,

the lines of travelling lights. The lines and nodes where the lights are, do not remain, taken together, the same even a single moment. There are at any time nodes and lines where lights are not.

Suppose we choose the hour of deep sleep. Then only in some sparse and out of the way places are nodes flashing and trains of light-points running. Such places indicate local activity still in progress. At one such place we can watch the behavior of a group of lights perhaps myriad strong. They are pursuing a mystic and recurrent manoeuvre as if of some incantational dance. They are superintending the beating of the heart and the state of the arteries so that while we sleep the circulation of the blood is what it should be. The great knotted headpiece of the whole sleeping system lies for the most part dark, and quite especially so the roof-brain. Occasionally at places in it lighted points flash or move but soon subside. Such lighted points and moving trains of light are mainly ar in the outskirts, and wink slowly and travel slowly. At intervals even a gush of sparks wells up and sends a train down the spinal cord, only to fail to arouse it. Where however the stalk joins the headpiece, there goes forward in a limited field a remarkable display. A dense constellation of some thousands of nodal points bursts out every few seconds into a short phase of rhythmical flashing. At first a few lights, then more, increasing in rate and number with a deliberate crescendo to a climax, then to decline and die away. After due pause the efflorescence is repeated. With each such rhythmic outburst goes a discharge of trains of travelling lights along the stalk and out of it altogether into a number of nerve-branches. What is this doing? It manages the taking of our breath the while we sleep.

Should we continue to watch the scheme we should observe after a time an Impressive change which suddenly accrues. In the great head-end which has been mostly darkness spring up myriads of twinkling stationary lights and myriads of trains of moving lights of many different directions. It is as though activity from one of those local places which continued restless in the darkened main-mass suddenly spread far and wide and invaded all. The great topmost sheet of the mass, that where hardly a light had twinkled or moved, becomes now a sparkling field of rhythmic flashing points with trains of travelling sparks hurrying hither and thither. The brain is waking and with it the mind is returning. It is as if the Milky Way entered upon some cosmic dance. Swiftly the head-mass becomes an enchanted loom where millions of flashing shuttles weave a dissolving pattern, always a meaningful pattern though never an abiding one; a shifting harmony of sub-patterns. Now as the waking body rouses, sub-patterns of this great harmony of activity stretch down into the unlit tracks of the stalk-piece of the scheme. Strings of flashing and travelling sparks engage the lengths of it. This means that the body is up and rises to meet its waking day. Dissolving pattern after dissolving pattern will, the long day through, without remission melt into and succeed each other in this scheme by which for the moment we figure the brain and spinal cord. Especially, and with complexity incredible, in that part which we were thinking of, the roof-brain. Only after day is done will it quiet down, lapse half-way to extinction, and fall again asleep. Then at last, so far at least as the roof-brain, motor acts cease. The brain is released from the waking day and marshals its factors for its motor acts no more (MohN pp. 176-178).

As regards the mind of man, Sherrington says, "Of man we know even more confidently than of any other concrete life that his mind is correlated with his brain" (MohN, p.187). And G. G. Simpson has to say this about the correlation between the body and the mind: "Mind is not a thing or an aspect of a thing; it is a process that occurs in the body. We should no more argue about the distinction of mind and body than about the distinction of, say, digestion and body or respiration and body."[69] And in a brilliant passage quoted below, Carl Sagan tells us about the strange composition of our brain and its inherent capacity to reach sublime heights of rational thinking and creative insights:

Like all our organs, the brain has evolved, increasing in complexity and information 5 content, over millions of years. Its structure reflects all the stages through which it has passed . The brain evolved from the inside out. Deep inside is the oldest part, the brainstem, which conducts the basic biological functions, including the rhythms of life – heartbeat and respiration. According to a provocative insight by Paul Mac-

Lean, the higher functions of the brain evolved in three successive stages. Capping the brainstem is the R-complex, the seat of aggression, ritual, territoriality and social hierarchy, which evolved hundreds of millions of years ago in our reptilian ancestors. Deep inside the skull of everyone of us there is something like the brain of a crocodile. Surrounding the R-complex is the limbic system or mammalian brain, which evolved tens of millions of years ago in ancestors who were mammals but not yet primates. It is a major source of our moods and emotions, of our concern and care for the young. And finally, on the outside, living in uneasy truce with the more primitive brains beneath, is the cerebral cortex, which evolved millions of years ago in our primate ancestors. The cerebral cortex, where matter is transformed into consciousness, is the point of embarkation for all our cosmic voyages. Comprising more than two-thirds of the brain mass, it is the realm of both intuition and critical analysis. It is here that we have ideas and inspirations, here that we read and write, here that we do mathematics and compose music. The cortex regulates our conscious lives. It is the distinction of our species, the seat of our humanity. Civilization is a product of the cerebral cortex.

The language of the brain is not the DNA language of the genes. Rather, what we know is encoded in cells called neurons – microscopic electrochemical switching elements, typically a few hundredths of a millimeter across. Each of us has perhaps a hundred billion neurons, comparable to the stars in the Milky Way Galaxy. Many neurons have thousands of connections with their neighbors. There are something like a hundred trillion, 10^{14}, such connections in the human cerebral cortex.[70]

Carl Sagan says something very interesting about the architecture of our consciousness: "The neurochemistry of the brain is astonishingly busy, the circuitry of a machine more wonderful than any devised by humans. But there is no evidence that its functioning is due to anything more than the 10^{14} neural connections that build an elegant architecture of consciousness."[71]

Julian Huxley holds the view that mind is "an operative part of life's mechanism." On page 86 of his book *Evolution in Action* he writes:

Life has two aspects, a material and a mental. Its mental aspect increases in importance during evolutionary time. Later animal deployments have reached a higher level of mental organization than earlier ones ; the higher animals have a larger mental component in their make-up. This fact leads to a conclusion – that mind is not a pale epiphenomenon, not a mere "ghost in the machine," to use Professor Ryle's phrase, but an operative part of life's mechanism.[72]

In a more lucid passage on the same page of his book, Huxley writes:

For a biologist, much the easiest way is to think of mind and matter as the aspects of a single, underlying reality – shall we call it world substance, the stuff out of which the world is made. At any rate, this fits more of the facts and leads to fewer contradictions than any other view. In this view, mental activities are among the inevitable properties of world substance when this is organized in the form of the particular kind of biological machinery we find in the brain.[73]

Sherrington makes some very important observations on the nature and function of the mind. He says that "Mind, for anything perception can compass, goes therefore in our spatial world more ghostly than a ghost. Invisible, intangible, it is a thing not even of outline, is not a 'thing.'" And then he talks about the perceptible world. "All that space-time continuum contains" and talks about the relationship between the perceiving mind and the perceived world." He says,

They have this in common – we have already recognized it – they are both parts of one mind. They are thus therefore distinguished, but are not sundered. Nature in evolving us makes them two parts of the knowledge of one mind and that one mind our own. We are the tie between them. Perhaps we exist for that (MohN,pp. 256-257). 'But he draws our attention to a very important fact about our knowledge of our own mind, which is a very disturbing fact. He writes:

Man's analysis of his sensible world seems to have outstripped his analysis of his own mind. It may be said that to analyse the sensible world is in truth to analyse the mind. But asked whether that were what he was after in analyzing the sensible world, man would surely reply, 'No, my object was to understand better the world which I perceive.' Having that intent he has in recent centuries prospered in his object. The scientific description of the sensible world from of old, even after the intellectual heyday of classical Greece, seems in observation and inference sadly superannuated to a reader of today. After a halt of many centuries, the study of the physical world strode forward. With the study of the mind it has been different. There, as regards analysis of the mind, the difference between classical Greece and now is by a modern reader felt to be far less. It may be argued that the analysis of mind as compared with that of analysis of the physical world was early relatively advanced. If so, it has, as compared with physical science, advanced relatively slowly since. The fact remains that ways of thought regarding the mind would seem during the last 2000 and odd years not to have changed to anything like the extent to which ways of thought about the perceptible world have changed (MohN, p.246).

Then Sherrington dwells at some length on the nature of Nature. There was a time when the "natural world... looked at by the moralist, assured him from every nook and corner that a loving father had devised it, loving what He had made." But modern perception of this world is, Sherrington says, "perhaps nearer to the judgement of Philo in Hume's 'Dialogue,' " pronounced as follows:

'Look around the universe. What an immense profusion of beings animated and organized, sensible and active! You admire the prodigious variety and fecundity. But inspect a bit more narrowly these living existences. How hostile and destructive to ach other! How insufficient all of them for their own happiness!' (MohN,p.270)

Sherrington says that our newer knowledge of the universe is similar to what Aristotle found in it: " 'evil is more plentiful than good, and what is hateful is more plentiful than what is fair.' " He presents a scientist's perception of nature in these words; "Nature is a scene of interaction, and between living things interaction can be cooperation or conflict. Nature exhibits such cooperation, but she is burdened with conflict like a nightmare. Beauties it presents, joys it contains, but a blight of suffering infests it (MohN, p.271.).

It is in this world that man is doomed to live and his resources are his only support and strength. We saw above what advice G. G. Simpson and Richard Carrington gave us to re-orient our lives in order to live as crown of creation, which we have been claiming to be. In the closing passage of his book, Sir Charles Sherrington, too, makes a strong plea to us to discharge our responsibilities since we are "as yet Nature's noblest product:"

> the human mind, such as it is, is left the crown of mind to which human life in all its needs has direct access. Compared with a situation where the human mind beset with its perplexities had higher mind and higher personality than itself to lean on and to seek counsel from, this other situation where it has no appeal and no resort for help beyond itself, has an element of tragedy and pathos. Ours is a situation which transforms the human spirit's task, almost beyond recognition, to one of loftier responsibility. It elevates that spirit to the position of protagonist of a virility and dignity which otherwise the human figure could not possess. It raises the lowliest human being conjointly with the highest, Prometheus-like, to a rank of obligation and pathos which neither Moses in his law-giving nor Job in all his suffering could surpass. We have, because human, an inalienable prerogative of responsibility which we cannot devolve, no, not as once was thought, even upon the stars. We can share it only with each other (MohN, pp. 304-306).

But we have seen above that below the cerebral cortex there are layers, though thin, of reptilian and mammalian brains in the human skull. It is no wonder therefore that aggression, blind faith, irrationality and similar negative pulls have made the world of human affairs miserable. It appears that in most of us these negative pulls have an upper hand. J. B. S. Haldane sounds correct when he writes, "Man of today is probably an extremely primitive and imperfect type of rational being. He is a worse animal than the monkey."[74] But Julian Huxley believes that evolution has been moving in a progressive direction. However, he says that for this to happen further "the brain's level of performance" has to be "genetically raised – in acuteness of perception, memory, synthetic grasp and intuition, analytic capacity, mental energy, creative power, balance and judgement." But he also says that although "Progress is a major fact of past evolution,…it is limited to a few selected stocks. It may continue in the future, but it is not inevitable; man , by now become the trustee of evolution, must work and plan if he is to achieve further progress for himself and so for life."[75]

We have covered briefly the cosmic-inorganic and organic- biological phases of evolution. Now psycho-social phase is on concurrently with the previous two phases. Psychologists and social scientists can tell us what is actually going on now and what are the future prospects of man's existence because man is now the dominant species and it is he who can either drive the engine of evolution forward or bring it to a grinding halt or even destroy himself and all life on the earth. Literature is the highest intellectual product of this phase of evolution and it holds up the mirror to the ethos of this phase. Literature today has to perform this task and evaluate the worthiness of man to play his role as the "trustee of evolution" with the long perspectives, put together here, as background.

We shall close this Chapter with one more quotation – the last paragraph in Carl Sagan's much-acclaimed book already referred to above:

> For we are the local embodiment of a Cosmos grown to self-awareness. We have begun to contemplate our origins: star-stuff pondering the stars; organized assemblages of ten billion billion billion atoms considering the evolution of atoms; tracing the long journey by which, here at least, consciousness arose. Our loyalties are to the species and the planet. We speak for Earth. Our obligation to survive is owed not just to ourselves but also to that Cosmos, ancient and vast, from which we spring.[76]

CHAPTER TWO
Philip Larkin's Aesthetic of Poetry

In the previous chapter we said in our concluding words that literature today has to evaluate, at metaphysical level, the worthiness of man to play the role as "the trustee of evolution." Philip Larkin, in his major poems, attempts to do this evaluation. As we have seen above and shall see in the succeeding chapters of this work, serious creative writers and scientists are concerned at the sorry condition of man's existence and want it to be radically changed in the light of the new world order revealed by human consciousness operating in different fields of knowledge. Philip Larkin is one such writer. In this chapter we will see what his poetic vocation aims at in this direction. We shall quote his views on poetry and his task as a poet to show this. Here we must make it clear that Larkin is not a theorist of poetry like, say, Coleridge, Matthew Arnold or T. S Eliot. He himself made this point clear when he said, "I find it hard to give any abstract views on poetry and its present condition as I find theorizing on the subject no help to me as a writer"(RW, p.79). But his views and opinions on poetry and his task as a poet are very important to understand his poetry and the long perspectives to which it is attached as if to the navel cord.

We shall first quote the following sentence which occurs in his interview with the *Observer*: "Deprivation is for me what daffodils were for Wordsworth"(RW,p.47). The word "deprivation" here needs to be explained because Larkin is not talking about social or economic deprivation, but about deprivation of an altogether different kind. People are deprived of a worldview that they need to have. It is an imperative need today. Deprived of it, they are literally dying, as Saul Bellow, whom we have quoted above, put it and as Larkin himself tells us in his poem "Nothing to be Said." What Wordsworth does as a nature poet in his short lyric is important. He sees a thread of thrill and joy running through the daffodils (thousands of them) "Fluttering and dancing in the breeze" like "the stars that shine /And twinkle on the milky way." Then, when the poet is alone in his room in vacant or passive mood, his soul is filled with pleasure and it dances as the daffodils danced "Beside the lake, beneath the trees." What Wordsworth does here is to show the spiritual aspect of beauty and joy natural phenomena, terrestrial (daffodils) and celestial (the stars on the milky way), possess and then shows its link to his own human heart . The poet's purpose here is to show spiritual link between nature and human soul and thereby bring about spiritual elevation of man.

Philip Larkin's task as a post-modern poet is of a different kind. He has to make man aware of his real status in the universe, a status which is both humbling and ennobling. He finds that most of us are deprived of this awareness. He makes this very clear in these lines in his poem "Reference Back:"

> Truly, though our element is time,
> We are not suited to the long perspectives
> Open at each moment of our lives (TWW,p.40).

He is of the view, and in this he is in the company of mainstream scientists, creative writers and thinkers, that unless man has this awareness his future as a species is endangered. But he is a poet, not a scientist or philosopher. He transmutes scientific-philosophic truths into poetic creations. It is therefore necessary to know what he thinks of himself as a poet. He has made a number of observations in this regard and it is necessary to examine some of these observations. As our first example in this regard, we will consider his observation in reply to the question of the interviewer for the *Paris Review* as to why he wrote and for whom: "…you write because you have to. If you rationalize it, it seems as if you've seen the sight, felt the feeling, had this vision, and have got to find a combination of words that will preserve it by setting it off in other people. The duty is to the original experience. It doesn't feel like self-expression, though it may look like it. As for *whom* you write, well, you write for everybody. Or anybody who will listen" (RW, pp. 58-59).

There is an urge in the poetic self to create. This means that there is something of great value in what the poet has seen, what he has felt, and in the vision arising from the sight and the feeling. "Here," the opening poem in *The Whitsun Weddings*, best illustrates this poetic process. The first twenty-four and a half line sentence, covering the first three stanzas and half of the first line of the fourth and last stanza, spans many sights in a particular region in real time in England. Philip Larkin's poetic consciousness feels the feelings that these sights arouse in him. Then in the next two short sentences in the last stanza, the ground is prepared for the vision that the sights and the feelings give rise to. In these two sentences, we see the four elements of the medieval world – fire, earth, water and air (the sky) – at work and when we are face to face with them we feel that a new kind of perspective is going to open before us. In the last one and a half lines, which also constitute the last sentence in the poem, we have the long perspective or the poet's vision unfold before us. In the last stanza, that is, in its seven and a half lines, and not earlier, the word "Here" , which is also the title of the poem, occurs thrice, which is significant in that the word tells us again and again that here we can see the elements – the elements which have created us in a long and often erratic process of evolution – at work. And then in the last one and a half lines in the poem we have the vision. The vision is that of the sea facing the sun. These are the two elemental phenomena that began creating, and are still creating, life on earth. The poet calls the sea facing the sun "unfenced existence." It is also "untalkative, out of reach." Water impregnated with energy (energy on our earth means the energy of the sun) is existence, whether in the seas or on land. Man has fenced life on earth and also mortgaged his existence – mortgaged to what? To a kind of life that obfuscates the true perception of his existence and so this existence is untalkative to him and also out of his reach. And finally the poet finds a combination of words that will preserve for a long time the sights he saw, the feelings he felt and the vision he had.

Our next quotation is from Larkin's "Statement" which was published in *Poets of the 1950s* edited by Robert Conquest: "I write poems to preserve things I have seen /felt (if I may so indicate a composite and complex experience) both for myself and for others, though I feel that my prime responsibility is to the experience itself, which I am trying to keep from oblivion for its own sake" (RW, p. 79). The last clause in this sentence is worth paying close attention to. In his poems (that is, in what we deem his best poems), Larkin tries to preserve something from oblivion for its own sake. The experiences in these poems are uniquely felt and of permanent value. Now these experiences may mean different things to different people. For Larkin they are meaningful in relation to long perspectives, as we have put together in the preceding chapter, *vis-a vis* the kind of life we live. This kind of life is not in conformity with the truth of things and so human civilization is in a bad shape, is, in fact, in ruins, as William Golding rightly holds.

Another very important observation Larkin makes regarding his vocation as a poet in reply to the question of the interviewer for the *Observer* ("Do you feel terribly pleased when you've written one," that is, a poem?) is as follows: "Yes, as if I've laid an egg, and even more pleased when I see it published. Because I think that's a part of it. You want it to be seen and read, you're trying to preserve something. Not for yourself, but for the people who haven't seen it , or heard it or experienced it" (RW, p. 52)

Here Larkin makes two very important points about poetic creativity. The first point is that writing a poem is as sublime a creative act as a mother giving birth to a child. And just as a mother is immensely pleased to see her baby in good health, Larkin is pleased to see his poem published because he wants it to be seen and read. A mother, too, wants her baby to be seen and loved by people around her. The other point that Larkin makes here is that the poem should be preserved for "the people who have not seen it, or heard it or experienced it." This point is of utmost importance in evaluating the worth of a poem. A poem must be a fine creation in which the sight seen, the feeling felt and the vision the poet had must cohere in a fine combination of words. Then this creation is worth preserving because it will please, aesthetically speaking, and elevate the spiritual self of the reader in whatever place and at whatever point of time he happens to read it. The pleasure and ennobling influence will be felt by the reader because he has not had the experience laced with the vision the poem encapsulates. To illustrate the points Philip Larkin makes in the observation under consideration, we can refer to "The Trees," a very short and simple poem in *High Windows* (p. 6). Poets have written about trees, but in Larkin's trees we see sights, feel feeings and have a vision that are uniquely creative and specific to the individual talent of the poet. The poet must have felt immense pleasure in writing this poem. And the vision that he had and which is enshrined in the particular verbal structure is of universal and permanent importance for mankind.

And in reply to one of the questions of the interviewer Larkin spoke about Hardy's "wonderful dicta about poetry:" " 'The poet should touch our hearts by showing his own,' 'the poet takes note of nothing that he cannot feel,' 'the emotion of all the ages and the thought of his own' – Hardy knew what it was all about" (RW, p. 67). What Larkin finds valuable in these dicta is that poetry has its solid foundation in feelings and emotions that the poet's heart has felt and which touch the reader's heart. By way of illustration we can refer to the epics of Homer. Written some three thousand years ago, these epics have as their settings a civilization and its mores that appear very unfamiliar, often barbarian and brutish to us. But even now they give the reader the greatest aesthetic pleasure and also bring to him a lot of spiritual riches and wisdom. It is because the feelings and emotions of the characters in these epics are of all the ages. And then the genius-specific thought of Homer so shaped and wove them (the feelings and emotions) into his works that they attained perennial charm and strength.

And in an essay entitled "The Poetry of Hardy," Larkin expresses similar ideas but in different words. He writes: "Hardy taught one to feel rather than to write – of course one has to use one's own language and one's jargon and one's own situations – and he taught one as well to have confidence in what one felt." In the same essay Larkin wrote: "In almost every Hardy poem in the 800 pages, barring one or two…there is a little spinal cord of thought and each has a little tune of its own, and this is something you could say of very few poets" (RW, pp. 175-176).

Here Larkin refers to the three basic constituents or ingredients we find in Hardy's poetry and which also constitute the hallmark of a good poem. First, it is feeling. Feeling can be superficial or deep and multidimensional. It is the second kind of feeling that springs from the deepest depths of the poet's being and goes deep into the reader's heart that is enshrined in a good poem. This kind of feeling to arise from a soul and touch a soul is the privilege of a poet and of a reader of poetry with a very refined sensibility. Then there is, in a good poem, a little spinal cord of thought. The term "spinal cord" is very important. It is the spinal cord of thought that makes a poem stand erect; without it the poem will sag. .Now, again, thoughts can be trivial or deep, serious and of permanent value. The value of a poem depends on the value of its thought suffused with feeling. Finally, a good poem has a tune of its own. Tunefulness must be related to the feeling and thought in the poem. We can mention Hardy's little poem "The Self-Unseeing" in which the three ingredients are so organized as to form an organic whole of great beauty and perfection. We can find the same kind of organization in Hardy's major poems. The poem "The Whitsun Weddings" is a superb instance of this kind of organization. But because Larkin's England has changed considerably from the England of the time in which Hardy lived, Larkin uses in his poem his "own language," his "own jargon," and his "own situations."

"The Whitsun Weddings" spans a range of feelings whose integrity is never in doubt – in this respect Hardy and Larkin are alike. And as in Hardy's poem, referred to above, in Larkin's poem, too, feelings and thought are so interwoven that they form a beautiful design on its fabric. In the beginning of the poem, the poet-persona, in the situation he finds himself – "three-quarters empty train," "All windows down, all cushions hot," "all sense of being in a hurry gone" and the setting the train passes through – he feels drained of creative feelings. But even in this impoverished setting he sees (or feels) something procreative that he tells us about in the last two lines of the first stanza. It is a kind of wedding in the coming together of the elements of the medieval world – "sky and Lincolnshire and water meet." Fire in "the tall heat" sleeping "For miles inland" is already pervasive in the setting. So we have fire, sky, earth (Lincolnshire), water – the elements which have been creating life – plants, animals, man – on our planet. If the setting is impoverished it can be made rich because the procreative elements are still working. In the second stanza we have the same kind of depressing setting ending in the "acres of dismantled cars." The feelings of the poet do not overreach themselves but their objective correlatives are quite eloquent. Then the human scenes, which are the exact counterparts of the landscapes, open up. In the humanscape (if we may use such a term) we find cultural impoverishment and so the poet's first feeling is that of indifference which soon changes to one of curiosity. He watches or looks at groups of middle class (perhaps lower middle class) people, friends and relations of the newly-weds, who board the train at different stations for their honeymoon in London, with a feeling of superiority (one may say even of contempt at their superficialities and vulgarities). But as regards the just-married couples, he does not have feelings of superiority or contempt because he knows the sanctity or value of marriage as an institution. When the last couple gets on board and the train starts moving, the poet says to us, "And loaded with the sum of all they saw /We hurried towards London..." What the friends and relations saw departing did not amount to much. But the poet's feeling during "Some fifty minutes" of the journey from this point did amount to much. He knows that just as the coming together of the elements produce /create life on earth, marriage creates human society. This society is culturally deprived just as the landscapes are impoverished, not to say ugly, but it can be made healthy and beautiful. That is why the poet calls the "postal districts" of London "squares of wheat" and tells us "...and what it (the train) held /Stood ready to be loosed with all the power /That being changed can give." And, finally, as the train applied the brakes, there swelled among them a sense of falling and becoming somewhere rain. As regards the tune of the poem, we can only say that the poet uses his own language, his own jargon, his own situation and tunes them, with a minor variation, into a stanza pattern that Keats used for his classic "Ode on a Grecian Urn."

And now we quote the last two sentences from Larkin's essay on Emily Dickinson and Walter de la Mare entitled "Big Victims:" "Poetry is an affair of sanity, of seeing things as they are. The less a writer's work approximates to this maxim, the less claim he has on the attention of his contemporaries and of posterity" (RW, p. 197). A poet must have both the capacity and ability to see things as they are. But what does the expression "seeing things as they are" mean? Simply put, it means seeing the truths of things and phenomena, whatever his political leanings or religious faith may be. And for this to happen the artist must have, first and foremost, the world view we have put together in the preceding chapter with the help of great scientists who are also great thinkers, as will be evident from their views assembled together in the chapter. And the views of some of the great creative writers we have quoted in that chapter and those of other creative writers, philosophers and scientists we have quoted in other chapters of this work reinforce the imperative need of all of us to see things as they are. But it is easier said than done because, as Mikhail Sholokhov says (we have quoted his exact words in this work), truth has been a corpse a long time already and also because, as William Golding observes (we have quoted him too), we are damned with our own trivialities. However, a true artist, at least in his creations of permanent value, keeps his trivialities (of which we all are victims) at bay, resurrects the truth, breathes life into it, and gives us glimpses of it.

And now we will go to Larkin's essay entitled "Pleasure Principle." At the very outset of this essay, he tells us how a poem gets written:

> It consists of three stages, the first is when a man becomes obsessed with an emotional concept to such a degree that he is compelled to do something about it. What he does is the second stage, namely, construct a verbal device that will re-produce this emotional concept in anyone who cares to read it, anywhere, any time. The third stage is the recurrent situation of people in different times and places setting off the device and re-creating in themselves what the poet felt when he wrote it (RW, p. 80).

The first stage in the process of poetic creation is the inception or birth of an "emotional concept" in the poet's imagination. The word "concept" can have philosophical halo or aura. It is "an idea or mental image corresponding to some distinct entity or class of entities" (O.E.D.) and is suffused with emotion and demands to be incarnated as a poetic creation – a demand so compelling that the poet cannot help meeting it. The idea is of great value and demands to be perceived and understood by sensitive people, anywhere, any time. Then the poet has to construct a verbal structure to make the concept or idea appear in all its emotional suffusion. The emotional concept thus incarnated has such power and value that it is re-incarnated in the reader's imagination in any place and at any time. This is the secret of the perennial value of a work of art and Larkin tried to achieve permanence for his emotional concepts in his poetic creations.

In the same essay, Larkin wrote: "But at bottom poetry, like all art, is inexorably bound up with pleasure, and if a poet loses his pleasure-seeking audience he has lost the only audience worth having, for which the dutiful mob that signs on every September is no substitute" (RW, p. 81-82). I read somewhere that Robert Frost said that poetry begins in pleasure and ends in wisdom. It was Aristotle who, some two and a half millennia ago, told us how poetry gives us pleasure. We quote below some lines from the opening paragraph of Chapter IV of *Poetics* (Trans. S. H. Butcher):

> Poetry in general seems to have sprung from two causes, each of them lying deep in our nature. First, the instinct of imita-

tion is implanted in man from childhood, one difference between him and other animals being that he is the most imitative of living creatures, and through imitation learns his earliest lessons; and no less universal is the pleasure felt in things imitated. We have evidence of this in the facts of experience. Objects which in themselves we view with pain, we delight to contemplate when reproduced with minute fidelity; such as the forms of the most ignoble animals and of dead bodies. The cause of this again is, that to learn gives the liveliest pleasure, not only to philosophers but to men in general.

And our last quotation is from Larkin's "Introduction to *All What Jazz*." Here he writes, "In a humanist society, art – and especially modern, or current art – assumes great importance and to lose touch with it is parallel to losing one's faith in a religious age" (RW, p.292). Ours is not a religious age, we live in a humanist society. In this kind of society literature provides the same kind of spiritual mainstay to those who seek fulfillment as religion used to provide a kind of *nirvana* to those who sought it in its realm. We remember that Matthew Arnold said (we have quoted him in this work) that a time would come when poetry would replace religion. Larkin assigns a very high position, and rightly so, to poetry and his major poems have the depth and sublimity of feeling and thought that, we believe, will live up to this high position.

In the next three chapters we have analysed thirty of Philip Larkin's poems selected from *The Less Deceived, The Whitsun Weddings* and *High Windows*. The reader will judge whether the analyses reveal the pleasure the poems intended to give and whether their value is such that it will give them the permanence that works of art have.

CHAPTER THREE
Poems from *The Less Deceived*

CHURCH GOING

Simon Petch says that ' "Church Going" is the best-known poem'[1] in *The Less Deceived* and David Lodge called it "Larkin's most popular poem."[2] There was a fairly detailed discussion of the poem in the interview Larkin gave to Ian Hamilton for the *London Magazine* in November 1964. Hamilton referred to the general opinion that "Church Going" was "a kind of 'representative attitude' poem, standing for a whole disheartened, debunking state of mind in post-war England" and asked Larkin how he felt about its "enormous popularity." Larkin's detailed reply regarding the popularity of the poem and its supposed religious character was quite clear and so it is reproduced below:

> I think its popularity is somewhat due to extraneous factors – anything about religion tends to go down well; I don't know whether it expresses what people feel. It is of course an entirely secular poem. I was a bit irritated by an American who insisted to me it was a religious poem. It isn't religious at all. Religion surely means that the affairs of this world are under divine surveillance, and so on, and I go to some pains to point out that I don't bother about that kind of thing, that I'm deliberately ignorant of it – 'Up at the holy end,' for instance. Ah no, it's a great religious poem; he knows better than me – trust the tale and not the teller, and all that stuff.

Of course the poem is regarding going to church, not religion – I tried to suggest this by the title – and the union of the important stages of human life – birth, marriage and death that going to church represents...

To a further remark by Hamilton that the poem seemed to be " a debate between the poet and the persona" Larkin's reply was again very clear:

> Well, in a way. The poem starts by saying, you don't really know about all this, you don't believe in it, you don't know what a rood-loft is – why do you come here, why do you bother to stop and look round? The poem is seeking an answer.[3]

These observations of the poet are significant. But to understand the poem we shall trust the tale and shall see that the poem corroborates what the poet has said above.

We shall now come to the poem. The first two stanzas move with breathless speed. A bored, uninformed man, as the persona modestly introduces himself later in the poem, drops in on a church during daytime. He often visits churches when he is sure that nothing is going on inside, which implies that he never attends a service in a church. He steps inside, lets the door "thud shut" and mutters to himself: "another church." He looks around and sees

> matting, seats and stone,
> And little books, sprawlings of flowers, cut
> For Sunday, brownish now; some brass and stuff
> Up at the holy end; the small neat organ,
> And a tense, musty, unignorable silence,
> Brewed God knows how long.

He takes off his cycle-clips in "awkward reverence," moves forward and moves his hand around the font, looks at the ceiling which seems new, wonders whether it has been cleaned or restored, mounts the lectern, peruses a few "hectoring, large-scale verses" and pronounces "here endeth," whose echoes snigger briefly. Here it may be mentioned that the persona's cycle-clips have provoked sneering remarks from certain high- brow critics. But it is precisely the cycle-clips, though they place the persona on a lower social rung, that represent the majority of people even in a developed country like England. And it is necessary that this majority reject the superstitious practices of the church. Individual exposure of such practices even by a great man like Tolstoy led to his excommunication by the Russian Orthodox Church. The ordinariness Larkin invests his persona with is intentional. It is people like him who, possessed of the right kind of perception, should reject the church and its superstitious practices. As Larkin made it clear in the abovenoted interview, the poem is about church going. John Wain referred to the pun intended in the title of the poem.[4] And now we shall refer to the views of two critics on the opening stanzas of the poem. Keith Sagar writes:

> What we first become aware of as we begin to read "Church Going" is a tone of voice, ordinary, conventional, casual, perfectly fitting the speaker, a mild bore who has left his bicycle propped against a gravestone. He enters the church only when 'there's nothing going on;' the building itself is undistinguished, just another church in another suburb. He neither knows nor cares about churches, their accoutrements, the acts of worship which take place there, the faith they serve. His attitude is, if not quite disrespectful, at least flippant.[5]

We disagree with Keith Sagar in that the persona's attitude is neither disrespectful nor flippant; he is only expressing the mainstream view of the inefficacy of this institution.

And referring to the one and a half lines – "Hatless, I take off/ My cycleclips in awkward reverence" – closing the first stanza, David Lodge writes:

> That line-and-a half must be the most often quoted fragment of Larkin's poetry and the way in which the homely "cycleclips" damps down the metaphysical overtones of 'reverence' and guarantees the trustworthy ordinariness of the poetic persona is indeed typical of Larkin. But if his poetry were limited to merely avoiding the pitfalls of poetic pretentiousness and insincerity it would not interest us for long. Again and again he surprises, especially in the closing lines of his poems, by his ability to transcend – or turn ironically upon – the severe restraints he seems to have placed upon authentic expression of feeling in his poetry.[6]

Although Larkin's persona said that this or any other church was not a place worth stopping at, he did stop and often stops at churches. But he always wonders why he does so and what he should look for in them. He also says that like faith, superstitious practices of the church will also one day meet their natural death and, therefore, wonders what will happen to churches when they fall completely out of use. Perhaps a few cathedrals, with their parchment, plate and pyx, locked in cases, will be on show and the rest will be let rent-free to rain and sheep. Perhaps people will avoid them as unlucky places. In the next stanza, the speaker's distrust in the efficacy of the church in sustaining any longer the superstitious faith of the people is very clearly expressed, although the superstitions may continue for some time because, as George Santayana observes, "superstition and moral truth" are "the two ingredients of religion."[7] Perhaps, after dark, some dubious women, with their children, may come to a church and make them (the children) touch a particular stone lying there, or they may pick simples in the compound of the church as a cure for cancer. Stones do not cure ailments or bring good luck and to believe that simples can cure cancer is pathetically absurd. What the poet says here is of very great importance. Anthony F. C. Wallace, in his book *Religion: An Anthropological View*, is right when he says: "Religion is based on supernaturalistic beliefs about the nature of the world which are not only inconsistent with scientific knowledge but also difficult to relate even to naïve human experiences. Magic does not make the rains come. The gods do not win battles at man's request, and witches do not make the cattle barren."[8]

But the word "cancer" in this stanza is of crucial importance. Our culture today is afflicted with deadly cancer and the church is nothing more than an ordinary medicinal herb which might be of some use in pain in bone-joints or in common cough and cold. The church with "some brass and stuff/ Up at the holy end" is nothing more than that herb. Even so, "dubious" women may come "on some / Advised night" to see "walking a dead one." These poor women have nothing better to hold on to in the hours of physical, mental, moral and spiritual crises in their life. And the number of people in their situation suffering from deprivations of serious nature is very large. But superstitions also, like belief, will die and then, the persona rightly thinks and says so, what will remain of churches will be "Grass, weedy pavement, brambles, buttress, sky." But the poet says:

...it held unspilt
So long and equally what since is found
Only in separation – marriage, and birth,
And death, and thoughts of these.

The ingredient of superstitions over time that had silted the church has dispersed. But the church had also moral truth as its second ingredient, which held together for a long time three important passages of rites in the life of man – birth, marriage and death — into a kind of unity. Children were and are still baptized here, marriages were and are still solemnized here and the dead were and are still buried in its yard. Anthony F.C. Wallace speaks about the significance of important passages and the rituals or rites associated with them:

> In all societies there are two types of mobility or passage, to the successful accompaniment of which ritual is directed: role change and geographical movement. In both cases the person undertaking the passage from one state to another must abandon their certain attachments and habits and form new ones; they must, in other words, learn. Role changes occur more or less regularly and predictably in the life cycles of individuals; and although these role changes and their timing vary from one culture to another, they often maintain a general connection with physiological maturation. Birth, puberty [also marriage] and death are universal objects of ritual, for at these times the individual enters into a new relationship to the world and to the community, subject to new opportunities, new dangers, and new responsibilities.[9]

And mourning rituals are one of the classic examples of rites of passage. Wallace writes:

> An individual, not long ago committed to the living and to whom the living were emotionally attached – in either positive or negative way or both – has died. The departed soul and the survivors must be released from each other; otherwise, the living will remain in their frustrated devotion and the departed soul will be unhappy. Once again the goal of ritual is to separate effectively the living from the dead, to ac-

complish the transition, to bring about the incorporation of the dead into its proper place of the hereafter and to reconstitute the mourners with each other and with the community.[10]

There used to be an emotional link between these rituals and the Church. It used to play a significant role in investing the rituals of birth, marriage and death with moral and spiritual values. Keith Sagar also says the same thing when he writes:

Larkin is thinking, of course, of the three great Christian Ceremonies,
christening, wedding, funeral, which, whether we regard them as sacramental
or not, ritualize the great crises of human experience, give them form and
dignity and recognition as constituting not the fortuitous experiences of
individuals helpless and naked in a world of obscurely felt compulsions, but
the essential framework or rhythm of all human experience.[11]

But here, too, the church has been losing ground and unable to hold these three most significant points in man's existence unspilt. So the persona asks himself, "for which was built/ This special shell?" But even though he has no idea what this accoutred, frowsty barn is worth, it pleases him to stand here in silence.

The last stanza, as is usual with a Philip Larkin's poem, is very complex. In this stanza we are made to seek answer to the question what this "accoutred, frowsty barn" of a church is worth. The words "shell" and "barn" are important. First the persona calls the church a serious house on a serious earth. The earth is a serious place from the point of view of human existence as it is here and here alone that man has lived so far and can live in future too. And the church is a serious house. In what sense? A house is a building for human habitation. Man chose this house long ago and in its "blent" air – air blended with moral, spiritual, even sublime emotions, thoughts and ideas – "all our compulsions meet" and are "recognized and robed as destinies." What are our compulsions or irresistible desires? We shall at this point go to a philosopher to understand the nature of religious compulsions.

William James, in his book *Varieties of Religious Experience*, says that all religions appear to meet "in a certain uniform deliverance" which consists of two parts: "(1) An uneasiness and (2) Its solution." Uneasiness is a sense that "there is something wrong about us as we naturally stand." And "The solution is the sense that we are saved from the wrongness by making proper connection with the higher power." When a man moves from stage one to stage two, he "identifies his real being with the germinal higher part of himself." He then "*becomes conscious that this higher part is coterminous and continuous with a MORE of the same quality, which is operative in the universe outside of him, which can keep in working touch with, and in a fashion get on board of and save himself when all his lower being has* gone to pieces *in the wreck.*"[12]

This, according to William James, is the authentic religious experience and he is absolutely right. The Church was supposed to be the mediator between man's "germinal higher part" and "more of the same quality which is operative in the universe outside of himself." In common parlance, it was supposed to be the gateway to heaven. This was a fatal flaw in the founders of the Church and since there is no heaven anywhere in the universe, the Church indulged in superstitious practices to keep the faith of the masses engaged. It is therefore no wonder that the Church today is an empty shell, an accoutred frowsty barn.

However, the speaker says, there will always be someone who will "be surprising/ A hunger in himself to be more serious." This "surprising" hunger for spiritual upliftment will make him gravitate towards this ground because he once heard that this was the proper ground "to grow wise in, even though so many dead lie around." The last line of the poem is, at first sight, puzzling, though of crucial significance. The so many people lying in their graves in the churchyard had not grown wise in this ground, that is, in the Church. The Church had never been able to prise open the lid of ignorance on the "germinal higher part" of their selves and connect it to the "more of the same quality which is operative in the universe outside" of them. On the contrary, as Tolstoy tells us, the Church practiced something very different. To quote his own words: "…Church doctrine is theoretically a crafty and harmful lie and practically a collection of the grossest superstitions and sorcery which completely conceals the whole of Christ's teaching."[13] Larkin is not as harsh in his denunciation of the Church doctrine as Tolstoy was – Tolstoy had reason to be – but he cannot gloss over the superstitions and deceptions practiced by the Church. Larkin's persona is also not disrespectful to the so many lying dead in this ground ; he is only sad that the Church did not impart to them the kind of religious experience William James talks about, and they died in ignorance in which they were born.

Despite Philip Larkin's assertion that "Church Going" is a secular poem – and despite John Wain pointing out the intended pun on the title of the poem, that is, the Church is going – some critics have interpreted it as if it were a great religious poem. They say that the persona in the poem first appears as a clown with a flippant attitude towards the Church, but gradually, as the poem progresses, he corrects himself and sees it as the embodiment of true religion. For example, Terry Whalen writes: "Indeed it is an ostensibly bored and sardonic figure who crashes about in 'Church Going,' viewing most sacred objects and surroundings with a musing that gives to his agnostic humanism an oddly religious glow."[14] shall we say intentionally? The persona deliberately created by Larkin – as Conrad created Marlow in some of his novels to convey some profound but deeply disturbing, in fact, tragic perceptions vis-s-vis man's destiny – tells us very clearly that church-going is now a meaningless ritual and the Church itself is of little efficacy in our crisis-ridden world as simple is in cancer. The comparison of the church to simples is interesting also because this medicinal herb is now only of historical importance. The first reference to simples we find in Aeschylus' masterpiece *Prometheus Bound.* Prometheus tells us that before he came to men's help they knew of no drugs that they could use to get rid of their many ailments and so simply wasted away, "until," he says, "I showed them the blending of mild simples wherewith they drive out all diseases." Then we find two references to this herb in Virgil's *Aeneid* (Dryden's Virgil, Bk.4, 1 743 & Bk.12. 1 592). In the first reference, Virgil speaks of its "baleful Juice;" in the second reference, he shows the inefficacy of the juice of this herb to heal the mortal wound suffered ny the hero at the hands of Turnus. Then this herb is seen in *Romeo nd Juliet* and *Hamet* too. But in these plays it is shown to be used in making poisonous potions.

Philip Larkin is not anti-religion, no sensible person is. In a later poem, viz. "Water," he makes it clear that today there is an urgent need for a new religion and if he were asked to do something about it, he would construct a religion of water. Like all things on earth religion also has been evolving, as any student of cultural anthropology will tell us. And Philosophy tells us truths about the essential nature of religion. It is time we gave serious thought to do something of the kind Larkin wants to do in "Water." T

Deceptions

"Deceptions" is Philip Larkin's one of the major poems although he has been criticized by several critics, chief among them Janice Rossen, for his alleged sympathy for the rapist rather than the victim of the rape . We quote below a few lines from Janice's comment on the poem:

> In 'Deceptions' Larkin addressed the problems of violence and sex when a rape results, and the event here is not distanced by satire but rather brought close by focusing on its victim and her agony. The poet shows compassion for the girl's suffering; yet at the same time, the poem remains problematic because the poet also shows a great deal of sympathy with the man who has attacked her, and thus he ends the poem with a marked detachment from the woman's suffering, which he begins the piece in describing.[1]

But such criticism seems to be misplaced. First of all we must remember that Larkin is the first poet to, so to speak, exhume the long-ago buried poor country girl raped in London and later forced to become a prostitute. And he exhumes her with all her pain and suffering that she experienced ("gulped") at the outrage committed on her inherent dignity that she had as a virgin. This was tantamount to total violation – crushing underfoot – of the dignity of a girl's existence as a human being.

The reason why Larkin wrote this poem deserves our serious attention. Here one is reminded of a somewhat similar story entitled "Martha" by Khalil Gibran – the story of a poor innocent country girl raped by a rich rake from a city and then forced to become a prostitute in a city slum. This girl, still young, is now dying. A young college student, on vacation, hears of the girl's suffering and comes to her dirty, dilapidating room and hears from her the story of her seduction by the rake and later, taking advantage of her material needs, how she was raped by the rake's many friends and finally forced to become a prostitute. The student, sitting beside her death-bed like a priest granting her absolution, speaks these words of consolation to her:

' "You are oppressed, Martha, and he who has oppressed you is a child of palaces, great of wealth and little of soul. You are persecuted and despised, but it were better that a person should the oppressed than that he should be the oppressor; and fitter that he should be a victim to the frailty of human instincts than that he should be powerful and crush the flowers of life and disfigure the beauties of feeling with his desire. The soul is a link in the divine chain. The fiery heat may twist and distort this link and destroy the beauty of its roundness, but it cannot transmute its gold to another metal; rather it will become more glittering... Ay, Martha, you are a flower crushed beneath the feet of the animal that is concealed in a human being. Heavy-shod feet have trodden you down, but they have not destroyed that fragrance which goes up with the widow's lament and the orphan's cry and the poor man's sigh toward Heaven, the fount of justice and mercy. Take comfort, Martha, in that you are the flower crushed and not the foot that has crushed it."'[2]

Khalil Gibran's story has a religious tinge, whereas Larkin's poem is entirely secular and so the real country girl in his poem, raped, like Martha, when a virgin of sixteen, and now in her forties a coarsened prostitute in the slums of London when Mayhew interviews her, speaks thus: ' "You folks as has honour, and character, and feelings, and such... can't understand how all that's beaten out of people like me. I don't feel. I'M USED TO IT."'[3]

The gold of her soul does not glitter now; the rapist transmuted it into base metal, and she cannot be consoled, as Martha was consoled on her death-bed, that she will get justice in Heaven simply because there is no such place in the universe. But both Khalil Gibran and Larkin are right on one point: the oppressed is less deceived than the oppressor. In a letter to George Hartley, Larkin wrote: "the agent is always more deceived than the patient because action comes from desire, and we all know that desire comes from wanting something we haven't got, which may not make us any happier when we have it. On the other hand suffering – well, there is positively no deception about that. No one imagines their suffering."[4] We shall soon see that Larkin's observation regarding desire has confirmation in Jean-Paul Sartre's view of it. We shall also see what the Buddha says about desire or lust in his Fire Sermon.

Larkin does not, like Mayhew, address the ageing prostitute in the slums of London, but the poor, innocent and homeless country girl of sixteen drugged and raped at night in a brothel and suffering terribly in the room the following morning. The poet here does not use a persona, as he does in many of his poems. He speaks to the girl in his own person and empathises with her in her suffering and the beginning of the poem is remarkable:

> Even so distant, I can taste the grief,
> Bitter and sharp with stalk, he made you gulp.

The poet travels back in time, goes into the room in the London brothel in which the violated girl is lying in intense pain and, as if holding her hand, speaks the above words. He also tastes the grief that the rapist made her gulp, that is, forced down her physical as well as spiritual throat while doing the heinous deed. The poet in Larkin is here at his noblest and the difference between Mayhew the sociologist and Larkin the poet is very clear.

There follows a single sentence covering the next five and a half lines of the first stanza. It is morning following the night of the crime. In the morning light, London looks bright and beautiful: the poet calls it "bridal London." In those days London, which had not yet become a crowded and ugly metropolis – John Betjeman calls it "slough" and a "mess" and wants it bombed out of existence[5] – must have looked like a beautiful bride in the morning sunshine – we remember the beauty of London in the early morning sun as seen from the Westminster Bridge in 1802 in Wordsworth's sonnet. But in sharp contrast to the bridal London, this girl, who, too, should have been a beautiful bride brimming with fulfillment and joy on such a morning, as the bride in "The Wedding Wind" was on the morning following the consummation of her marriage the previous night, has been so trampled upon and crushed by an animal concealed in a human being that the "bridal London bows the other way." It is the entire city of London – the whole heart of a country – that denies the poor girl what was her due, to be fulfilled as a bride. Outside the brothel room, we see the "sun's occasional print" and "the brisk brief/ Worry of wheels in the street," that is, with the start of a new and bright sunlit day, the activities of life that had remained arrested during the night, have, with their worries and all that, begun to flow like a stream – life is indeed a stream flowing along the passage of time. And as the day advances, the light, which in the morning appeared only as the sun's occasional print, becomes "tall and wide." This light is the light of the day but it is also the tall and wide light in the mind or consciousness of the ruined girl. It is "unanswerable," it does not account for her ruin: for what sin has her life been so utterly destroyed? But it spans the entire length and breadth of her consciousness and enters its deepest depths. And this cruel light "Forbids the scar to heal." The wound inflicted on the poor girl's soul by the bestial cruelty of the rapist is so deep that it can never be healed. But here we are reminded of these lines in Dostoevsky's *The Karamazov Brothers*: "People talk sometimes of bestial cruelty, but that is a great injustice and insult to the beasts; a beast can never be so cruel as a man, so artistically cruel."[6]

So this tall and wide and unanswerable light of the sun as well as the waking consciousness of the girl cannot tell her what devilry in man (And again we are reminded of this sentence in *The Karamazov Brothers*: "I think if the devil does not exist, but man has created him, he has created him in his own image and likeness."[7]) has put a permanent blister on her soul.

Instead, this light "drives/ Shame out of hiding." In her drugged state, which was the metaphor for the darkness of the night, the shame had remained hidden. But now it is not only driven out of hiding, but also covers the entire extent of her consciousness with such intensity of pain that she feels that the light of the day mirrors her shame, so that the poet says:

> All the unhurried day
> Your mind lay open like a drawer of knives.

The imagery used here is entirely original and of a synaesthetic kind "which transfers meaning from one domain of sensory perception to another."[8] No other image could have conveyed the excruciating pain that filled the mind of the girl. Larkin's empathy for the suffering girl has the same depth of compassion and pity that Hardy had for Tess Durbeyfield. In the first stanza we find that the finest kind of artistic creativity draws its strength from its humane attitude towards the suffering of the oppressed.

It is the second stanza that gave rise to the charges, referred to above, which are of course misplaced. Here, too, the poet is speaking to the girl in his own person but he also states a painful truth of human civilization – the oppressed are less deceived than the oppressors. But, before that, Larkin makes it clear that he has not shifted his empathy from the victim to the perpetrator of the crime. He says,

Slums, years have buried you. I would not dare
Console you if I could.

This is a very sincere assertion of the fact that the suffering of the girl (Khalil Gibran adds to it other kinds of suffering – "the widow's lament, the orphan's cry and the poor man's sigh") is inconsolable. What can be more sincere than the poet's words that even if he could, he would not dare console her. In this respect this poem is very different than Khalil Gibran's romantic story, in which the college student consoles the dying woman that she will get justice in heaven. Justice can be secured on this earth only and nowhere else. But before that the malady that has been afflicting human civilization right from its beginning has to be tackled. This malady is "Desire." Larkin says that "suffering is exact, but where / Desire takes charge, readings will go erratic." The violated girl's suffering is extreme and exact: "her mind lay open like a drawer of knives." But the rapist's reading of his desire was erratic. Why? We will go to Sartre to know why. Sartre speaks of "the man who drinks to get rid of his thirst" and of "the man who goes to brothels to get rid of his sexual desire," and writes:

Thirst, sexual desire, in the unreflective and naïve state want to enjoy themselves; they seek that coincidence with self which is satisfaction, where thirst knows itself as thirst at the same time that the drinking satisfies it, when by the very fact of its fulfillment it loses its character as lack while making itself be thirst in and through the satisfaction. Thus Epicurus is right and wrong at the same time; in itself indeed desire is an emptiness. But no non-reflective project aims simply at suppressing this void. Desire by itself tends to perpetuate itself, man clings ferociously to his desires. What desire wishes to be is a filled emptiness but one which shapes its repletion as a mould shapes the bronze which has been poured inside it. The possible of the consciousness of thirst is the consciousness of drinking. We know moreover that coincidence with the *self* is impossible, for the for-itself attained by the realization of the Possible will make itself be as for-itself, that is, with another horizon of possibilities. Hence the constant disappointment which accompanies repletion, the famous: "Is it only this?" –which is not directed at the concrete pleasure which satisfaction gives but at the evanescence of the coincidence with self. [9]

So the satisfaction of sexual desire in a rapist has no real coincidence with the self, the self which is the touchstone of all values. And so the readings relating to the satisfaction of all perverted desires go erratic. There are rapists galore in human society clinging ferociously to their desires for power, for wealth, for torturing others, for killing, for subjugating the weak and the meek. And the perpetrators of these crimes are certainly more deceived than their victims.

And now we will go to the Buddha's "Fire Sermon," part of which is reproduced below. It is one of the two greatest sermons ever preached, the other being Jesus' Sermon on the Mount. T. S. Eliot, in his Notes to *The Waste Land*, says that Buddha's Fire Sermon "corresponds in importance to the Sermon on the Mount."[10] Addressing one thousand bhikkhus, the Buddha said:

"Bhikkhus, all is burning....
"Bhikkhus, the eye is burning, visible forms are burning...
Burning with the fire of lust....

"The ear is burning, sounds are burning, auditory consciousness
is burning ....Burning with
the fire of lust....,

"The nose is burning, odours are burning, olfactory consciousness is burning....Burning
with the fire of lust...

"The tongue is burning, flavours are burning, gustative consciousness is burning...Burning
with the fire of lust....

"The body is burning, tangible things are burning, tactile
consciousness is burning...
Burning with the fire of lust....

"The mind is burning, mental objects (ideas etc.) are burning, mental consciousness is
is burning...Burning with the fire of lust..." [11]

Unless man's being is purged of these lusts, his life will remain blighted. And the oppressors of various brands will go on inflicting inconsolable pain and grief on the weak. These oppressors in political, economic, social, even cultural domains have always been guilty of bad faith and their various desires (lusts) have behaved in a very erratic way, causing exact sufferings to the weak. The poet again says to the girl, "...you would hardly care/ That you were less deceived out on that bed,/ Than he was, stumbling up the breathless stair/ To burst into fulfilment's desolate attic." The use of the word "attic" here is significant, particularly so as it is "desolate." The rapist's fulfillment is an empty, utterly wretched attic.

All the senses of the rapist were burning with sexual lust, as the Devil, with his burning hatred of all that is good and noble, moves restlessly all the time in the infernal lake of burning sulphur. In this condition, he is seen "stumbling up the breathless stair." The pathetic fallacy used here deserves our notice. The rapist is stumbling up the stair breathlessly because he is in such tight grip of burning lust that he cannot breathe. And in this condition he bursts into fulfilment's desolate attic. The fulfillment his lust is seeking will be no fulfillment, it will only fill his soul with desolation. But this will be no consolation to the girl who is going to be ruined for life. This is a tragedy that has been enacted for billions of times since the beginning of civilization by the depravity of man's lusts resulting in the suffering (inconsolable) in the form of countless widows' lamentations, countless orphans' cries, and countless poor men's sighs. "Deceptions" is a tremendously powerful metaphor for all such sufferings.

I Remember, I Remember

In the interview with the *Observer*, Philip Larkin said,

> I was wondering whether in the new *Oxford Dictionary of Quotations* I was going to be lumbered with 'They fuck you up, your mum or dad.' I had it on good authority that this is what they'd been told is my best-known line, and I wouldn't want

it thought that I didn't like my parents. I did like them...

Anyway, they didn't put that line in. Chicken, I suppose.... If someone asked me what lines I am known for it would be the one about mum and dad or 'Books are a load of crap' – sentiments to which every bosom returns an echo, as Dr. Johnson said – or, rising a little in the spiritual scale, 'What will survive of us is love,' or 'Nothing, like something, happens anywhere.' They did include that one, actually (RW, p.48).

So we can say that the last line of the poem "I Remember, I Remember" stands high in the spiritual scale. We shall soon see what this 'spiritual scale' really means. It is a comment on, and for that reason it stands apart from, the rest of the poem. It is also the inevitable conclusion derived from what goes before it. So we shall go to the poem to see what it is about. We find here a persona who seems to be just past his adolescence. He is travelling in a train with a friend . He is also narrating to us how he passed his adolescence in Coventry. Larkin himself is the persona in the poem as he wrote in an essay "Not The Place's Fault" how he composed this poem:

> In January 1954 I wrote a poem called 'I Remember, I Remember'(included in *The Less. Deceived...*) after stopping unexpectedly in a train at Coventry, the town where I was born. and lived for the first eighteen years of my life. The poem listed, rather satirically, a lot of things that hadn't happened during the time, and ended:
>
> 'You look as if you wished the place in Hell,'
> My friend said, 'Judging by your face.' ' Oh, well,
> I suppose it's not the place's fault,' I said.
>
> 'Nothing, like something, happens anywhere.'
>
> The poem was not of course meant to disparage Coventry, or to suggest that it was, or is, a dull place to live in, or that now I remember it with dislike or indifference, or even can't remember It at all.[2]

And in a letter to Harry Chambers in August 1972, Larkin wrote," I'm afraid people may think it is a considered account of my childhood, which of course it isn't."[1]

Here it will be in place to quote the views of some psychologists on this crucial period, that is, adolescence in a child's life. First we quote Gary A. Davis, according to whom

> "Typically independent, confident, and self-assertive adolescents often involve themselves in radical , non-conforming and imaginative situations. Their curiosity, which draws them towards the complex and ambiguous, extends both inward, rendering them introspective and fantasy-prone, and outward, making them energetic and persistent.

> " Identification of these traits, however, is not sufficient; adolescents must be trained to be creative in order to approach their education, interpersonal relations, and ultimately their careers from broader, more flexible perspectives."[2]

Our second quotation is from *Encyclopedia of Psychology* (vol. I):

> Adolescence is a period of many changes ranging from the biological changes associated with puberty, to the social /educational changes associated with the transitions from elementary to secondary school, and to the social and psychological changes associated with the emergence of sexuality. With such diverse and rapid changes comes a heightened potential for both positive and negative outcomes. And, although most individuals pass through this developmental period without excessively high levels of 'storms and stress,' a substantial number of individuals do experience difficulty,,,

Changes in Cognition

> Cognitive changes during this developmental period involve increase in adolescents' ability to think abstractly, consider the hypothetical as well as the real , engage in more sophisticated and elaborate information processing strategies, consider multiple dimensions of a problem at once, and reflect on oneself and on complicated problems.[3]

The persona in this poem is, as stated above, a young man perhaps just past his adolescence and is travelling in a train with a friend. The train stops at a railway station. "Watching men with number-plates /Sprint down the platform to familiar gates," he exclaims, "Why Coventry!" and adds: " 'I was born here." He "leaned far out," trying to look for a "sign"

> That this was still the town that had been mine
> So long, but found I wasn't even clear which side was which.

A man, like a plant, has roots where he is born. Through its roots a plant gathers water and minerals from the soil, sends them up along the stem to each and every one of its numerous, hundreds of thousands of its leaves. These leaves make food for the plant and send it to each and every one of its trillions of cells. The gathering of water and minerals is contingent on the fertility of the soil and the making of food on the availability of sunlight. Favourable atmospheric conditions are also necessary for the plant's good health.

Man as an organic form of life is not very different from a plant. The soil of Coventry or, for that matter, of numerous other places is all right for the growth of human crop. But what about the sunshine, that is, the bright light of truth in which alone the growing adolescents can prepare hygienic food for their mental, moral, spiritual growth? And the atmospheric conditions in which the plant has a healthy growth are analogous to the total culture of the place in which a child is born and brought up. This culture is good or bad depending on the availability or non-availability of the sunlight of truth about everything. But we can say with complete assurance that no such cultural ecology is allowed to develop anywhere in the world, not that such ecology cannot be cultivated.

Philip Larkin has borrowed the title of his poem from a poem by Thomas Hood (1799-1845) entitled "Past and Present."[4] The first line in each of its four stanzas is "I Remember, I Remember." it is a typical sentimental-romantic poem with the persona glorifying his long past childhood and bewailing his present condition. His condition is so lamentable that he often wishes that "the night [when he was a child] had "borne" his "breath away." He remembers the various kinds of flowers in his garden and says, "Those flowers made of light!." He remembers where he used to swing when the air would run fresh to him and tells us as follows:

And thought the air must rush as fresh
To swallows on the wing;
My spirit flew in feathers then
That is so heavy now.

And the fever on his brow is so heavy that "summer pools could hardly cool" it now. Finally he tells us that he is now "farther off from Heaven /Than when I was a boy."

Larkin's poem belongs to an altogether different kind. When the train left Coventry railway station and his friend said, "Was that...where you have your roots?" the persona wanted to retort, "No, only where my childhood was unspent," but he did not. He, however, added to himself – " just where I started." He started his life, he was born, in Coventry and he remained where he had started even when, in terms of years, the period of his childhood and almost all of his adolescence had ended. This was something tragic as we shall soon see how. But this is how most children's childhood remains unspent. Here we are reminded of the following lines in Matthew Arnold's essay "The Function of Criticism:"

> The mass of mankind will never have any ardent zeal for seeing things as they are; very inadequate ideas will always satisfy them. On these inadequate ideas reposes, and must repose,the general practice of the world. That is as much as saying that whoever sets himself to see things as they are will find himself one of a very small circle; but it is only by this small circle resolutely doing its own work that adequate ideas will ever get current at all.[5]

The period from childhood to adolescence is of crucial importance in the life of any child. It is a period during which an adolescent should not only be allowed but also helped to see things as they are, that is, they must see things in the sunlight of truth, nothing but truth. Their impressionable minds will then develop in such a progressive direction that they will acquire adequate ideas valuable for man's progress. But, as Arnold rightly points out, the world lives and manages its affairs with very inadequate ideas and so most, if not all, children everywhere grow up without their latent faculty of perception being allowed to develop to the extent that they can see things as they are. But the seeds of perception are there in every child. By the time we are grown up these seeds are desiccated and dead for want of fertilizers and moisture and sunlight in the form of right kind of cultural atmosphere and our life is eaten up with trivialities.

Now let us see how or in what sense Larkin's childhood and adolescence remained "unspent" in Coventry. He gives us a list of things that did not happen to him during this period. Not that these things would have made any difference. First, as regards his garden, he says, "I did not invent /Blinding theologies of flowers and fruits." Romantic theologies of flowers and fruits, or theologies of any other kind are of a blinding, not awakening nature. Then he says that he was "not spoken to by an old hat." No small-town elderly person ever spoke encouragingly to him. Then he says with wry humour:

> And here we have that splendid family
> I never ran to when I got depressed.

Nor were the boys there "all biceps and the girls all chest" that we find in popular or pulp fiction. Nor was there his friends' "comic Ford" and invitation from them to him to spend, say, an occasional weekend on their farm where he could be "really" himself. There was of course the "bracken" near his house. He assures us that, "come to that," he will show it to us. But in this bracken he

> never trembling sat,
> Determined to go through with it, where she
> Lay back and all became a burning mist.

That is, promiscuous or transient sex relationship that, again, we find aplenty in pulp fiction. Had he ever had such relationship the orgasm would have only given him the sensation of "a burning mist," something not worth writing home about. Nor was there "a distinguished cousin of the mayor" to read his "doggerel" and praise it to his father thus: *There/Before us, had we the gift to see ahead"*. This whole monologue of the persona is bitter satire and it makes his face express a strange kind of bitterness so that his friend observes, " 'You look as if you wished the place in Hell…judging from your face.' " To this the persona replies, "Oh well, /I suppose it's not the place's fault." Whose fault was it then that his childhood passed away, was lost "unspent?" it was the fault of the culture of the place which had nothing of that "something", that is, the sunlight of truth in which alone can the mind of an adolescent do a kind of photosynthesis, that is, prepare valid postulates relating to healthy intellectual, moral, cognitive, spiritual development of his self. The psychologists we have quoted above tell us that adolescence is a period of crucial importance in the life of a growing child. During this period the adolescent is "typically independent, confident and imaginative" and often wants to involve himself in "radical, non-conforming and imaginative situations." Besides, puberty, which brings with it profound physical and psychological changes in the adolescent – according to anthropologists, puberty is one of the rites of passage – is also a period of rapid cognitive development. The dictionary gives us the meaning of "cognition" thus: "the mental action or process of acquiring knowledge through thought, experience, and the senses.> perception, sensation, or intuition resulting from this." During this period adolescents should know the truth, nothing but the truth about everything. It will give their mental-spiritual self the required spinal cord that can help this self transcend all trivialities, all blindnesses, all narrownesses, in short, all falsehoods that have been choking the growth of human culture. But the tragedy of this culture is that , as Mikhail Sholokhov (we have quoted him elsewhere in this work) says, truth has been a corpse a long time already. And so Larkin's poem ends with the statement concerning this tragedy:

Nothing, like something, happens anywhere.

This one-line sentence is written within inverted commas and stands apart from the rest of the poem. So it can be taken as a quotation stating a general /universal truth. But it is also the inevitable conclusion from what goes before it in the poem. And because it is a most succinct and at the same time a comprehensive comment on how we live, it is bound to become one of the famous one-line sentences in world literature. Nothing in this way of life is "something," that is, the truth. If this is true and if human civilization is allowed to keep going without this "something," what is going to be the future of this civilization? It is only this "something" that can enrich human culture, which is now in a very poor shape, and keep it moving in the right direction and help mankind realize their great potentials in various fields. But the tragedy is that nothing like this truth guides man's life anywhere in the world of today. Philip Larkin is not a pessimist ,as he is sometimes alleged to be and tauntingly called "kid Sophocles." Sophocles, who lived and wrote two and a half thousand years ago, still remains one of the greatest creative writers of the world and his name should be mentioned with reverence. And if Larkin is a pessimist, what about William Golding, Harold Pinter and Doris Lessing, Nobel laureates all, whose visions of life are darker than that of Philip Larkin, and what about the visions of many creative writers and scientists whom we have quoted in Introduction above. The dictionary meaning of Pessimism is this: "Philosophy a belief that this world is as bad as it could be or that evil will ultimately prevail over good." No creative writer worth his salt can be a pessimist in this sense. But no creative writer worth his salt will either say that God is in heaven and all is right with the world. And the "something" in the last line of the poem means truth which can, if only man so decides, become the guiding principle of human culture.

"I Remember, I Remember" led some critics to presume that Larkin's childhood was not happy. The Interviewer for the *Observer* asked Larkin to tell him about his childhood, adding, "Was it really as 'unspent' as you suggest in one of your poems?" In reply, Larkin said that "it was all very normal" and that he had "friends whom he played football and cricket with and Hornby trains and so forth" (RW, p.47).The word "unspent" here needs a little bit of explanation. It means that the persona's childhood and adolescence did not develop, as it should have developed, in a cultural climate conducive to such development. Then the Interviewer for *Paris Review* asked him this question: "Was your childhood unhappy?" Philip Larkin's reply was as follows,

My childhood was all right, comfortable and stable and loving, but I wasn't a happy child, or so they say. On the other hand, I've never been a recluse, contrary to reports: I've had friends, and enjoyed their company. In comparison with other people I know I'm extremely sociable (RW,p.66).

And in the essay from which we have quoted some lines above, Larkin describes how he spent his adolescence in Coventry. It was a normal adolescence. The theme of "I Remember, I Remember" has, as its starting point, the poet's personal experience in retrospect and its importance lies in its universal significance, the last line of the poem makes this very clear. It is also Larkin's first major poem in which his treatment of Deprivation, a major theme in his poetry, is seen very clearly by the reader.

Chapter Four
Poems from *The Whitsun Weddings*

HERE

Simon Petch says that this poem "gives us a comprehensive overview of the world of *The Whitsun Weddings*" and that "It literally sets the scene for most of the poems in the book."[1] It is a significant observation and will receive our due attention in the course of our analysis of the poem. At the moment we will focus our attention on the poem or, more precisely, on the train journey the poem describes. Andrew Swarbrick writes this about the journey and what he thinks the poet wants to say:

The poem describes a journey to the north-east coast of England (near Hull where Larkin lived latterly) and the different locales through which the poet passes, from 'rich industrial shadows' through the 'large town' (Hull itself

) to a coastal 'beach of shapes and shingle.' It is a literal journey through a recognizably contemporary England; at the same time, the journey is also an imaginative flight away from modern urban materialism towards a vision of solitary freedom, 'unfenced existence,' symbolized by the sea and sky stretching beyond the beach.[2]

That the journey describes real landscapes and humanscapes is never in doubt: "The shining gull-marked mud" of the poem, which was photographed by Larkin himself (this beautiful photo can be seen in the monograph *Philip Larkin's Hull and East Riding* by Jean Hartley[3]), bears witness to this fact. But it is not a flight from modern urban materialism. Larkin's poetry derives its strength from his presence in real locales in real time and among real, that is, common people, just as Thomas Hardy's great novels derived their strength from the soil and people of Wessex in real time. In fact, as the title of Lolette Kuby's book on Larkin makes it clear, Larkin, though an uncommon poet, wrote poetry for the common man. He is uncommon in the sense that he could feel on his poetic pulse the highest ideas in various fields of knowledge and make this knowledge worthwhile as it is scientific humanism in the same sense in which Hardy understood scientific humanism.

Donald Davie, in his book *Thomas Hardy and British Poetry*, quotes from "Apology" (dated 22 February 1922) with which Hardy prefaced his post-First War collection of poems, *Late Lyrics and Earlier:*

> looking down the future these few hold fast to the same: that whether human and kindred animal races will survive till the exhaustion or destruction of the globe, or whether these races perish and are succeeded by others before that conclusion comes, pain to all upon it, tongued or dumb, shall be kept to the minimum by loving-kindness, operating through scientific knowledge, and actuated by the modicum of free will conjecturally possessed by organic life when the mighty necessitating forces –unconscious or other –that have "the balancing of the clouds," happen to be in equilibrium which may or may not be often.[4]

Davie rightly and with becoming humour observes that Hardy "had no talent for discursive prose and this document cannot be read without exasperation" and writes down his comment as follows:

The last part of this inelegant sentence makes it forgivable to think of Hardy, even today, as a pessimist; for introduction of the words "free will," and the immediate qualification of them in clause after clause, phrase after phrase, mirror quite comically how in Hardy's system there is indeed a margin for human choice but the slimmest margin possible. Cramped and intermitted as that area of freedom may be, Hardy, however, is quite clear about what should motivate our actions within it –it is "loving kindness, operating through scientific knowledge." This is what I have meant so far, and shall mean in what follows, by "scientific humanism."[5]

Julian Huxley, who is not only a great biologist but also a fine humanist, has to say something important about "scientific humanism." In chapter XIII of his book *The Uniqueness of Man*, he elaborates on his concept of this philosophy of life. He asks: "What are the aims before humanism?" and himself answers, "One phrase, to my mind, really contains them all: to have life and to have it more abundantly." But he says, "like all one-phrase programme, this needs amplification and definition," and writes:

A humanism that is also scientific sees man endowed with infinite powers of control should he care to exercise them. More importantly, in the perspective of scientific knowledge it sees man against his true background –a background of irresponsible matter and energy of which he is himself composed, of the long and blind evolution of which he is himself a product. Humanity thus appears a very peculiar phenomenon– a fraction of the universal world-stuff which, as a result of long processes of change and strife, has been made conscious of itself and of its relations with the rest of the world-stuff, capable of desiring, feeling, judging, and planning. It is an experiment of the universe in rational self-consciousness.[6]

It is this scientific humanism, which constitutes the core of Larkin's poetic self, that moves like a searchlight across the locales of the poem. Of course this humanism is tinged with Hardy's kind of "loving kindness."

The first thing that arrests our attention in this poem is the long opening sentence spanning the first three stanzas and half of the first line in the fourth stanza, that is, a total of twenty-four and half lines. The next thing one notices is that this sentence does not seem to have a subject. Barbara Everett says that " 'Here' begins with a 'Swerving east...' that carries the enormous three-stanza image-loaded opening sentence swinging through the poem with an extraordinary, spacious momentum."[7] The linguist H. G. Widdowson has analyzed the elaborate structure of this as well as that of the three sentences in the last stanza. He draws our attention to the three clauses in the first sentence, each beginning with the word "Swerving," And the interesting thing about them is that the second clause is more complex than the first and the third clause is more complex than the second. Widdowson also draws our attention to the absence of a subject in this sentence. Now absence of the subject here is of utmost significance for the thematic interpretation of the poem. Instead of the subject appearing as per the requirement of the code, there appears the main verb "gathers" as the first word in the first line of the second stanza. Widdowson comments on it thus:

> The first word of the second verse takes us completely by surprise. It is neither a continuation of the pattern, nor the long - awaited subject, but a finite verb. Now we can only conclude from this that there must be a subject somewhere which we have missed, concealed somewhere in the complex structure of the first verse. What gathers? Search as we may, however, we shall find no satisfactory candidate.[8]

Another perceptive comment on this long sentence has been made by David Trotter in his book *The Making of the Reader*. He speaks of the reader being "taken aback by the enormous opening sentence, which buffets across three intricate stanzas before beaching on the fourth." Continuing, he writes:

> The length of the sentence announces Larkin's determination that this time the event described (a swerving night-journey into the north-east of England) should last until the poem ends, and that it should produce *by some logic of its own* the necessary shared meaning. If the length of the sentence startles, then so should another feature: the absence of a grammatical subject. Who is the agent of this journey? Who or what is it that, in the long-delayed main clause, 'gathers' to the surprise of a large town? A traveller in a train, presumably. But the traveller does not draw attention to himself, and

so insist on the eccentricity of his point of view; he does not remove his bicycle-clips, or define a British Rail sandwich. He is a spectral presence, a hole in the syntax.[9]

The subject of the long sentence is not a person like the frequenter of empty churches, or the "death- suited" poet himself returning from his alma mater, but the objective human consciousness spanning the various fenced locales covered by the poem. In the last sentence the same consciousness speaks of the "unfenced existence" of which we shall know more later. At the moment we shall concentrate on the talkative, as opposed to "untalkative," and within reach, as opposed to "out of reach," locales covered by the long sentence that runs parallel to the train journey which the poem describes. This is the logic of the long sentence, an astounding linguistic performance in its own right. But Larkin does not believe in virtuoso linguistic performance of any sort. He is a visionary poet of his own kind. The poem is a poetic vision spanning the various locales in it for a very significant purpose. The purpose is to make us cognize and meditate upon the whole setting to understand our position in the scheme of things here in this world which has, so to say, umbilical cord-link to the unfenced existence of the elements that make the whole cosmos. Unless we have this visionary perception, we cannot understand the poem, nor can we understand the meaning and purpose of our existence.

The long sentence, running parallel to the train, seems to cover five locales: (a) "rich industrial shadows;" (b) fields/ Too thin and thistled to be called meadows/ And now and then a harsh-named halt, that shields/ Workmen at dawn;" (c) "solitude/ Of skies and scarecrows, haystacks, hares and pheasants/ And the widening river's slow presence,/ The piled gold clouds, the shining gull-marked mud;" (d)a "large town" with its "domes and statues, spires and cranes" clustering "Beside grain-scattered streets, barge-crowded water/ And residents from raw estates" pushing "through plate-glass swing doors to their desires" – their desires being limited to such things as "Cheap suits, red kitchen ware, sharp shoes, iced lollies" – these residents, "a cut-price crowd" are "urban, yet simple," and the city's "mortgaged half-built edges," where this locale ends; and (e) "wheat-fields," with fast shadows, "running high as hedges,/ Isolate villages" where loneliness clarifies "removed lives." The journey ends here and so does the sentence. The human presence or that of other creatures in the setting covered by the sentence also ends here.

In the remaining seven and a half lines of the last stanza we have a differ-ent kind of setting. This setting is devoid of any kind of human presence. This absence is gradual. In the preceding locale, which lay outside the "mortgaged half-built edges" of the city of Hull, in which we saw "isolate villages," not the crowds of the city; this locale was better because loneliness clarified the lives of the people there; also, "wheat-fields" ran "high as hedges." And now, start-ing with the second half of the first line in the last stanza to the first half of the seventh line, we are made to prepare ourselves to have the perception in the last one and a half lines that is of the utmost value for man. And here we will go again to the linguist H. G Widdowson who comments on them thus:

> In the five simple finite structures which occur immediately after the word "clarifies" there is a reference to all four me-dieval elements: leaves thicken and weeds flower (earth), waters quicken (water), the silence is like heat (fire) and air ascends (air). Remote and hidden from the urban world is an existence where elemental life-forces are at work, an essential simplicity apart from the complexity of the immediately per-ceptible reality of urban life and indeed from appearance of nature seen in similar terms. It seems reasonable to suggest that the complexity of the syntactic patterning in the text which creates bafflement in the reader reflects what the writer sees as a confused complexity in perceptible reality. As this yields to a simple vision of elemental natural life, so there is a corresponding simplicity in the patterning of the lan-guage. But the awareness of elemental existence is elusive and ultimately beyond communication – "untalkative and out of reach."[10]

From the second half of the first line to the first half of the penultimate line of the last stanza we find palpable existence of the four mediaeval sub-stances and no human presence at all. In the preceding scene, we saw "isolate villages" where "loneliness" clarified "removed lives." The "wheat-fields, run-ning high as hedges" also testified to the presence of human existence there. In the still earlier scene we saw congested human presence lacking in clarity in the city of Hull, as seen in "cut-price crowds," "salesmen and relations," "grim head-scarfed wives" and others of the same kind as might be seen in "grain-scattered streets," in the "Pastoral of ships," in "tattoo-shops," and so on. The people in such locales are far removed from the life of the elements. They have no idea how the elements operate in organic nature including themselves. And there is something more in the poem which is beyond the comprehension of the poor but "simple" crop of humanity that we find here. The poet says that "past the poppies" and "beyond a beach/Of shapes and single" there is "in the bluish neutral distance,"

> unfenced existence:
> Facing the sun, untalkative, out of reach.

The vast sea facing the sun is a great metaphor signifying the mysteries of life. It was the seas that, impregnated by the sun, gave birth to life on earth. Man himself came into existence in the process of evolution that began with this impregnation millions of years ago. But man has so distanced himself from the source of his origin and fenced his existence within such narrow and ugly landscapes and has also made the affairs of his life so commonplace and trivial that this source does not now talk to him and is also beyond his reach. Had he not done so he would have been in communion with the unfenced existence of the elements and the quality of his life would have been better. We must never forget what Julian Huxley, whom we have quoted above, says about the uniqueness of man, "an experiment of the universe in rational self-consciousness" with "infinite power to control if we only care to use it." So far we have not as a species cared to do so. It was time we heard the voice of the bard and of great men like Julian Huxley.

And now we can say that Simon Petch's observation, referred to at the beginning of this essay, is correct. The best poems in *The Whitsun Weddings* – "Mr Bleaney," "The Whitsun Weddings," "Days," "Water," "Dockery and Son," "Nothing to be Said," "Home is so Sad," "First Sight," "Essential Beauty," "Toads Revisited," "Send no Money," "Ignorance" – are all pleas to man to be aware of his uniqueness and re-orient his life and his civilization accordingly. And in " An Arudel Tomb," the last poem, which is as great as any other in the volume, there is an emphatic rejection of the kind of man's history as shaped and handed down to us by the ruling elite over the ages, again with a plea to us to make a better history for the future.

Mr Bleaney

"Mr Bleaney" is a poem about human condition. It is also one of the poems in which the persona is the poet himself. All such poems – "Here," "The Whitsun Weddings," "Water," "Dockery and Son," "Forget What Did," "Sympathy in White Major," for example –come straight from the poet's personal experience and tell us what the poet wanted or wants to do to make us aware of certain very important truths that should be the guiding principles of our life. In what follows here we will see how the message this poem gives us should help us to reorient our life, if only we have the necessary will power to do so.

A single man, looking for a one-room accommodation, comes to what seems to be a boarding- house where Mr Bleaney lived for a long time until death removed him altogether from the world. The landlady, who shows him round the room, speaks about Mr Bleaney and the poem opens with these words:

'This was Mr Bleaney's room. He stayed
The whole time he was at the Bodies, till
They moved him.'

Here, at the very beginning of the poem, we are presented a very great composite metaphor. Mr Bleaney, with all that his name connotes, is Everyman. His meagerly furnished room is the metaphor for the puny, cocoon-like world of our existence that we spin around us; we live in it all our life until we are pushed into the limitless and bottomless pit of the darkness or nothingness of Death.

Mr Bleaney lived in this room, which the would-be tenant is having a dekko at, all the time he worked with the Bodies – a car-assembling works. In the passage quoted below, Larkin himself tells us about a personal experience of a similar kind which identifies him with Mr Bleaney.

We are not told about Mr Bleaney's antecedents because, cut off from his familial and social roots, he simply floated on the surface of life. In the second stanza of the poem, the landlady purveys food for our thought some more information about Mr Bleaney. She says, " 'Mr Bleaney took/ My bit of garden properly in hand.'" But the garden, seen through the window of the room, is merely "a strip of building land,/ Tussocky, littered." A garden is a place where samples of nature's beauty (beautiful plants, flowers, fruit-trees) give us aesthetic pleasures and even sublime perceptions. Andrew Marvell's "Thoughts in a Garden" gives us such pleasures and perceptions. The climax of aesthetic pleasure is reached in Marvell's poem when he says:

> What wondrous life is this I lead!
> Ripe apples drop about my head,
> The luscious clusters of the vine
> Upon my mouth do crush their wine;

And so on. And we have a live feel of the poet's spiritual pleasure in his garden when he says:

> Here, at the fountain's sliding foot
> Or at some fruit-tree's mossy root,
> Casting the body's vest aside
> My soul into the boughs does glide.
> ;
> There, like a bird, it sits and sings,
> Then whets and claps its silver wings,
> And, till prepared for longer flight,
> Waves in its plumes the various light.

Mr Bleaney's garden, on the other hand, is a sad reflection on the total lack of aesthetic and spiritual dimensions of his self. Whatever self he had, it was like a bit of land, littered with rubbish and discarded objects. The symbolism here is all too clear. Life was meant to be a beautiful garden, given the mental, intellectual, spiritual endowments man was blessed with. Luigi Pirandello writes in his play *Six Characters in Search of an Author*: "nature employs the human imagination as an instrument to pursue its work of creation at a higher level."[1] But "the human imagination" in Mr Bleaney was so impoverished that it was unemployable by nature for any kind of creation at a higher level. It was not that Mr Bleaney was an evil or vicious man. All that we gather about him from the poem goes to show that he was an entirely harmless, in fact, a lovable person. However, what is worrisome is that most of us sail in the same boat with him in our life's voyage. The poet himself, to say nothing of us the common people, steps into Mr Bleaney's shoes, as we shall see soon. The pity, in fact, the tragedy is that, barring a few scientists, philosophers, creative artists and thinkers, most of us are bankrupt of any wealth of imagination that can be used for any higher-level creation. Mr Bleaney was one of us. His inner self was not fertile enough to yield a crop of imagination rich enough for use for a higher-level creative work of nature.

The inside view of the room in which Mr Bleaney lived for a long time is equally depressing. The "flowered curtains," falling to "within five inches of the sill" (they are short, besides being ugly), are "thin and frayed." As regards the other items of furniture in the room, we see a bed, an upright chair and a 60-watt bulb. The furnishing is so meager that there is not even a hook behind the door on which one could hang one's clothes, nor is there any room for books or bags. The man wanting the room – the poet himself – is obviously an intellectual since he has books. Also his self is not so shrunk and shabby and grown so dry as that of Mr Bleaney. And yet, surprisingly enough – and it is an unpleasant surprise to us – he says impulsively: "I'll take it." And take it he does. Why does he do it? Because his ordinary self is not very different from Mr Bleaney's. Now he lies "where Mr Bleaney lay" – on a "fusty bed" – and stubs his fags "On the same saucer-souvenir" on which Mr. Bleaney used to stub his fags. We feel alarmed, alarmed because if a poet becomes a Mr Bleaney who else shall do the creative thinking at a higher level which we desperately need. However, the saving grace is that the poet feels uneasy and he shares his unease with us in the words quoted below:

> The first two-thirds of the poem, down to 'But if,' are concerned with my uneasy feeling that I'm becoming Mr Bleaney, yes. The last third is reassuring myself that I'm not because he was clearly quite content with his sauce instead of gravy, and digging the garden and so on, and yet there's doubt lingering too, perhaps he hated it as much as I do.[2]

But even here the poet in Larkin maintains some distance from his predecessor. We saw that he had books, whereas Mr Bleaney didn't have any. Also, he calls the radio set in the room, which Mr Bleaney "egged on" the landlady to buy, a "jabbering set" – why? – and stuffs his ears "with cotton wool" when it is turned on. We know that the news and views it airs are mostly jabbering related to the superficialities and externalities of life, if not damn lies and frauds dished out by the established order to perpetuate themselves in power. Mr Bleaney, on the other hand, used to listen to it, we can be sure, with interest, even with avidity as most of us now watch TV, which has replaced the radio set and performs its function more brazenly.

The poet now knows all about Mr Bleaney's life : what were his habits, what time he came home from work, his preference for sauce to gravy, how he kept trying hard without success to be part of a winning team in the four football pools in which he betted. With regard to the "yearly frame" of Mr Bleaney's life, the poet says that "Frinton folk" used to put him up for his summer holidays and he spent his Christmas holidays with his sister at Stoke – both places equally small and obscure. All this information must have been purveyed to the persona-poet by the landlady, which he, in turn, purveys to us. This shows that he has come closer to Mr Bleaney and his own normal (routine) habits and activities are, we can reasonably guess, not very different from his predecessor's.

The last two stanzas make the poem remarkable. They consist of only one sentence, whereas the preceding five stanzas consist if six sentences. In these two stanzas may be found the philosophical underpinning of the poem. This underpinning is also the spinal cord of thought that keeps the poem erect and disseminates the light of wisdom of the truest kind. Mr Bleaney is not a remote figure; he is one of us, but he lived a shrunken kind of life. It was simply devoid of the livingness of life. The poet's life itself seemed to be merging with Mr Bleaney's life when he started living in the room in which Mr Bleaney had lived and died. Here we are reminded of these lines in Sartre's *What Is Literature?*: "We are no better than our life, and it is by our life that we must be judged..."[4] The kind of life that we, like Mr Bleaney, live will finally lead to the atrophy of life itself in us.

In these two stanzas(They constitute another composite metaphor), we are given a supposedly inside view of Mr Bleaney's life. This supposition is that of the poet himself, which is significant. Mr Bleaney was completely unaware of the third dimension of his being, not that it did not exist. Also, as Larkin said above, he was often dissatisfied with his existence, but he knew of no other frame of human existence. So when a cold wind arose and "tousled the clouds," Mr Bleaney, watching the out- of- the- ordinary and somewhat threatening (only slightly so) spectacle, would lie down on his "fusty" bed, thinking that this was the home that provided him safety. But he would also grin and shiver because, try as he would, he would not shake off his dread. What dread? The dread that "how we live measures our nature." D. H. Lawrence tells what kind of life that people like Mr Bleaney, who is one of us, live will lead to:

"God cannot do without man." It was a saying of some great French religious teacher. But surely this is false. God could do without the ichthyosaure and the mastadon. These monsters failed creatively to develop, so God, the creative mystery, could dispense with them. In the same way the mystery could dispense with man, should he too fail creatively to change and develop. The eternal creative energy could dispose of man, and replace him with a finer creative being. Just as the horse has taken the place of mastadon.[5]

The kind of life man has been living – Mr Bleaney's life is typical of this kind of life – will result in him having, at the end of the day, nothing more to show than Mr Bleaney did at the end of his life – a "hired box" of a room, that is, a coffin. And that will serve him right.

The greatness of this poem lies not in there being a superior self, that is, the poet, passing judgment on the indistinguishably puny self of Mr Bleaney. The poet knows only too well that his poetic self, that is, the transcendentally aware self, is awake and active only while engaged in poetic creation. At all other times his ordinary self lapses into the same kind of somnambulism, metaphorically speaking, in which Mr Bleaney lived all his life and we too, exceptions apart, live the same kind of life. This is a deeply disturbing part of our existence. The social, political, economic, educational, even cultural setups controlling our life have, more often than not, played us false. Even religion and philosophy have often been stuck in "imprecisions" and have not shed off many of their unscientific postulates. So they have exercised constraints on man's consciousness and, therefore, most of us live and die like Mr Bleaney.

Here a reference to an article entitled "The Conditional Presence of Mr Bleaney"[6] by the linguist H. G. Widdowson seems to be in place. He says that "the appreciation of this poem depends, in some degree at least, on an understanding of the peculiarities of certain grammatical features. These have to do with person, tense and conditional clause." Widdowson says that the poem comprises two scenes. The "spatial" setting of both scenes happens to be the same – Mr Bleaney's room. But the "temporal" setting of scene one differs from that of scene two. He says that the first scene is presented in "theatrical mode with dialogue and description of décor…" This scene ends with the first half of line 10. The characters in this scene are the landlady and the new lodger (the persona). We have already discussed above this scene. But an important point that Widdowson makes is that the persona remains here a detached observer. In the second scene (from the second half of line 10 to the end of the poem) the persona is the only character, but instead of being merely an "onlooker" he is now the "participant." Also, now he seems to be drawn closer to the dead Mr Bleaney. He takes a decisive step in this direction, as we have seen above, when he takes Mr Bleaney's room, sleeps in his fusty bed and stubs his fags where Mr Bleaney used to stub his. But we have also seen above that his merger with Mr Bleaney's self is not complete.

Then, in the next six lines (ll 15-20), the persona tells us about the daily (routine) as well yearly frame of Mr Bleaney's habits. The information about these habits was purveyed to him by the landlady, but the fact that he now knows all about them and, in turn, purveys them to us shows his interest in his predecessor's life and also that Mr Bleaney now seems to be a presence in his life. In fact, as Widdowson says, "The first person present of the new lodger merges with the third person past of the previous one. Mr Bleaney, though not present, is nevertheless a presence in the second scene of the poem." He adds: "The consequence of this convergence of person and time reference is worked out in the last two stanzas."

And the last two stanzas consisting of one very complicated sentence is, Widdowson rightly observes, a syntactic "hybrid." He compares it to imagined "medieval monsters like the basilisk," and says, "The basilisk, or cockatrice, was part reptile and part domestic fowl, and had a mysterious effect on men." This last sentence comprises a long, very complicated conditional clause and the last three words "I don't know," seem, at first sight, to constitute the main clause. In that case the conditional clause will actually be subordinate noun clause. It is true that a noun clause, like an adverbial clause of condition, can begin with "If." But a noun clause normally follows, not precedes, the main clause. But if we treat it as adverbial clause of condition, which it apparently appears to be, the last three words in the sentence cannot function as the main clause. Then this extremely complex structure presents another problem. Widdowson says that an if-noun clause is in the past tense, "the simple past tense is used to make reference to a possible event in the past time. This event may or may not have taken place, but the temporal context is firmly fixed in the past." But with adverbial clauses of condition the matter is somewhat different. With the help of the following two sentences Widdowson explains the difference:

(1) If he stood here, he would see the clouds.

(2) If he stood here, he would have seen the clouds.

His comment on the value of the tense in the two sentences is as as follows:

> The utterance of sentence (1) expresses the hypothetical pos-
> sibility of the third person appearing in the present: it refers
> to a state of affairs alternative to that which actually obtains.
> [The second sentence], on the other hand, refers to a possible
> state of affairs in the past. Since in the poem there is no in-
> dication in a main clause as to which of these values for the
> past tense is indicated, the ambiguity remains unresolved. We
> do not know, as we read through the last two stanzas, whether
> reference is being made to a possible state of affairs in the
> past or in the present....For, although all of the activities re-
> ferred to in last two stanzas are, by virtue of the if clause, rep-
> resented as hypothetical activities of Mr Bleaney, as phrase
> follows phrase the reader recognizes that what is being ex-
> pressed are the present lodger's own actual experiences, for
> why else would he be led to wonder whether Mr Bleaney un-
> derwent them?

So, Widdowson says, the "if" clause here "is a syntactic hybrid, part ad-verbial and part nominal." But why does Larkin create a linguistic cockatrice in the last two stanzas? The answer is not very far to seek. The poem seems to symbolize a journey – a journey from the outer world which shapes our life , our habits (listening to the jabbering set, our preference for sauce to gravy,etc.), all of which shpe our spiritual self. This spiritual self is a chaos whose objective correlative is the linguistic cockatrice of the last two stanzas. We have seen above what Pirandello says about what nature requires of man. We have seen what Sartre says: man must be judged by the kind of life he lives. We have also seen what Lawrence says: man will be superseded if he fails to develop cre-atively. And because Mr Bleaney has merged with the poet-persona, the latter cannot shake off the dread: "That how we live measures our own nature." This dread is a kind of emanation from the supposed activities – supposed by the poet – of Mr Bleaney described in these stanzas, activities that naturally fol-lowed the kind of life he lived. But our own activities are not very different in kind. Mr Bleaney is shown as cowering before something that appears to him threatening. And because he has by now completely merged with the new lodger (the poet), the dread is actually the poet's, and it should we ours as well. No other kind of linguistic structure could have conveyed this dread.

Nothing to be Said

In the first stanza of his poem "Nothing to be Said" (*The Whitsun Weddings*, London: Faber & Faber 1964,pt. 1979,p. 11), Philip Larkin says that " Life is slow dying"

> For nations vague as weed,
> For nomads among stones,
> Small-statured cross-faced tribes
> And cobble-close families
> In mill-towns on dark mornings

These lines cover almost all of mankind – billions of men and women inhabiting the planet now. What is a very disturbing thing is that people comprising whole nations live life as vague as that of weeds. Weeds, we know, are unnecessary growth in a cornfield; they can and do destroy crops unless we weed them out. They do not produce anything that we need; and they live a very vague life in that their growth is never healthy and they are completely unproductive. But why is the human condition in such a tragic situation? We can find clues to the answer to this question in the following two passages. The first is from a book titled *From Fish to Philosopher* (Boston: Little, Brown &Co.,1953,p.184) by a biologist, Homer W. Smith:

> Thomas R. Lounsbury, a nineteenth-century professor at Yale's Sheffield Scientific School, was not far wrong when he remarked that we must regard with profound respect the infinite capacity of the human brain to resist the introduction of useful knowledge. Granting the force of the sardonic comment, by way of explanation it must be emphasized that the brain is basically just as conservative as any organ of the body: it works by repetition, and an organ that works by repetition can only learn by repetition – by being forcibly inscribed with new channels.[1]

Our second quotation is from Saul Bellow's novel *Mr Sammler's Planet* (Delhi: Universal Book Stall, 1969; rpt. 1970, p.89):

What if some genius were to do with "common life" what Einstein did with "matter"? Finding its energetics, uncovering its radiance. But at the present level of crude vision, agitated spirits fled from the oppressiveness of "the common life", separating themselves from the rest of their species, from the life of their species, hoping perhaps to get away (in some peculiar sense) from the death of their species.[2]

Useful knowledge, that is , truth, and nothing but truth (no obfuscations, please) about life in general and man's life in particular, can only be forcibly inscribed with new channels in the human brain. But, sadly for all of us, there is no Einstein to find the energetics, uncover the radiance of common life and forcibly inscribe them with new channels in the brain. So the oppressiveness of this life is slowly but surely driving human species to death.

In the first four lines of the second stanza, Larkin says that the "separate ways/ Of building, benediction" as well as "Measuring love and money" are also "Ways of slow dying." We shall again quote Saul Bellow, this time the following lines from his novel *Henderson the Rain King* (Penguin Books 1959,rpt. 1975, p. 124): "... the world, the world as a whole, the entire world, had set itself against life and was opposed to it – just down on life, that's all-"[3] So Larkin is not wrong when he tells us that our common life, with all its paraphernalia of building, benediction, measuring love and money, is down on life and is moving inexorably towards slow death. Now what is "building"? It should mean building different institutions –political, socio-economic, educational, cultural and so on with firm foundations in truth and justice. Unfortunately this has not been the case and the different ways of building them by different peoples are all ways of slow dying. Then comes "benediction." The dictionary meaning of this word is: "Christian prayer that asks God to protect and help someone." Now to call "benediction" a way of slow dying is a serious matter. We shall here refer to the views of an eminent scientist to show that Larkin is not being irresponsible. In his much-acclaimed book, *Evolution: The Modern Synthesis* (London: George Allen & Unwin,!942, rpt. 1974,pp.577-578), Julian Huxley writes:

The future of progressive evolution is the future of man. The future of man, if it is to be progress and not merely a stand-still or a degeneration, must be guided by a deliberate purpose ....Before progress can begin to be rapid, man must cease being afraid of his uniqueness, and must not continue to put off the responsibilities that are really his own to the shoulders of mythical gods or metaphysical absolutes.[4]

So seeking the blessings and protection of God will not lead to future evolution of man, but only to his progressive degeneration. Then we come to "Measuring love and money" which, the poet tells us, are also "Ways of slow dying." Love is the essential principle of creation and creativity. Its extent and depth are immeasurable and unfathomable. To measure it, that is, dole it out in small measures for use only on certain occasions and leave vast expanses of life barren of it is a sure way of slow dying. As regards man's way of measuring money, the less said the better. It is either too little or too much. Most people – nomads among stones; small-statured, cross-faced tribes; cobble-close families in mill-towns and suchlike – have too little money, while the thieving rich amongst us, squandering big sums on garden parties and similar extravaganzas, have too much of it.

The first three lines in the third and last stanza, quoted below, appear to be somewhat puzzling:

Hours giving evidence
Or birth, advance
On death equally slowly.

Hours giving evidence of what? Obviously of man's life without foundation in truth, which is indeed a serious matter. Can we afford to turn a blind eye to what Shakespeare said more than four hundred years ago in these great lines in his *Measure for Measure*: "There is scarce truth enough alive to make societies secure, but security enough to make fellowships accursed" (III,ii. ll. 229-231)? Birth of a child is also advance on death slowly because the child is kept ignorant of the truth about life, the world, the ultimate reality.

But the tragedy is that "saying so to some/ Means nothing; others it leaves/ Nothing to be said." There are pig-headed people to whom true facts about life mean nothing. Their brains have been made immune to the percolation of truth into their consciousness. Then there are people, and their number is legion, to whom "it leaves / Nothing to be said." These people have perverse psyche. They are educated, knowledgeable people but their psyche resists introduction of useful knowledge, that is, truth. Nothing therefore can be said to them because their consciousness will not allow truth to enter and percolate it. In short, the human condition today is tragic and the species, with deadening encumbrances of building, benediction, measuring love and money, the day spent in hunting pigs or giving garden parties, is inching towards slow but sure death.

We shall close our discussion of this poem with a quotation from Carl Sagan's book *Cosmos:*

> From an extra-terrestrial perspective, our global civilization is clearly on the edge of failure in the most important task it faces: to preserve the life and well-being of the citizens of the planet. Should we not then be willing to explore vigorously, in every nation, major changes in the traditional ways of doing things, a fundamental redesign of economic, political, social and religious institutions?[5] (p. 358)

Naturally the Foundation will Bear Your Expenses

"Naturally the Foundation will Bear Your Expenses" is a very serious poem and deserves close critical attention of the reader. Larkin himself, in the interview given to Ian Hamilton for the *London Magazine* in 1964, emphasized the seriousness of the theme of the poem and deplored the low level of critical understanding (of the above- average reader) that misunderstood and misinterpreted it. He spoke at some length on that occasion:

> Well, that was rather a curious poem. It came from having been to London and having heard that A had gone to India and B had just come back from India; then when I got back home, happening unexpectedly across the memorial service at the Cenotaph on the wireless, and what used to be called Armistice Day, and the two things seemed to get mixed up together. Almost immediately afterwards *Twentieth Century* wrote, saying that they were having a Humor number and would I send something funny, so I sent that. Actually, it is

as serious as anything I have written and I was glad to see that John Wain has picked it up, quite without any prompting from me, in an article in the *Critical Quarterly*. Certainly it was a dig at the middleman who gives a lot of talks to America and brushes them up and does them on the Third and then brushes them up again and puts them out as a book with Chatto. Why he should be blamed for not sympathizing with the crowds on the Armistice Day, I don't quite know. The awful thing is that the other day I had a letter from somebody called Lal in Calcutta, enclosing two poetry books of his own and mentioning this poem. He was very nice about it, but I shall have to apologise. I've never written a poem that has been less understood; one editor refused it on the grounds, and I quote, that it was 'rather hard on the Queen'; several people have asked what it was like in Bombay! There is nothing like writing poems for realizing how low the level of critical understanding is; maybe the average reader can understand what I say, but the above average often can't.[1]

As regards the dig at Professor Lal in the poem and Lal being daft enough to think that Larkin, in his poem, has paid homage to his poetic pretensions, it is best to let the matter rest there. The poem is a serious indictment of the modern-day elitist world whose so-called intelligentsia have a low level of critical understanding not only of literature, but of all serious ideas, be they philosophical, scientific, economic, sociological, or whatever. That these pseudo-intellectuals have grabbed positions of power in a very important sphere, that is, academia, is, to say the least, condemnable. But they have been spawned by a socio-political-economic setup that cannot stand any truthful scrutiny because, as Emile Durkheim observes, "As far as social facts are concerned, we still have the mentality of primitives."[2] The academic in the poem is the typical product of a system which, on the social-political-economic level, is run by his true counterparts, that is, wheeler-dealers in big business and political circles.

Larkin, as we have seen above, was appreciative of the comment on this poem by John Wain in his article in *Critical Quarterly*. We shall refer to this article later. First we will have a look at the poem itself.

The persona in the poem is out and out a bourgeois academic nourished on, and now spewing, intellectual superfluities, if not downright lies. But he has contacts across countries and the contact men are his true pals. Less than three weeks ago he delivered a lecture in Berkeley, U.S.A. And he is now going to Bombay to deliver the same lecture there. Hurrying to the airport in a taxi to catch his plane – he calls it his "Comet" – he leafs through the lecture-notes. In London it is a dark November day, while there will be warm sunshine in Bombay. Samuel Butler, in his *The Way of All Flesh*, speaks of an ideal November day in England thus: "weather was cold and raw – the very ideal of a November day…".[3] Hundreds of thousands of the rich Westerners, to escape the freezing cold of their native lands, tour in tropical countries to enjoy the warm sunshine in them. The persona in the poem is going to kill three birds with one stone of his lecture tour. He will impress his listeners with his superfluities couched in incomprehensible jargon – there is no dearth of Indians in intellectual circles of a glittering kind being overawed by a white-complexioned academic from a Western university. Secondly, it will be a real pleasure trip for him in that he will enjoy not only the warm winter sun in Bombay but also the warm hospitality of his hosts – Indians are known for extending hospitalities to their guests. Finally, it will be a free trip to India as the Foundation will bear all the expenses of his tour, which is the most outrageous aspect of the tour. There are Foundations funded by governments to sponsor such tours of well-connected but mostly spurious scholars.

The last two lines of the first stanza are stunningly powerful in that they bring to glaring light the darkness of the man's design:

> Perceiving Chatto darkly
> Through the mirror of the Third.

He has dark designs to get his lectures published by Chatto & Windus through the mirror of the BBC's Third Programme. If the lectures are aired on the BBC they will acquire the necessary sheen for publication by a reputed publishing house.

The second stanza throws a very harsh light on the character of the persona. While proceeding to the airport, his taxi was delayed by the crowds of people who, after attending the Cenotaph congregation on the Armistice Day to pay tribute to the British soldiers killed during the First World War, were crossing the road. The academic, who recalls the day (11 November) only when he is airborne, calls the crowd "colourless and careworn." And then in a crude manner he ridicules the solemn ceremony of laying wreaths on the Cenotaph by dignitaries including the Queen:

> That day when Queen and Minister
> And Band of Guards and all
> Shall act their solemn-sinister
> Wreath-rubbish in Whitehall.

He calls the solemn ceremony "sinister" and wreath-laying "rubbish." He does not stop at that. He goes on to call such ceremonies "mawkish nursery games" and, with a touch of indignation, says, "O when will England grow up?" implying that he alone of the Britons is really grown up. This man is guilty of what Sartre calls "bad faith." Sartre distinguishes bad faith from lies as follows:

> Frequently this [bad faith] is identified with falsehood. We say indifferently of a person that he shows signs of bad faith or that he lies to himself. We shall willingly grant that bad faith is a lie to oneself, on condition that we distinguish the lie to oneself from lying in general....The essence of the lie implies in the fact that the liar actually is in complete possession of the truth which he is hiding....The ideal description of the liar would be a cynical consciousness, affirming truth within himself, denying it in words......the one who practices bad faith is hiding a displeasing truth or presenting as truth a pleasing untruth. Bad faith then has in appearance the structure of falsehood. Only what changes everything is the fact that in bad faith it is from myself that I am hiding the truth. Thus the duality of the deceiver and the deceived does not exist here. Bad faith on the contrary implies in essence the unity of a *single* consciousness.[4]

All walks of life have been infested with people with bad faith from the beginning of man's history. The bad faith in us – particularly in those of us who rule the academia as well as the political, economic, social, even cultural and religious spheres – has darkened the human scene.

In a naked display of his bad faith the academic tells us that he is superior to his fellow countrymen because while they engage in "mawkish nursery games," he "outsoars the Thames" and "dwindles off down Auster." The use of the classical word "Auster" to tell us that he is travelling south and then the name dropping indulged by him in using the unfamiliar Christian name – Morgan Forster – instead of the well-known initials E.M.Forster are superb touches that expose this man's bad faith. And, as Simon Petch[5] points out, his sterile southward journey is contrasted with Forster's journeys to India that produced a classic like *A Passage to India*. And his contemptuous attitude to his country and his countrymen stands in sharp contrast to Forster's profound understanding and evaluation of British culture in his novels. The contrast between him and Forster is clinched when he says that in Bombay he will greet Professor Lal, his contact and pal, who once met Morgan Forster. Whereas Forster, a great thinker by any standards, met many genuine Indian intellectuals during his several visits to India, appraised himself of Indian culture as well as of the constraints this culture was handicapped with, once presided over the P.E.N. conference held in India and, most important of all, in the dark Marabar caves perceived what only sages perceive – the origin of man's existence and the darkness at the core of his being – this academic will only meet and interact with pseudo-intellectuals and practice, through his lecture, intellectual hocus-pocus.

Now a mention must be made of the perceptive article, referred to above, by John Wain. Part of this article, reproduced below, is devoted to the analysis of this poem:

> Personally I would not call that light verse; I take it to be deeply felt satiric poetry. It is a strong blast of direct feeling, the kind of thing Larkin is not supposed to do. (Supposed, that is, by the reviewer who takes this poem to be unsuccessful light verse.) What comes through is a deep antipathy to the *New Statesman* intellectual with his automatic contempt for the slow, devious logic of the English popular mind, his opportunism which proceeds by "contacts", and his glossy internationalism which makes him feel that his fate is not really bound up with England's. Larkin, who is so commonly said to feel in negatives, has a strong positive here; he identifies with the puzzled, mournful crowds lining the streets at the Armistice ceremony, trying in an inarticulate fashion to show that , while they cannot comprehend the nature of the earthquake that was the First World War, they still wish to show some feeling for the men who died in it. 'When will

England grow up?' is the kind of superior-irritable mood that one senses behind, say, the *New Statesman's* 'This England' column; the definition of 'growing up' is 'coming to share the attitude of me and myLondon cenacle.' Larkin's poem is a magnificent growl of rejection, a voice from the 'other' England which, between the cynicism of Fleet Street, the vulgarities of the glossies, and the metropolitanism of the clever weekly Press, seldom gets a hearing.ProfessorLal, who makes it the mainstay of his career that he once met E.M.Forster so cosily known here by his Christian name, ia a type one meets everywhere in the world of international 'culture;' the middleman of high intellectual fashion catching jet planes from Berkeley to Bombay with his rapidly-assembled lecture-notes in his briefcase, exists by virtue of the network of Professor Lals, and what the poem is saying (tacitly but strongly) is that the real work of civilization is going on elsewhere if it is going on at all.

What John Wain says about the theme of the poem is true and apt. It is shallow intellectualism, "vulgarities of the glossies" and "the metropolism of the clever weekly Press" that have usurped the position legitimately belonging to genuine intellectualism whose object is to enlighten human consciousness. The result has been deplorable and a very skewed order not only in academia but in other fields also – politics, economics, even culture and religion – now rules the roost because men of bad faith are in control everywhere.

Home is so Sad

According to Andrew Motion, the inspiration for writing "Home is so Sad" came from Larkin's visit to his mother in 1955. He writes;

> it wasn't anger he felt when he arrived to see his mother in Loughborough but sadness – the feeling he distilled in "Home is so Sad," which he finished on New Year's Eve after he had returned to Pearson Park. The poem stands as a coda to "The Whitsun Weddings" and "Self's the Man:" in the former he sees love at its most enviable; in the latter he reminds himself of its realities. Now he explains where his sense of the realities comes from: his parents. His mother's house preserves all the odds and ends ('the pictures and the

cutlery/ The music in the piano stool. That vase.') which represents the original good intentions of a couple making a home together. But all that remains of their 'joyous shot at how things ought to be' is faded home. What will survive of us, the poem says, is not love but the wish to love – and indelible signs of how the wish has been frustrated.[1]

The inspiration to write this poem may have come to Larkin from his visit to his widowed mother's home and what he saw there, but the poem, a fine work of art, far exceeds in range and depth of perception of real life. Larkin's poetry at its best is concerned with man's existential condition – what it should be and what it actually is. This yawning gulf between the two is a matter of utmost concern for the poet, as it is for great scientists, philosophers, thinkers in various fields of knowledge, and as it should be even for ordinary people like us, otherwise man will have no future. Home in this poem is a symbol for our planet. Seen from the outer space, our earth looks very beautiful, but we have made it very ugly, so much so that sooner than we suppose it may not be able to sustain organic life at all. It will be in place here to quote a passage from Saul Bellow's novel *Mr Sammler's Planet:*

> And we know now from photographs the astronauts took, the beauty of the earth, its white and its blue, its fleeces, the green glitter afloat. A glorious planet. But wasn't everything being done to make it intolerable to abide here, an unconscious collaboration of all souls spreading madness and poison.?[2]

And that is what has already happened in the future anticipated and visualized by the poet and presented as the setting of the poem. It is, in the Larkin canon, one of those poems which open a vast vista of very valuable perceptions which mankind can turn a blind eye to at their peril. And since the poem has a fine philosophical ambience it is only proper to go to a philosopher for some help to attempt a viable exposition of this poem. Martin Heidegger, in the chapter entitled "Building Dwelling Thinking" in his book *Poetry Language Thought*, poses the following two questions and also seeks their answers:

"1. What is it to dwell?
 2. How does building belong to dwelling?"[3]

He takes an Old English and High German word *Buan* for building and says that "it means to dwell." He writes: "Now to be sure that the old word *buan* not only tells us that *bouen*, to build, is really to dwell; it also gives us a clue as to how we have to think about the dwelling signifies."[4]

Heidegger takes another word *bin* and says that the "old word *bauen*, to which the *bin* belongs, answers: *ich bin, du bist* mean : I dwell, you dwell." Continuing, he writes:

> The way in which you are and I am, the manner in which we humans *are* on the earth is *Buan*, dwelling. To be a human being means to be on the earth as a mortal. It means to dwell. The old word *bauen*, which says that man is in so far as he *dwells*, this word *bauen* however *also* means at the same time to cherish and protect, to preserve and care for, specially to till the soil, to cultivate the vine. Such building only takes care – it tends the growth that ripens into its fruit of its own accord. Building in the sense of preserving and nurturing is not making anything. Ship-building and temple-building, on the other hand, do in a certain way make their own works. Here building, in contrast with cultivating, is a constructing. Both modes of building – building as cultivating, Latin *colere*, *cultura*, and building as raising up of edifices, *aedificare* – are comprised within genuine building, that is, dwelling.[5]

Heidegger asks, "in what does the nature of dwelling consist" and gives a very lucid answer:

> The Old Saxon *wuon*, the Gothic *wunian*, like the old word *bauen*, mean to remain, to stay in a place. But the Gothic *wunian* says more distinctly how this remaining is   e x p e r i - enced. *Wunian* means: to be at peace, to be brought to peace, to remain in peace. The word for peace *Frieda*, means free, *das Frye* and *fry* means: preserved from harm and danger, preserved from something, safeguarded. To free really means to spare. The sparing itself consists not only in the fact that we do not harm the one whom we spare. Real sparing is something *positive* and takes place when we leave something be-

forehand in its own nature, when we return it specifically to its being, when we "free" it in the real sense of the word into preserve of peace. *The fundamental character* of *dwelling is this sparing and preserving.*[6]

The home in Philip Larkin's poem "Home is so Sad" is very much concerned with "dwelling" and "building." This home is very sad and stays "exactly" as it was "shaped" – built as well as furnished – to man's perverted concept of comfort. Man has left the earth without ever having learned to dwell – exceptions like the Buddha, the Christ and some others remain exceptions. The Buddha attained Nirvana, or supreme enlightenment, under a tree and died on a mat in a grove formed by two large trees. And he and the Christ wandered from place to place, alleviating the sufferings of people and teaching them how to dwell.

The home in Larkin's poem "withers" because it is "bereft/ Of anyone to please." Its allurements have failed to win the occupants back, the occupants having already been consigned to the dark void of extinction in which innumerable creatures in the irreversible march of evolution have regularly vanished. And it withers also because it has no heart "to put aside the theft/And turn again to what it started as" – "A joyous shot at how things ought to be." Its theft consists of "the pictures and the cutlery/ The music in the piano stool" and "That vase," which must have cost the owner a fortune. All these expensive items of furnishing and presumably many more, commonly seen in super rich people's houses, such as astronomically expensive tapestries, flower-pots with exotic plants, fabulous wall-to-wall carpets on the floor, horns of killed deer, hides of tigers and cheetas adorning the walls, and many more things beyond the imagination of the common man. Larkin rightly calls these possessions of home "theft." Unlike any other creature since the beginning of life on the earth, man has been given to thieving and the thieving has been increasing in direct proportion to the strides of human civilization. The theft has accumulated to the extent that man has completely lost sight of the fact that "dwelling" means saving the earth – "setting it free into its own presencing." It is true that home started as a joyous shot at what things ought to be. Man does need home. For a long time starting with his advent on the earth he lived a hard life in caves. The Neanderthalers, who lived "between some 160,000 and 40,000 ago," [7] lived in "encampments consisting of a group of rough tents clustering round a central hearth" that would be "probably spread far and wide across the countryside…. But with the onset of colder conditions caves were increasingly in demand, and the Neanderthalers often had to fight stern battles with their animal occupants, such as the giant cave bear and the cave lion, and perhaps also with rival families of their own kind."[8] Even our own forebears, the *homo sapiens*, who took control of the earth between 40,000 and 35,000 years from now, lived for thousands of years partly nomadic life, "compelled to follow the seasonal migrations of the herds,"[9] which they hunted for food. Life for these people was very hard, what with "a constant struggle to provide food and shelter for themselves and their families under conditions that would horrify the pampered city workers of today."[10]

It was only in the Neolithic era, between 8,000 and 7,000 B.C., with the first settled civilizations in Mesopotamia and the Nile valley, and soon thereafter in India and China, that man built himself, first, "permanent camps… partly of skin tents and partly of more solid structures of wood, turves and piled-up stones…" Later they made houses of mud, sometimes with foundations "made of stone."[11] Still later, in ancient Egypt, they made houses of sun-baked mud bricks. People of the Indus Valley civilization made houses of burnt bricks.

But as the human civilization marched forward, the rich and mighty, having amassed huge wealth, started building extravagantly and atrociously large luxury houses. Castles, chateux, manors of the feudal-aristocratic world were built, owned and lived in by those who never knew the meaning of dwelling and building. They knew only of thieving and spoliation. And their modern-day descendants – the big bourgeoisie, billionaires and multi-billionaires – have ransacked and disfigured the planet to build luxury houses. The fortunes spent on the landscaping and interior decoration of these houses, to say nothing of the money spent on their construction, take our breath away.

Judged by the quality of life lived by these people – and quality alone can sustain and lead forward further evolution of human species – they are, to use Larkin's own expression, "a cast of crooks and tarts." And, again, judged by such parameters as intelligence with strong moral and spiritual fibres; philosophical vision that can transcend the limits of daily, routine life; scientific perceptions that can sift healthy grains of truth from all kinds of falsehood that have befouled human civilization; deep feelings that can empathise with the sufferings and deprivations of the masses in many places on earth, elevating and ennobling powers of great works of art, these crooks and tarts are what they are, the bane of human species, and yet they call all the shots in every walk of life.

The home is accursed with a lot of stolen wealth, but it has no heart to put aside the theft and "turn again to what it started as" – "a joyous shot at what things ought to be." Home is necessary for man to perform the daily duties allotted to him by the very nature of life and also to preserve the earth. But the joyous shot fell wide long, long ago. And the poet says "you", that is, *we* "can see how it was." The word "was" is followed by a colon. We know that a colon links a general statement to an example. All the items of furnishing listed in the last two lines of the poem are the theft the home was stuffed with as a result of which the joyous shot fell wide long ago to the eternal shame of man and man himself went extinct.

"TOADS" and " TOADS REVISITED"

Our analysis of "Toads" and "Toads Revisited" will be prefaced with a quotation each from Khalil Gibran and D. H. Lawrence. Regarding the kind of work that we should do, Khalil Gibran says,

> Work is love made visible.
> And if you cannot work with love but only with distaste, it is better
> that you should leave your work and sit at the gate of the
> temple and
> take alms of those who work with joy.[1]

And the first five stanzas of Lawrence's poem entitled "Work" run thus:

> There is no point in work
> unless it absorbs you
> like an absorbing game.
>
> If it doesn't absorb you
> if it is never any fun
> don't do it.
>
> When a man goes out into his work
> he is alive like a tree in spring,
> he is living, not merely working.

When the Hindus weave thin wool into long, long lengths
of stuff
with their dark hands and their wide dark eyes and their still
souls absorbed
they are like slender trees putting forth leaves, a long white
web of living leaf,
the tissue they wear,
and they clothe themselves in white as a tree clothes itself in
its own foliage.

As with clothes, so with houses, shops, shoes, wagons or cups
or loaves.
Men might put them forth as a snail its shell, as a bird that leans
Its breast against its nest, to make it round,
as the turnip models its round root, as the bush makes flowers
and gooseberries,
putting them forth, not manufacturing them
and cities might be as once they were, bowers grown out
from the busy bodies of people.[2]

These two quotations serve as perspectives on the nature of work that man should do. But both Khalil Gibran and Lawrence are being romantic about their view of work. Philip Larkin's "Toads" and "Toads Revisited" are about the nature of our civilization that makes us do toad work to keep our body alive and in material comfort but destroys our soul in the process. A number of Larkin critics have made perceptive comments on the two poems. M. L. Rosenthal says that "Toads" is a "complaint against the toad work that squats on man's life unless he is willing to relinquish his bourgeois comforts and security."

And in his comment on "Toads Revisited," he writes:

In the new poem Larkin looks with a disinterested eye at the world of those whom the world does excuse from "the toad work," mainly because they are "stupid or weak," and decides that he is better off than they after all....

His catalogue of refugees from work – "palsied old step-takers," "hare-eyed clerks with jitters," convalescents "still vague from accidents," and the like – is clever and full of a kind of dismay, though of course deliberately oversimplified. Though the poem in a sense repents a life dominated by work, it actually carries the same meaning: the uselessness of trying to break of the particular set of conditions of a very specialized kind of bourgeois professional life. The charm of the ending lies in its humorless surrender to the 'inevitable' while mustering up the morale to accept without bitterness, ' *faute de mieux*, a way of life alien to human nature. 'Toads Revisited' is saturated with a kind of nostalgia for an old, now forsaken romantic dream of freedom.[3]

According to John Wain, one of the principal themes of Larkin's poetry " is certainly choice, the act of choosing." He refers to three poems – "'Toads," "Self is the Man" and "Dockery and Son - as mainly concerned with the problem of choice and writes:

the individual is constantly being faced with choices, and these choices, large and small, add up to the large multiple act of choice that we call life-style. Choice of a life-style is one of Philip Larkin's recurrent themes. What kind of person am I, how is my kind of person best fulfilled and expressed in how I live? All life, from trivialities to grave, momentous decisions, finds itself included in this collective choice, for 'how we live measures our own nature.' Very often, the poet compares his life-style with that of others; sometimes the others are people who seem to reap all the advantages of life with very little effort and sacrifice, even such effort and sacrifice as is exacted by the toad work.[4]

The two "toad" poems together raise serious questions regarding the life-style the modern Industrial-bourgeois-consumerist civilization compels people like the persona in the poem to adopt. The persona himself is not an individual in revolt against this order. In fact, he is a typical product of this dispensation.

His plight is not very different from that of Mr Bleaney, but he is articulate – and Mr Bleaney is not, because he never held an executive rank as the persona in the poem does – to express his unease. It is in fact disgust that he feels for this life-style. It resembles Shakespeare's "ugly and venomous," toad, but unlike Shakespeare's toad, it does not wear "a precious jewel in his head." The work the persona is compelled to do to live a decent life (everybody's right) sits like a dirty, poisonous toad on his life. The very thought of such a brute sitting on one's body, to say nothing of one's life, which is a far more precious possession than the body, is sickening in the extreme. This poison in fact eats into the very vitals of a man's being and destroys it so that his life degenerates and degenerates until he becomes a mere cog in the wheel of the juggernaut of the system. The persona does not live like a big bourgeois who squanders money right and left to maintain his extravagant life-style. He has only to pay a few bills on account of eating healthy food, residing in reasonably comfortable digs, wearing clean and decent clothes, pursuing intellectual/academic interests, and suchlike. But the toad-work that he is compelled to do, and which soils his vey soul for six days of every week, just to pay such bills, is "out of all proportion."

It is not that the persona does not want to work. He knows, as any other man does, that work is worship and that only in and through work – socially useful, creative work –that a man can realize himself. We quote below lines from Eugene O'Neill's *The Hairy Ape* and from George Orwell's *Keep the Aspidistra Flying* which tell us how much of the glamour of the bourgeois world depends on toad work exacted from people like the persona in the two poems. In *The Hairy Ape*, we have these lines:

Scene Five: Stage direction

In the rear, the show windows of two shops, a jewellery establishment on the corner, a furrier's next to it. Here the adornments of extreme wealth is tantalizingly displayed. The jeweller's window is gaudy with glittering diamonds, emeralds, rubies, pearls, etc. fashioned in ornate tiaras, crowns, necklaces, collars, etc. From each piece hangs an enormous tag from which a dollar sign and numerals in intermittent electric lights wink at the incredible prices. The same in the furrier's. Rich furs of all varieties hang there in a downpour of artificial light.

Long's comment on this show is: '…one of these 'ere would buy grub for a starvin' family for a year.'[5]

And in Orwell's *Keep the Aspidistra Flying*, we find these powerful lines:

It was an American paper of the more domestic kind, mainly adverts with a few stories lurking apologetically among them.

And what adverts! Quickly he flicked over the shiny pages. Lingerie, jewellery, cosmetics, fur coats, silk stockings flicked up and down like the figures in a child's peepshow. Page after page, advert after advert. Lipsticks, undies, tinned food, patent medicines, slimming cures, face-creams. A sort of cross-section of the money-world. A panorama of ignorance, greed, vulgarity, snobbishness, whoredom and disease.[6]

The persona in the poem, with his loaf-haired secretary in a stylish office, has to cater to the needs of the people who lord it over in this world. No wonder the work that he has to do to keep his body and mind together sits on his life like an odious brute whose poisonous secretion goes deep into his soul, threatening to kill it. So he asks himself: "Can't I use my wit as a pitchfork /And drive the brute off?" But the tragedy is that a similar toad sits deep inside his soul too.

The poet would like, after driving the brute off, to live on his wits just as lots of people live on theirs. This because the bourgeois-consumerist order will not allow him to live a comfortable life otherwise. But who are these people? They are, first, "Lecturers, lispers/ Losels, loblolly-men, louts." John Skinner's comment on the use of these people here is as follows:

> If the inclusion of Lecturers among the rank of social para-sites is a private Larkin joke (one with which we are familiar), the other categories mentioned hardly seem appropriate. Neither louts or lispers are immediately associated with quick-wittedness; losel is a highly obscure word and loblolly-man another term of which no one need be ashamed to confess ignorance.[7]

The heavy alliteration here and lumping together of disparate characters including those who either do not exist and whose identity is uncertain are used just to show the alternative to toad work. There is another alternative: "Lots of folk", that is, gypsies, "with fires in a bucket eat windfalls and tinned sardines" and they seem to like their life-style. Many gypsies are or were shop-lifters, or rich people were sometimes generous enough to bestow tinned sardines on them. But they are never rich. They do not have money to buy their nippers footwear and their "unspeakable" wives, because undernourished, look like whippets. But these people do not have toad work sitting on their chests and corroding their lives with its sickening poison.

If the persona had been courageous enough he would have shouted: "Stuff your pension," thereby getting rid of toad work. But he knows that "that's the stuff/ That dreams are made on."

By bringing the Shakespearian touch to his words here, Larkin wants to tell us that the feeling expressed here is genuine but it is steeped in sadness. The sad fact is that he cannot shout the imprecation at the toad work because, as he tells us in all honesty, "something sufficiently toad-like/ Squats in me, too." What is almost tragic about this fact is that this toad's hunkers at the very core of his soul are "heavy as hard luck" and "cold as snow." This is a terrible spiritual condition for a man to be in and, as we know what Larkin himself said – "poetry is an affair of sanity, of seeing things as they are" (RW p.197) – and as R. P King says, "for Larkin, poetry is a way of being honest," and that Larkin "believes that a poet must write only about that he feels deeply,"[9] These lines speak of the deep anguish in the speaker's soul. But, as stated above, he is no revolutionary out to fight the system. On the contrary, he says, if the toad work were not squatting on his soul, he would "blarney" his way to "getting/The fame and the girl and the money/All at one sitting."

The last stanza of "Toads" is remarkable for the spiritual-metaphysical truth it conveys. The speaker is oppressed by two toads. The first is the "toad work" (an ugly, sickening, poisoning brute) that the system – a system in which much of the work done is socially unnecessary and ethically abhorrent – imposes on his life and which, try hard as he may, he cannot drive off with the pitchfork of all the wit at his command. This is the outer toad. Then there is an inner toad of metaphysical nature that is more brutal and seems, with its hunkers heavy as hard luck and cold as snow, to crush and deaden his spiritual self. What exactly is this other toad? The speaker says that it is not that "one bodies the other / One's spiritual truth." What the poet means is that the toad work he is compelled to do need not necessarily sully the spiritual truth of his being. But the existential situation for a man becomes very worrisome if he is bedeviled by both the toads. It becomes then impossible for him to get rid of either. But what exactly is the inner toad? Here we are put in mind of these lines in Julian Huxley's book *Evolution*: The *Modern Synthesis:*

The poet spoke of letting ape and tiger die. To this pair, the cynic later added the donkey as more pervasive and in the long run more dangerous. The evolutionary biologist is tempted to ask whether the aim should not be to let the mammal die within us, so as the more efficiently to permit the man to live.[10]

It is a dirty, dark, ignoble patch on the spiritual self of man inherited from lowly forms of life – his forbears – in course of geological eras that has made him a coward so that he cannot drive away this brute, which is corroding his very soul, to get spiritual liberation.

In his poem, "Address to the Beasts," W. H. Auden says that we are, all told, worse than beasts, which he speaks with thus:

> For us who, from the moment
> we are first worlded
> lapse into disarray,
>
> who seldom know exactly
> what we are up to.
> and, as a rule, don't want to

Very few of the beasts find human beings "worth looking at." To them "all scents are sacred/except our smell…" Beasts are "Endowed from birth with good manners" so they "wag no snobbish elbows," they "don't leer," they "don't look down …[their] nostrils,

> nor poke them into another
> creature's business."

Their "habitations/ are cosy and private, not/ pretentious temples." They have, of course, "to take lives/ to keep…[their] own," but they "never/ kill for applause." The poet speaks to them:

> Compared with even your greediest,
> How Non-U
> our hunting gentry look.

And although they "cannot engender/a genius like Mozart/neither can… [they]"

plague the earth
with brilliant sillies like Hegel
or clever nasties like Hobbes.[11]

The people who wield power in social, political and economic arenas are
worse than the beasts in Auden's poem. They have at the lowest level of their
brain a thin layer of the reptilian brain. It is these people who force us to do
toad work and since we all have, exceptions apart, a dark ugly and degenerate
patch in the metaphysical structure of our being, we do not muster enough
courage to shout, "Stuff your pension." It is possible and, therefore, we must
try to cleanse our self of the degrading and degenerate impurities. Then we
shall enjoy work as worship and have the choice of a better life-style.

"Toads Revisited" is in a sense a sequel to "Toads" but the vision here is
darker. In "Toads" we found that people not subjected to toad work were either
gypsies or those living on their wits. Here we meet altogether different characters. But first we should take a look at the first seven lines of the poem. The
poet, taking a walk "around the park" feels, and rightly so, that it is better than
work, that is, toad work. The park, with its "lake, the sunshine,/The grass to
lie on" is certainly a nice place, nice because a man here can see himself in kinship with the elements – water, sunshine and earth(grass) from which he has
sprung. Not only that, he has another attraction here,

> Blurred playground noises
> Beyond black-stockinged nurses

Tiny tots, even with their noises, are always nice company , as one sees in
them as yet unspoiled human selves. And so the poet concludes, it is "Not a
bad place to be" – "to be" what? To be one's essential self in communion with
both the elemental and unblemished human presences.

But immediately thereafter, as if he has made some mistake, he says, "But
it doesn't suit me." The reason why he says this is that here one meets "of an
afternoon"

> Palsied old step-takers,
> Hare-eyed clerks with the jitters,
> Waxed-fleshed out-patients

Still vague from accidents,
And characters in long coats
Deep in the litter-baskets.

One cannot like to be where such characters spend their time sitting on benches and grass or loitering around in the park. They are stupid or weak and so not fit to do toad work. The persona exclaims in disgust: "Think of being them!" We saw in "Toads" that they who dodged toad work lived on their wits. The persona wanted to be one of them. If he had enough courage he would have given a shit to toad work and 'blarneyed' his way to getting the fame, the girl and the money, all at one sitting. The speaker is a bourgeois and needs the comforts, though not the luxuries, of bourgeois life. So he just cannot bear to be one of the characters we find in the lines above. All these characters live on charity. When dinner-time comes they are given bread. They can only sit by "some bed of lobelias," turning over "their failures." They have "Nowhere to go but indoors," where they have "No friends but empty chairs." The poet, or for that matter anybody worth his salt, cannot "Think of being them." This he says a second time. And this is reinforced with a "No" with which the penultimate stanza begins.

The last two stanzas of the poem make a painful reading. The persona has no choice but to keep doing toad work to keep himself a respectable member of the bourgeoisie. So he says:

No, give me my in-tray,
My loaf-haired secretary
My shall-I-keep-the-call-in-Sir.

He is a well-paid executive working for a business house which makes luxury goods of the kinds described by O'Neill and Orwell above. He has in-and-out trays on his office table. He has a loaf-haired secretary who receives telephone calls for him and asks whether she should keep a particular call for him or dispose it of at her own level. John Skinner says that the word "Call" here has "semantic reverberations…with its allusion – at least – to a telephone call and an *existential call* to a world of freedom beyond toads, but possibly also the *call of death* implied in the final stanza."[12] The question asked in the lines " What can I answer/ When lights come on at four/ At the end of another year?" most certainly allude to death the toad work will drive him to. So with a heroic resignation he asks his inner toad:

> Give me your arm, old toad,
> Help me down Cemetery Road.

This last couplet has full rhyme in contrast to all other off-rhymed couplets. Colvin Bedient comments on the form in Larkin's poetry in general and the two toad poems in particular:

> Then the unconscious rightness of his forms, 'Toads' being, for example, appropriately restless in alternating uneven trimesters and dimeters, 'Toads', again, troubled with alternating off-rhyme and 'Toads Revisited' calmer in off-rhymed couplets, full rhyme kept in reserve for the *entente cordiale of* 'toad' and 'Road.' There is the frequent perfection of his metrical spacing; the easy way his words fall together; the tang and the unsurpassed contemporaneity of his diction and imagery; the fluent evolution of his poems.[13]

In his major poems – both the toad poems are major poems – Philip Larkin makes his vision and form coalesce in a uniquely successful manner. The vision here is extremely significant. The toad sitting on the very metaphysical fabric of his being has to be driven off, otherwise work, the medium in which man can fulfill himself and take human culture forward, will degenerate, has, in fact, already degenerated for the most part into toad work.

Here we may have to face a problem. A reader of these two poems may ask: What have they got to do with the long perspectives in which we have tried to evaluate Larkin's poems in this book? We can say in reply that their true merit can be judged only in the long perspectives. We have seen above that human brain has three layers: the reptilian layer, the mammalian layer and the cerebral cortex. There are men, and their number seems to be legion, in whom the reptilian layer is stronger than the other two layers and it is these people who rule the roost in the skewed civilization of ours. Then there are those, and they constitute almost the entire human population, in whom the mammalian layer sits like an ugly toad on their very soul. So they (and we include ourselves among them) are timid, irrational, controllrd by blind faith and are easily intimidated. The persona in the two poems, who represents us all suffering at the hands of our masters with the reptilian layer dominating their brain, has therefore no choice but to suffer the spiritual indignity he tells us about just to earn enough to pay a few bills.

WATER

"Water" is one of those poems which give us scientifically and metaphysically correct perception of some of the vital truths of our existence. Today, more than ever, man needs a new religion. George Bernard Shaw, in his play *Major Barbara*, gives us the right kind of advice in this matter when he says,

> Well, you have made for yourself something that you call a morality or a religion or what not. It does not fit the facts. Well, scrap it. Scrap it and get one that fits. That is what is wrong with the world at present. It scraps its obsolete steam engines and dynamos, but it wont scrap its old prejudices and its old political constitutions. Whats the result? In machinery it does very well; but in morals and religions and politics it is working at a loss that brings it nearer bankruptcy every year. Don't persist in that folly. If your old religion broke down yesterday, get a newer and better one for tomorrow.[1]

It is not that religions have become useless and, therefore, need to be discarded out of hand. But the established religions that we have are inadequate today for two important reasons. Firstly, many basic elements of the established religions – such as the existence of a personal god, belief in Heaven and Hell in any conventional sense, existence of a soul without a body, existence of another world or afterlife, and so on – do not, as Shaw says, "fit the facts." Secondly, the evil in man over the ages has become so insidious that it has warped his vision, thus making him unable to see the truths about the real nature of things. This evil is not extraneous to man's self. And this self is not an immortal substance. As William James rightly puts it: "our entire feeling of spiritual activity, or what passes by that name, is really a feeling of bodily activities whose exact nature is by most men overlooked." The spiritualists, William James writes, believe that "The soul... exists as a simple spiritual substance in which the various psychic faculties, operations and affections inhere." And "The consequence of the simplicity and substantiality of the soul are its incorruptibility and natural immortality." James rightly disagrees with such a theory of the Soul. "By spiritual self," he means, "a man's inner or objective being, his psychic disposition, taken concretely."[2] This soul or spiritual self is as much corruptible or mortal as our body is. And just as we need water to keep our body clean and healthy (we of course need several other things for this purpose), we need a religion of water for our Soul.

Association of water with all religions as a purificatory element is well known. Thomas Mann in his masterpiece, *The Magic Mountain*, writes that 75% of man's body is water, 20% protein and only 5% other substances.[3] The physicist Werner Heisenberg writes that "Water is the condition of life" and says that Aristotle ascribed to Thales, the 6th century Greek philosopher, the statement that "'Water is the material cause of all things.'"[4] One of the characters in William Golding's *Darkness Visible* speaks thus about the importance of water in Christianity, "They used to build churches by holy wells. Over them sometimes." And he adds: "Water is holiness."[5]

So Philip Larkin says that if he "were called in/ To construct a religion" he "should make use of water." Here the phrasal verb "called in" is significant. One of its dictionary meanings is "to ask someone to come and see you to help you with a difficult situation." We are passing through a difficult phase, in fact, a prolonged crisis in our cultural evolution. So if the poet in Larkin is asked to help us out of our difficulty he will construct a religion of water. Again, the word "construct" is important. So far religions are supposed to have been revealed by God to the prophets – Buddhism of course is an exception. Today the urgently required religion will have to be painstakingly constructed. Here it will be in place to quote the very first paragraph in Julian Huxley's book *Religion Without Revelation*:

> I have called this book *Religion Without Revelation* in order to express at the outset my conviction that religion of the highest order and fullest character can co-exist with a complete absence of belief in revelation in any straightforward sense of the word, and of belief in that kernel of revealed religion, a personal god.[6]

Here we should take note of the fact that the first sentence in the poem is a conditional sentence Type II. This means that the world being what it is – very perverse – is not likely to call the poet to do the worh that is very necessary for its cultural evolution. But in the unlikely event of the world approaching the poet, he will do his duty by mankind and construct a new religion that is urgently needed by man.

Philip Larkin's religion of water also presupposes absence of belief in revelation as well as absence of belief in a personal god. However, some people may think it presumptuous of him to think that he can do what the founders of great religions have done. But we should remember what Matthew Arnold said about poetry eventually replacing religion as well as philosophy:

> Our religion has materialized in fact; it has attached its emotion to the fact, and now the fact is failing it. But for poetry the idea is everything; the rest is a world of illusion.

And

> what now passes with us for religion and philosophy will be replaced by poetry [because] our religion, parading evidences such as those on which the popular mind relies now; our philosophy, pluming itself on its reasonings about causation and finite and infinite being, what are they but the shadows and dreams and false shows of knowledge? The day will come when we shall wonder at ourselves for having trusted to them, for having taken them seriously; and the more we perceive their hollowness, the more we shall prize 'the breath and finer spirit of knowledge' offered to us by poetry.[7]

Larkin does not reject religion and philosophy per se. He only says (and here he is in the good company of many philosophers, scientists, creative artists and thinkers in many other fields of knowledge) that there is an urgent need for a new kind of religion. What is his original thought about the matter is that his religion will make use of water. "Going to church," according to the tenets of his region, "would entail a fording/ To dry, different clothes." To approach his religion, our cognitive self, after some kind of purificatory fording, will have to put on "dry, different clothes" of power of perception to imbibe, assimilate and absorb this religion. Some sort of intellectual and spiritual rejuvenation will be necessary to live this kind of religious life.

As far as the liturgy of this religion is concerned, it will not employ the liturgy of any of the established religions. But liturgy is an important appendage of every religion and so Larkin's religion too will have its liturgy, but of an altogether different kind. It will have "images of sousing" and "A furious, devout drench." These images and this drench will purge the devotee's whole range of consciousness as also his perverse beliefs, including belief in a supernatural order. The drench has to be furious precisely for this reason.

Then we have the strikingly original last stanza of the poem in which the poet says that he should, as the last step in the process of constructing a new religion, "raise in the east /A glass of water/Where any-angled light/ Would congregate endlessly." Here we quote the following remarkable lines from Erwin Schrodinger's book *What is Life? with Mind and Matter*:

> Suppose that you could mark the molecules in a glass of water; then pour the contents of the glass into the ocean and stir the contents of the latter thoroughly so as to distribute the marked molecules uniformly throughout the seven seas; if then you took a glass of water anywhere out of the ocean, you would find in it about a hundred of your marked molecules.[8]

It is said that 18g of water contains 6.02×10^{23} (that is, twenty-one zeroes after 602) molecules of water. But what does Larkin's glass of water, with its mind-boggling number of molecules and raised in the east, signify and symbolize? It signifies human brain. Our brain is the glass of water. Just as a glass of water contains an incredibly immense number of molecules, our brain (also called "grey matter") is packed with an incredibly large number of cells called neurons. Julian Huxley tells us about their number as follows: " As Professor J. Z. Young has set forth in his recent book *Doubt and Certainty in Science*, the number of cells in our 'thinking parts' alone – the cerebral cortex of our brain – is about seven times the total human population of the world and their organization is of a scarcely conceivable complexity."[9] Fritjof Capra writes: "The structure of the human brain is enormously complex. It contains about ten billion nerve cells (neurons), which are interlinked in a vast network through 1000 billion junctions (synapses)."[10] The total number of molecules in those cells must be countless.

We know that water makes a ray of light change its direction when it enters it at an angle. A straight ray of light will go straight into it. Any number of rays of the sun, when a glass of water is raised in the east, will enter it at different angles and, together, will illumine the countless molecules there. Now this whole process of the rays of light congregating endlessly on the water's surface, getting refracted while entering it and collectively illuminating all the molecules, and sometimes even forming a spectrum there, becomes a beautiful metaphor. There are today various fields of knowledge. Each field radiates light. These many-angled rays of light should congregate endlessly on the surface of our brain, be refracted while entering it and illumine every one of the countless molecules of the 10 billion cells there. Then our brain, with all its cells thus illuminated by the truths in all fields of knowledge, will be fully enlightened. The refracted rays of knowledge will also sometimes form spectrum in our brain. Then our sense of our selves, our consciousness of the world, our deepest and purest thoughts, desires and emotions will have scientific-philosophical authenticity and we shall have real self-realization, which is the true end of religion.

Some thinkers have said that religion implies belief in "spiritual beings" or it is "a felt practical relationship with what is believed in as a supernatural being or beings." Julian Huxley says that they "should have remembered that one of the great religions of the world, namely Buddhism in its original and purest form, does not profess faith in any supernatural being..." He refers to the observation of Renan that "'Buddhism is Catholicism without God' and that 'this atheist religion has been eminently moral and active in good works.'" The most sacred life-consciousness of the Enlightened One was perfectly illumined by many-angled rays of knowledge from various fields of knowledge so that he perceived the ultimate truth and purpose of man's being as very few have perceived them. This most transcendental awareness is Nirvana.

Julian Huxley is for the removal of the "superposed" belief and its corollaries, but he says people may ask what will then remain of the reality. His answer is as follows:

> a great deal. That reality includes permanent facts of human existence – birth, marriage, reproduction and death; suffering, mutual aid, comradeship, physical and moral growth. It also includes other facts which we may call the facts of the spiritual life, such as the conviction of sin, the desire for righteousness, the sense of absolution, the peace of communion; and those other facts, the existence and potency of human ideals, which like truth and virtue and beauty always

transcend the concrete and always reveal further goals to the actual. It also includes facts and forces of nature outside and apart from man – the existence of matter and of myriads of other living beings, the position of man on a little planet of one of a million suns, the facts and laws of motion, matter, and energy and all their manifestations, the history of life. I say that it includes these; it would be more correct to say it includes certain aspects of all these and many other facts. It includes in their aspect of relatedness to human destiny; and it includes them as held together, against the cosmic background, by a spirit of awe and reverence.[11]

Man's further evolution as a species depends on such an awareness and him re-orienting his life and activities in conformity with it. But for that, Julian Huxley says, "the brain's level of performance" must be "genetically raised – in acuteness of perception, memory, synthetic grasp and intuition, analytic capacity, mental energy ,creative power, balance, and judgement."[12] Philip Larkin's poem is a fervent plea for genetically raising of the brain's level of performance. If such a breakthrough does not take place man will either destroy himself with his destructive nature or speedily come to an evolutionary dead end. But the problem, as the philosopher John H. Hick puts it in his book *Philosophy of Religion* (rpt. Pearson India, 1915, p.43), is this: "All the evidence suggests that humanity gradually emerged out of lower forms of life with a very limited moral awarenesss and wih very crude religious assumptions."

Philip Larkin's proposal to use water to construct a new and urgently needed religion has fine scientific underpinning. Sir Charles Sherrington in his great work, *Man On His Nature*, tells us that "Water is a great menstruum of 'life,' " and adds: "It makes life possible. It was part of the plot by which our planet engendered life" (MohN, p. 105).

The Whitsun Weddings

Writing in 1979, Donald Davie called Philip Larkin "the central figure in English poetry over the last twenty years." Continuing, he wrote:

there has been the widest possible agreement, over this period, that Philip Larkin is for good or ill the unofficial laureate of post-1945 England. Some may have criticized what Larkin does with the truths he discovers, what attitudes he takes up to the landscapes and the weather of his own poems; but those landscapes and that weather – no one, I think, has failed to recognize these. And this is just as true if we think of landscapes and weather metaphorically; we recognize in Larkin's poems the seasons of present-day England, but we recognize also the seasons of an English soul – the moods he expresses are but our moods too, though we may deal with them differently. On the literal level, at any rate, no one denies that what Larkin says is true; that the England in his poems is the England we have inhabited.[1]

The landscapes presented in "The Whitsun Weddings" are, or were, the real landscapes of the period in England. But it is not a realistic poem. The landscapes are metaphorically rich. In his sonnet no. 84, Shakespeare wrote:

Lean penury within that pen doth dwell
That to his subject lends not some glory.

Larkin's poem lends much glory to the real scenes and setting of his poem. Our attempt here will be to see how from the real landscapes Larkin distils great poetry, or how he invests them with deep metaphorical significances. Also, we will see the fine correspondence between the outer and spiritual landscapes.

The persona in the poem is only the veiled poetic self of Philip Larkin. In fact, as A. T. Tolley observes, "The 'I' [in the poem] is clearly Larkin, the librarian leaving Hull late on a Saturday afternoon for a week-end in London."[2] One of the great merits of Larkin as a poet is that he sees his self as nothing more than the common denominator of the ordinary selves of his countrymen and regards the act of writing poetry as cleansing his spiritual self. This self of the poet boards one Whitsun afternoon (one-twenty, to be precise) a train at Hull bound for London. This train becomes the metaphor for life in the mid-twentieth century England. As the persona boards the train, his mental state and the corresponding interior of the train are glimpsed at in the opening lines of the poem:

That Whitsun, I was late getting away:
Not till about
One-twenty on the sunlit Saturday

Did my three-quarters-empty train pull out,
All windows down, all cushions hot, all sense
Of being in a hurry gone.

Though it is a bright, sun-lit afternoon, both the inside of the train and the poet's mind are, for the most part (three-fourths in each case) unoccupied; the windows of both the coach and the poet's mind are down; the seats meant for passengers in the train and the space meant for serious thoughts in the poet's mind are hot, that is, not imaginatively warm enough to be procreative. And, consequently, there is no sense of hurry either in the train or in the poet's mind. Nonetheless, the journey begins because life is movement in time. Philip Larkin himself tells us about the real journey that he once undertook and which forms the theme of this uniquely successful poem. He says that one Whit Saturday,1955, he caught

a very slow train that stopped at every station and I hadn't realized that, of course, this was the train that all the wedding couples would get on and go to London for their honeymoon [;] it was an eye-opener to me. Every part was different but the same somehow. They all looked different but they were all doing the same things and sort of feeling the same things. I suppose the train stopped at about four, five, six stations between Hull and London and there was a sense of gathering emotional momentum.

Every time you stopped fresh emotion climbed aboard. And finally between Peterborough and London when you hurtled on, you felt the whole thing was being aimed like a bullet – at the heart of things, you know. All this fresh, open life. Incredible experience. I've never forgotten it.[3]

And, while returning the compliment paid him by Poetry Book Society in selecting "The Whitsun Weddings" as their choice for 1964, Larkin wrote: "Some years ago I came to the conclusion that to write a poem was to construct a verbal device that would preserve an experience indefinitely by reproducing it in whoever read the poem."[4] Larkin also said that for him writing poetry meant preserving experience: "it seems as if you have seen this sight, felt this feeling, had this vision, and have got to find a combination of words that will preserve it by setting it off in other people."[5] We shall try to see how the sights, the feelings and the vision are preserved in the combination of words that takes the shape of "The Whitsun Weddings." First, the sights caught from the window when the train starts moving until we come to the end of stanza two. First "the backs of houses;" then "a street/Of blinding windscreens;" then "the fish-dock" from which the smell of fish floating in the air can be inhaled in the train. Then the first stanza ends with these lines:

> The river's level shifting breadth began,
> Where sky and Lancashire and water meet.

James Naremore comments on these lines thus: "... the last two lines are lyrical, even majestic, though they seem to have grown quite naturally out of the flat tone of the preceding verses. The enclosed, arid heat of the opening has been replaced by a feeling of space and water."[6] Here, in the four medieval elements (the sky, earth and water and fire, that is, the pervasive heat in the setting), from which all life on the earth is made, the cognitive self of the poet sees the procreative power of the elements and we understand its significance. The stanza closes with a full-stop as if a wide window that had surveyed a moving setting shut when the poet had the vision. Barbara Everett comments on these lines as follows:

> In this description of the flat, airy country south of Hull there
> is another 'wedding,' too, in the lying together of those nat-
> ural powers – sky, land, water – whose simple beauty and
> strength the human beings emerging from a modern urban
> society cannot help so comically and pathetically lacking.[7]

It is from this wedding of the elements that organic life in its multifarious forms is born on the earth. And, likewise, it is from the weddings of men and women that human society owes its existence. These facts have to be kept in mind while reading the poem.

The second stanza is the second wide window opening, as it were, after a wink of the eye, on the moving setting. As in the first stanza, in it, too, there are two sentences. The first sentence covering the first three lines tells us of the "tall heat" sleeping "for miles inland" and of the "slow and stopping curve" of the southward movement of the train. It appears that the sleeping heat outside has made Larkin's poetic consciousness sluggish so that he uses "we" for both his and the train's slow movement; in this state the window of his self perceives the scenes thus:

> Wide farms went by, short-shadowed cattle, and
> Canals with floatings of industrial froth;
> A hothouse flashed uniquely: hedges dipped
> And rose: and now and then a smell of grass
> Displaced the reek of buttoned carriage-cloth
> Until the next town, new and nondescript,
> Approached with acres of dismantled cars.

Donald Davie's very perceptive comment on these lines is as follows:

> The slow canals have wound through many a poem about England since T. S. Eliot's *Waste Land* but never under such a level light as this. For in the poem as a whole ("The Whitsun Weddings"), the tone of the describing voice is scrupulously neutral, it affords no handle at all for reflections like "A canal and not a river," "Tainted water, not fresh." There is no meaning, no "placing" in the way pre-industrial things like farms, cattle, hedges, and grass are interspersed with industrial things like chemical froth and dismantled cars. And for Larkin indeed this seems to be one of the rules of the game; there is to be no historical perspective; no measuring of present against past. Canals and smashed cars come along with hedges and cattle simply because they come along like that in any railway journey through England, as we all know. And precisely because poem after poem since *The Waste Land* has measured our present (usually seen as depleted) against our past (usually seen as rich), Larkin's refusal to do this is refreshing – at last, we recognize with relief, we can take all that for granted, take it as real.[8]

Here we can make one or two points. The tone of Larkin's "describing voice" is "neutral" because the poet-persona's organic consciousness is the growth of the soil of contemporary England – an England whose soil does not appear to have much fertility, literally as well as metaphorically speaking. This accounts for the apparent lack of a very fertile imagination at work in the poet. We find diminishment of fertility both in the natural world – hedges, not luxuriant growth of plants and trees; the occasional smell of grass displacing "the reek of buttoned carriage-cloth;""short-shadowed cattle," culminating in complete infertility in "acres of dismantled cars," to say nothing pf "Canals with [toxic] floatings of industrial froth" – and in the sluggish consciousness of the poet.

But in Larkin's poetry, particularly in his great poems like the present one, this realism lifts us to a very important level of awareness of life and its meaning, as we shall soon see. Colvin Bedient refers to St.-John Perse's remark that "Poetry… never wishes to be absence, nor refusal," and observes, "certainly in 'The Whitsun Weddings' Larkin grants it the presence of the world, as he grants the world its presence."[9]

Another important thing that we notice in the first two stanzas of the poem is that not a single man or woman is seen in the setting covered by the moving train. Nor do we see anyone other than the persona himself on the train The reason obviously is that landscapes are prior to man in time. Man then comes and acts upon and is acted upon by the landscapes. The landscapes seen through the train window by a poetic self show how man has acted upon them. And we shall soon see how these landscapes have acted upon men and women of the time.

The second stanza, like the first, is end-stopped, that is, it ends with a full-stop. The next four stanzas (stanzas 3-6) are run-on. There are, of course, internal full-stops in them. The seventh stanza ends with a semi-colon. In these four stanzas the humanscape of the contemporary Eng-land unfolds itself. It is a significant humanscape because a dozen marriages that have been solemnized bring, at different stoppages of the slow-moving train, the participants (brides and grooms and their relations and friends) in these marriages on the scene. Significantly, the poet does not give even a glimpse of the faces, and the expressions on the faces, of the newly-wed couples. Only the friends and relations who come to the railway stations to see them off are made vivid to us.

Barbara Everett says: "Poems like 'Here' and 'The Whitsun Weddings' have – as their titles suggested – a perfectly clear 'literal' sense, an allusion to time and place, that may be a little ironical but that is a part of their meaning" and "To propose a further meaning is merely to extend the levels on which we read."[10] The uniqueness of these poems lies in the fact that both the 'literal' and 'metaphorical' are an organic unity in them as they are in life. But now we will see how the humanscape unfolds itself in the next four and the first three lines of the penultimate (seventh) stanza. The persona tells us that at first he

> didn't notice what a noise
> The weddings made
> Each station that we stopped at:

because, as he says, "sun destroys/The interest of what is happening in the shade." Here the poet is making a general statement and so we should pause and think why this happens. We saw earlier that, looking through the window of the train at "the tall heat that slept/ For miles inland," the poet's consciousness, finding itself moving alongside the moving setting that was infertile, not to say ugly, seemed lost in contemplation. And so he did not think at first that what was happening in the shade at railway stations was of any interest. In the light of the sun we have a clear perception of things as they are, but in the shade our perceptions need some kind of transcendence. So when the persona heard the "whoops and skirls" of the friends and relations of the newly-wed couples down the railway platforms he thought that "the porters [were] larking with the mails / And went on reading." He is obviously an intellectual who is not much interested, to say nothing of participating, in the drama of ordinary human life going on around him, presumably because he thinks it is no more than a farce which, sadly, it has become in most of its aspects. We find the humanscape in the poem analogous to the natural setting seen through the train's window in the first two stanzas. We can even say that that setting is the objective correlative of the human setting in the poem. But a poet, who is true to his salt, has to work with whatever human material is at his disposal. So Larkin is drawn into this drama although at first he seems to be contemptuous of what he see:

> grinning and pomaded, girls
> In parodies of fashion, heels and veils,
> All posed irresolutely, watching us go,
>
> As if out on the end of an event
> Waving goodbye
> To something that survived it.

Here we see Larkin as an observer of and a participant in this ordinary, not to say farcical drama. First he sees the girls in "parodies of fashion" because they belong to lower middle class. But "out on the end of an event" they are seen "Waving goodbye / to something that survived it." What did survive the event? It is something that, ideally speaking, transforms human life with value-addition in marriage. It is the poet who perceives this beautiful poetry of life even amidst the whole tawdry show. No wonder, he says,

> Struck, I leant
> More promptly out next time, more curiously,
> And saw it all again in different terms:

Following the colon after the word 'terms' come snapshots of fathers, mothers , an uncle of the couples and of the girlfriends of the brides. Fathers have "broad belts" under their suits and their foreheads are "seamy"; mothers are "loud and fat"; an uncle is seen "shouting smuts." And the girls with their "perms", their "nylon gloves and jewellery substitutes" and their dresses – "lemons, mauves, and olive-ochres" – are "Marked off unreally from the rest." These are middle class people who constitute the majority in a developed country like England. The visuals of the fathers, mothers, an uncle, girls, even children presented here are of real people in a real society in historically verifiable time, just as the setting presented in the first two stanzas is real in time and place, as Donald Davie testifies above. And the marriage parties have come just after the receptions held in "cafes,""banquet-halls up yards," "bunting-dressed/Coach-party annexes." Nicholas Marsh tells us about the social status of these places:

> The speaker's satiric tone comes across from the oxymoronic effect of 'banquet-halls' (associated with palaces and high society) 'up yards' (conjuring up a community hall, or an outbuilding of a small country-town hotel) and of 'bunting-dressed' (celebration) 'coach-party annexes'(seedy commercialism).[11]

It may, however, be emphasized here that the poet's attitude is not one of satirizing or sneering at the social status or mores of these people.

"All down the line," the poet says, "Fresh couples," accompanied by relations and friends, came. And as the train, with the poet and the couples moved, the rest, having "thrown the last confetti and advice," stood on the platforms. To the persona the faces of each of them "seemed to define / Just what it saw departing." The children's faces expressed frown "At something dull." Fathers' faces expressed happiness experienced as never before at "Success so huge and wholly farcical." We wonder how a huge success can be farcical. And "The women shared/ The secret like a happy funeral." The words "happy" and "funeral" do not normally collocate, so what is the point in putting them together? The point is that the funeral is that of the virginity and it is happy because of the consummation in the marriage. Finally, the "girls, gripping their handbags tighter, stared/ At a religious wounding." The expression "religious wounding" arrests our attention. It takes us back in time to primitive societies in which "wounding" used to be part of religious rites; there used to be something mysterious about such wounding. To these girls the consummation in marriage has something of the mystery of religious wounding.

The different attitudes to the weddings are realistic but they have a tinge of something mysterious. However, says the persona,

> Free at last,
> And loaded with the sum of all they saw,
> We hurried towards London.

Free at last of the crudities and vulgarities and ordinariness of the relatives and friends of the couples, "We", that is, the persona and the couples, hurried towards London. Now the poet-persona identifies himself with the married couples as he uses the pronoun "We" here. And they are "loaded with the sum of all they [the relations and friends] saw." We have seen above what the children saw, what the fathers, the women and the girls saw and felt as the couples departed. The sum of what they all saw did not amount to much – not anything approaching the profound transformation that the rite of passage (marriage) is supposed to effect in the lives of the newly wedded couples.. But for Larkin the poet there is, in this "sum of all they saw," material enough to write a great poem with.

Now, as the train approaches London, landscape reappears, but it is a different landscape from the one we saw in the first two stanzas of the poem. The poet says, "Now fields were building-plots, and poplars cast/ Long shadows over major roads…An Odeon went past, a cooling tower/ And someone running up to bowl." This went on "for/ Some fifty minutes, that in time would seem/ Just long enough" for them to "settle hats and say

I nearly died."

Why nearly died? The poet's earlier detachment and withdrawal from life nearly died. The couples, too, as they are approaching London, are going to be born to a new life that the rite of passage has brought about in them. The poet is now interested in the dozen couples "sitting side by side" and watching the landscape. These couples are unreflecting and passive spectators. So

none
Thought of the others they would never meet
Or how their lives would all contain this hour.

But the poet, true to his calling, was thinking. He says

I thought of London spread out in the sun,
Its postal districts packed like squares of wheat
There we were aimed.

These lines contain much food for thought. Even in the landscapes we passed through in the first two stanzas we did not come across any squares of wheat and so squares of wheat in London are an impossibility. But the poet likens London's postal districts packed with towney people to wheat fields and implies that each man in these districts is like an ear of wheat in a field. Just as wheat gives man his bread whereby man gets strength and energy, each man even in London's postal districts, which seem to have poor human culture, has the potentiality to be productive to give the species strength and energy. Larkin made this very point when, in reply to a question of the interviewer for *Paris Review*, he said, "The line 'Its postal districts packed with squares of wheat' refers to London, not England. It doesn't seem 'diminutional' to me, rather the reverse, if anything. It's meant to make the postal districts seem rich and fruitful" (RW, p. 74).

The landscape appears again as the train approaches the London railway station. Here we see "walls of blackened moss:"

And as we raced across
Bright knots of rail
Past standing Pullmans, walls of blackened moss
Came close

Landscape and humanscape interact. Man acts upon landscape and is acted upon by it. And now "the frail/ Travelling coincidence" is nearly over. The coincidence of travelling together was frail because it was of a very short duration and also because no sharing of thoughts and feelings took place either among the couples or between the poet and any of them. But the poet has understood its significance and so he writes

and what it held
Stood ready to be loosed with all the power
That being changed can give.

Who have changed and what is the power of this change? First the persona himself. He at first appeared as withdrawn, then thought himself superior to the people in the marriage parties, then slowly was drawn into the feelings of these people. He is changed considerably in the process. The couples are also changed though they say nothing about it. It is for poetry to fathom the inmost depths of even those feelings that remain inarticulate and make the reader enter them.. This only poetry or art is capable of doing because, as John Dewey says, art is "the greatest intellectual achievement in the history of humanity."[12]

Thus loosed with all the power of being changed, there "swelled" in the couples, as the "tightened brakes" of the engine "took hold,"

A sense of falling, like the arrow-shower
Sent out of sight, somewhere becoming rain.

John Wain's comment on the last word – "rain" – in the poem is significant:

The last word of the poem is crucial: the 'rain' which falls somewhere – it doesn't matter where – is the age-old emblem of fertility and the renewal of life, the nourishment that Hopkins cries out for in the terrible line

Mine, O thou lord of life, send my roots rain

The human actors in this scene, who will set up home and mate and keep the human spectacle going, are unreflective; their world is concrete and immediate; if we are to have any such thing as 'art' – whether poetry or any of the other arts – their actions need to be completed and interpreted by a brooding imaginative vision playing over them from a point of detachment. In a sense the poet's involvement is greater than theirs; he sees and understands just what it is that each participant feels, and then puts them together to form one complete experience, felt in its directness by no one, yet present in the atmosphere and available to that contemplative imagination that makes 'art'[13].

In "The Whitsun Weddings" the poetic shelf of Philip Larkin, using very ordinary, not to say impoverished, settings, natural as well as human, creates a work of art of universal and permanent significance. The poet presents both the natural setting and the humanscape as they are – impoverished, not to say ugly. But he does not, for that reasn, calls his world a waste land. By presenting the weddings of the elements and of men and women with due regard he tells us that procreation in the two worlds has not stopped. All that is needed is to raise the quality of these procreations, which is, unfortunately, a very difficult task. But, as Colvin Bedient rightly observes, Lakin grants his poem the presence of the world and this world the presence of great poetry so that "The Whitsun Weddings" will always be counted among the brightest gems in the treasure-house of English poetry.

DAYS

"Days" is a poem with a fine philosophical aura and we have to enter this aura and get illuminated by it. To do this we shall essay a modest interpretation of the piece. In the first stanza the first and last lines are questions. The first question – "What are days for?" – is followed by four lines, which, we can say with some assurance, constitute a comprehensive answer to the question. The answer is related to life's livingness, wakefulness and its essentially joyous nature in its existence in days.

Man's or, for that matter, any creature's life on this earth is measured only in terms of days. In fact there is no concept of days anywhere in the universe except on our earth and so there is no life beyond days for any organic structure – man, animal or plant. Martin Heidegger says: "the being of human reality …is being-in- the- world."[1] My life has no being beyond the days allotted to it. Days come in unending successions, waking every day whatever lifeforms exist for particular periods to engage in tasks allotted to them, and thereby helping them to realize life in its joyous wakefulness, not just in the physical sense, but also in its intrinsic mental, moral, spiritual, even transcendental senses. Therein lies the fulfillment, nay, the immortality of the human spirit. But does man find himself happy during his days in this world? Here we are reminded of what a character in Bernard Shaw's play *John Bull's Other Island* says about the world having been reduced to a place of "torment and penance" or, to be precise, "hell."

> The world, sir, is very clearly a world of torment and penance, a place where the fool flourishes and the good and wise are hated and persecuted; a place where men and women torture one another in the name of love; where children are scourged and enslaved in the name of parental duty and education; where the weak in body are poisoned and mutilated in the name of healing , and the weak in character are put to the horrible torture of imprisonment, not for hours but for years , in the name of justice. It is a place where the hardest toil is a welcome refuge from the horror and tedium of pleasure, and where charity and good works are only for hire to ransom the souls of the spoiler and sybarite. Now, sir, there is only one place of horror and torment known to my religion; and that place is hell. Therefore it is plain to me that this earth of ours is hell.[2]

Days are only on this earth; successions of days are spans of life of different creatures. Nothing of life extends beyond days for any individual or any species of organic life. But the world of man's existence being what it has become – hell – the poem asks of us its second question: "Where can we live but days?" The question must needs be solved satisfactorily so that whatever days are allotted to a man's life he must live in them truly, realizing what George Santayana calls his "ideal immortality." Elaborating on this expression, Santayana writes: "Ideal immortality is a principle revealed to insight; it is seen by observing the eternal qualities of ideas and validities, and the affinity to them native to reason and the cognitive energy of mind." [3] Also, man, in order to realize this kind of immortality, must be happy in his days, that is, his essential self, that is, his soul must be in harmony with the universe .

We can attain this immortality and harmony only in our days. But the poet says:

> Ah, solving that question
> Brings the priest and the doctor
> In their long coats
> Running over the fields.

This is the second and last stanza of the poem. The voice of the poet here acquires a somber tone. The priest and the doctor in their long black and white coats, respectively, running over the fields to solve this question appear to be threatening figures. But why do they appear threatening? First, let us see what a doctor thinks of a man's soul – the centre of man's true livingness, transcendental wakefulness and joy. In Bernard Shaw's play *The Doctor's Dilemma*, Doctor Ridgeon, reacting to the accusation – "Don't you see that what is really dreadful is that to you living things have no souls" – says "with a skeptical shrug:" "The soul is an organ I have not come across in the course of my anatomical work." To this, Jennifer, the heroine of the play, replies bitterly: "You know you would not dare to say such a silly thing as that to anybody but a woman whose mind you despise. If you dissected me you could not find my conscience. Do you think that I have none?" [4] If a doctor dissected me, he would not only not find my conscience, but also my consciousness, my moral sense and my spiritual self with its longing for transcendental meaning of my existence. But it is precisely these dimensions of my being that are real me. It is, therefore, not surprising that in Virginia Woolf's novel *The Years*, a character named Peggy, herself a brilliant doctor, says, "Doctors know very little about the body, absolutely nothing about the mind." [7] What Peggy seems to mean is that sensations, feelings, emotions that constitute the livingness of the body in the world and cognitions, perceptions, consciousness, transcendental awareness that constitute the livingness of the mind, again in the world, are beyond the scope of medical science.

As opposed to Ridgeon's denial of the existence of the soul in living things, C. G. Jung, in the lines quoted by Erwin Schrodinger in his book *What is Life?*

with Mind and Matter, and reproduced below, says that the soul is something "in which all knowledge is rooted" and "all science… is a function of the soul:"

All science *(Wissenschaft)* however is a function of the soul, in which all knowledge is rooted. The soul is the greatest of all cosmic miracles, it is the *conditio sine qua non* of the world as an object. It is exceedingly astonishing that the Western world (apart from very few exceptions) seems to have so little appreciation of this being so. The flood of external objects of cognizance has made the subject of all cognizance with-draw to the background, often to apparent non-existence.

Schrodinger's comment on Jung's observation is: "Of course Jung is quite right."[5]

This soul is the very essence of man's being and the "reality" of this being is "being-in -the world," as Heidegger rightly tells us. Our life can therefore have fulfillment only in the days that span it. The doctor, though he can and does cure many of my physical and some of my mental ailments, can be of no help in solving the question: "Where can we live in but days?"

And as far as the capability of the priest is concerned, he is less qualified than the doctor to be of any help in the matter. He will tell us that this world is a vale of tears and true happiness is to be had only in the after-world in which God has his abode. A very strong rebuttal of this erroneous – and, shall we say, dictated-by-vested-interests, too – view of life comes from no less a person than Tolstoy in the following passage in an essay bearing the title "Did Jesus Believe in Immortality?":

according to the doctrine of our Churches, human life, the supreme good that is known to us, is but a very small portion of another life of which we are deprived for a season. Our life, according to this conception, is not the life that God in-tended or was obliged to give us. Our life is degenerate and fallen, a mere fragment, a mockery of life, compared with the real life which we think God ought to give us. The principal object of our life, according to this theory, is not to try to live this mortal life comfortably to the will of the giver of life; or to render it eternal in the generations of man, as the Hebrews believed; or to identify ourselves with the will of the Father, as Christ taught; no, it is to believe that after this unreal life the true life begins.[6]

Sir Charles Sherrington, whom we have already quoted above and quote here again, says that life is "an energy system" and it is "so woven into the fabric of Earth's surface that to suppose a life isolated from the rest of that terrestrial world even briefly gives an image too distorted to resemble life" (MohN, p.79).

And an important philosopher like A. J. Ayer rejects the priestly view of after-life and a transcendent god:

It is common to find belief in a transcendent god conjoined with belief in after-life. But In the form it usually takes, the content of this belief is not a genuine hypothesis. To say that men do not ever die or that the state of death is prolonged insensitivity, Is indeed to express a significant proposition, though all the available evidence goes to show that it is false.[7]

So we see that neither the doctor nor the priest can solve the question asked in the last line of the first stanza. It is , however, nobody's case that medical science and religion have no place in man's life. Both have designated roles in our life. The role of medical science is obvious – to keep us physically and mentally fit, a pre-condition for living a life of truly transcendent experiences. The priestly belief in a transcendent god and the conjoined belief in after-life is philosophically unsustainable. But religion is necessary for man – the kind of religion described/ defined by Alfred North Whitehead: "Religion is a force of belief cleansing the inward parts. For this reason the primary religious virtue is sincerity, a penetrating sincerity. A religion, on its doctrinal side, can thus be defined as a system of general truths, which have the effect of transforming character when they are sincerely held and vividly appreciated."[8]

Thus we cannot but agree with Tolstoy that "the supreme good" known to us is our life on this earth as there is no life anywhere else. This supreme good must be informed by "a system of general truths...sincerely held and vividly appreciated." But what is life? G. G. Simpson tells us that it is a "hierarchy of organization." Continuing, he writes,

The hierarchy runs more or less from the subatomic through atoms, molecules, cells, tissues, organs ,individuals, specific populations, communities, and biomes, comprehensive biological systems, to the whole realm of the organic and its environments in space and time.[9]

Up to a certain level in this hierarchy medical science has a vital role to play. Beyond that general truths not only enshrined in true religion but in many other fields of knowledge have to be taken recourse to and Herculean efforts have to be made by man to transform the hell that our world has become into heaven in which man can live a full life and fulfill himself. This is all the more necessary because, as Albert Camus famously said, man "is deprived of the memory of a lost home or the hope of a promised land."[10]

Ambulances

"Ambulances" is a poem about how life is completely annihilated in death. This and three other poems – "The Building," "The Old Fools" and "Aubade" (Larkin's swan song) – have Death as their main theme and they are all very powerful poems. Their power lies not in the poet's obsession with death but because they tell us what life – being alive – really means and how death completely and for ever destroys a living organic structure. "Life is the gift of nature; but beautiful living is the gift of wisdom,"[1] so goes a Greek adage. And they who understand what beautiful living really means, have, in fact, tasted the unique sweetness of beautiful living – as a poet like Philip Larkin must have savoured it in aesthetic experience while writing some of his great poems – cannot but feel intensely the tragedy of death. The people who are shown as about to die in "Ambulances," "The Building" and "The Old Fools" did not have the wisdom that could have given them a beautiful life. Even the persona in "Aubade," who does understand what death actually means, has not lived a beautiful life. And now we will try to understand what the poem "Ambulances" tells us.

The annihilation of life that is going to take place in this poem is that of a haphazard, meager kind of human existence, but the loss of even such existence, never to be resurrected in all eternity in the same individual life, in saddening in the extreme. The poet says that ambulances, "closed like confessionals," keep coming to the kerbs so that, in the end, all streets in the city are visited, which simply means that everywhere people die. "They (ambulances) thread /Loud noons of cities" to reach the kerbs. The expressions " closed like confessionals" and "loud noons of cities" need our special notice. Confessionals are closed cabins in which sinners, sitting alone, confess their sins and seek absolution from the priest who hears the confession but is hidden from the sinners. In the ambulances the sinners are already dead or about to die and therefore past making any confessions. Nor are there any priests to grant them pardon. The sinners have already died or will die without making a clean breast of their sins. Then the pathetic fallacy in "loud noos" is very telling. Loud noons are contrasted with the somber silence in the confessionals-like ambulances . The noons are noisy with the words of routine, commonplace exchanges among people performing commonplace tasks in the streets of the city. Words used while expressing even trite, banal feelings are signs of life's livingness. The streets are loud with such words, they are vibrating with life although this is a life of superficialities. The ambulances are shorn of even such life. They have only "deadened" silence in them. These ambulances are painted "Light glossy grey with arms on a plaque." People look at the passing ambulances and their glances are expressive of pity and sorrow. But the ambulances do not give back any of these glances because the dead or the dying man lying is in no position to do so.. The poet in these lines in the first stanza tells us about the difference between life – even noisy superficialities and sad , silent glances that are expressions of life – and death , an expressionless and silent void. All this we find in the first stanza which appears to be a sort of Prologue to what comes in the rest of the poem .There follow four stanzas, the first three of which, unlike the first stanza, are not end-stopped, that is , they do not end on a full stop. There are three full stops in the middle of the four stanzas and a final full stop at the end of the poem. The spacing of the periods is significant as it tells us how to read the poem.

The next sentence covers the whole of the second stanza (six lines) and the first four lines of the third stanza. These ten lines have to be read in one breath with only slight pauses where commas occur: there are no other punctuation marks. . A dying man is brought on a stretcher from a house and "stowed" in the ambulance. It is "a wild white face" overtopping "Red stretcher- blankets." This man is now only a commodity which can be stowed in some place. Present on the scene are "children strewn on steps or road" and "women coming from the shops /Past smells of different dinners." They only see "momently" the "wild white face" being carried away on the stretcher. But they

sense the solving emptiness
That lies just under all we do,
And for a second get it whole
So permanent and blank and true.

Children and women of lower middle class do not have any deep, not to say philosophical, awareness of the difference between life and death. The housewives coming from shops (where they had gone to buy groceries for their dinners) passed houses, from which smells of dinners floated out, have just reached the scene under discussion. The savoury smells of dinners should have enveloped their olfactory sense in some kind of pleasant sensation. But both the children present on the scene and the women reaching it "sense," though only momently, "the solving emptiness/That lies just under all we do." Death is "the solving emptiness," that is, it solves the problem that life is, but only emptiness remains when life is solved and gone. And this emptiness "lies just under all we do." Sophocles writes these great lines in *Ajax:* "For I see the true state of all us that live - /We are dim shapes, no more, and weightless shadow"(ll.125-126). And Doris Lessing, in her novel *The Grass is Singing*, tells us this about the distance between life and death in the context of the imminent death of its protagonist, Mary Turner, "between her and the fatal darkness was a short strip of daylight."[2] If one may say so, it is only on a thin, brittle crust spread over the vast, unfathomable ocean of Death that life, as we know it, exists. Death is nothing but emptiness that lies just under all our activities that go by the name of Life. Or we can say that our lives are mere bubbles on the surface of a large and deep river, that is, Death. Here it seems necessary to remind ourselves that Philip Larkin is a poet who lays bare before us the truth behind every phenomenon, every institution, every commonly held belief that he deals with in his poems. And this act of laying bare the truth is done in the consciousness of ordinary, common men and women for a very valid and important reason. Here also, in the last two of the four lines quoted above , it is the children and women representing the common man who get the truth whole – the truth which is "So permanent and blank." This is very noteworthy. It is not philosophers and thinkers who are present on the scene and it is not their perception of "the solving emptiness...so permanent and true " that Larkin is speaking of. He is firmly of the belief, and rightly so, that any qualitative change in our existence will have its foundation in the upgraded and updated consciousness of the common people. All our social, educational, cultural planning should have as its target this uplifting of a truly philosophical-scientific nature.

The ambulance , with its door fastened after the dying man has been stowed in it, leaves the scene. And the women whisper, "*Poor soul....*at their own distress." Now, what is their distress? The answer to this question can be found in the next seven lines, that is, the whole of the fourth stanza and the first line of the fifth stanza (except for the last word in this line). Something ("the sudden shut of loss") is "borne away in [the] deadened air" inside the ambulance. The expression "sudden shut of loss" is an example of linguistic creativity. It can mean a loss that is suddenly shut inside the ambulance or loss of life suddenly shut in the eternal darkness of death. It is a loss

> Round something nearly at an end,
> And what cohered in it across
> The years, the unique random blend
> Of families and fashions,

The loss is around the dying man in the ambulance. Everything around or in the body – such as force, motion, sensations, which are the basic elements of life – is nearly at an end. But there were more important things that have been suddenly shut in the deadening silence of the ambulance. These were "the unique random blend /Of families and fashions" that "cohered" in the person of the man (now dying) "across /The years" of his life. Some of the words in these lines need explication. First, the word "cohered," that is, stuck together. What were the things that stuck together across the years in this man's life. The answer is the rest of the third and fourth lines – "the unique random blend /Of families and fashions."

Man is a social animal and, as such, every man has a social self. But a man has also an individual self. Both the selves are unique in each person because no two individuals are identical. The social and individual selves in a man start, from birth on, connecting themselves to other individuals in society and also to prevalent ideas, beliefs, values and, of course, fashions. And there is something uniquely organic in these connections in each case. In the case of the dying man here, and most of us are hardly any different from him, the connections established with families and fashions were, though unique, yet random.

Each individual has his own unique way of forming connections, as in each case these connections differ from those in other cases. But the connections are random because neither human society nor the life of an individual is properly organized and managed. So the entire web of our life is nothing but a random or tangled web of connections. The threads in this web are also weak, but they are organic because they have their origins in the individual's sensations, feelings, emotions, perceptions, cognitions for whatever they are worth.

But all these connections that cohered across the years in the life of the individual, now dying, have now begun to loosen and will soon be snapped for ever. The traffic parts to let the ambulance pass so that it can put the man in a room where he will be "Far /From the exchange of love" and therefore "unreachable." These expressions occur in the last sentence in the poem. This sentence covers the last word "Far" in the first line and the remaining five lines in the last stanza of the poem. This sentence has an intricate structure, but it can be analysed and made clear. The traffic parts to let the ambulance go so that , far from the exchange of love and, therefore, unreachable, the dying man may lie in the room . The traffic (read "the world"), in so doing, brings closer what is left to come, that is, death, "And dulls the distance all we are." This last clause(which is also the last line of the poem) of the sentence is a deviant linguistic structure and therefore carries a weight of ambiguity. T he distance is made dull. The clause also says that all we are is the distance. The poet seems to convey to us a message. The message is that when death comes it makes the distance that all we are dull, that is, the distance between us and death is made less sharp and clear which simply means that we find ourselves very close to it. The poet also uses the expression "all we are," which, again, has a haze of ambiguity. This "all" should mean that all that we are does not amount to much. And the poet does not leave room for any exceptions among us, not even for himself. We have quoted earlier in this work Heidegger's observation, quoted by Sartre, that the reality of life can be understood only in its relationship with the world. It is the reality of our existence made known to us that the world really is. When that reality is lost, there is only Death. Devoid of this reality, even when it does not amount to much, as was the case with the dying or already dead man, and as it will be the case with us, too, given the kind of life we live, there is only the vast and limitless void of darkness, that is, Death.

FIRST SIGHT

"First Sight" is a poem with a vast range and depth of meaning. In his "Farewell to a Friend," Kingsley Amis refers to some of Larkin's poems (including "First Sight") in one paragraph and comments on them in the next paragraph. The two paragraphs run thus:

> But of course, permanently and universally, his poetry tells us everything about him as well as other things he does. Visible Philip Larkin is there and no mistake—-'Toads', ' I Remember, I Remember', ' A Study of Reading Habits,' 'Posterity', 'This Be the Verse' with its over-quoted mum-and-dad opening – and invisible Philip too, strongly, unparaphrasably personal but never self-centred, often amazingly remote and distanced from any interest of his own that could reasonably be inferred by any outsider: 'Wedding Wind,' 'Deceptions,' 'At Grass,' 'MCMXIV' – all about those men, nothing about him at all—-'First Sight' – about the lambs in the snow, 'The Explosion.'

> Poems like these reduce the rest of us to cloddish wonderment that a man such as we know him to have been should have been able to think of things like that, let alone set them down with such fidelity, precision and tact: that the worthwhile secret is something that neither his poetry nor anything else is going to tell us about. But this kind of bafflement is a normal response to an artist of the first rank.[1]

In "First Sight" the poet is thinking of something very important on our behalf and his thought takes the artistic shape of a "tiny poem of crystalline delicacy and strength,"[2] as John Press put it.

From the above two well-judged comments on the poem, two points are clear. There is a vision – a vision that in a fine work of art becomes, in the words of the anthropologist Richard Carrington, "the key to a new level of awareness"[3] – enshrined in the poem. This vision, when we perceive and cognize it, reduces us to cloddish wonderment. Then there is the shrine of verbal structure. In an article entitled "Taking a Poem to Pieces," J. McH Sinclair has analyzed this structure, so we shall concern ourselves with the vision the poem enshrines. The poet creates a beautiful verbal structure and embeds symbols in it to achieve his end. And the symbols used here conform to the description of a symbol by Albert Camus: "A symbol...assumes two worlds of ideas and sensations, and a dictionary of correspondences between them."[4]

The first symbol used in the poem, and with which the poem begins, is "lambs." Obviously, lambs stand for babies. Lambs and babies were much beloved of Jesus, who is often referred to as the Shepherd. These lambs also bleat and their warm breath "clouds the air" on the snow-covered scene. The warmth or energy of life makes itself felt in the freezing air with below zero degree temperature. Our toddlers also, at the corresponding stage of their lives, try to give articulation to life's energy in and through their speech which, at this stage, consists of a few single words spoken at a time. It is at this stage when both lambs and toddlers, "stumbling to and fro," that is, trying to walk steadily and surveying the world around them in their own nascent light of consciousness, "Meet a vast unwelcome" and are allowed to know "Nothing but a sunless glare." Both "a vast unwelcome" and "a sunless glare" are beautiful symbols.

Now the lambs in the poem merge with the being of toddlers. The little ones "stumble to and fro" both literally and metaphorically. Their consciousness has not yet attained cognitive steadiness, but they try to grasp the truth underlying things, appearances around them. But they only meet a vast unwelcome which is a sunless glare which is "a wretched width of cold." These are beautiful metaphors that tell us that our toddlers, right from the beginning, are made to live in a world of speech, thought and action in which, as Larkin told us earlier, "Nothing, like something, happens anywhere."

Julian Huxley, in his book *Religion Without Revelation*, refers to the "graded organization of the mind." In our mind there is "a hierarchy of different levels, with the degree of dominance of the higher levels varying from time to time." Huxley says that when the control of the higher "centres is weakened or removed, the lower centres have free play in ways which are not possible when they are acting in subordinate capacities."[5]

Now the problem with human civilization has been that its affairs in various fields – religious, social, economic, political and so on – have been conducted for far too long by men with minds in which lower centres have had free play or in which the higher centres have had very weak control over the lower centres. Such people constitute the authorities in various fields and the dispensations imposed by them attack our toddlers as soon as their consciousness starts stumbling to and fro trying to grasp the truth of things. Toddlers and young children are particularly vulnerable because their minds are completely open to "suggestibility" at this stage. As to what incalculable harm is caused by this "suggestibility" in the religious field to the children Julian Huxley writes:

> The fact that religious instruction is usually begun very young, buttresses with all kinds of alien strength and makes certain religious feelings and ideas take root so deeply and so unconsciously that it is extremely hard for the growing mind to break away from them without great difficulty, and often indeed profound sense of sin. This depends partly on the greater suggestibility of the child, partly on the fact that impressions made in childhood gather round themselves all sorts of strong emotional associations.[6]

So the child's first sight in the prevalent religious field – irrespective of the hold of a particular religion therein – makes the lower centres in the organization of his mind dominate the higher centres throughout his life. It is only one in a million, that is, very few who come to understand truths about religion and re-orient their religious perspective in the light of the truths. Other fields of man's civilization are equally frozen. According to many Christians, man's history on the earth is nearly 5000 years old, while many Hindus with ossified minds believe that man has inhabited the earth for billions of years.

In the very interesting opening paragraph of his book *A Brief History of Time*, Stephen Hawking tells us how when "a well-known scientist (some say it was Bertrand Russell)" in a lecture on astronomy said that our earth orbits in empty space around the sun, which, in turn, "orbits around the centre of the stars called our galaxy," a little old lady reacted, saying that what he said was "rubbish." She also said that the earth was flat and rested on the back of a "giant tortoise." When the scientist, with "a superior smile," asked what supported this tortoise, the lady said, "You're very clever, young man, very clever...But it's turtles all the way down."[7]

When an important character in Naguib Mahfouz's novel *The Cairo Trilogy*, says to his father that he wants to know about the origin and destiny of Man, the father gets a very unpleasant surprise and asks him if he does not know that the origin of Man is Adam and his destiny is either paradise or hell-fire. There are still millions, if not billions, of people across countries who either know nothing about, or do not believe in, or even angrily reject the theory of Evolution. And, almost universally, we lack vital knowledge of our life in relation to the universe and the world and of our own make. As Carl Sagan, in his brief introduction to Stephen Hawking's book, says,

> We go about our daily lives understanding almost nothing of the world. We give little thought to the machinery that gen-erates the sunlight that makes life possible, to the gravity that glues us to an Earth that would otherwise send us spinning off into space, or to the atoms of which we are made and on whose stability we fundamentally depend.[8]

And if we thought of the economic and political strait-jackets imposed on humanity over the ages by the ruling elites with the lower centres dominating their minds, there would flash upon our mind's eye a long history of oppres-sions, miseries, degradations and countless deaths of hapless masses caused by poverty, disease, famines and mindless wars. Here we are put in mind of two modern plays – Bertolt Brecht's classic, *Mother Courage and Her Children* (1939), and *Bingo* (1974) by Edward Bond. Both the plays have firm basis in real socio-economic- political conditions in particular historical periods. *Mother Courage* is set in certain periods during the Thirty Years War (1618-48) involving mainly Sweden, Denmark, Spain, France and Germany. These countries, though Christian, professed either Catholicism or Protestantism, and wanted to establish, through war, the dominance of their cherished faith. In man's civilized history this war was perhaps the most disastrous one before the Second World War.

Brecht's play is sub-titled 'A Chronicle of the Thirty Years War.' In this war, Mother Courage loses her three children, who represent Bravery, Honesty and Pity (Kindness}. It happens because wars are cowardly, dishonest and piti-less (cruel). And "the Song of the Wise and the Good" sung by Mother Cou-rage and the Cook with choric comments in scene Nine of the play makes a comprehensive comment on our civilization right from the biblical times until now – a civilization in which the famed wisdom of Solomon brought him low and so it is better to have no wisdom; a civilization in which the legendary bravery of Julius Caesar, who "sat like God on altarpiece" availed nothing and "they tore him limb from limb/While his prestige still did increase" and so it is better to have no bravery; a civilization in which the spotless honesty of Socrates, "Who always spoke the truth" for which all mankind should owe him thanks, only brought him low as he was made to drink hemlock, and so it is better if we have no honesty; it has been a civilization in which the unselfishness of St. Martin, the fourth century A.D. Bishop of Tours and the patron saint of France, who gave away his cloak to a beggar to save him from death by cold, but which resulted in the death of both by cold, was brought low for his unselfishness and so it is better if we are not unselfish. Finally, ours has been a civilization in which the common people, though they have kept "God's Ten Commandments" and have always shown "strict godliness," yet their godliness has only brought them low. Mother Courage and the Cook tell us the brutal truth concerning their lives and the lives of common people throughout man's civilized history:

> That's how it is with us. We're law-abiding folk, we keep to ourselves, don't steal, don't kill, don't burn the place down. And in this way we sink lower and lower and the song proves true and there's no soup going. And if we were different, reward, only vices. Such is the world, need it be so?[9]

The action of Brecht's play begins in the second decade of the 17th century. The action of Edward Bond's *Bingo* also takes place in the second decade of the 17th century England – in the hometown of Shakespeare, to be precise – and is concerned with Shakespeare's retired life and death there. Out of the population of two thousand people of this townlet seven hundred are destitutes. In the Introduction to his play, Bond claims that "It is based on the material historical facts so far as they're known, and on the psychological truth so far as I know it." He calls the English society of the time "Goneril-society – with its prisons, workhouses, whipping, starvation, mutilation, pulpit-hysteria and all the rest of it." He also says that Shakespeare as a property-owner "supported and benefited from this Goneril-society."

Shakespeare had thought that his retired life at his beautiful house, the New Place, with its large park and orchard amidst fine natural setting would be happy. But the scenes of poverty, misery, degradation all around him as well as his loveless family life sometimes make him think of going back to London. But London, too, holds no charm for him. He says to himself:

> I'm stupefied at the suffering I have seen. The shapes huddled in misery that twitch away when you step over them. Women with shopping-bags stepping over puddles of blood. What it costs to starve people. The chatter of those who hand over prisoners, the smile of men who see no further than the end of a knife. Stupefied. How can I go back to that? What can I do there? I talk to myself now. I know no one will ever listen.[10]

Benedict Nightingale, reviewing this play in the New Statesman, wrote:

> How is it (we're to ask) that a man whom we worship for his humanity could bear to live in a society we know to have been so cruel? How can we, his descendants, bear to live in a society directly derived from it?[11]

So it is only proper to call this world "a wretched width of cold" in which the new ones, while still stumbling to and fro in their effort to get a firm foothold on life, meet "nothing but a vast unwelcome."

The second and last stanza of the poem is a sort of counterpoint to the first stanza. In the first stanza, the lambs were stumbling to and fro and also making their first attempts at articulating the urge for self-expression of life in them. What they met with and where they found themselves we have seen above. The innocent lambs sit by their mother ewe, waiting. Waiting for what? They have no idea. But something "hidden round them [is] waiting too." This thing is, in the words of the poet, "Earth's immeasurable surprise" which will be "Utterly unlike the snow." The phrase "Immeasurable surprise" is important and needs to be properly explicated. In the literal context of the poem it means the spring season with bright, warm, life-giving and life-sustaining sunshine. It is utterly unlike the winter's snow-covered landscape which symbolizes frozenness leading to numbness of the senses and even to death. This sunshine, which is literally the giver of all life on this earth, has, as a symbol, perhaps the vastest dictionary of correspondences between two worlds of ideas and sensations. This sunshine is hidden but waiting to replace the sunless glare of the winter snow in the wretched width of cold that our world has unfortunately become. Sunshine also symbolizes truth as opposed to ignorance symbolized by snow. Truth is always there , waiting to appear and make things bright and beautiful. But the lambs, says the poet, "could not grasp it if they knew." The problem, as Naguib Mahfouz puts it, is "not that truth is harsh but liberation from ignorance is as painful as being born.[12] William Golding, in reply to a literary magazine's questionnaire, said: "I am very serious. I believe that man suffers from an appalling ignorance of his own nature. I produce my own view, in the belief that it may be something like the truth."[13] And in Harold Pinter's *Homecoming*, Teddy, the Professor of Philosophy with a Ph. D. degree in the subject, reacting to his father's desire to know something about his critical works, addresses the whole family – his father, his uncle, his two brothers and his wife (a cast of crooks, pimps and tart) – gathered there, and says:

> You wouldn't understand my works. You wouldn't have the faintest idea of what they were about. You wouldn't appreciate the points of reference. You're way behind. All of you. There's no point in sending you my works. You'd be lost. It's nothing to do with the question of intelligence. It's a way of being able to look at the world….To see, to be able to see! I'm the one who can see. That's why I can write my critical works….You're just objects. You just…move about.[14]

We are, most of us, way behind, not able to look at the world as great philosophers, great artists, great scientists, great thinkers in various fields of knowledge look at it; we are just objects; we just move about although we may be very intelligent. This because right from the time we were toddlers, through our adolescence, and even past those periods, whenever we have had the first sight of anything, any phenomenon, it was so tailored as to give us a vast unwelcome and so the world looked like a wretched width of snow. There can be, in this very world, a spring with bright, warm, life-invigorating sunshine if truth in all fields of knowledge – scientific, philosophical, theological, art and literature, socio-economic-political, and so on – is allowed to shape the destiny of mankind. But it is easier said than done. Mikhail Sholokhov writes in his masterpiece, *And Quiet Flows the Don*, "What the people want is the truth, but it's always being buried and earth heaped over it. They say it's been a corpse a long time already."[15]

But why does such a sorry situation exist in human society? So far as educated, knowledgeable people are concerned, it is because faulty education is imparted to them. Samuel Butler tells us in his novel *The Way of All Flesh* what education did to his hero: "By far the greater part... of his education had been an attempt, not so much to keep him in blinkers as to gouge his eyes out altogether."[16]

We shall end our analysis of the poem with a quotation from a British anthropologist, Ashley Montague. This passage is an eloquent comment on how the culture in Europe makes every child grow up into an adult who is a cripple in his mind and heart:

Fundamentally, man is quite an intelligent animal, but he is a victim, alas, of the two-handed engine of his culture which distorts his mind and renders him unintelligent. Outworn traditional teachings have made of Western man a shockingly unintelligent creature who lives under the continuous and unrelieved domination of a chaos of ideas more degrading, more stupid, more idiotic, and more saddening than it may ever be possible to describe. This confused morality has, without question, been substantially responsible for his present deplorable state. For the processes and patterns of thought of every child born into the Western world today have been conditioned according to the prescriptions of these teachings, so that culturally Western man has come to be a function entirely of the reigning spirit of confusion and prejudice. And since in his conduct he functions without effort as a victim of confusion and prejudice, he arrives at the belief that it is thus "natural" to act and think. In this way is produced the mentally and spiritually bludgeoned individual who gropes his way confusedly through life – and whose number is legion.[17]

Dockery and Son

The title of the poem "Dockery and Son" puts us in mind of Dickens's novel *Dombey and Son*. It is not that Philip Larkin's poem is an imitation or parody of Dickens's novel. But both Dombey and Dockery wanted a son. Dombey got a son when he was forty-eight, while Dockery got one when he was much less than half his age. The reason why Dombey desperately wanted a son is clearly given in the novel:

The earth was made for Dombey and son to trade in, and the sun and the moon were made to give them light. Rivers and seas were formed to float their ships; rainbows gave them promise of fair weather; winds blew for or against their enterprises; stars and planets circled in their orbits to preserve inviolate a system of which they were the centre.[1]

Dombey was a typical business magnate spawned by the *laissez-faire* economy that ruled the roost in England of his time. He wanted his business empire to be called <u>Dombey and Son</u> and only a son could have given it that name. Larkin, too, mentions the reason why Dockery wanted a son when he was only nineteen or twenty. But that comes later in the poem. We shall follow the poem in its movement.

In this poem, as in several other of his poems, the persona is Philip Larkin himself. As the poem opens, we find him in St John's College, Oxford, from where he graduated with a first class Honours in English in 1943, some nineteen years before. He visited Oxford in 1962 to attend the funeral of his predecessor as librarian of Hull University[2] and so he is "Death-suited" although he wrote this poem in 1963, that is, a year later. And as "Death-suited" he comes to his *alma mater*. Larkin uses this expression for a very important reason. When we are "death-suited" we have perceptions that go deep into the meaning and worth of life. And it is in this state that he meets his erstwhile Dean with whom he has a short conversation or, rather, it is the Dean who does the talking. He asks Larkin if he remembers a contemporary of his named Dockery – he was a year or so junior to Larkin – and Larkin nods. The Dean says that his son is now a student here. Then the Dean asks him if he keeps in touch with... But before his question is completed Larkin starts thinking,

> Or remember how
> Black-gowned, unbreakfasted, and still half-tight
> We used to stand before that desk, to give
> 'Our version' of 'these incidents last night'?

In this context, we quote the following lines from Kingsley Amis's essay "Oxford and After:"

> To outward view, Philip was an almost aggressively normal undergraduate of the non-highbrow sort, hard-swearing, hard-belching, etc....going to the English Club but treating

its sessions as Incidents in beery nights out, being fined by
the Dean (I wish we had more than the tiny but exact glimpse
near the start of 'Dockery and Son').[3]

Philip Larkin is now no longer the Oxford undergraduate as described by
Amis. His essential self has undergone a sea-change, a metamorphosis and is
now the self of a poet who, as Blake put it, "present, past and future sees." But
Amis's comment is significant in that it shows that Larkin's poetic experience
here, which is of great value for all of us, has a real-life touch. Also the meditation of a "death suited" person, which the poem is, gives it some genuine
metaphysical content in the Sartrean sense of the term. The poet tries the door
of the room in which he lived for three years, but it is locked . He writes:

I try the door of where I used to live:

Locked. The lawn spreads dazzlingly wide.
A known bell chimes. I catch my train, ignored.

Barbara Everett calls "Dockery and Son" an Oxford poem and writes: "…
for three lines in it frame wonderfully a human dream about the 'dreaming
spires,' the 'city of lost causes,' the place where the constrained mathematics
don, Lewis Carroll, wrote about the magic garden that the innocent could
never lastingly get into…"[4] The poet was in this magic garden for three years
but now he cannot enter it. He now has to live – in fact lives – in a different
world in which most of us, if not all of us, are condemned to live. Also he is
now a poet and as such he can't live in a magic garden but must face the world
of his time and allow the presence of poetry in it. It is no wonder that he is ignored by the city containing the magic garden, dreaming spires, but a city of
lost causes. But though ignored by the magic garden, yet, before leaving the
place, he has a glimpse of " the dazzlingly wide" lawn spread in the sun and
also hears the "known bell" chime. And then he catches the train that will take
him back home.

Nietzsche, in his *Birth of Tragedy*, writes: "The realm of poetry does not
lie outside the world." Larkin knows this very well and his poetry is always located in the world of lived life and real time. He perhaps also knows about the
great task that, Nietzsche says, art has to perform: " …art is the supreme task
and the truly metaphysical activity of this life."[5] "Dockery and Son" is firmly

located in the world of the poet's life and time and it has rich metaphysical content, as we shall soon see. As the train starts moving, "Canal and clouds and colleges subside/ Slowly from view." The magic garden and its environs thus subsided and the poet left alone on the train, poetic meditation begins. But serious meditation – meditation that concerns life, its meaning, the destiny of man – takes time to take off the ground. But the process starts – starts with thinking about Dockery and his son, who is now , the Dean told him, at Oxford. He says to himself that he must have been born in 1943 when he himself was twenty-one. And since Dockery was junior to him, it follows that he begot a son when he was only nineteen or twenty. He tries to recollect details concerning Dockery at college because he was not one of his close friends. He recollects that Dockery was "that withdrawn/ high-collared public schoolboy" who shared rooms with a boy called Cartwright, who was killed, perhaps in the War. The train of thought released by the case of this public schoolboy begins moving in the poet's mind with this kind of start: "Well, it just shows/ How much...How little." But thoughts like this being of a serious nature, tax the mind and the poet being tired because of his travel, yawns and falls asleep. He awakes "at the fumes/ And furnace-glares of Sheffield," where he has to change the train – do "the fumes and furnace-glares" symbolize the hell that our world has become? It is in this world of fumes and furnace-glares that Philip Larkin with a poetic self has to live and it is here and here alone that his art has to perform the difficult task which Nietzsche speaks of.

While waiting for his train at Sheffield railway station, Larkin tells us that he "ate an awful pie." This "awful pie' has received notice of critics. Blake Morrison writes:

> A detail such as the 'awful pie' could have no place in a poetry that demands sparseness, visual sharpness and an eschewal of the prosaic. But that 'awful pie' is crucial here in establishing the poet as a man who notices such things – a man whose sure grasp of the commonplace encourages us to trust his insights into deeper and more serious questions about fate, free will, heredity, time, the purpose of life (according to the Movement's aesthetic, the less special or gifted a person, the more he is to be relied on).[6]

The distinctive quality of Larkin's poetic sensibility is that it reflects itself in ordinary, everyday experiences of life. But this sensibility has dimensions and levels that are laced with intellectual, philosophical, even transcendental awareness that make his poems worthwhile and of enduring value.

After eating the "awful pie," Larkin, like an ordinary branch-line rail passenger, not as a celebrated poet, walks "along/The platform to its end." Why does he do so? To "see the ranged/ Joining and parting lines reflect a strong/Unhindered moon." This is an unusual, not to say a strange way of looking at the moon. But we have to remember that the poet is "death suited" and ever since he tried to open his college room and found it locked and was told about Dockery's son now being at Oxford, he has been trying to probe the deeper meaning, purpose and fate of life. The adjectives "strong" and "unhindered" used here for the moon are important: "ranged/Joining and parting" rail lines have a shine that can, on a clear moonlit night, reflect the moon in the way the poet wanted to see it. Standing close to the lines and looking at the moon, the poet perceives something deep and mysterious. The poet's meditation is going to have a corresponding depth and mystery. But this is not an easy task. Philosophers, sages,, thinkers, creative artists, scientists have been trying over the ages and across cultures to solve these mysteries, but only with partial success. As Larkin is a creative artist of high rank, he must also contribute his share in the effort. Standing all alone at the end of the platform and looking into, and not at, this moon, he descends into its depths and we know that the moon's surface is a lifeless desert.. And what does he find there? There is no bright, romantic world here, but only the hard steel of railway lines reflecting the desert. And so his meditation starts thus:

> To have no son, no wife
> No house or land still seemed natural.
> Only a numbness registered the shock
> Of finding out how much had gone of life,
> How widely from the others.

This is, for the poet, the moment of existential stock-taking as well as a moment of creation of a fine work of art. Bertrand Russell describes the state of a creative mind at such moments in these words:

> Every one who has done any kind of creative work has experienced, in a greater or less degree, the state of mind in which after long labour,,, truth or beauty appears, or seems

to appear, in a sudden glory – it may be only about some small matter, or it may be about the universe. The experience is, at the moment, very convincing; doubt may come later, but at the time there is utter certainty. I think most of the best creative work, in art, in science, in literature, and in philosophy, has been the result of such a moment.[7]

To have no son, no wife, no house or land had not seemed unnatural to Larkin. It was his own decision not to have these possessions and there have been people who have lived this kind of life. But what happened to the poet at this moment was that something of profound importance was registered on his consciousness. It suddenly experienced numbness and this numbness registered a shock – the shock "Of finding out how much had gone of life." The pity or even the tragedy of human existence is that it goes on getting expended continuously after reaching the optimal growth which is also called the "log phase." And we are hardly ever aware of this slow but sure loss of life. But when we , if ever, become aware of it and also understand that we have missed all that we should have had, all that would have enabled us to understand the value of life, our organic-transcendental self registers a shock. And in the case of Larkin there is a collateral awareness: not only that much of life has gone, it has gone much widely from the life of other people, Dockery being an example of these people. In reply to a question by the interviewer for *Paris Review* whether as a bachelor he did not feel that he was an outsider, Larkin said, "Samuel Butler said, Life is an affair of being spoilt in one way or another" (RW, p. 65).

So now Larkin begins to wonder why Dockery begat a son when he was only nineteen. He first thinks that Dockery must have "taken stock/ Of what he wanted, and been capable/ Of," but he rejects this line of thinking – "No, that's not the difference" – and starts thinking on a different line: "rather/ how convinced he was he should be added to!" The poet's mind has been trying hard to understand the truth as to how and why a man's life takes a particular course rather than another. Blake Morrison observes: "The speaker's puzzling process is dramatized by the inclusion of hesitations and qualifications such as 'now,' 'No, that's not...' 'rather,' and 'they are more a...,' which give the impression of a man struggling to make a sense of a difficult problem."[8] Then there follow the following two crucial lines:

Why did he think adding meant increase?
To me it was dilution.

The words "adding," increase" and "dilution" are of crucial importance and have to be understood in their full scientific and philosophical connotations. A man begetting children just goes on adding to himself: two, three, four, and so on. As we know, these additions (children) are mere repetitions or replications of the progenitors. Regarding the "degree of permanence in hereditary properties," Erwin Schrodinger writes in his *What is Life? with Mind and Matter*:

> what is passed on by the parent to the child is not this or that peculiarity, a hooked nose, \ short fingers, a tendency to rheumatism, haemophilia, dichromasy, etc. Such features we may conveniently select for studying the laws of heredity. But ... it is the whole (four-dimensional) pattern of the 'phenotype,' the visible and manifest nature of the individual, which is reproduced without appreciable change for generations, permanent within centuries – though not within tens of thousands of years – and borne at each transmission by the material structure of the nuclei of the two cells which unite to form the fertilized egg cell. [9]

There is, of, course, what is called Mutation but it, as Schrodinger says, "is a small step in the development of the species." Also, "In order to be suitable material for the work of natural selection, mutations must be rare events, as they actually are."[10]

So we see that our children are not genetically better engineered to bring about "increase" in the quality of human existence and so we cannot but agree with the hero of Samuel Butler's novel *The Way of All Flesh* when he says, "If a man is to enter into the Kingdom of heaven, he must do so, not only as a child, but as a little embryo, or rather as a little zoosperm – and not only this, but as one that has come of zoosperms which have entered into the Kingdom of heaven before him for many generations."[11]

We have also seen above what J. B. S. Haldane says about the direction of evolution. So it is not surprising that to Larkin the "addition" is not "increase" but "dilution."

Larkin, therefore, asks, "Where do these innate/ Assumptions come from? " What are these assumptions and how can they be called innate? One of these assumptions is that our sons are our "increase." There are many such assumptions which we live by. These assumptions arise "Not from what/ We think truest or most want to do." Those things (the truest or what we most want to do) "warp tight-shut, like doors." We saw above that Larkin's erstwhile room at Oxford was locked. But a locked room can be opened, whereas tight-shut, warped doors cannot possibly be opened. The assumptions controlling our lives and actions are

more a style
Our lives bring with them: habit for a while,
Suddenly they harden into all we've got

And how we got it ; looked back on, they rear
Like sand-clouds, thick and close.

John Wain has drawn our attention to "sand-clouds" which are hardly ever seen in England: "I wonder how the image of sand-clouds (a sight very rarely met with in the British Isles) came to Larkin's mind. But it is altogether effective, the image of something as uncontrollable as an ordinary atmospheric cloud but more solid, more threatening (to be caught in a sand-cloud can't possibly do you any good), and apt to pursue people who journey across deserts."[12] And to be caught in a sand-cloud that is "thick and close" can be, even as a thought, terrifying .But Larkin the poet is passing through a desert that man's life seems to have become. Our habits, when they harden into all we have got, are such sand-clouds. And the pity is that they embody something – "For Dockery a son, for me nothing,/Nothing with all a son's harsh patronage." Then follow the last four lines of the poem, which are, John Wain says, "perhaps the bleakest in all English poetry."[12] But, as he rightly points out, they are not cynical, sickening or hysterical as some modern literary works he cites in his essay are.

Larkin's poem is not a cry of despair. It says that life is first boredom. Life as embodied in our organic structure should enjoy itself so long as it lives. But the habits that are inculcated in us in our very childhood are so trite and trivial that we hardly ever have a glimpse of truth that has beauty ingrained in it. The penultimate line of the poem – "And leaves what something [i.e. Truth] hidden from us chose" – is a very important element in the poet's meditation on life lived by people in general. A character in Dickens's *Dombey and Son* says something very valuable about habits sans Truth controlling our life:

> I have good reason to believe that a jog-trot life, the same from day to day, would reconcile me to anything. One don't see anything, one don't hear anything, one don't know anything, that's the fact. We go on taking everything for granted, and so we go on, until whatever we do, good, bad, or indifferent, we do from habit. Habit is all I shall have to report, when I am called upon to plead to my conscience on my death-bed. "Habit," says I; "I was deaf, dumb, blind, and paralytic to a million things, from habit." "Very businesslike indeed, Mr What's-your-name," says Conscience, "but it won't do here."[13]

Life sans Truth is tasteless and, therefore, a boredom. We do not use it, it simply "goes." And when most of this kind of life is frittered away, fear grips us, the same kind of fear and terror that gripped Marlowe's Faustus at the moment of reckoning, because then we realize, too late, its value. It is true that even when we use it well, it will go. But then, as Stephen Weinberg says (we have quoted him above), it is lifted above the level of farce and acquires some of the grace of tragedy. But the pity is that most of us do not know, are never taught, how best to use it. And so, when we see it is going to desert us, fear grips us because then we see that we are going to be lost in eternal darkness of death.

Essential Beauty

publicity – advertising – is the dirtiest ramp that capitalism
has yet produced: George Orwell

"Essential Beauty" seems to have been inspired by a great passage in Socrates' speech on "absolute beauty" in Plato's *Symposium*. Part of the passage is quoted below:

> And the true order of going, or being led by another, to the things of love is to begin from the beauties of earth and mount upwards for the sake of that other beauty, using these

as steps only, and from one going on to two, and from two to all fair bodily forms, and from fair bodily forms to fair practices, and from fair practices to fair sciences, until from fair sciences he arrives at the science... which has no other object than absolute beauty, and at last knows which is beautiful by itself alone. This...is that life above all others which man should live, in the contemplation of beauty absolute; a beauty which if you beheld, you would see not after the measure of gold, and garments, and fair boys and youths, whose presence now entrances you...But what if a man had eyes to see true beauty – the divine beauty, I mean, pure and clear and unalloyed, not infected with the pollutions of the flesh and all the colours and vanities of mortal life – thither looking, and holding converse with the true beauty simple and divine? Remember how in that communion only, beholding beauty by which it can be beheld, he will be enabled to bring forth, not images of beauty, but realities (for he has hold not of an image but of a reality), and nourishing true virtue will properly become the friend of God and be immortal, if immortal man may. Would that be an ignoble life?[1]

Larkin's poem presents two sets of pictures – one set in the form of giant advertisement hoardings in frames and the other in the form of glimpses of real life lived in ugly, small towns. The first set covers the first stanza and also cuts into part of the second stanza. The poem consists of two very complex stanzas of sixteen lines each with very complex sentence-structure and equally complex rhyming pattern.

The frames in which the hoardings are fixed are "as large as rooms" and "face all ways/ And block the end of streets." There is a hoarding advertising giant loaves. Another hoarding advertising custard screens graves. The juxtaposition of "custard" and "graves" sets our teeth on edge. Then there are hoardings which "cover slums with praise / Of motor-oil and cuts of salmon." There is a very sinister hoarding advertising cigarettes that we are made to see only towards the end of the poem. These hoardings, shining "Perpetually," are "sharply-pictured groves /Of how life should be." The brazenness of such preposterous claims takes our breath away. But this is not all. In a hoarding "high above the gutter," we see "a silver knife" sinking "into golden butter," an action that seems as if some big cat's teeth were sinking into the soft flesh, say, of a stag. The rhyming together of "gutter" and "butter" establishes a sickening connection between the two. Then we find a glass of milk standing in the meadow in one of the hoardings and also "well-balanced families, in fine /Midsummer weather." The members of these families owe everything they have – they have nothing of substance in them, "only their smiles, their cars… their youth" – to the small cubes of butter, towards which they all stretch their hands. Then there are other pictures:

> the deep armchairs
> Aligned to cups at bedtime, radiant bars
> (Gas or electric), quarter- profile cats
> By slippers on warm mats.

These hoardings do not reflect "the rained-on streets and squares" that are part of the whole real setting with slums and graves and gutters. But they do reflect a kind of life lived by a class of people (the bourgeoisie) who rule the roost in society. These people have made our world a place described in the following words by Katherine Anne Porter in her story "Pale Horse, Pale Rider:"

> Closing her eyes she would rest for a moment remembering that bliss which had repaid all the pain of journey to reach it; opening them again she saw with a new anguish the dull world to which she was condemned, where the light seemed filmed over with cowebs, all the bright surfaces, the sharp planes melted and formless, all objects and beings meaningless, ah, dead and withered things that believed themselves alive. [2]

The poet in Larkin makes no secret of what he thinks of the life of these people. He says that though they dominate outdoors, that is, the world, the hoardings depicting their life

> rise
> Serenely to proclaim pure crust, pure foam,
> Pure coldness to our live imperfect eyes
> That stare beyond this world.

We have seen above what Socrates says about the kind of life "above all others which man should live." And we know that Socrates was a seeker after truth about all aspects of life. So Larkin is fully justified in calling the life of these people pure crust, pure foam, pure coldness; but our eyes, though imperfect – imperfect because we are ordinary men and women, not seers and sages – are live and can stare beyond their world, "seeking the home/ All such inhabit." But there they see nothing that is "made/ As new or washed quite clean" as the hoardings try to create the illusion in us. What they see are described in the rest of the poem (ll 22-32). First we see white-clothed tennis players in "dark raftered pubs." They are having a drink after their usual practice in their club. The pubs are dark, not shining like the "sharply-pictured groves" in the hoardings. Nor are these pubs looking "As new and washed quite clean," to say nothing of there being no "radiant bars (Gas or electric)" or warm mats of the hoardings. In a letter in 1955 to Patsy Murphy, Larkin wrote: "I'm passing through an anti-English phase at present – they are miles uglier and noisier and vulgar than the Irish; the pubs here are nightmares of neo-Falstaffianism, coughing laughter well soused with phlegm."[3]

In such a pub we can also see a boy "puking his heart out in the Gents." The boy's health is blighted and stands in sharp contrast to the "Well-balanced families" in the pink of their health in the hoardings. Then we see the pensioner who pays half a penny more to buy a brand of tea known as "Granny Gravesclothes Tea." He buys this tea "To taste old age." In old age food and drinks seem to lose their taste, so the pensioner goes in for this brand of tea, but it will taste only old age and not what cups of nightcap at bedtime give to those seated in "deep armchairs" in cosy, warm rooms in the hoardings. And finally we see "dying smokers" sense something. What do they sense? They "sense[not see] /Walking towards them through some dappled park/As if on water that unfocused she/No match lit up, nor drag brought near." The smokers are dying of cancer.

To the dying smokers the "she" in the hoarding appears "unfocused" as if on water because their sense- perception is dimming. No match seems to lit up her face nor does it appear that anything can drag her close to them. She seems to be getting dimmer and beyond their approach. This girl, advertising cigarettes, had, with her sexual appeal, lured them and they took to smoking with the disastrous result that we see now. They had thought her the ultimate bliss of sexual fulfillment but she is receding from them. The truth, however, is that while the smokers are dying, the girl "stands newly clear" and "smiling" as before. She seems to recognize them as her victims to be lost soon in the darkness of death. And this recognition seems to make her smile. After this recognition, she herself goes dark.

We shall now again revert to the passage from Socrates' speech. The crass materialism of the present-day bourgeois civilization puts up such advertisements just to delude us into believing that what they show constitute "essential beauty" – Socrates' "absolute beauty" – and we should live their kind of life. Can we, in this context, forget the tragedy that is shown to take place in Theodore Dreiser's masterpiece *An American Tragedy*? These hoardings are tainted with the touch of ugly, rained-on streets, slums, graves, gutters, blighted youth, old age soon going to taste death and, finally, the darkling vision of the smokers soon to be extinguished in the vice-like grip of cancer. In short, it is a blighted civilization with no future whatever the promoters of this civilization may claim. It is a far cry from what Socrates says man's life should be. Man should have risen, step by more steps, to a height at which contemplation of "beauty absolute," should have been the guiding light of his life. He was created for this high purpose. Instead he has been pulling himself down into the cesspool of a degenerate way of life, and yet he is so presumptuous as to claim that their way of living – guzzling delicacies and swilling expensive drinks at the expense of the common people – is how life should be.

Martin Bruce's comment on this poem is as follows:

> "Essential Beauty"... traces the disparity between the illusory world of billboards, "these sharply- pictured groves/ Of how life should be," and the imperfection of of real existence, "where nothing's made /As new or washed quite clean," and concludes with the sober facts of sickness, old age, and death which advertising rarely recognizes. [4]

There is something intrinsically pernicious in human psyche that is responsible for this sad condition of the world. Sickness, old age and death, and their attendant sorrows and sadness, made the Buddha renounce the luxuries of a royal palace and seek light – that light which alone can bring Grace to man's life. Jesus, too, renounced worldly comforts and tried to alleviate the sufferings of man and also tried to infuse in him that divine light which alone can save the world.

But our rich men, the bourgeoisie – can one, in this context, forget D.H. Lawrence's poem, "How Beastly the Bourgeois Is" – with their blighted moral sense have been trying, though only unsuccessfully, to put a gloss on their de-generate way of life by putting up giant hoardings which , even to our imper-fect but live eyes, proclaim pure crust, pure foam, pure coldness. We quote below some lines from the beginning and end of Lawrence's poem:

> How beastly the bourgeois is
> especially the male of his species –
>
> Presentable, eminently presentable –
> shall I make you a present of him?
>
> Isn't he handsome? Isn't he healthy? Isn't he a fine specimen?
> Doesn't he look a fine clean Englishman, outside?
> Isn't it God's own image ? tramping his thirty miles a day
> after partridges, or a little rubber ball?
> wouldn't you like to be like that, well off and quite the thing?
> … … …
> How beastly the bourgeois is!
> Standing in their thousands, these appearances, in damp
> England
> what a pity can't all be knocked over
> like sickening toadstools, and left to melt back,
> into the soil of England.[5]

But the pity is that these people cannot be knocked over. They are in firm control of the levers of power in all fields of life and brazenly advertise their way of life as a model and care a damn for the ugly realities of common people's life.

An Arundel Tomb

A poem like "An Arundel Tomb" is "criticism of life" in the best sense of the term. It is a meditation on love as the value-adding element in life *vis-a- vis* the sterility of life lived by a medieval knight (an earl of Arundel) and his wife. Philip Larkin wrote this poem – a classic – after visiting the Arundel Tomb on which he saw sculptured the effigies of the long dead knight and his wife. James Booth gives us important background information about this tomb and the original and later renovated effigies:

Larkin has misdated the effigies, and more particularly their attitude of 'clasped' hands. By a delightful irony, the tomb of Chichester Cathedral which inspired the poem is not in fact pre-baroque, but a comprehensively reworked Victorian version of sculptor Edward Richardson (1812-69). The original effigies, which presumably (but not certainly) depicted a fourteenth-century Earl of Arundel and his wife, had been defaced centuries before, during the Reformation and the Civil War. When Richardson started his work in the 1840s the original mutilated figures had become separated, the knight had no arms below his shoulders and the lady's right hand was missing. It was even uncertain on which side of her husband she had originally lain, and it was Richardson's decision to place her to the knight's right with her right hand held in his. Though the holding of hands is not unknown in original monuments, a medieval knight would more usually have his hands pressed together in prayer…Moreover, the consolatory expressions of the hands in Richardson's version, not flatly palm to palm, but with her hand, fingers limply bent, resting in his large male palm, seems distinctly Victorian in spirit rather than medieval. In the *Monitor* television programme of 1964 Larkin expressed wry amusement at the unintended anachronisms in his poem.[1]

Larkin obviously ignored the re-worked effigies and the effigies in his poem are supposedly the original and still undamaged ones as they serve his artistic purpose. What the poet has tried here with tremendous success – Larkin's poem puts us in mind of poems like Donne's "Ecstasy" and Keats's "Ode on a Grecian Urn" – is to show the sterility of the life of the ruling elite – knights and their ladies of the Middle Ages – in England. The same sterility afflicted the life of aristocratic ruling class of the age across countries. It was a life of great pomp and show, but hollow inside. Our life, more especially the life of the people at higher rungs of society, is no less hollow, but that is a different matter. People at these rungs have constituted the privileged or ruling class. Doris Lessing asks of us a very pertinent question about the life-style of this class: "Has there been a time in our country when the ruling class was not inside its glass bell of respectability or of wealth, shutting its eyes to what went on outside?"[2] What was tragic about the medieval civilization was that although the ruling aristocracy wielded absolute power over the masses, did acts of valour in the battle field, showered favours on those loyal to them, lived in castles and palaces in great comfort and luxury, maintained private militias, sometimes even granted pensions to indigent artists and writers, they did nothing to alleviate the sufferings of the masses, nor did they contribute anything to the progress of human culture. In fact it was a dark age in the history of human culture. In Dickens's *Dombey and Son*, Mrs Skewton, the faded beauty and accomplished coquet of yesteryear, now in her seventies – Dickens sarcastically calls her Cleopatra – tells us about the "glories" of this aristocratic civilization in these words: "'Those darling bygone times...with their delicious fortresses, and their dear old dungeons, and their delightful places of torture, and their romantic vengeances, and their picturesque assaults and sieges and everything that makes life truly charming! How dreadfully we have degenerated!'"[2] But "An Arundel Tomb" is not a poem of historical nature. It may be called an elegy in that their period is now only seen as a "scrap of history." Our age will also, because of our "days and ways" prove to be no better, the poet seems indirectly to warn us.

We will begin our analysis of the poem with a look at its last line: "What will survive of us is love." One is reminded of a dialogue between Scipio, the poet, and Caligula, the hero in Albert Camus' play *Caligula*, in which Scipio says, "All I know is that everything I feel or think turns to love." Caligula replies: "That, Scipio, is a privilege of noble hearts."[3] Few, if any, members of the ruling elite anywhere, anytime, particularly of the Middle Ages, have had noble hearts and whatever they felt or thought hardly ever turned to love. This lack of nobility in the ruling class has been the cause of immense sufferings and deprivations of men and women throughout history.

The first stanza of the poem describes the effigies in stone. The sculpted figures, though created by an artist (sculptor) present a sharp contrast to the paintings on Keats' urn. Their faces are "blurred"- -a very telling symbpl - and they "lie in stone." Their life was a tissue of lies and they have, ever since their death, lied in their stone effigies too. Here a reference to an essay "Lies" by Christopher Ricks in his book *The Force of Poetry* seems to be in place. He says that "lie/lie is...simply the most important pun in the language." Elaborating on the importance of this pun, he writes:

> The importance of the *lie/lie* pun is that it concentrates an extraordinarily ranging and profound network of truth-testing situations and postures. It brings mendacity up against

those situations and postures which constitute the great moments or endurances of truth: the child-bed, the love-bed, the bed of sleep and dreams, the sick-bed, the death-bed, the grave.... And even perhaps the modern secular counterpart to the confessional's kneeling: the psychiatrist's couch."[4]

In none of the truth-testing situations in their lives did this couple prove true to themselves or to each other. The blurred faces are symbolic of the lies that permeated their being. And their "proper habits" (the phrase is steeped in bitter irony) are "vaguely shown/As jointed armour, stiffened pleat." The "jointed armour" and the "stiffened pleat" are the objective correlatives of the metallic hardness of the Earl's heart and the stiffness, not gracefulness, of the Countess's disposition. And to cap it all, their little dogs are sitting at their feet – the poet calls it "faint hint of the absurd." If they had any softness in their nature it exhibited itself only in such habits as their fondness for their pets.

In the second stanza, the damning description of the sculpture continues. The "plainness of the pre-baroque" piece of sculpture does not "involve," that is, does not engage or attract the eye. There was nothing intrinsically worthwhile spiritual in their nature that could have appeared in an artistic creation (sculpture) which could have attracted (involved) the eye and made it linger on it. However, there is something in it that one sees "with a sharp tender shock." What is it that gives one this shock? The Earl's "left- hand gauntlet" is clasped in his right hand and the left hand is holding the countess's hand. This must give one shock because a lover does not make his beloved hold his left hand. James Booth says that "Larkin ruefully acknowledged" the "inaccuracies, when they were brought to his attention," in his depiction of the effigies, "and also the fact that 'it should be "right-hand gauntlet," not left-hand.' "[5] But all the inaccuracies are intended as they serve the poet's purpose. In the re-worked effigies the Earl is seen holding his wife's right hand with his right hand. And in this particular case the poet leaves us in no doubt when he says that one sees with a sharp tender shock the earl's left hand holding the countess's right hand. Here one is reminded of the first three stanzas of Donne's "Ecstasy"

Where, like a pillow on a bed,
    A pregnant bank swelled up, to rest
The violet's reclining head,
    Sat we two, one another's best.

Our hands were firmly cemented
With a fast balm, which thence did spring;
Our eye-beams twisted, and did thread
Our eyes, upon one double string;

So to intergraft our hands, as yet
Was all the means to make us one,
And pictures in our eyes to get
Was all our propagation.

Larkin could not but have had "The Ecstasy" in his mind when he wrote the lines under consideration in his poem. "They" in Larkin's poem "would not think to lie in stone so long." They did not have in their life any pretension to true love and naturally they could not have thought of their lying in stone so long about their love after their death. Then "such faithfulness in effigy" can mean that their faithfulness to each other in their conjugal life was not at all real. It "was just a detail friends would see." It was the friends of these high and mighty who made the sculptor depict as true what was a lie. Here one is reminded of a passage in Samuel Richardson's novel *Pamela*, in which Mr B. tells Pamela some home truths about the conjugal life of the spoiled young men and women of aristocratic families – the ruling elite – of his time. Part of this passage is quoted below:

> So great is the difference between what they both [the hus-
> band and the wife] expected *from*, and what they found *in* each
> other, that no wonder misunderstandings happen, and ripen
> to quarrels; that acts of unkindness pass, which, even had the
> first motive to their union been *affection*, as usually it is not,
> would have effaced every tender impression on both sides.

> Appeals to parents and guardians often ensue! If, through
> friends, a reconciliation takes place, it hardly ever holds; for
> why? The fault is in the minds of *both*, and *neither* of them
> will think so: so that the wound (not permitted to be probed)
> is but skinned over; rankles still at bottom, and at last breaks
> out with more pain and anguish than before. Separate beds
> are often the consequence; perhaps elopements; if not, an un-
> conquerable indifference; possibly aversion. And whenever,

for appearance sake, they are obliged to be together, every one sees, that the yawning husband, and the vapourish wife, are truly insupportable to each other; but separate, have freer spirits, and can be tolerable company[6]

And the renowned historian G. M. Trevelyan tells us something more revealing about the institution of marriage in the Renaissance England. He writes:

Wife- beating was a recognized right of man, and was practiced without shame by high as well as low. Similarly, the daughter who refused to marry the gentleman of her parents' choice was liable to be locked up, beaten, and flung about the room, without any shock being inflicted on public opinion. Marriage was not an affair of personal affection but family avarice, particularly in the 'chivalrous' upper class.[7]

And this institution must have been in a worse shape in the fourteenth century.

Then the sculptor's "sweet commissioned grace" did something more: it was

Thrown off in helping to prolong
The Latin names around the base.

The idea was that the names in Latin, prolonged in depicting their medieval ranks, would glorify them and impress future generations so much as to make them revere the two. But the Earl's friends, who, like him, belonged to the ruling elite

would not guess how early in
Their supine stationary voyage
The air would change to soundless damage,
Turn the old tenantry away;

The expression "stationary voyage" is laced with wry humour ('voyage' cannot be 'stationary'), but what the poet means is that their friends would not guess that quite early in their voyage in the realm of the dead, that is, not long after their death, "The air would change to soundless damage" and "Turn the old tenantry away." Soon after they died, the air quietly damaged the sculpted names and their feudal titles. The word 'tenantry' here is significant. The dictionary meaning of this word is: "the tenants of an estate." The titles of the medleval figures were the tenantry in the cathedral in which they were buried, but the air not only corroded the titles, it drove them away from there. The age of the feudal lords came to an end, sooner than the lords had thought, in the social history of the country. The friends would not have guessed how soon the visitors ("succeeding eyes") began "to look, not read."

However, the effigies, as we saw them above, "Rigidly persisted, linked, through lengths and breadths of time," because their supposed glory as well as their supposed love for each other, depicted by the sculptor, made the common people look at them with awe for a long time even after their tenantry had been driven away from the social life of the people. We know that history often lies, especially in glorifying the elite culture. The linked effigies persisted, though "rigidly," perhaps also because the sculptor's "sweet commissioned grace" had tried to show their souls steeped in love for each other. Here we need to know something of what psychology says about the three basic dimensions of true love: : "(a) intimacy, which mainly includes central features of love, such as feeling free to talk about anything, honesty, openness, and understanding; (b) commitment, which mainly includes love features of intermediate centrality, such as devotion, protectiveness, commitment, putting the other first, and sacrifice; and (c) passion, which mainly includes peripheral features, such as euphoria, excitement, heart rate increases, sex appeal and sexual passion."[8] None of these components of true love , we can be sure, existed between the earl and the countess.

Then we come across the most beautiful lines in the poem:

> Snow fell, undated. Light
> Each summer thronged the glass. A bright
> Litter of birdcalls strewed the same
> Bone-riddled ground. And up the paths
> The endless altered people came.

On the one hand, the high and mighty couple were snowed up in wintry death forever – they had had no worthwhile achievements to their credit in their lifetime, so no cloud of glory trailed in their stationary voyage. On the other hand, the rhythms of the livingness of life continued to succeed one another down the ages and generations. Each summer the warm, pleasant, life-giving light of the sun thronged the glass-panes in the cathedral. And although the ground here was "bone-riddled," that is, the graves in the cathedral were riddled with the bones of the long-dead upper crust of society, the bright, cheerful chirpings of birds – the poet has a beautiful expression, "A bright/ Litter of birdcalls" – strewed this ground, as if beautiful flowers were strewn on this otherwise gloomy ground. The rhythm of life continues uninterrupted despite man casting ominous shadows over earth by living a kind of life unworthy of his status. The lords and ladies of the Middle Ages are dead and gone and their heyday is now laid over by wintry snow because theirs was a wintry Age. But first the light of the summer sun brightened the place, then the cheerful songs of birds spread as it were the aroma of life over the whole gloomy ground. Then came the people, later in origin than birds – "Endless altered people came" "up the path." Generations of men not only kept coming into existence, but also came endlessly altered. These endlessly altered people came in tides and washed out their identity. That was bound to be. Humankind keep changing, though slowly, down the ages; the "endless altered people" were more and more different from the masses of the fourteenth century who virtually worshipped these lords and ladies, ironically called "the nobles." Change is inevitable. So what is the present status of the long-superseded knights and their ladies? The poet tells us this with the clarity of thinking that is the hallmark of a true artist:

> Now, helpless in the hollow of
> An unarmorial age, a trough
> Of smoke in slow suspended skeins
> Above the scrap of history,
> Only an attitude remains:
>
> Time has transfigured them into
> Untruth.

Now in the hollow of this "unarmorial age," the nobles, who lived at a sublime height of glory in their own age, are helpless and their age is regarded as an age of low achievement – a "trough." And in this trough above the scrap of their history they lie like "slow suspended skeins" of smoke that had made the human scene of their time hazy. Their supposedly glorious past is now a mere scrap of history. The word "scrap" is sharply satirical. Their history is now utterly insignificant, something that has been discarded, like scrap iron. On this scrap-heap they now appear as only an attitude. And time has "transfigured them into/ Untruth." The word "transfigured" is steeped in the bitterest kind of irony. The dictionary meaning of "transfigure" is to "transform into something more beautiful or spiritual." But Time has transformed them into Untruth. The poem is a warning to us as well – "how we live measures our own nature." And the last line of the poem, "What will survive of us is love," is a comprehensive comment on human existence. As we have seen above, "love is a privilege of noble hearts." The "stone fidelity," depicted by the "sculptor's sweet commissioned grace," the two worthies "hardly [ever] meant" in their conjugal life. However, it "has come to be \Their final blazon." The verb "blazon," used here as a noun, is very significant. The dictionary meaning of this verb is "to be written or shown on something in a very noticeable way." The stone fidelity, though non-existent in the Earl and his wife, but depicted by the artist (the sculptor) at the behest of their aristocratic friends, has come to prove something very important:

> Our almost instinct almost true:
> What will survive of us is love.

These last two lines are tricky. It is not the love of the twain – it was non-existent – that has survived, but the artist's vision regarding love that makes us almost instinctively recognize as almost true the "blazon" that "What will survive of us is love." Christopher Ricks says that the last line of the poem can be said with both a classical and a romantic intonation. He writes:

> What Larkin achieves is an extraordinary complementarity; a classical pronouncement is protected against a carven coldness by the ghostly presence of an arching counter-thrust, a romantic swell of feeling; and the romantic swell is protected against a melting self-solicitude by the bracing counterthrust of a classical impersonality. The classical intonation for the line says something *sotto voce*: 'What will survive – and not just mount, shine, evaporate, and fall – of us is love.' The romantic intonation says something different *sotto voce*: 'What

will survive of us – of us too, ordinary modern people in an unarmorial age, uncommemorated by aristocratic art or by a Latin inscription – is love.[9]

We stated above that "An Arundel Tomb" put us in mind of Keats's "Ode on a Grecian Urn," particularly its last two lines. The closing two lines of Larkin's poem emerge as naturally from what has gone before in the poem as these lines of the great Ode, "'Beauty is truth, truth beauty, – that is all/ Ye know on earth, and all ye need to know" conclude Keats's poem. Without joining in the enormous amount of critical discussion of these lines we shall simply quote a few words from the philosopher John Dewey' book *Art as Experience*:

> There has been much dispute as to what Keats meant in his famous lines... and what he meant in the cognate prose statement – "What imagination seizes as beauty must be truth." Much of the dispute is carried on in ignorance of the particular tradition in which Keats wrote and which gave the term "truth" its meaning. In this tradition "truth" never signifies correctness of intellectual statements about things, or truth as its meaning is now influenced by science. It denotes the wisdom by which men live....And in Keats's mind it was particularly connected with the question of justifying good and trusting to it in spite of the evil and destruction that abound.[10]

The last line in Larkin's poem is also very important. Nothing of value (e.g. "truth" and "beauty") has survived of the way of life lived by the ruling elite of the Middle Ages and so their history is now a mere scrap. Larkin wants us – all of us everywhere – to know that love alone will survive of us. Will Durant quotes George Santayana as to what Laplace, on his deathbed, thought of love: "Laplace is reported to have said on his deathbed that science was mere trifling, and that nothing was real but love."[11] The paintings on Keats's Urn are works of art. Referring to Schopenhauer's view on painting, Will Durant writes: "...the painter sees, in the person whom he paints, not merely the individual character and feature, but some universal quality and permanent reality for whose unveiling the individual is only a symbol and a means."[12] The effigies on the Arundel tomb, in sharp contrast to the paintings on the Urn, had nothing to show in their characters and features by way of any universal quality and permanent reality and so, naturally, "Time has transfigured them into Untruth."

Chapter 5
Poems from *High Windows*

Sympathy in White Major

In one of his essays on Hardy's poetry, Larkin wrote, "in every Hardy poem , barring one or two about the death of Edward II and that sort of thing, there is a little spinal cord of thought and each has a little tune of its own, and this is something you can say of very few poets"(RW p. 176). The same can be said of each of Larkin's poems that appeared in *The Less Deceived*, *The Whitsun Weddings* and *High Windows* and his last great poem "Aubade" that appeared after *High Windows* (1974). "Sympathy in White Major" has its own spinal cord of thought that we must try to locate. But we face difficulty in our effort to do so. Barbara Everett begins her "brilliant analysis" of the poem with a reference to Clive James's difficulty with it. Clive James found the second poem in the triptych "Livings" and "Sympathy in White Major" obscure. Everett's introductory remarks on the poem, reproduced below, can be helpful in deciphering the code that the poem is:

'Sympathy in White Major' (CP,168) is a linguistically fairly simple, almost monosyllabic poem, whose three stanzas describe a man (the poet, or 'I') who pours himself out a large drink and hears as from a toastmaster his social virtues celebrated in warm clichés. The style is mostly commonplace, the situation being downrightly imagined: the drink fills a stanza, elaborately detailed, and the clichés of praise load every rift with ore. If the poem strikes a reader as obscure, the reason must lie not in the area of paraphrasable meaning but in 'how to take it' – the absence of a sense of why the man and the drink and the fantasies of praise frankly matter at all. The answer to this does not lie in the paraphrasable content... but in the ordonnance of the whole. Rather than offering a strong logic of statements whose syntax follows what we like to think of as normal colloquial usage, the poem works by an interaction (or Juxtaposition) of striking images.[1]

The poem is, in fact, not paraphrasable. No word, no phrase, no sentence is difficult enough to need elucidation. But just as Barbara Everett mentions Clive James's difficulty with this poem, George Hartley also says that Clive James found two poems in *High Windows* obscure: "Clive James found two poems in *High Windows*, 'Sympathy in White Major' and the middle section of 'Livings,' cases of 'over-refinement leading to obscurity.'"[2] The poem indeed presents difficulties to the reader for the reasons mentioned by Everett. Therefore, the reader should first enjoy the dazzling brilliance of the technique employed here. Each of the three eight line stanzas is one sentence comprising one complete statement. The third stanza seems to be the logical sequence to the first. The second stanza seems to be an interruption to put in something very important. This stanza can be probed to locate the "little spinal cord" that gave the poem what it needed to be a successful work of art. Then there is a persona within a persona in the poem, or we can say that there is a persona and his alter ego. In the first stanza, we find how the persona pours himself a large drink and then, lifting it up, says "in private pledge:/ *He devoted his life to others.*" The use of "He" here gives the persona praised an identity separate from that of the persona who pours the drink. The pouring of the drink can be seen as a detailed and brilliant ritual. An anthropologist's definition of the ritual is:

Ritual may be defined as stereotyped communication, solitary or interpersonal, which reduces anxiety, prepares the organism to act, and (in social rituals), coordinates the preparation for action among several organisms, and which does all this more quickly and reliably than can be accomplished (given the characteristics of the organisms and circumstance) by non-stereotyped, informational communication.[3]

This ritual is necessary and important because the persona is going to talk about his success or failure as a poet. Success is very important in art because, as Larkin himself wrote: "In a humanist society, art – and especially modern or current art – assumes great importance, and to lose touch with it is parallel to losing one's faith in a religious age."(RW p.292)

This observation requires our serious attention, particularly because it says that in the modern world art is the mainstay of man's spiritual life. To perform this high/ sublime function modern art has to tell man the truth, the whole truth, about cosmos, about the terrestrial existence, and also about the psycho-social realities of human existence. This means that art today has to discharge the same functions that religion once performed, that is, to provide the much-needed sustenance to man's life for further human progress. As Julian Huxley put it in his book *Evolution: the Modern Synthesis:* "True human progress consists in increases of aesthetic, intellectual, and spiritual experience and satisfaction."[4]

It was this great task of furthering human progress by making his poetry provide the kind of sustenance man needed that Larkin as a poet undertook. In this task he only partially, if at all, succeeded. He need not and is not ashamed of this fact because even the greatest of men have had only partial success in making man move forward along the path of progress. Khalil Gibran in one of his poems (" Song of Man") says that he went to great sages and prophets to understand the truth:

; I heard the teachings of Confucius;
I listened to Brahma's wisdom;
I sat by Buddha under the Tree of Knowledge;
Yet here am I, existing with ignorance
And heresy.

I was in Sinai when Jehova approached Moses
I saw the Nazarene's miracles at the Jordan,
I was in Medina when Mohammed visited.
Yet here I am, prisoner of bewilderment.[5]

In view of the facts stated in these lines, Larkin the poet could not have hoped that he would succeed in bringing back the lost displays – the truth about everything – to man and thereby change the quality of his existence appreciably. Thomas Mann is right when he says, "no matter how much it [Life] has been redeemed by becoming literature, it keeps right on sinning ."[6]

So in the very title of his poem the poet seeks our sympathy. Larkin's poem owes its title to the poem *Symphonie en Blanc Majeur* by the French poet Theophile Gautier. Barbara Everett has discussed the theme of Gautier's poem and its influence on the painter who painted pictures of women in white. Larkin could not have liked either Gautier's poem or the pictures inspired by it because they had nothing to do with the sublime task that modern or current art has to perform. Larkin's poem is , as Barbara Everett tells us, "marvelously clear...clear as whiteness is blank," but whiteness, the poet tells us in the last line of the poem, is not his favourite colour. The task of literature or art is to cleanse the darkness sitting like a poisonous toad at the heart of man's being. But the uncanny as well as sparkling, clinking clarity of the scene in the poem is symbolic of the sparkling clarity of both thought and technique in Larkin's poetry. But this clarity was needed to make man understand the crisis facing his civilization and thereby make him realize the urgent need for change in his lifestyle. Larkin, we may be sure, assimilated the best thoughts in various fields of knowledge and found the vast gulf between what man should have lived like and what kind of life he has actually lived, and rightly felt that man has no future unless he re-cast his whole way of life and made it conform to "the fundamental facts of nature," as Thomas Mann put it in a different context. We quote below the passage in which this phrase occurs. Mann writes,

> The world as normally arranged is conducive to man's needs and his pleasures In life.... I won't go so far as to say that the whole natural order of things, for instance the size of the earth, the time it takes to revolve on its axis and about the sun, the division between day and night, summer and winter

– in short, the whole cosmic rhythm, if you like to call it that – was especially arranged for our use and behoof; that would be cheek, I suppose and simple-minded into the bargain. It would be teleological reasoning, as the philosophers express it. No, it will be truer to say that our needs are – thank God that it should be so – in harmony with the larger, the fundamental facts of nature.[7]

Larkin's poetry was an effort at persuasion in this direction. The task was daunting, if not impossible to accomplish. Despite this, the poet lifts his glass, filled "up to the edge" with gin and tonic, and says in "private pledge" that his poetic self devoted his life to others, that is, making man aware of the whole truth. But what did the poet actually do in this regard? Of this we are told in the second stanza.

Other people wore human beings "like clothes in their days." They wanted name and fame and for that they made use of men. They wanted to be heroes. This happens not only in literature but in many fields of life. These heroes, though they stir people into some kind of action that does serve some immediate purpose that earns them great fame, their ideas and motivating power do not bring about that kind of change that J. B. S. Haldane spoke of in his *Causes of Evolution* and which we referred to earlier in this work. This kind of radical change is the imperative need of human civilization because, as Haldane wrote in the same book and, again, we have quoted him above, that man is a most primitive and imperfect rational creature and that he is a worse animal than monkey. Julian Huxley also wrote these striking lines in his book referred to above: " The poet spoke of letting ape and tiger die. To this pair, the cynic later added donkey, as more pervasive and in the long run more dangerous. The evolutionary biologist is tempted to ask whether the aim should not be to let the mammal die within us, so as the more effectively to permit the man to live." [8]

Larkin the poet devoted his life to others to bring about this kind of change in man because he knew, as any thinking person should know, that without such change man's future is not secure. So he says that unlike other people who wore human beings as clothes in their days, he set himself the task of bringing "to those who thought" he "could the lost displays." What are the displays that are lost to man? And who were "those" people who thought Larkin the poet would bring them these displays? People, as Sholokhov said, want the truth and Saul Bellow said that people want even an iota of truth as they are literally dying for want of it. We have already referred to these views above. The lost displays alone can give us truth about everything , from the cosmic dance of matter in space to the strange activities of each cell in any organic structure, truth about all institutions (religious, socio-political-economic, cultural) set up by man, as well as truth about man's real origins and nature. Dostoevsky rightly said : "Everything passes, only the truth remains." [9] It is these truths that have become the lost displays and the poet in Larkin (not Larkin himself) tried to bring them to those who hungered for them. But success proved elusive. He says, "It didn't work for them or me." What exactly happened? It is not that truth is hard to come by and success cannot be attained. Dostoevsky expresses his views in this regard thus: "Believe me, this dream [the kingdom of heaven on earth] ...will come to pass without doubt, it will come, but not now, for every process has its law. It's a spiritual, psychological process. To transform the world, to recreate it afresh, men must turn into another path psychologically." [10]

Dostoevsky wrote these words in 1880. Today we cannot be that optimistic. But re-creation of a new world is possible. Whether man will fulfill the pre-conditions necessary for such a task that Dostoevsky points to is an open question. Philip Larkin the poet undertook the task. It did not work either for him or for those for whom he undertook it. This was bound to happen. The process of change will be long and arduous and there will be setbacks. But the setback in Larkin's case was not disheartening. He tells us:

> But all concerned were nearer thus
> (Or so we thought) to all the fuss
> Than if we had missed it separately.

The effort was only partial success – the assertion that all concerned were nearer to all the fuss is qualified by the clause, *Or so we thought*. Had they all tried separately, they would not have achieved even partial success. It has to be a co-operative effort over a considerable period of time to transform man's recalcitrant mind besotted with so many lowly desires and jibbing at every step forward. Here the second stanza, which contains the spinal cord of thought of the poem, ends.

The laudation of the social self of Larkin, which had begun with *"He devoted his life to others"* in the last line of the first stanza, resumes in the third and last stanza and in the first seven of the eight lines of the stanza; "every rift is loaded with the ore of clichés," as Barbara Everett rightly puts it. There are many readers of literature (in fact, most) who are given to showering laudations on a writer, who becomes well-known, without having decoded the message of the artist. The clichés are uttered while the social self of the poet is holding the glass of wine. Barbara Everett refers to a poem by Mallarme entitled "Salut" and says that the persona is saluting Larkin the poet. As we pointed out earlier, pouring out of the wine is a ritual. The salute was part of the ritual.

And here we shall once again go to the last line of the poem, "Though white is not my favourite colour." George Hartley, in the essay referred to above, comments on this line as follows:

> 'The whitest man,' a phrase from the days of the British raj, guyed in Edwardian Music Hall, is turned into an ambiguity in the last line. Whiteness or moral worthiness, Is also the whiteness of the man untainted by experience, but finally it denotes cowardice: the white feather sent to the Major who wouldn't volunteer for active service, the musical-military pun in the title.[11]

I think this line can be interpreted thus: It was those men who, without deciphering the codes that his poems were, showered on him cliché-ridden praise, in which "the whitest man" was one of the clichés. The poet specifically disowns this in the powerful last line. He only knows too well that no man, not even a poet, can be called the whitest man simply because there are dark spots in our make. Writing poetry is a cleansing operation (bringing about *catharsis*) at the spiritual level in the poet himself as well as in the readers of his poetry.

The Trees in Philip Larkin's "The Trees"

Except during the nine months before he draws the first breath, no man manages his affairs as well as a tree does.

G. B. Shaw

Philip Larkin's poem "The Trees" seems to be a plea to man to re-vitalize his civilization because 'entropy' seems to have set in in it, which bodes ill for the future of man's existence as a species. The plea is made by the trees in the poem and they seem to have a right to do so. Philip Larkin shows a scientifically accurate perception of the life of trees and, relying on that – "a scientific truth" – he creates, to borrow Naguib Mahfouz's words, "general philosophy for existence reaching far beyond science."[1]

Carl Sagan, in his book *Cosmos*, says something interesting about man's fundamental relationship with trees:

> At the very heart of life on Earth – the proteins that control all chemistry, and the nucleic acids that carry the hereditary instructions – we find these molecules to be essentially identical in all the plants and animals. An oak tree and I are made of the same stuff. If you go far enough back, we have a common ancestor.[2]

Much earlier, Henri Bergson expressed the same idea in the following words: "…it seems to us most probable that the animal cell and the vegetable cell are derived from a common stock, and that the first living organism oscillated between the vegetable and animal form, participating in both at once."[3]

Carl Sagan repeatedly points out the unity between man and the tree in his abovementioned book. On page 52, he writes:

> We humans look rather different than a tree. Without a doubt we perceive the world differently than a tree does. But down deep, at the molecular heart of life, the trees and we are essentially identical. We both use nucleic acids for heredity; we both use proteins and enzymes to control the chemistry of our cells.[4]

In a sense plants seem to be a life-form of superior merit because it is they which give all animals – and man has "only recently evolved from animals"[5] – all they need to exist. Anthony Huxley makes it very clear in his book *Plant ant Planet* when he says that "The evolution of animals could not have occurred without that of plants before them" and that "Plants arise, live, mate, fruit and die in their many different ways without needing any assistance from mankind at all,"[6] whereas man cannot exist without them.

The trees in Philip Larkin's poem "The Trees" try to teach man a thing or two how to bring out the best in his organic structure – a miracle of the creativity of nature – so as to be worthy enough to carry the torch of Life along the right path to a destination where all creation, animate and inanimate, on our beautiful planet may live in perfect harmony because, as Carl Sagan rightly observes, "we are, all of us – trees and people, angler fish and slime molds and paramecia – descended from a single and common instance of the origin of life in the early history of our planet."[7] In fact, as Henri Bergson says, "There is no manifestation of life which does not contain, in a rudimentary state – either latent or potential – the essential characters of most other manifestations."[8] And as regards the familial relationship between the animal and plant life, he says this:

> no definite characteristic distinguishes the plant from the animal. Attempts to define the two kingdoms strictly have always come to naught. There is not a single property of vegetable life that is not found, in some degree, in certain animals; not a single characteristic feature of the animal that has not been seen in certain species or at certain moments in the vegetable world.[9]

With this brief introduction, which throws light on the basic familial relationship between plant and animal [man], which also points out that plant is a life-form on which man is a parasite, we shall approach Larkin's beautiful short poem. The first stanza runs thus:

> The trees are coming into leaf
> Like something almost being said;
> The recent buds relax and spread.
> Their greenness is a kind of grief.

The trees here are deciduous. Their leaves fall annually in autumn because deciduous trees are not active in winter. Anthony Huxley writes that leaves on any tree age but annual "disposal" of leaves on "the deciduous tree or winter-resting plant" is "essential" because the tree "must not be active in winter." He also tells us this about the new leaves on deciduous trees: "Young deciduous leaves are bright green, which is due to the penetration of light right into the cells, where internal reflection makes every chloroplast operate fully."[10] Paul Morel in *Sons and Lovers* is also an amateur painter, who takes delight in painting leaves and trees. When Miriam asks him why he likes his last painting and Paul asks her to search for an answer, she says, "I don't know. It seems so true." Then Paul says, "It's because – it's because there is scarcely any shadow in it; it's more shimmery, as if I'd painted the shimmering protoplasm in the leaves, and not the stiffness of the shape. That seems dead to me. Only the shimmeriness is the real 'living.'"[11] It is this beautiful shimmeriness in the protoplasm of millions of cells in each of the numerous leaves on the trees that makes them "Like something almost being said." The phrasal verb "coming into" means "inherit money or property." The trees were despoiled of their leaves in autumn and winter, which means that they were deprived of the vitality of life, but with the start of spring they are going to inherit something precious, that is, a new life shimmering in the protoplasm of the cells in the bright new leaves on them. Anthony Huxley writes that when deciduous shrubs and trees lose their leaves in winter there is a "remarkable and rapid transformation from a full-scale food-making factory to a complete shutdown situation" and that the "plants very largely curtail their metabolism" although "the roots are seldom entirely inactive." But with the onset of "the new growing season" the roots start pumping "food into the thrusting forth of new leaves and fresh growth;" and as the food is thrust upwards, "buds, which are actually minute shoots,"[12] appear on the stem. The poet is talking of "recent buds" and says "their greenness is a kind of grief." The dictionary meaning of the word "grief" is "intense sorrow, especially caused by someone's death." Whose death is implied in this grief? The question asked in the second stanza of the poem will supply the answer and we will come to it by and by. At the moment we will concentrate on the buds and leaves and their greenness. Anthony Huxley tells us how leaves emerge from buds: "Leaves emerge from their buds in a miraculous unfolding and expansion of compressed tissues, lubricated by mucilage from special glands."[13] Larkin says that "the recent buds" – some buds remain dormant for quite some time – "relax and spread," that is, the new buds, after their birth, which must have involved creative effort tinged with pain, enjoy being themselves in the bright and warm sun and then they open out into hundreds of thousands of new leaves in which the trees find their fulfillment, which is manifested as "something almost being said."

L. Oken, an early nineteenth century botanist, wrote: "A leaf is a whole plant."[14] And Agnes Arber says that the leaf is "an effective assimilating, breathing and transpiring organ."[15] Plants, of course, do not have the language that we humans use, not even the languages that animals and insects use. But this does not mean that they do not have the faculty of perception and of being aware of certain sensations. Anthony Huxley writes:

> Larger animals feel heat and cold, wind and rain, fatigue and pain, and various degrees of trust, affection and sexual pleasure. Human beings add to these all kinds of emotional and intellectual perceptions and one might add confusions. In such terms plants do not feel; but if we apply one of the main definitions of the word – 'to perceive or be aware of through physical sensation' (Webster) – they most certainly do.[16]

Even a human being, when he reaches the state of total self-realization – as great mystics do – that is, when the very essence of life coalesce with emotional-intellectual- transcendental perceptions, he will find it extremely difficult to express in words that state of total, one may say divine, self-fulfillment. For the trees in Larkin's poem coming into leaf is that state of fulfillment. All parts of the trees are acting in unison and to the best of their capacity. The trees are engaged in self-maintenance with vigour to fulfill the purpose of their life. Agnes Arber refers to Spinoza's idea of "self-maintenance" and comments on it as follows:

> He [Spinoza] gave it the following formulation: "The effort by which each thing endeavours to persevere in its own being is nothing but the actual essence of the thing itself;" moreover, at an early date, he had definitely identified it with life. He thus set the principle in the forefront of biology by making the urge towards self- maintenance not merely a character of living things, but the very gist of life itself.[17]

The trees, with their recent buds relaxing and opening out miraculously into bright green leaves, are expressing their "urge towards self-maintenance" and displaying the actual essence of their being. But the leaves' greenness is a grief – intense sorrow as if caused by some dear one's death – to the poet. And this brings us to the second stanza of the poem:

Is it that they are born again
And we grow old? No, they die too.
Their yearly trick of looking new
Is written down in rings of grain.

The question posed in this stanza is very significant and seeks a correct answer. The cells in the stem-nodes which bring forth buds never age. The ageing in a tree takes place only in the stem (trunk). It is this miracle in the life of trees that they get a new life every summer. In the case of man the cells in his body keep ageing and getting replaced by new ones. But the cells in the brain remain the same from beginning to end though ageing takes place in them too. However, as Julian Huxley points out, "…in human beings, mental structure may continue to develop throughout life even up to old age – we need only to think of Verdi or Titian."[18] Here it will be in place to quote a sentence from Erwin Schrodinger's book *What is Life?* with *Mind and Matter*: "The nervous system is the place where our species is still engaged in phylogenetic transformation; metaphorically speaking, it is the 'vegetative top' … of our stem"[19] . This similarity between the cells in the stem-nodes in trees and those in the human brain provides the poem its spinal cord. There is another important thing about the life of a tree that distinguishes it from that of a man. In man's life, after the log phase, that is, the period of optimal growth, senescence begins, that is, life starts deteriorating with age. In trees, the movement of life is throughout upwards, with slowdowns alternating with renewed growths. Today senescence has set in not just in the life of one individual but in the whole of human civilization. William Golding calls this senescence 'entropy', which is a more appropriate term in the context. In *Darkness Visible*, part of the dialogue between Sophy and her father runs thus:

' "We're not wholesome, are we?"
"That's a good word."
"You, Mummy, Toni, me – we're not the way people used to
be. It's part of
the whole running down."
"Entropy." '[20]

Sophy and her sister, Toni, are exquisitely beautiful and their father is a handsome, educated and sophisticated man. Yet, paradoxically, they are not wholesome. This is so because of the whole running down or the entropy that is afflicting the human scene today. It is this awareness of entropy set in in human civilization that fills the poet with grief. Orhan Pamuk rightly observes in his novel *Snow*: "Only people who are very intelligent and very unhappy can write good poems."[21] "The Trees" is certainly a good poem.

The poet asks, "Is it that they [the trees] are born again/ And we grow old"? The answer to the first part of the question is, in a sense, yes, as will be evident from what has been said above about the life of trees. Senescence does not take place, as it does in man after the log phase, in the stem-nodes of trees – the numerous nodes which push forth buds which open out as bright green leaves in the spring season. But the poet knows very well that all life-forms, from mayflies, which are very short-lived, to the stars, which live for billions of years, are subject to death. So he says, "No, they die too." But before they die they keep renewing themselves every spring. The poet calls their miraculous ability to renew their life again and again a "trick written down in rings of grain." The following passage in Anthony Huxley's *Plant and Planet* tells us how these rings in the stem of trees work to enable them to renew their life again and again:

> In woody dicots…including gymnosperms, a process called secondary thickening produces an arrangement in which there is an ever-widening central core of xylem. Cut across, this core is seen to have rings, each composed of larger or smaller cells, the larger produced in spring when growth is at a peak and overall expansion takes place, the smaller and denser in summer and winter as growth slows down. Every year a new ring is formed, and its width can tell how good a season it was, while the number of rings tells us the exact age of the tree.[22]

Every year a new ring of living cells that gives the tree a new life completes its life and then is converted into hard wood in which the cells are dead. But before that happens, another ring of living cells begins to form so that the uptake of water and mineral salts from the roots continues and in the spring this uptake is most vigorous into the stem-nodes. The trees in the poem seem to be experiencing a good spring because of which the leaves are so bright green that they seem to be saying something and causing grief to the poet because of his being painfully conscious of his own senescence-afflicted self and of the entropy that has touched the present human condition. And this brings us to the third and last stanza of the poem:

> Yet still the unresting castles thresh
> In fullgrowm thickness every May
> Last year is dead, they seem to say,
> Begin afresh, afresh, afresh.

Every May the thickness of the trunk is fullgrown as the cells in the castle-like ring in this season are larger and send water and mineral salts up to the stem-nodes with unresting vigour. Last year's ring became hard wood with dead cells. All such rings formed in the years gone by are hard wood. Fritjof Capra writes in his book *The Web of Life:* "As the tree grows, there is only a thin layer of living cells around its perimeter just beneath the bark. All the wood inside, more than ninety-seven percent of the tree, is dead."[23] So we can say that trees, with just three percent of their stems alive, keep renewing themselves every spring because the cells in the stem-nodes, which give birth to buds and leaves, never age. And they tell us also to forget about the last year and renew ourselves with a new spring in our life. This is possible though difficult – difficult because man has allowed his life to sink in the winter of many kinds of ignorance and falsehood. Naguib Mahfouz, in the following lines, points to this difficulty, but advises us to liberate ourselves into a new spring of enlightened existence: "The problem is not that the truth is harsh but that liberation from falsehood is as painful as being born. Run after truth until you're breathless. Accept the pain in recreating yourself."[24]

Later, in the same novel, Mahfouz writes: "The duty common to all human beings is perpetual revolution, and that is nothing other than an unceasing effort to further the will of life represented by its progress toward the ideal."[25] But what is the ideal? The following passage in Ages Arber's book, already referred to in this essay, can help us understand the nature of the ideal:

> the relationship within the plant, of the whole and part, recalls a certain conception of relation of man to the universe, which, though occurring inclassical literature, did not reach its fullest expression until the Middle Ages. According to this conception, man, the microcosm, was regarded both as one

of the innumerable constituents, which together make up the universe, and also as a mirror or symbol of that universe, seen, as it were, through a diminishing glass. In other words, man offers, within the limitations of his finiteness, a parallel to the total universe. So, comparing small things with great, we may call a shoot a microcosm of the whole plant: while a leaf; a leaflet; a leaf-lobe; or even the hair to which a lobe may ultimately be reduced; is a microcosm of the whole shoot.[26]

The perception of a similar make of his being – a mirror of the universe seen, as it were, through a diminishing glass – and living up to that perception should be the ideal man should strive for.

Agnes Arber refers to Aristotle's theory of causation. Aristotle identified four primary causes of the existence of any object/organism/phenomenon: (a) Material Cause, (b) Efficient Cause, (c) Final Cause, and (d) Formal Cause. With a simple example of a Roman road, she explains the meaning and significance of these causes:

"(1) The Material Cause: the earth, stones, etc. used in the road making.
"(2) The Efficient Cause: the forces set in motion by the labour employed in the construction.
"(3) The Final Cause: the purpose of facilitating travel from place to place, which is the reason for which the road is made.
"(4) The Formal Cause: the idea of road making which preexisted in the Roman Mind."

Agnes Arber says that for "studying organic form" these four causes may be fitted into two categories – "the mechanical or physiochemical causes (material+ efficient causes) and the teleological causes (final + formal causes)."[27]

Regarding the physiochemical causes of our physical organization, Sir Charles Sherrington says this in his book *Man on his Nature*:

Biology analyses the organism in the instance of ourselves and many others like us into an assemblage of quasi-independent minuter living things. It clinches that finding by showing that each of us for a short time lives as one such single unit. Physical science, with its units of a different order, carrying out on us search for its units finds that they likewise make us up. It finds us like the rest of what it has examined, a mass resoluble into units of what it calls 'energy'(MohN, p. 166).

What Sherrington says about the physiochemical causes of man's being is scientifically accurate and true. But teleological causes equally well shape his being. Agnes Arber refers to Kant's views regarding the two categories of causes thus:

Towards the end of the eighteenth century, Kant, looking at the matter from the standpoint of the philosopher, seems to recognize frankly the irreducible existence of the two types of cause. He noted that, in the animal body, many parts might be explained through laws of a merely mechanical kind...but he added:

"Yet the cause that accumulates the appropriate material, modifies and fashions it and deposits it in its proper place, must always be estimated teleologically ..." Borrowing the oft-quoted expression, with which Kant illumined another occasion, we may say that mechanism without teleology is blind, while teleology without mechanism is empty.[28]

Trees are true to the teleology of their being. They give us pure air to breathe in and prepare food for all animals on the earth. It is because a tree, to use Spinoza's words again, "perseveres in his own being," which is nothing but its actual essence. Trees realize their essence by renewing their life again and again with the help of the unageing cells in their stem-nodes. The billions of miraculously organized cells in man's cerebral cortex can be used until quite late in his life for creative purposes. The trees in Larkin's poem – we must always remember that trees are the original form of life on earth, while, in "evolutionary terms", we are but "a blink of the eye"[29] – give us very important advice which we can ignore only at our peril. The advice given in all seriousness is very important: "Last year is dead.../Begin afresh, afresh, afresh." Nietzsche, through his Zarathustra, tells us the same thing:

The time has come for man to set himself a goal. The time has come for man to plant the seed of his highest hope. His soil is still rich enough. But one day this soil will be poor and domesticated and no tall tree will be able to grow in it. Alas, the time is coming when man will no longer shoot the arrow of his longing beyond man, and the string of his bow will have forgotten to whirl![30]

Man should put his none too glorious history behind and make a fresh beginning. Then he will be true, like the tree, to the teleology of his being. This seems a tall order – with regard to the deplorable human condition, the very first sentence in Samuel Beckett's masterpiece, *Waiting for Godot*, says, "Nothing to be done"[31] – but man has no choice.

LIVINGS [I]

"Livings" is a triptych, that is, three separate poems are linked to each other in some kind of relationship to form a whole. At first sight it is not clear how they form a whole because they seem to stand quite independent of each other. Also, Barbara Everett says that Clive James referred "to the second part of 'Livings' – as also to another poem in this volume [*High Windows*], 'Sympathy in White Major' – as being distractingly obscure…"[1] John Wain also found "Livings II" as "Larkin's most opaque poem."[2] However, attempts have to be made to decode the message that the triptych wants to convey.

The first poem does not seem to present much difficulty and seems quite amenable to a straightforward explication. But to say this about any Larkin poem may be risky because each of his great poems leads us from everyday world and commonplace things to a world of translucent, even transcendent ideas. Richard Hoggart rightly observes that serious artists "purify the language and educate the emotions of the tribe."[3] And since our language of everyday use is not exactly pure and our emotions are, more often than not, uneducated and crude, great effort on the part of an ordinary reader of poetry like the present writer is needed to understand even partially a work of art.

In the first poem of the triptych we come across a small- town businessman who, as he himself tells us, deals with "farmers" who deal in "things like dips and feeds," that is, his business is in agricultural line. Every three months he visits a particular town, where he stays at a particular hotel for three days to finalize deals for supply of things like dips and feeds. He carries a lean old bag, which the boots takes into a "single" room in which he hangs his hat.

He goes to the dining room, where he drinks one beer. Then he has dinner. While eating dinner ("from soup to stewed pears"), he reads the local paper, in which he comes across news of births and deaths, properties for sale, proceedings at the police court, adverts regarding availability of motor spares. Later, he moves into the Smoke Room. He drinks whisky there. There are people there, such as Clough, Margetts, the Captain, Dr Watterson. They talk about such matters as

> Who makes ends meet, who's taking the knock,
> Government tariffs, wages, price of stock.

The smoke puffed out by these people hangs under the light. There are comic pictures on the wall which nobody pays attention to. Then the sound of dominoes being played in the Bar is heard. The unnamed businessman stands a round of drink to the domino players. This is all that his evening's engagements in the hotel amount to. This is how businessmen of his class staying in not very expensive hotels display the normal activities of their life.

Later, he takes a walk in the square, which is empty. While walking, he sees that

> a big sky
> Drains down the estuary like the bed
> Of a gold river, and the Customs House
> Still has its office lit.

These lines from the third and last stanza of the poem have a different setting, that is, outside the hotel, from that of the rest of it and the two images that come within the businessman's ken are important. The images contrast with each other. The first image has two natural or elemental phenomena – the sky and the estuary – as its constituents. These constituents unite – the sky "drains down the estuary." And this sky looks like "the bed /Of a gold river." There is something unique about this image. An estuary is the tidal mouth of a large river. The golden sky is so reflected in the river that it appears that, passing through its mouth, the sky has become the river's bed. The image here reminds us of Larkin's creative power that can suddenly raise the register of his poetic discourse from the commonplace, everyday, even coarse speech to a sublimity of thought clothed in equally sublime language. The beauty of the image lies in the fact that it is alive, it is seen as a process.

In sharp contrast with this image is the image of the Customs House with its office still lit. But this image, too, is very important. Earlier, in the Smoke Room, we saw the inmates talk about "Government tariffs, wages, price of stock" and how these things affected people. Customs House stands for foreign trade, whereas the talk of the people in the Smoke room was related to domestic business. The significance of the talk and the Customs House will be clear in the last line of the poem.

Finally, while drowsing "Between ex-Army sheets" on the bed, the businessman wonders why he keeps coming to this place. It is the deep discontent of his "lean" life that makes him think so – the lean old leather case that he carries symbolizes his life. The business was his father's but now that the father is dead, it belongs to him. And in the last line he says to us, "t's time to change, in nineteen twenty-nine." It was the year in which the Great Depression set in in America, spread like a wild fire throughout the country and engulfed the whole of Europe except the communist Russia . We quote below the following passage on this crisis from H. G. Wells's *A Short History of the World:*

The great crash began, as nobody who lived through it can forget, at the end of October in the year 1929, in Wall Street, the financial quarter of New York. Soon the shares of even the best companies were worth barely a quarter of what they once were, and for others no buyers could be found....

There had been commercial crises before, but this was unheard of in its violence. Its effects were maximized, not only by the disastrous 'foreign debts' and tariffs policy...but by some particular results of uncontrolled private ownership and enterprise. The gambling in shares had been extended so widely that bucket shops were opened everywhere, and labourers and stenographers bought and re-sold things as one sixty-fourth of a share in General Motors....Soon factories, mills and shipyards were closing down; unsaleable expensive cars piled up and their owners sold apples in the streets; farmers went bankrupt and their lands went wild. At the beginning of 1933, it was estimated, nearly twenty million people were facing starvation. ,

Wells says that the disaster did not remain confined to America alone. Soon "it spread wider than any plague since the Black Death." British "pound broke and lost a fifth of its value... London had been the financial centre of the world, and international trade was now in chaos. "[4]

The protagonist (the unnamed middling businessman) feels that it is time to change. But change to what? He is now in a blind alley and he cannot see his way out of this alley. The atmosphere of the poem has something ominous about it. The talk in the Smoke Room and the Customs House working till late in the evening are indicative of the rumblings of the coming storm.

[II]

As stated above, critics like Clive James and John Wain have found the second poem in the triptych obscure or opaque. The persona in this poem is a light-house- keeper, who is, at this moment, in his room in the lighthouse and is looking down at the sea from that height, which is seventy feet from the sea level. He sees this in the first stanza:

> The sea explodes upwards,
> Relapsing, to slaver
> Off landing-stage steps-

Waves rise and fall and in this process "they slaver/ Off landing- steps" at the port. The word "slaver" is significant. The saliva running from the mouth of the waves wet the dirty landing-stage steps and cleanse them of the dirt on them. The sea washes clean all the dirt and filth that we may cause to be heaped up. On the fringes of the falling waves or ebbs suds are running. The lighthouse-keeper apostrophizes them thus: "Running suds, rejoice!" Geoffrey Leech says that an apostrophe is used as "the kind of dramatic licence whereby words are addressed to someone who is unable to hear them or reply to them." Further, he says: "In direct address we can express our attitude to a person or thing with great subtlety, and this is perhaps the chief advantage of apostrophe for the poet."[5]

The poet, in addressing the suds, expresses his attitude with great subtlety. We shall see what this subtlety amounts to. There are more apostrophes in this poem. As the waves fall or recede, "Rocks" on the shore "writhe back to sight" and

Mussels, limpets,
Husband their tenacity
In the freezing slither-

The poet attributes animate sensation "writhe" to the rocks with a purpose. Then the creatures like mussels and limpets, lowly creatures though they are, cultivate their tenacity which enables them to hold on to the rocks even in adverse circumstances when the "freezing slither" of the tides strikes them with great force. They do not lose their hold. The life force working in them, though in an attenuated form compared with the same force working in the humans, keeps them going in very difficult situations because this force has not been weakened in them by any perversity as it has been in us by our various perversities. That is why the lighthouse- keeper- poet apostrophizes them and says: "Creatures, I cherish you!" One may venture a guess here and say that Larkin is officiating for the lighthouse -keeper so that the poem acquires a unique kind of atmosphere and wraps itself in it.

During the day the sea looks like "the salt/ Unsown stirring fields," over which the "sky builds/ grape-dark" canopy. The sky and the sea create, or rather re-create, a world which existed on our earth when life began on it. In this world there is, however, an intrusion—that of a radio set that the lighthouse-keeper has. But the radio, rubbing its legs, looks like, or so it seems to the poet, a beetle or some such sea creature. When such a creature, by its very nature, rubs its legs while flying, a droning sound is produced and the radio, "Telling" the lighthouse-keeper "of elsewhere," produces the sound that to the creatures of this world and in the atmosphere of this world means nothing more than droning. Here we are in a world in which the present-day world of ours, as presented in the first and third poems of the triptych, is completely alien and the radio bringing to the keeper news of this world tells him of "elsewhere," the elsewhere that did not exist in the geological eras before the advent of man. In those eras the oceans and the seas had not been sown with inequities by the boats and ships built by man. And of what does this redio-beetle tells the lighthouse-keeper? It tells him of

Barometers falling ,
Ports wind-shuttered,

Fleets pent like hounds,
Fires in humped inns
Kippering sea-pictures—

The man is annoyed at the trivialities purveyed by the radio. The weather report tells the lighthouse keeper: barometers are falling; ports are shuttered by the wind; fleets are pent in the harbor like hounds in their kennel; and humped inns are keeping sea-pictures on their warm walls. But the normal activities of man now, as we saw in "Livings I" and will soon see in "Livings III,' as well as in this poem itself, are completely entangled in trivialities in all walks of life. So he shouts: "Keep it all [the banal babbling of the radio set] off!" Again it is an apostrophe, but this time it is shouted at the radio set. And this apostrophe is different from the two earlier ones. The first, addressed to the running suds, told them to rejoice. In the second, the lighthouse- keeper told such very primitive sea-creatures as mussels and limpets that he cherished them for cultivating their tenacity to survive in "freezing slither." So we see that the three apostrophes work very subtly and are integral to the meaning of the poem.

And after dismissing the radio set and the "elsewhere," he brings us back to his adopted world, the sea-shore from where he watches approvingly activities of a different sort of life. Now it is night. He says, "By night, snow swerves…/ Through the stare travelling / Leather- black waters." But before we pay close attention these words demand, it will be in place to say something about the parenthesis used here – "O loose moth world" – that occurs between the lines "By night…" and "Through the stare…" There is, above the surface of the sea at this place at this hour of the night, a loose world of moths. This is a world all right. It is not only man's world that is world; man must know that he is only one of the million species inhabiting the earth and insects constitute three-fourths of the total land population. Besides, more than one hundred and fifty thousand species live in the seas and oceans. But the world of moths is loose. They do not live in a close-knit social organization. Gradually, in the course of evolution, social life of animals became more and more complex resulting in close interdependence and interrelatedness of individual existences. But loose or close-knit, the life of each species is a world in its own right.

Now we come to the lines "By night"—-etc. quoted in the previous paragraph: "By night snow swerves/ Through the stare—" What is this stare? It is the light that flashes from top of the lighthouse. In this "stare," huge blocks of ice, or icebergs, are seen "travelling leather-black waters." In this brilliant light, the lighthouse- keeper sets his plate and spoon and has dinner. After eating, he takes out his "divining- cards." Telling fortunes with these cards seems to be his favourite pastime. But the poet does not tell us whose fortune he divines – his own or that of mankind. Here it will be in place to quote the last sentence in Fred Hoyle's much-acclaimed book *The Nature of the Universe:* "Perhaps the most majestic feature of our whole existence is that while our intelligences are powerful enough to penetrate deeply into the evolution of this quite incredible Universe, we still have not the smallest clue to our own fate."[6]

The world of "Livings II" is at many removes, perhaps at the furthest remove, from the worlds of Livings I &III. But here, too, there are mad intrusions from such worlds. The first intrusion was from the radio set at which the lighthouse- keeper shouted: "Keep it all off!" And in the last two lines we find another intrusion, that of the "Lit shelved liners" groping "like mad worlds westward." These luxury liners used to carry pampered bourgeoisie from Europe, mainly England, to America, the land of plenty. John Wain comments on this part of the poem thus: "…the liner in the second one ["Livings II"] is obviously a thirties job, one of those mad floating palaces in which the rich and important crossed the Atlantic before the airlines destroyed them (the palaces, not the rich and important)."[7] These liners were so many mad worlds and they groped.

The words "mad" and "groped," used here, are significant and need our close attention. The world of the big bourgeoisie wallowing in all kinds of luxury is mad. And their whole life, or rather their life's activities, are nothing but gropings in a dark tunnel that their life's passage in time is. And this brings us to "Livings III."

[III]

"Livings" as plural of "living" means the way we live, but it is an unusual usage and so it attracts our notice. In "Livings I" we saw a very undistinguished businessman emotionally living a very lean life that his "lean leather-bag" symbolized, and anticipating the storm of great depression that swept across America and the countries of Europe preceding the Second World War. He felt that it was time to change the course of human affairs, but saw no way to do it, nor were the millions to be affected by the catastrophe in a position to do anything to avert it. In "Livings II," we saw both animate and inanimate forms of life acting with force, energy and tenacity in adverse conditions. This way of living was at the furthest remove from the so-called civilized life of man.

In "Livings III," we find ourselves once again in the civilized world, but a somewhat unfamiliar world. We are taken back in time (in the mid-eighteenth century) to the academic world of Oxford or Cambridge. This world should symbolize the intellectual height attained by a particular civilization. But it tells us a different story. The Dons of a particular college are having dinner. The Master is away. One of the Dons – he seems to be the speaker here – says, "Nocturnal vapours do not please." These words, put within brackets and forming a whole line appear puzzling. Is the Master the nocturnal vapours and, if so, does it mean that he, or rather his ideas, like the vapours at night, obfuscate realities? Whatever be the case, the Dons feel more at ease in the absence of the Master. The port goes round faster than it does when the Master is present and topics of small talk are raised with greater ease. And what are the topics? Firstly, they discuss which advowson, that is, a vacant benefice, is the fairest and who, after taking his degree, will adorn it. Then they talk about the money the sale of wood at Snape will fetch. There is perhaps a forest at Snape, with trees of commercial value, that belongs to the college. Then they discuss the names for the sexual organs that are on the outside of a woman's body. They also discuss why Judas looks like Jack Ketch, the common executioner of the seventeenth century whose barbarity at the execution of political offenders was terrifying.

In the second stanza, the trivialities of the Dons' dinnertime talk are momentarily kept in abeyance to give us a glimpse of the setting of the poem, that is, the dining-hall. The candlelights first grow thin, then broaden. Their butler, appropriately named 'Starveling', piles logs at the fireplace and sets, just behind the screen, jordan, that is, chamber-pot so that the Dons may piss into it with greater convenience than taking the trouble of going to the bogs for the purpose.

Once again our attention is focused on the Dons. They have drunk so much that both their temper and complexion are heated. And so, the poet tells us, "Oath-enforced assertions fly." But what are the subjects that oath-enforced assertions are related to? Not some serious academic/ intellectual/ philosophical/ socio-economic issues. The heated and oath-enforced discussions are about (a) rheumy fevers (b) resurrection (c) regicide (d) rabbit pie and suchlike.

What a falling down on the part of the leaders of the intellectual world supposed to be concerned about the challenges facing human civilization and showing man the path leading to a better future! But they were never, in the whole course of their academic career, whether at school or college/ university, taught to serve society as "kindly light" in which people could see the truth of things, re-organize their life and re-orient their thinking. Had it happened, the world would have become a better place. But the world of the businessman in the first of the triptych and that of the Dons here are, qualitatively speaking, more or less the same and their livings or ways of life are foregrounded on the settings symbolizing the world of their life. The setting of "Livings III" is described in the third and final stanza.

The fields around the college are cold and muddy; the cobbled streets close by the college are still in the cold evening. No light of intellect and wisdom radiates from the college. A sizar, a poor undergraduate receiving financial assistance from the college and required to do certain menial duties as part of his upkeep, is shivering with cold at his studies. He does not have the luxury of a fireplace which the Dons, while guzzling food and swilling drinks, have. Then we see a kitchen cat making a kill. The kitchen obviously is infested with rats. The college bells, regularly chiming, discuss time's "gradations" (a beautiful word both denoting and connoting the time expended or wasted). And, in keeping with the ambience of futility, wastage and reprehensible ("oath-enforced") assertions, we find "prayers and proofs" on dusty shelves. Even those who profess faith in religion pay scant regard to it.

After the phrase "prayers and proofs" in the sixth line of the last stanza, there is a colon, which is followed by the last two lines that run thus and close the poem:

> Above, Chaldean constellations
> Sparkle over crowded roofs.

The New Caxton Encyclopedia tells us this about the Chaldeans:

> Inhabitants of an ancient land called Chaldea, whose boundaries cannot be exactly defined. Biblical and Greek writers referred to the whole of Babylonia as Chaldea, but it was originally only the southern and south-western parts, espe-

cially between the mouths of the rivers Tigris and Euphrates, which then flowed separately into the sea. The city of Ur, 'Ur of the Chaldees' in the Bible was the home town of Abraham. The inhabitants of Chaldea were one of the Semitic people of the region. Biblical and classical writers also used the word 'Chaldea' to apply to astrologers and magicians, probably because most of the priests and 'wise men' of Babylonia came from Chaldea.[8]

It was the Chaldeans who, more than three thousand years ago, discovered the constellations referred to by Larkin. In Thomas Mann's classic, *The Magic Mountain*, we get some interesting information about the "magnificent" astrological/astronomical discoveries made by them. Hans Castorp, the hero of the novel, while talking to his cousin, gives him this information:

Why, you know what the zodiac is – the primitive heavenly signs: Scorpio, Sagittarius, Capricorn, Aquarius, and the rest. How can you help being interested in them?....They were known to the Chaldeans too...those Arabic-Semitic necromancers, who were so well-versed in astrology and soothsaying. They knew and studied the zone in the heavens through which the planets revolve; and they divided it into twelve signs by constellations, the *dodecatemoria*, just as they have been handed down to us. Magnificent, isn't it? There's humanity for you!....

....
I like to think about the Chaldeans when I lie and look at the planets they were familiar with– for, clever as they were, they did not know them all. But the ones they did not know I cannot see either. Uranus was only recently discovered by means of the telescope – a hundred and twenty years ago.... ... ...
I call it recently...in comparison with the three thousand years since their time. But when I lie and look at the planets, even the three thousand years get to seem 'recently,' and I begin to think quite intimately of the Chaldeans, and how in their time they gazed at the stars and made verses on them – and that is humanity too.[9]

The reference to the Chaldeans in the last two lines of the poem is very significant. These semi-nomadic people, without the benefit of modern university education and without telescopes, observatories and equipment required for astronomical discoveries did something significant, on which Thomas Mann's hero rightly comments: "There's humanity for you!"

On the contrary, our Dons at the dining-table here seem to be degenerate samples of humanity. The dining room seems to be a place of darkness, while the Chaldean constellations sparkle over the crowded roofs of the colleges.

Now the question that arises is: Do the three "Livings" that seem to be separate poems form a single whole? The answer should be that they constitute a whole. In "Livings I" we saw two different worlds. First we saw the world of trade and commerce in which we saw unease in the talk of the inmates of a hotel and a sense of premonition of the imminent catastrophe the young businessman had while lying on his bed in the hotel room. The other world is only glimpsed in the image of the golden sky draining down the estuary and making the river bed golden. The catastrophe overwhelmed the world of human affairs whereas the world of elements maintained its calm beauty. The catastrophe happened because the edifice of trade and commerce has its foundation in greeds and lies.

In "Livings III," Larkin went more than two hundred years back in time when he wrote it and took us into the dining room of a real university college of England, it does not matter whether it was Oxford or Cambrige. We found a very unflattering picture of the dons there while the Chaldean constellations sparkled over the crowded roofs of the university buildings. The constellations have sparkled for billions of years, since much before man came into existence, and will continue to sparkle long after man has ceased to exist, which, judging by the quality of life man has been living, may be sooner than we think.

In "Livings II" we find ourselves in a world far removed from the worlds of the poems preceding it and following it. Here we are in the world of the elements – the sea and the sky – and that of certain creatures (e.g. mussels, limpets, loose moth worlds) fostered by them. But into this world also the worlds of the other two poems intrudes. The lighthouse-keeper tries to "keep off" the broadcast of the beetle-like radio set from this world but cannot do anything about the intrusion of the 'Lit shelved liners" that "Grope like mad worlds westward."

The last two lines in each poem provide the spinal cord of thought to the poem.

"FORGET WHAT DID"

The title of the poem "Forget What Did," like that of "Sympathy in White Major," at first sight appears puzzling. But Prof. James Booth in an email told me about the source of this title. He wrote: "In Chapter 2 of Susan Coolidge's girls' classic *What Katy Did* the sisters read the diary of their 'pale, pudgy' six-year-old brother, Dorry, and find, alongside entries like 'played, or Had rost befe for diner, and cabage, and potato', several which read simply 'Forgit what did.' Larkin chose the title of his poem well and we will soon see in this coice the genius of the poet.

The persona suddenly decided to stop the diary. This sudden decision "Was a stun to memory," that is, it stunned his memory. Here the use of the verb "stun" as a noun is important in that it catches our attention and makes us think what the line in which the word occurs actually means. The next line – "Was a blank starting" – is also puzzling. What can the phrase "blank starting" possibly mean? The next stanza, quoted below, further complicates the matter:

> One no longer cicatrized
> By such words, such actions
> As bleakened waking.

"Cicatrized," used here as a transitive verb, does not seem to have an object and so we ask: cicatrized what? Then one can ask, do "such words, such actions" refer to "bleakened waking"? Then we find the adjective "bleak" used as an adjectival participle, which should mean that the waking in the persona is bleakened, that is, it has become or been bleak. Then the verb "cicatrize" presents another problem. The dictionary meaning of "cicatrize" is "heal by scar formation." What was the wound that could no longer be healed? So we find that the first two stanzas of the poem present several lexical and syntactic as well as semantic problems.

But these problems arose because of the matters related to the persona's sudden decision to stop the diary. Here it will be in place to have a look at the syntactic structure of the poem. The poem is divided into six stanzas comprising three sentences. The first two stanzas form a unit of one sentence, the next two together make the second sentence and the last two stanzas make the third sentence. So the poem consists of three units, each unit a sentence covering two stanzas. We shall try to interpret it unit-wise.

In the first unit, the persona says that "stopping the diary" stunned the memory simply because memory, the store-house of happenings, was used to be recorded regularly in the diary. These happenings are, with most of us, related to our ordinary, everyday, routine life. W. H. Auden, in a short poem entitled "Short Ode to the Cuckoo," says, "in my diary,/ ...I normally enter nothing but social/ engagements and, lately, the death of friends." But he records once in a year something holy too when he hears the song of the cuckoo although, "Compared with arias by the great performers/ such as the merle," her song (a "two-note act") "is kid-stuff." Auden writes, "I /scribble year after year when I first hear you,/ of a holy moment."[1] But what we usually write in our diaries have nothing to do with matters of tremendous significance, with the meaning, purpose and potentialities of our existence. But the stopping of the diary was also, the persona says, "a blank starting." How can a starting be blank? Simply put, there was a blank after the diary stopped. Perhaps something could happen later that might be called a starting. Then what the persona says in the second stanza, which is part of the same sentence which began the poem, can be understood as " By such words, such actions/ As bleakened waking" a man "no longer cicatrized." The persona after using "cicatrized" as a transitive verb, intentionally leaves it hanging in the air without its object. But the verb here naturally refers to some wound that cannot be healed by the words and actions of "bleakened waking." Now the word "bleak" has several meanings. *The Concise Oxford English Dictionary* gives the following meanings of the word "bleak:"

Adj. 1. bare and exposed to the elements: a bleak moor – charmless and inhospitable, dreary. (of the weather) cold and miserable. 2 (of a situation) not hopeful or encouraging.

So "bleakened" can mean made "dreary," "charmless." "cold and miserable" "not hopeful or encouraging" and so this kind of waking is woefully inadequate to heal the wound although, even when the wound is healed, the scar will remain to remind the bearer of the wound that was. The meaning of "a blank starting" and of the wound that cannot be cicatrized will be clearer in the last section (the last two stanzas) of the poem. In the meantime we will struggle with the middle section (the third and fourth stanzas) which comprises the second sentence.

The first line of the third stanza is "I wanted them over," which means that the persona wanted the words and actions of "bleakened waking," which used to get recorded in his diary, to be over and done with. The next two lines in this stanza are : "Hurried to burial/ And looked back on." Not only did the persona want the words and actions of bleakened waking to be over, but he also wanted them to be hurriedly buried and looked back on as he moved forward in the direction in which he could have real awakening. But how did he want the past (words and actions of bleakened waking) to be looked back on? He tells us this in the fourth stanza:

> Like the wars and winters
> Missing behind the windows
> Of an opaque childhood.

For a grown up man the windows of childhood become opaque. The horrifying perceptions of wars and experiences of cold, freezing winters one may have had in his childhood disappear behind these windows. The words "wars" and "winters" and "the windows/ Of an opaque childhood" are beautiful metaphors. "Wars" stands for all kinds of discords in human society; sometimes they erupt, volcano-like, into wars. "Winters" stands for hate that we the grown-ups are, more often than not, afflicted with. Children are the worst victims of these discords and this hate. They have traumatic experiences of discords and hate. But as they enter adolescence these traumatic experiences go missing behind the windows of opaque childhood. In the very beginning of adolescence new windows begin to open one after another. These windows open on larger and larger vistas which reveal to the cognitive self of the adolescent perspectives on life that can help him to understand the world around him and his own self in the world. But many, or rather most, of us do not bother to make use of these high windows and live a life of imprecisions and ignorance and finally die "old fools." Many of us write diaries which contain only records of experiences that are mere husks of experiences of a transcendental kind which should guide our life. But these husks form the habits that control our lives and these habits in course of time harden so much in us that we are never able to separate the chaff from the wheat. Larkin refers to this kind of hardening in "Dockery and Son." He says that these habits later become "all we've got," but, "looked back on, they rear/ Like sand-clouds, thick and close." The persona in this poem was in such sand-clouds when he decided to stop the diary. This was, however, a very crucial decision and so the stopping of the diary, besides being a stun to the memory, was a "blank starting" inasmuch as the persona did not know in the beginning what to do with the blank that followed the decision. It is very hard to break with habits that become *all we've got* and form new habits that can help us to perceive things as they really are. This is not only so with individuals but with a whole way of life – a way of life in which people are never allowed a chance to see the deeper and higher levels of things and phenomena and not allowed to let these levels shape and guide their way of life. So a stage in human culture, that is, in "the customs, ideas, and social behavior of a people or group" (dictionary meaning of the word "culture") is reached when any qualitative change in it seems impossible to bring about. This is the central theme of Harold Pinter's masterpiece *No Man's Land*.

But the persona in Philip Larkin's poem did finally take a decision. And this brings us to the last section of the poem comprising stanzas five and six. But before looking over these stanzas, which constitute or form the spinal cord of the poem, it is necessary to point out that the diary in the poem is a metaphor of profound significance. The diary here is the mind or consciousness of the persona. For a long time, well beyond adolescence, we can be sure, only commonplaces or husks of the life-sustaining grains of realities had been stored in the persona's consciousness. And that inflicted a wound therein. The persona realized that this wound would not cicatrize by the words and actions of bleakened waking. So the decision to stop the diary, that is, not to allow the chaff and husks of realities to further deepen the wound was correct. But the decision left the persona bewildered as to what his consciousness should record then.

And so the persona asks in the first line of the fifth stanza: "And the empty pages?" Our consciousness, with many pages, is a diary. The pages should be filled out not with words and actions of bleakened waking but with the words and actions of ripeness of our fully awakened and perceptive self. The pity is that most of us are either never awake from birth to death or, at the utmost, we spend all our life in a state of bleakened waking only. It will be in place here to quote the following lines from Francois Mauriac's short story "A Man of Letters:"

We creators...belong to a minority who are awake. That is why we are afraid of ourselves. You say you are not afraid of yourself? Believe me! The majority of men are asleep. All those restless Anglo-Saxons, all those criers at the Bourse, in Parliament – they are asleep, old boy! The dope of business is as good as the dope of politics. It is terrible to be for ever awake, incapable of sleep, attentive and lucid by profession.[2]

Therefore, the persona says:
Should they ever be filled
Let it be with observed

Celestial recurrences,
The day the flowers come,
And when the birds go.

We know that the modal "should," like any other modal, has a number of meanings. The meaning of "should" here is *formal real condition*, "referring to a possible event or situation" (COED). It is possible that the pages of the diary-cum- consciousness of the persona will be filled. But his condition is that if they are ever filled, they will be filled with the following "observed" phenomena: "Celestial recurrences/ The day the flowers come/ And when the birds go." First, the celestial recurrences. Now what are these cosmic phenomena that occur again and again? Obviously, the coming into existence, and dying out, of the stars; the occurrences of the supernovae; formation of black holes and similar singularities in cosmos. These celestial recurrences will first be observed and then recorded in the diary of the persona's consciousness. But the recording of the "observed celestial recurrences" will cover only some, not all, pages of the consciousness. Some further pages will contain the record of the march of evolution of organic-biological life on the earth, reaching a point when plants, the first form of life on our planet, gave birth to angiosperms, that is, plants of a large group that started bearing flowers. The persona will observe flowers come to bloom on the stems of plants – what metabolism in the physiology of plants pushes that energy that causes inflorescence. In an interesting passage in his book *Plant and Planet*, Anthony Huxley tells us how a flower is viewed by different kinds of people:

To the average human eye the flower, however ephemeral, is an object to be cultivated for decorative purposes, in garden or vase, or to cause admiration, amazement and occasionally revulsion when seen in the wild. To the taxonomist, it is the means of establishing the plant's classificatory status and its affinities in the vegetable kingdom. To the enquiring mind, every flower, however insignificant, has, if examined carefully, intricacy, ingenuity and unity of purpose which create a beauty and interest of their own."[3]

Philip Larkin has the enquiring mind of, if one may say so, the philosopher of science. He will observe the entire process of transformation of energy into flowers and record this observation on the pages of his consciousness. This is not a romantic longing, but an imperative need. Milton, in *Paradise Lost*, tells us about the value of flower in the structure of a plant in the following lines:

From the root
Springs lighter the green stalk, from thence the leaves
More airy, last the bright consummate flower
Spirits odorous breathe. (Book V. ll479-482).

Just as the "consummate flower" has odorous spirit that breathes delicate, soul-suffusing fragrance, man's consciousness emanating from his unbelievably complex organic structure is a kind of light that illumines his own being as well as vast expanses of space and time. The study of the flower as the consummation of a plant's existence will help Larkin to understand the nature of human consciousness because this consciousness is the efflorescence of his existence. No less a person than Buddha said that consciousness has its basis in matter. We quote his very words on this point:

" 'Consciousness may exist having matter as its means (rupupayam), matter as its object (ruparammanam), matter as its support (rupatatittam), and seeking delight it may grow, increase and develop, or consciousness may exist having sensation as its means...or perception as its means...or mental formations as its means, mental formations as its object, mental formations as its support, and seeking delight it may grow, increase and develop.

" 'Were a man to say: I shall show the coming, the going, the passing away, the arising, the growth, the increase or the development of consciousness apart from matter, sensation, perception and mental formations, he would be speaking of something that does not exist.' " [4]

Then the consciousness will observe and then record the mystery of death. When an animal life-form – be it any animal or man – dies, disintegration of the organic structure that the man or the animal was takes place. The incredibly complex structure in which the constituent parts, beginning with cells and ending with tissues, co-operate with each other in various groups and also live their individual lives incessantly throughout the life-span of that structure, falls apart and the whole structure disintegrates and this is death. The persona's consciousness will observe the entire process of this disintegration and record it on its pages. Thus the blank pages of the diary will be filled .

William Faulkner, in his novel *The Town*, tells us that poets "are not really interested in facts: only in truth: which is why the truth they speak is so true that even those who hate poets by simple natural instinct are exalted and terrified by it."[5] The present poem is a typical example of a poet interested in the truth of things and the truth the poet speaks of is so true that we are exalted by it. This truth is the imperative need of our culture today. Sir Charles Sherrington, lauding the historian for what he has been doing with human civilization, wants the natural history to be similarly written and interpreted. In an impassioned passage in his *Man on his Nature*, he writes:

He[the historian] has much enlightened us. Histories of kings, of cities, of countries, of this political movement or that, of philosophies, and of the chequered records of peoples and their leaders. Sometimes he has taken a whole continent's story of civilization....But there is yet this other theme at once comprehensive and intimate. The history of our planet, all that it comprises and has done and made. It asks to be written, so that all read our planet's becoming which contains our own. It asks to be undertaken, after the same manner as was undertaken not so many centuries back the myth of the nine-fold heavens and of man's life at the fixed centre, set forth so that all pious Christendom could hear. This story of our planet in its newer light to be a frame to set our lives against and within it is a story not remote from us because it is our own. The planet in travail with its children. With the

Universe as heroic background for what to us is an intimate and heroic epic (MohN, pp.252-253).

And now we ask: What exactly is the title of this poem? Our answer should be: "Forget What (Bleakened Waking) Did." When Larkin stopped his diary, he was no better than the six-year-old Dorry, a pale, pudgy boy. Fortunately, however, he realized that his poetic self was destined to do something of value for mankind and so he bade farewell to his bleakened waking before it could do irreparable damage to his consciousness, which is the acme of our being.

High Windows

"High Windows" appears an easy poem, the language of the first four stanzas – all quatrains – is commonplace and the theme is all-too-familiar permissiveness of the present generation of boys and girls. But in the fifth and final quatrain, the poem attains an altogether new intensity and sublimity of both language and thought. This intensity and sublimity – they are not of romantic kind – constitute the spinal cord of thought of the poem.

Barbara Everett shows the poem's French connections in Mallarme and Baudelaire although, she rightly observes, it is a completely English poem and the poet's own creation. But the connections are interesting. Quoting the last two lines of the poem – "And beyond it, the deep blue air that shows/ Nothing, and is nowhere, and is endless" – Ms Everett writes:

> The radiant colour and the 'nothingness' are too Mallarmean to be only coincidentally similar. *L'azur* (the blue) is Mallarme's most consistent and philosophical symbol delineating both the necessity and absence of the ideal, an ideal which we imprint on the void sky by the intensity of our longing; his poetry is full of *'De l'eternal azur le sereine ironie* (the calm irony of the endless blue). The poem of Mallarme in which the image becomes most definitive is *'Les Fenetres'* (the Windows), which compares the state of the poet, sickened by existence and enduring the perpetual life-giving suffering of an always despairing and then re-purified idealism, to that of an old man dying in a dreary hospital, his face wistfully pressed to the windows, longing for the blue sky outside.[1]

Ms Everett goes on to say that Mallarme's *Les Fenetres* is "dependent on two superb prose-poems by Baudelaire," one of which has the same title as Mallarme's poem. However, Ms Everett rightly points out that "'High Windows' is not the same as 'The Windows' in Mallarme and Baudelaire" and that Larkin, by making the windows "High gives them a certain metaphysical or even ecclesiastical status..." She also says that " 'High Windows' is 'Les Fenetres' Englished and brought up to date."[2]

Larkin seems to have borrowed only the title of Mallarme's and Baudelaire's poems for writing an altogether different poem. His poem begins with a glimpse of the human condition brought up to date in England. It opens "modishly" with a "violent, random flatness" and "with a savage irony":

> When I see a couple of kids
> And guess he's fucking her and she's
> Taking pills or wearing a diaphragm
> I know this is paradise.

This is not paradise. It is a humanscape on which most sacred of human passions – the passion to procreate and gradually raise the qualitative level of human existence as a species – has been completely degraded. An instance of this degradation can be cited from William Golding's novel *Darkness Visible*. Sophy, a virgin who comes of an educated and sophisticated family, has her first sexual encounter with a van driver whom she picks at random. She finds him quite competent in performing his part of the sexual act because "He hurt her more than she had thought possible." After finishing his part, the driver pulls out, wipes himself, zips his trousers and looks down at her with triumph and says, " 'You were a virgin. Well. You aren't, now. I've had you, see?" Sophy takes out the tissues she has brought with her and wipes a treacle of blood from her thigh. The man says "in high humour and to no man in particular 'Had a virgin!.'"[3] Sophy looks curiously at the man, who is "now evidently delighted with life," and the following dialogue takes place between them, beginning with Sophy's question:

> " 'Is that all?'
> "What d'you mean?"
> "Sex. Fucking."
> "Christ. What did you expect?' "[4]

And as she is going back home, her thought on her first sex-experience runs thus:

> She was still in the grip of her astonishment at it meaning so little. It was so trivial an act when you subtracted the necessary and not-to- be repeated pain. of the first time. It meant nothing at all. There was little more sensation to it than feeling the inside of your cheek with your tongue – well, there was a little more but not much.[5]

And first thing she does when she reaches home is go to the bathroom and wash herself out as she is "faintly repelled by the mess of blood and spunk." And as she is at it, she has the disgusting and nauseating feeling of her own turd entering her womb where a little while before the penis of the van driver had entered: "...and she came on the other shape, lying opposite the womb but at the back, a shape lying behind the smooth wall but easily to be felt through it, the rounded shape of her own turd working down the coiled gut and she convulsed, feeling without saying but saying every syllable – I hate, I hate I hate!"[6]

Both "High Windows" and *Darkness Visible* were written in the seventies of the 20th century – in 1974 and 1979 respectively. In the early years of that century, D. H. Lawrence, while writing *Sons and Lovers*, could describe love-making consummating in sex-experience in terms of the supreme awareness of life-force manifesting itself in the eyes of the lovers, in the upward "thrust of manifold grass-stems, in the cry of pewits, and the wheel of the stars." Lawrence writes about this supreme awareness of Paul Morel at the moment of his and Clara's experience of consummation:

> All the while the pewits were screaming in the field. When he came to he wondered what was near his eyes, curving and strong with life in the dark, and what voice was speaking. Then he realized it was the grass, and the peewit was calling. The warmth was Clara's breathing heaving. He lifted his head and looked into her eyes. They were dark and shining and strange, life wild at the source staring into his life, stranger to him, yet meeting him; and he put his face down on her throat, afraid. What was she? A strong, strange, wild

life that breathed with his in the darkness through hour. It was so much bigger than themselves that he was hushed. They had met, and included in his meeting the thrust of the manifold grass-stems, the cry of the peewit, the wheel of the stars.[7]

Philip Larkin's kids – the fucking and diaphragm- wearing kids – belong to the same category to which the van driver and Sophy belonged. He says that life for these kids is paradise, the same paradise that everyone old have dreamed all their lives. These kids are not condemned, they are living out the fantasy of their fathers and mothers and of their grandparents as well. In their fantasy their progenitors had desired "pushing aside all bonds and gestures as an outdated combine harvester." What are "bonds" and "gestures"? Bonds means "force or feeling, that unites people." The love of the kind Lawrence speaks of in the passage quoted above establishes or should establish very deep and sacred bond between two souls based in mutually- shared pure feeling of life's livingness and beauty. "Gesture" is an action performed to convey one's feelings. Pushing aside all bonds and gestures, everyone young is now sliding down to endless happiness, Larkin says with a most damning irony. Our kids are not sliding down themselves but also desecrating the most sacred and exalted human bonds and gestures.

High Windows was published in 1974 when Philip Larkin was fifty-two years old. Forty years before that he must have been twelve. He wonders whether when he was approaching his teens, anyone, looking at him, had thought that for him as well as for boys and girls of his generation it would be a wonderful life without there being God or without "sweating in the dark/ About hell and that," or "having to hide" what one thought of the priest. In short, there would be no restraint on permissiveness simply because these restraints would have lost their credibility. Naturally, without these restraints and in the absence of any alternative faith, pursuit of pleasures becomes the sole passion (and also the soul-passion) of man. But, as Henry James tells us in his novel *The Europeans*, "in pleasure there are tremendous distinctions."[8] At one extreme there is the pig's pleasure of feeding on filth and garbage, at the other end there is pleasure embedded in the transcendental awarenesses of the prophets, creative artists, genuine philosophers and so on. In between, there are other distinctions. Aesthetic pleasure, pleasure inhering in ethical values and altruism, pleasure inhering in pursuit and acquisition of knowledge are among the pleasures that elevate and ennoble man. On the other hand, pleasures derived from fulfillment of bodily appetites (that is, sensual pleasure), love of adornment, acquisitiveness, personal vanity, pride of wealth and so on are those that hinder our spiritual growth and debase us. The kind of pleasure that our fucking and getting-fucked kids enjoy is, as William Golding says, "part of the whole running down" and is symptomatic of Entropy in human culture. In order to arrest this "running down" or "long slide" we have to perceive what Philip Larkin's high windows open on: "the deep blue air, that shows/ Nothing, and is nowhere, and is endless."

Today scientists – physicists and astro-physicists – have to say a lot about this "Nothing...nowhere and endless." Some 14 billion years ago, our universe was "infinitesimally small and infinitely dense,"[9] Stephen Hawking tells us. Then this universe exploded with a big bang and, in only a tiny fraction of a second, "the radius of the universe increased by million million million million million (one with thirty zeros after it) miles."[10] In this endless universe "there are some hundred thousand million" galaxies "that can be seen with modern telescopes, each galaxy containing some hundred thousand million stars." [11] As far as our galaxy – the Milky Way – is concerned, it is "about one hundred thousand light years across and is slowly rotating around its centre about once every several hundred millions years. Our sun is just "an ordinary, average-sized yellow star, near the inner edge of the spiral arms"[12] of the galaxy. And the wonder of wonders is that "the universe looks identical in whichever direction we look, and this would also be true if we were observing the universe from anywhere else."[13] So this universe is a "Nowhere." And in what sense is this tremendous show "Nothing"? It is Nothing because it is entirely non-human. D. H. Lawrence, in his novel *Women In Love*, writes: "Whatever the mystery that has brought forth man and the universe, it is a non-human mystery, it has its own great ends, man is not the criterion." And again in the same novel he writes: "the universe is non-human, thank God."[14]

Ms Everett's observation, referred to above, that by making his widows high Larkin gives a certain metaphysical and ecclesiastical dimension to his poem is important. Today, more than ever, man needs to know his true metaphysical and ecclesiastical bearings. But metaphysics, Sartre says, "is not a sterile discussion about abstract notions which have nothing to do with experience. It is a living effort to embrace from within the human condition in its totality."

[15]The living experience of the human condition from within can be roughly and briefly expressed in some such words as follows.

Man is made from the same stuff, that is, elementary particles-cum-waves, though mutated out of recognition, of which the universe (i.e. the galaxies, the stars, the interstellar matter) is made. As such, light , heat, energy are the guiding principles of his being. But he is also made from the same substance from which such lowly life-forms as reptiles and apes are made. G. G. Simpson, in his book *Biology and Man*, tells us that "man has slowly evolved from ape, reptile, fish, invertebrate, protist and ultimately from simple matter." [16]

So crudity, cruelty, perversity, brutality, treachery, chicanery, specious moral claims – most damaging of all, blind faith – are encoded in his D.N.A. But the ever energized and ever active elementary particles in his unbelievably complex organic structure, particularly in the cerebral cortex, are his saving grace. So alongside his many handicaps there is quite an active streak of light and wisdom in him that has enabled the species to produce some great and noble souls who have preserved human civilization and culture and also enriched it. But, to quote Sir James Frazer, "The world cannot live at the level of its great men." [17]We, men and women at the ordinary level, produce kids who are always "going down the long slide."

William James in his classic, *The Principles of Psychology*, says that man has three selves – the material, the social and the spiritual selves. These selves are composite in nature and cannot be detached from one another. The material self consists of our body, our clothes, our immediate family, our homes and our property. It is perverse to deny its existence as an organic part of our self. As regards man's social self, William James writes: "A man's social self is the recognition which he gets from his mates." He adds, "We are not only gregarious animals, liking to be in sight of our fellows, but we have an innate propensity to get ourselves noticed and noticed favourably by our kind." [18]About man's spiritual self, James writes:

> By the Spiritual Self, so far as it belongs to the Empirical Me, I mean a man's inner or subjective being, his psychic faculties or dispositions, taken concretely....These psychic dispositions are the most enduring and ultimate part of the self, that which we most verily seem to be. We take a purer self-satisfaction when we think of our ability to argue and discrim-

inate, of our moral sensibility and conscience, of our indom-
itable will, than we survey any of our other possessions.[19]

Most men allow their material self to gain an upper hand to the detriment
of his two other selves, particularly his spiritual self. The kids in Larkin's poem
are offspring of such men and women. So neither the grown-ups nor their kids
have any conception of the high windows of their spiritual self through which
they could relate themselves to the celestial phenomena and see themselves
made from the same stuff as that of the galaxies and the stars. Unless this relationship or our spiritual self is strengthened and made the foremost part of
our consciousness, "the running down" of our culture cannot be arrested. This
is a difficult task. As D. H. Lawrence says in *Lady Chatterley's Lover*, "If there's
got to be a future for humanity, there'll have to be a very big change from what
is now."[20]

The Old Fools

The world is as full of fools as a tree is full of leaves
                                                    — G. B. Shaw

The poem "The Old Fools" deserves our serious attention even though Philip
Larkin has been criticized for his alleged uncharitable attitude towards the old
people waiting for death, presumably in an Old Age Home. Perhaps the poet
is a bit harsh to them in the beginning of the poem. But we should remember
that in the poem "Ignorance" (*TWW,p*.39), Larkin tells us that we remain so
ignorant – "to know nothing, never to be sure/ Of what is true or right or real"
– throughout our life "That when we start to die/ Have no idea why." We
should keep in mind the fact that "The Old Fools" is a poem of extreme situation, giving rise to extremes of emotions. The poem appears very simple. But,
as is the case with Larkin's major poems, this simplicity is deceptive. Transcending the surface simplicity, the poem takes us into a realm of thoughts
about man's failure to understand the nature of his existence from beginning
to end along the passage of time. Senescence has set in in the organic structure
of these people on the verge of death so that "their mouth hangs open and
drools," they "keep on pissing," and "can't remember/ Who called this morn-

ing." But they cannot understand what has happened "To make them like this." So the poet angrily asks of us, "Do they somehow suppose/ It's more grown-up" when such unmistakable signs of physical and mental decay have appeared in them? The poet asks of us a second question: Could they, "if they only chose," change

> things back to when they danced all night,
> Or went to their wedding, or sloped arms all September?

They did only such things all their life, as most of us do during ours, and were never told by their teachers in school or college or by their mentors, if they had any in their social life, how from a single fertilized cell in the mother's womb the baby, when it is born, has twenty-six million million cells, and a grown up man's body is an organic structure of some 1000 billion cells, each cell living its own individual life as well as cooperating with others in a particular part of the body to form a particular organ and keep it functioning. They were never told how the various organs in our body, formed in this manner, built a cooperatives called the human body and how the metabolism going on in the body, or more precisely in the brain, gave birth to such properties as intellectual powers, consciousness, spiritual and transcendental urges, and so on. They were never told how this panoply of human existence has a very limited time-span during which all man's physical, intellectual, spiritual-transcendent powers having reached their acme, gradually start declining and the whole cooperative disintegrates, resulting in the final extinction of the individual's life for eternity. They do not know (for that matter, how many of us know ?) the difference between life and death. Sir Charles Sherrington tells us very lucidly about this difference:

> The difference is not one of ultimate nature but of scheme and degree of complexity. The atoms and sub-atoms are among Earth's commonest. 'Living' becomes a name for certain complexes of them, arrangements of which it may be said that they are organized integratively. i.e. to form a solidarity, an individual. It requires a heterogeneity which permits integration of its complex even if that latter be a single cell... .When its integrated coherence ceases, as sooner or later it will, it falls asunder into parts which are simpler and do not

form a solidarity; and that is called 'death'. And it is a mystery why, or rather how, life's moving equilibrium is not maintained longer. How, having started, it should wear out (MohN, pp. 75-76).

It is not only the old men in the poem but, exceptions apart, all of us remain fools all our life, deprived as we are of most of the truths relating to life in general on our planet, to say nothing of the truths relating to extra-terrestrial/ cosmic existence. Was Shakespeare not justified when he wrote these lines in *King Lear*:

When we are born, we cry that we are come
To this great stage of fools. (IV,vi,ll176-77).

The poet says that these old fools cannot be unaware of the change (senescence) that has taken place in their body and mind; they cannot say that they always behaved, as they do now, as "crippled and tight;" or that they used to sit through days, as they do now, "of thin continuous dreaming/ Watching light move." Their bodies are now crippled and their mind is now, more often than not, lost in thin continuous dreaming as it has lost the strength, if it ever had any, for any sort of serious thinking about life in general and human affairs in particular. Then, the poet asks, why are they not screaming at these deteriorations or decays which will soon snuff out their very existence?

In the second stanza, the poet tells us the scientific truth about how the end of man's existence, preceded by physical disintegration, is final and runs counter to the earlier non-scientific view of the re-incarnation of the soul. At death, our body, which is a unique structure of one trillion cells, breaks up and the cells start breaking loose of one another for ever, but we don't see this disintegration. The poet calls this extinction "oblivion." In the past, too, death used to be called "oblivion," but people thought that it would not be eternal but would end with the re-incarnation of the "immortal" soul. The poet expresses this idea in these lines:

It's only oblivion, true:
We had it before, but then it was going to end,
And was all the time merging with a unique endeavour
To bring to bloom the million-petalled flower
Of being here.

It was believed then that the oblivion that was death was all the time endeavouring to bring to bloom, that is , re-incarnate this million- petalled flower of life in this world. The being of man, when it is suffused with the essence of spiritual-transcendental awareness, becomes " the million-petalled flower." In other words, this being acquires a million petals of possible excellences of various kinds. In great men these possibilities are realized. But the belief that the soul will be re-incarnated with such possibilities and brought back into the world has now neither philosophical nor scientific backing or support.

So now we cannot pretend that the oblivion of death can be anything else but oblivion for ever. And the first signs of this irreversible and tragic oblivion can be seen in "the old fools" as "Not knowing how, not hearing what, the power/ Of choosing gone." This means that their being without the sweet, worthwhile kernel of the kind mentioned above, can be seen, to borrow Lucky's words in *Waiting for Godot*, to "waste and pine waste and pine" and to "shrink and dwindle."[1] This is a pathetic, in fact, a tragic condition for human consciousness to be in. Man's consciousness can be a vast panorama with exquisite profundities and sublimities illuminating cosmic phenomena rushing apart from each other with incredible speeds on the one hand and the dance of sub-atomic particles or energy-waves on the other. Erwin Schrodinger tells us that "the romance of the world that had existed many millions of years before it [the brain or mind], quite contingently, produced brains in which to look at itself" and that "conscious mind …is the stage, and the only stage on which the whole world-process takes place."[2] But the very looks of these old fools give unmistakable proof of them being dwindling, pining and shrinking: "Ash hair, toad hands, prune face dried into lines." The poet therefore asks, "How can they ignore it?"

The third stanza, with its central image of "lighted rooms" inside the head of old people, is remarkable for its poignancy of feelings. In these lighted rooms the total darkness of death has not yet enveloped their consciousness. There are still three-dimensional (not four-dimensional) rooms of light in their head. Their consciousness never had the fourth dimension of spiritual-transcendental awareness. In these lighted rooms they see now what they used to see long ago, people and their actions. Each person appears in these lighted rooms, the poet says, "Like a deep loss restored." They know these people, "yet can't quite name" them. Each of them is seen doing something exactly as what they were doing when the old fools saw them in the past. The poet says, "each looms/...from the known doors turning/ Setting down a lamp, smiling from a stair, extracting/ A book from the shelves." Sometimes they see in their dwindling and shrinking consciousness only the lighted rooms with

> chairs and a fire burning,
> The blown bush at the window, or the sun's
> Faint friendliness on the wall some lonely
> Rain-ceased midsummer evening.

We spoke above about the remarkable poignancy of feelings which this stanza seems to be steeped in. Here the poet is not at all being harsh to the old fools. They did not have the fourth dimension of human existence, but they were humans all the same and, as such, had feelings of organic nature that connected them emotionally to individuals who would appear or loom in their life at moments of particular significance. And in the beautiful lines quoted above – Philip Larkin's language enshrining poetic visions can rise to sublime heights when the occasion demands it – the setting is charged with delicate feeling. The old fools seem to be absorbed in it and are re-living, even in their dwindling and shrinking consciousness, fine experiences in their organic self that they lived a long time ago. They see, what they once saw, a bush blown at the window of the empty room, blown by the wind during a midsummer rain, and "the sun's/ Faint friendliness on the wall" in the evening when the rain had ceased. The pathetic fallacy in the expression "Faint friendliness" of the sun is exquisitely beautiful. Midsummer afternoon rain is refreshingly cool. And when the sun re-appears on the wall after the rain, its mild yet pleasant warmth gets connected in a friendly (pleasant) manner to the organic sensations of a man. The pleasantness of such scenes would seem to seep into and suffuse the organic self of these old fools. But the pity is that these people having lost almost all their organic vitality, do not now live "here and now" but "where all [such things] happened once." That is why, the poet tells us,

> they give

> An air of baffled absence, trying to be there
> Yet being here.

The old fools try to go to the long gone by days because then they experienced in their organic self such pleasurable sensations as described above. But they are actually here, so there is about them "an air of baffled absence."

But even those lighted rooms in which people appeared and actions took place long ago but had seemed to the old fools to belong to the present are now receding – "grow farther" – leaving behind only

> Incompetent cold, the constant wear and tear
> Of taken breath, and them crouching behind
> Extinction's alp, the old fools, never perceiving
> How near it is.

In place of those lighted rooms the old fools have now only incompetent cold and the constant wear and tear of taken breath in their mind or dimming consciousness. And these fools have now reached the last moments of their life and are "crouching behind/ Extinction's alp." But the pity is that they do not see, or seem to be aware of, the extinction-for-all-time that will swallow them any time now. That is why they remain quiet, otherwise they would have shrieked and screamed and acted, as Dylan Thomas asked his father to act in his poem "Do not go gentle into that good night:"

> Do not go gentle into that good night,
> Old age should burn and rave at close of day,
> Rage, rage against the dying of the light.[3]

Even Hall Summer's old cat died like a lion, defying Death:

> His look was a lion's
> Full of rage, defiance.[4]

The "peak" of "Extinction's alp" that is always visible to us wherever we go is not perceived by the old fools, to say nothing of them not being aware that it is very near them. Instead, they think that it is only "rising ground." That is, they cannot see death towering over the whole of lifescape (if one may use such a word) like a sky-high peak, telling us, wherever we are, that we cannot escape its watch over us. The state in which the old fools are is, according to the poet, "hideous inverted childhood." Naturally, they cannot say "What is dragging them back, and how it will end." They do not know whether it will come "at night," or when "the strangers come." But the poet says, "Well/ We shall find out." The poet here uses "We" which includes us all. It is a poet's task to predict such tragic moments. Philip Larkin wants us too to perform such tasks.

As is always the case with Larkin's major poems, "The Old Fools", too, has a fine metaphysical underpinning. The old fools, crouching below extinction's alp and not knowing what it is, and the physical and mental decay that has crippled them, are symbols of ignorance at the metaphysical level of their being that caught them in their very childhood and its miasma spread over and enveloped their cognitive self so that they remained fools and are going to die as such. And we, that is, most of us, are of their company. John Wain is right when he says that "the main thrust of Larkin's poetry is towards an increase of consciousness."[5]

The Card- Players

The analysis of this bizarre poem may follow a reference to a remarkable passage in Julian Huxley's book *Religion Without Revelation*, the passage in which Huxley views with scientific and philosophical accuracy and profundity the phenomenon that man is. He says that "each of our individual lives is unique, in a real sense ultimate, and reaches out to touch infinite heights and depths." In the next two paragraphs he elaborates on what he says in these lines. The two paragraphs are quoted below even at the risk of inviting objection to such a lengthy quotation:

> No one will turn his eyes upon himself and his own being and contemplate the spectacle in a spirit of detachment from practical details of everyday, so far as *sub specie aeternitasis*, but will come to feel something of reverence at what we may call the miracle of the mere existence of such an organization of material and mental qualities. If he has had some scientific training, his sense of wonder will be increased. This *man* is a small block of the general substance of which the universe is formed, just as is a stone, or a stream or a piece of bread. Not only, however, does it share with all other portions of substance which we call alive the power of maintaining its form and character in the midst of continual change, continually

building into itself new raw material of substance of less organized forms, and utilizing as the source of its own vital energy the breaking-down of other substance which it then discards; not only does it possess in common with them the power of reproduction, based in the amazing architecture of self-reproducing units which genetics has recently discovered in the chromosomes; but it has come to possess, as the result of many millions of generations of natural evolution, as the result of automatic forces working to preserve what from the point of utility is best worth having in the struggle of existence, the most surprising qualities. This piece of world-stuff possesses not only form and movement, but the capacity for knowing about other parts of the world, even stars a thousand light years off, events ten million years ago. It possesses the capacity for will, and with will and knowledge working together has learnt to control in notable degree both outer nature and its own nature. In some ways most extraordinary of all, it possesses the capacity for feeling, and for feeling in such a way that before some emotions all practical considerations fall away as unimportant; through feeling, this sentient portion of the world-continuum may be exalted to states which have value higher than anything else in the same world-continuum, and are often regarded as having absolute value.

Here is a mass of a few kilograms, of substance that is indivisible one (both its matter and spirit) by nature and by origin, with the rest of the universe, which can weigh the sun and measure light's speed, which can harness the tides and organize the electric forces of matter to its profit, which is not content with huts and shelters, but must build Chartres or the Parthenon; which can transform sexual desire into the love of a Dante for his Beatrice; which can not only be raised to ineffable heights at the sight of natural beauty or find "thoughts too deep for tears" in a common flower, but can create new countries or even heavens of its own, through music, poetry and art, to which it may be translated, albeit temporarily, from this practical world; which is never content with the actual, and lives by not bread alone; which is not only surmounting what it thought were the limitations of its nature, but, in individual and social development alike, transcending its own nature and emerging in newness of achievement.[1]

The above passage presents an ideal picture of man and his capabilities. It is true that man has been true to his salt in attaining great heights in the fields mentioned by Huxley and is capable of attaining greater heights in these and many more fields of knowledge. Unfortunately, however, it is only an infinitesimal minority of the human species that have done the species proud. Vast, overwhelmingly vast majority of men have lived, as Philip Larkin expresses it in a great simile, a life as vague as that of weeds. Julian Huxley, in his book *The Uniqueness of Man*, speaks of the "enormous range of individual variation in human minds" and writes: "The difference between a somewhat subnormal member of a savage tribe and a Beethoven or a Newton is assuredly comparable in extent with that between a sponge and a higher mammal."[2] The characters in "The Card-Players," who are an abomination of human existence, will perhaps rank even below a sponge because a sponge is used to make something, whereas these rotten characters are, even in their lifetime, nothing but lumps of carrion. There are four of them, three of whom are named: Jan van Hogspeuw (hogsvomit), Dirk Dogstoerd (dogsturd) and Old Prijck (Old Penis). The fourth card-player is not named, but he is no better. We are told what he does: behind the sleeping Old Prijck, he

> drinks ale,
> And opens mussels, and croaks scraps of songs
> Towards the ham-hung rafters about love.

Love is desecrated and made abominable in and through the scraps of songs that are croaked by him as if he were a frog singing them in its deep hoarse voice.

Now we will have a look at the setting of the poem and then see what the three characters, that is, hogspew, dogsturd and old prick do in their cave-like dwelling – the poet calls it "This lamp-lit cave." We know that not very long in the past our ancestors lived in caves amidst deplorable surroundings. The surroundings here are vividly painted by the poet. It is impenetrably dark outside the cave and "the rain /Courses in cart ruts down the deep mud lane." Immediately thereafter, the poet shows us what is happening "Inside." We shall enter the cave by and by after we have dealt with the outside. In lines 10-12, the description of the outside resumes. We are told:

Wet century-wide trees
Clash in surrounding starlessness above

This lamplit cave.

Two expressions here, "century-wide trees" and "starlessness," are unusual usage ; naturally, they require our close attention. Century-wide trees can mean trees whose life has spanned as wide a period as a century. Also it can mean that in the course of their long existence the trees have flourished and they now look as very wide umbrellas made of stems, branches, twigs and leaves. The degenerate human quartet in the cave, on the other hand, are already decayed and will soon become odious as ordure in their ignoble death. Then the surroundings of the cave-like dwelling are impenetrably dark, both literally and symbolically. This darkness is foregrounded in the starlessness of the night. It is in this context of the darkness outside that the dim figures with their befuddled and befouled consciousness are seen stirring inside. And what do they do?

The hogspew fellow "staggers to the door/ And pisses at the dark." He does this as if he were challenging the darkness to do its damnedest to the inner darkness coursing through his arteries, veins and nerves, or he may be telling us that the essence of his being is as hellishly dark as the darkness outside. Then we see the dogsturd chap pouring himself some more wine and then holding "a cinder to his clay with tongs,/ Belching out smoke." The expression "belching out smoke" has an ominous ring about it. The insinuation is that this fellow is a chimney from which quantities of smoke are belched out when he smokes. Old prick is snoring "with the gale" and "His skull face" is firelit. Outside, a strong wind is blowing; inside the cave snoring seems to be keeping time with the gale in the ominous darkness. What is very disturbing is that he has a skull face. The face is the book in which we read a man. If it is no better than a skull then we can only say that the man is dead qua man. The dogsturd fellow deals the cards. The hogspew chap, who pissed at the dark, "turns back and farts,/ Gobs at the grate, and hits the queen of hearts."

Here we are put in mind of the four card-players playing cards in a café In Jean-Paul Sartre's novel *Nausea*. They are described thus:

I make a great effort and turn my head. There are four of them. She bends over a red-faced old man with a pair of black-rimmed pince-nez on the end of his nose. He hides his cards against his chest and glances at me from under his glasses....smiles. His teeth are rotten. The red hand doesn't belong to him, it belongs to his neighbor, a fellow with a black moustache. This fellow with the moustache has huge nostrils which could pump air for a whole family and which eat up half his face, but in spite of that he breathes through his mouth, panting slightly. With them there is also a young man with a face like a dog. I can't make out the fourth player.[3]

Philip Larkin might have had these card players in his mind when he wrote his poem.

Larkin, always a serious poet, has written this poem to arouse in us extreme revulsion at the degeneration existing in human existence. In Sanskrit dramaturgy the theory of *Rasas* finds an important place. In his book *Natya-sastra*(7th/8th century AD), Bharata says that there are eight *rasas* and then he discusses each of them. But before doing that he tells us something important about the nature and function of *rasas* in drama. He asks , "But what is this thing called *rasa*?" And then he writes: "Here is the reply. Because it is enjoyably tasted, it is called rasa. How does the enjoyment come? Persons who eat prepared food mixed with different condiments and sauce etc., if they are sensitive, enjoy the different tastes and then feel pleasure (or satisfaction); likewise, sensitive spectators, after enjoying the various emotions expressed by the actors through words, gestures and feelings feel pleasure,etc." There are eight *rasas*, but we are here concerned with only one of them, *Bibhatsa rasa*.Regarding its function, Bharata writes: "Disgust is the Sthayi bhava of Bibhatsa rasa. It is stimulated by seeing or hearing whatever is undesirable, ugly, evil....[It] is produced by things which disturb the mind, like seeing something unpleasant or by wrong smell, touch, taste or sound." As to how it is expressed in acting, he says, 'It is to be acted by a leering mouth, by holding the nose, by hanging the head or walking stealthily."[4] Larkin's "The Card Players" is a poem soaked in bibhatsa rasa.

The "lamplit cave" in the poem is a sort of cesspool surrounded by impenetrable darkness. In the lane leading to this cave, rain courses through the cart-ruts, making it muddy and therefore almost unnegotiable. And century-wide trees clash in the surrounding starlessness above . In short, it is, symbolically speaking, cut off from the normal world and in it an extremely degenerate life, like rotting filth in a cesspool, exists. There are such cesspits of human life in many places in all societies. They pose a serious threat to the survival of human species.

The last line of the poem, separated from the rest of it, is the poet's indignant comment on this cesspit:

Rain, wind and fire! The secret bestial peace!

In point of expression of deep anguish and indignation felt at something gone disastrously putrid in the essential being of man, this line is comparable to the lines in *King Lear* in which Lear invokes , in the stormy night on the heath, the furies of nature to wreak havoc on earth; invites "sulph'rous and thought-executing fires" to "Singe" his "white head;" and asks the "all- shaking thunder" to

Strike flat the thick rotundity o' th' world. (III. ii. L 7)

Here Lear is seen shouting imprecations at the devilry of man on the heath on a dark night when wind, rain, thunder and lightning symbolizing the indignation of heaven itself seem to scourge the earth. The last line in Larkin's poem, as the last lines in several other of his poems, though separated from the rest of the poem, is an integral part of it and has, in fact, additional power in being a kind of distillation of what has gone before in the poem.

THE BUILDING

"The Building" is a poem about death, but it is not an ordinary death poem lamenting the loss of life. It is about the mental condition of the people on the verge of death. They are in a hospital. The hospital is a large, handsome building, in fact, "Higher than the handsomest hotel," whose "lucent comb shows up for miles," while, the poet ask us to "see,"

All around it close-ribbed streets rise and fall
Like a great sigh out of the last century.

The opulence of the building sharply contrasts with the humdrum ordinariness of its surroundings, which is very significant. The poet is careful not to call this building a hospital. Such mega hospitals have come up in many cities across countries. And in their height and handsomeness they vie with super luxury hotels. This comparison is important. The sponsors of such hospitals are big business houses who build them so that the patients of privileged classes may have a nice stay and expensive treatment in them. But just as the super rich clients of luxury hotels carry the meanness and selfishness of their ugly life into the midst of the opulence and glamour of these hotels and undergo no change for the better, the patients of this magnificent hospital building experience no well-being; on the contrary, they are "at that vague age that claims/The end of choice, the last of hope."

The ordinary aspect of the hospital's lounge or, more appropriately the waiting room for patients, appears like an airport lounge, but the people sitting on "rows of steel chairs" do not look like those who have travelled far by air; rather, they appear to have come from nearby places, but most of them will soon travel so far that no globe-trotter can even imagine. The vehicles that "keep drawing up/At the entrance are not taxis," but ambulances though the poet does not say so. The people "sit tamely" on steel chairs. Some of them are turning over the pages of "ripped" magazines kept in the hall. They are wearing "outdoor clothes" and have brought "half-filled shopping bags" because they have to stay here for a while. Their faces are "restless and resigned;" they cannot look otherwise, that is ,calm and hopeful. "Every few minutes," the poet tells us, "comes a kind of nurse/To fetch someone away." This, however, does not give them any kind of reassurance. Tea "at so much a cup" is available here. Some of the waiting patients drink it and then re-fit the "Cups back to saucers," or "glance below/Seats for dropped gloves or cards."

Who are actually these patients? The poet tells us:

> Humans, caught
> On ground curiously neutral, homes and names
> Suddenly in abeyance; some are young,
> Some old, but most at that vague age that claims
> The end of choice, the last of hope;

These "humans" are all rich patients, but they are now away from their cosy, luxurious dwellings; nor are they distinguished here as in their homes and society. They stand on a ground that is "neutral," that is, it has no colour of any positive feeling and at present may be called their immediate existential condition. It is in this condition that most of them will leave this world. Some will no doubt live for some time more; those that are young may live for many years to come. But they too will die in the same condition in which the very old/terminally ill patients are going to die here and very soon. But all of them are "Here to confess that something has gone wrong". The poet calls it an "error of a serious sort." There is here an implied comparison between the sinners' confessions to priests and the patients' confessions to doctors. Priests apply some sort of soothing balm on the guilty conscience of sinners and doctors try to remove the physical pain of patients. But just as man's sinful nature necessitated the building of many churches, big and small, including awe-inspiring cathedrals, so errors of serious nature in man's body have necessitated the setting up of hospitals like the present one, to which the poet draws our attention:

> see how many floors it needs, how tall
> It's grown by now, and how much money goes
> In trying to correct it [that is, "error of a serious sort"].

A lot of money used to go into the upkeep of magnificent cathedrals as well as maintaining the higher ranks of priests in great comfort and luxury. But the sins and perversions of humankind kept on multiplying. Similarly, the rich among us have begun to invest huge (astronomical) sums in the setting up of such hospitals to correct the wrongs in man's body. But the wrongs have not been eradicated; man's ailments keep on multiplying and such hospitals yield huge profits to their sponsors. It is nobody's case that religion and hospital are useless. But because of perversions of serious nature in both man's mind and body – perversions caused by his seriously wrong life-style–neither religion nor medical science has succeeded in eradicating them.

It is half past eleven, the busiest hour in a hospital "on a working day." Patients waiting in the hall are picked one by one and while they are being taken "To their appointed levels… their eyes/Go to each other, guessing" – guessing what fate is awaiting each of them. On the way they see someone, "wheeled past, in washed- to- rags ward clothes" This someone is perhaps dead or is soon going to die. . The patients, who see him, remain quiet because they see "This new thing held in common." The new thing is Death–a phenomenon that not only destroys the body of man but also brings about the disintegration of the whole complex of sensations, feelings, emotions, cognitions, consciousness and so forth that is formed from the properties of the organized structure (a cooperative) of a trillion cells (and countless molecules, atoms, elementary particles, electric charges) that an adult human body is. In short, Death is this kind of annihilation of man's life. Naturally a man who is inching inexorably towards it can only remain quiet when he sees somebody already in the maw of Death or just going to enter it.

What we have called the complex of the organized structure, which is man's body, is the essence of man's Being. Whatever the shape, symmetry, beauty or ugliness of this complex, it is man's Essence and its disintegration, even an intimation of this happening, cannot but unnerve him to the extent that he becomes speechless.

And Erwin Schrodinger, in his book *What is Life? with Mind and Matter*, in the following words, refers to the view of Aziz Nasafi, an Islamic Persian mystic of the 13th century, on the light that the life of any creature is:

> On the death of any living creature the spirit returns to the spiritual world and the body to the bodily world. In this however only the bodies are subject to change. The spiritual world is one single spirit who stands like unto a light behind the bodily world and who, when any creature comes into being, shines through it as through a window. According to the kind and size of the window, less or more light enters the world. The light itself however remains unchanged.[1]

This light, whatever its kind (it may be very hazy or of a transcendental kind) or size (it may be as minuscule as a pinpoint or vast enough to encompass the whole universe) is the living creature–a man, a reptile, an insect ,an amoeba. No creature wants to be deprived of this light because it will mean the end of its livingness. The patients being taken to different rooms are quiet and nervous because they know that

> Past those doors are rooms, and rooms past those rooms
> And more rooms yet, each one further off
> And harder to return from, and who knows
> Which he will see, and when?

At this point in the movement of the poem, the poet says to us: "For the moment, wait, /Look down at the yard" and also beyond the hospital gate. The yard "seems old enough." We see in it objects like "Red brick, lagged pipes," and also a man "walking...out to the car park, free." The word "free" arrests our attention. He is free for now because the grip of Death has not begun to tighten around him yet.

We also see

> Traffic; a locked church; short terraced streets
> Where kids chalk games, and girls with hair-dos fetch
> Their separates from the cleaners –

These are common enough scenes from the everyday life of ordinary people. But "a locked church" arrests our immediate attention. The patients on the verge of death can get no grace from the locked church. Also there is no link or connection between this "free" life and "the end of choice, the last of hope" which is now the mental condition of the patients in the hospital. And so the poet exclaims: "O world,/ Your loves, your chances, are beyond the stretch/ Of any hand from here!" This is a very sad condition for any man to be in, to live with the realization that the hopes, loves, chances of life, even of ordinary, commonplace life, are beyond his reach. Sir Charles Sherrington speaks of "the condition of 'anxiety'" and writes "none is...more far-reaching as a warper of the mind." (MohN, p. 228). The patients' minds are warped by the anxiety in them and no anxiety can be more mind-warping than that caused by the fear of approaching death.

But this world, with its loves, its hopes, its chances, is "unreal,/ A touching dream to which we are all lulled." From this dream we wake separately. In this unreal world "conceits/ And self -protecting ignorance congeal / To carry life." "Conceit" is a word with negative connotations: My opinion of myself and things around me are correct and worthwhile though this opinion is wrong. The poet has used the plural of conceit which simply implies all such opinions a man holds. And the expression "self-protecting ignorance" has very wide and deep implications. Right from the start when our consciousness begins to acquire the capacity or capability to understand the truth of things, which is *never* beyond our reach, we are kept in ignorance and a stage is reached in our life when the self feels threatened if truth is brought near it and so it seeks protection in conceits and ignorance. It is in this condition that most of us waste our entire life and the result is: a poor crop of humanity generation after generation. The use of the word "congeal" here is remarkably appropriate. When conceits and self-protecting ignorance congeal, it becomes very difficult, if not impossible, to make them melt with the life-giving warmth of truth and proper knowledge. If in any part of our body blood congeals our very life is threatened. But it is tragic that congealed conceits and self-protecting ignorance carry our life. However, they collapse when "Called to these corridors." The collapse in each patient takes place when the nurse beckons. At this moment one is face- to-face with Death and the protecting wall built around him or her falls and becomes debris. Not all of them are going to die right now. Some will come out by lunchtime or four o'clock after check-ups and with the doctors' prescriptions and advice, but the terminally ill patients, "not knowing it,"

> have come to join
> The unseen congregations whose white rows
> Lie set apart above–women, men;
> Old, young, crude facets of the only coin
>
> This place accepts.

The poet calls the rows of these patients "congregations," which has religious connotations.

With the approaching death and no protection of conceits and ignorance around them, and in place of their essential consciousness, if they had ever had any, they have now only its crude facets. And the hospital accepts "crude facets of the only coin." The only coin we have ever had is our body. We could have, if we had lived a better life, made the coin shine like gold. But we did not care. Now the terminally ill patients' bodies are coins on which are wrought crudities of the approaching Death. These crudities the hospital building – "this clean-sliced cliff" – accepts. It was meant to be a struggle to transcend the thought of dying. But it has not succeeded in its aim. It can succeed only if "its powers/ Outbuild cathedrals." Cathedrals – magnificent buildings – promised their adherents eternal life, that is, afterlife full of heavenly peace and happiness. They did not achieve success; today hardly any serious-minded person believes in afterlife. Superspeciality hospitals do not promise afterlife to their patients.

But they were and are being built and their sponsors think, even claim, that the patients , while undergoing expensive treatment and receiving proper care in them, will transcend the thought of dying or even evade it. But this has not happened so far. The poet emphasizes this point when he says that it – the struggle to transcend the thought of death –cannot happen

> unless its powers
> Outbuild cathedrals nothing contravenes
> The coming darkness

Howsoever luxurious care and expensive treatment may be provided to a man on the verge of the precipice, they cannot contravene the darkness in which the light of his life is going to be lost for all eternity, as Aziz Nasafi, whom we have quoted above, makes clear, although friends and relations of the patients about to die – the poet calls these friends and relations "crowds" – each evening try "with wasteful, weak, propitiatory flowers" to make them transcend the thought of dying. The propitiatory flowers they bring are weak and wasteful just as tithes and prayers offered in cathedrals did not give people afterlife full of heavenly joy and peace.

But what is the message of this beautiful poem? Neither religion nor medical science, despite all their claims, have been able to make man transcend the thought of dying when Death, with its eternal darkness, stands staring hard at him in the face. But we can transcend the fear of death as the Buddha did , as the Christ did, as Socrates did, as great thinkers or martyrs did. Such people lived a kind of life that can show us a path leading to a life of Enlightenment. But for that to happen we have to reorganize our life, overhaul it. As of now it is in a mess. Most of us, whether as seriously ill patients, or our friends and relations with their propitiatory (but weak and wasteful) flowers, or anonymous men and women seen as the traffic outside, or the kids chalking their games in the streets, or girls with hair-dos fetching their separates from the cleaners, have no idea why we live and how we die. And when we start to die – whether we are "women, men /Old,young" – we are "crude facets of the only coin." The only coin is our body, our sole possession. But at the approach of Death our only coin has crude facets, both physically and mentally/spiritually. Unless we get rid of our conceits and self-protecting ignorance congealing our lives, nothing will contravene the eternal darkness in which we men and women drown in a state of mind-warping anxiety, not to say in utter hopelessness.

Sad Steps

Philip Larkin borrowed the title of his poem "Sad Steps" from Sir Philip Sidney's sonnet no. 31 entitled "To the Sad Moon" in *Astrophel and Stella*. The first line of the poem, addressed to the moon by a sad lover, is

> With what sad steps, O Moon, thou climb'st the skies

It is a typical Elizabethan love sonnet. The sad lover, looking at the "wan face" of the moon silently climbing the skies, asks him if there, too, that is, on the surface of the moon (the poet calls it "heavenly place") " the busy archer his sharp arrows tries." He asks this of the moon because his own "long-with-love-acquainted eyes" can see that, like himself, the moon is lovelorn. So there is a fellowship between the sad earthly lover and the lovelorn moon and in the name of that fellowship he asks the moon to tell him;

> Is constant love deemed there but want of wit?
> Are beauties there as proud as here they be?

From what we know of Larkin's views on poetry and his self-imposed duty as a poet it is quite easy to see that "Sad Steps" is a very different kind of poem than Sidney's sonnet. It is also a post-modern poem of superior kind. One of the tasks post-modern poetry sets itself is to make man aware of his position in, and his relationship with, the whole universe. This is the imperative need of human civilization today because such awareness alone can make man see things as they are, which is very important for re-orientation of human culture today which is facing a crisis and the re-orientation can brook no delay.

Here it should be pointed out that there are five poems in *High Windows* - "High Windows," "Sympathy in White Major," "Forget What Did," "Sad Steps" and "Solar" – which are exclusively devoted to make man aware of himself in the sense described above. But it is not self-awareness for its own sake that is the concern of the poet. His concern is to bring about a qualitative change in human culture (which has been in a very poor shape) because such a change will help man to see things as they are by dispelling the haze of obfuscations that surrounds them

Seamus Heaney calls "Solar" and "Sad Steps" Larkin's sun and moon poems and writes: "Larkin, in *High Windows*, places his sun poem immediately after and in answer to his moon poem: 'Sad Steps' and 'Solar' face each other on the opened page like the two halves of his poetic personality in dialogue."[1] Similar is the case with "Forget What Did" and "High Windows;" they, too, face each other on the opened page. They may not be a dialogue between the two halves of a poetic self but they are about celestial phenomena with life on earth seen in long perspectives which these phenomena open. Similarly, "Sympathy in White Measure" is about the metaphysics (the poet calls it "the lost displays") of all phenomena, celestial and terrestrial. These poems and parts of a number of other poems provide the scientific-philosophical-metaphysical underpinning to Larkin's major poems like "Church Going," "I Remember, I Remember," "Here," "Mr Bleaney," "The Whitsun Weddings," "Dockery and Son," "An Arundel Tomb," "The Trees," "Livings," "Vers de Societe," "The Explosion."

And now we will come to "Sad Steps" to see what it is about. It is four o'clock in the morning. An elderly man well past his youth, we may be sure, "Groping back to bed after a piss," parts "thick curtains" and is "startled by/ The rapid clouds, the moon's cleanliness." The word "piss" establishes the man's old age, because old men make piss at least once at night. This man was, like any of us, once young and in all likelihood romantic as Sir Philip Sidney's sad lover is in his sonnet. The sky is "wind-picked" and "cavernous," that is, clear but vast and deep. Under this sky the gardens lie "wedge-shad-owed" – shadows of trees and plants are wedged into the open spaces in the gardens. The setting is romantic and the persona seems vulnerable to its al-lurements. Seamus Heaney writes: "The Renaissance moon of Sidney's sonnet sails close, and the invitation to the 'enormous yes' that love should evoke is potent." But, he writes, "Truth wins over beauty by a few points,"[2] and the persona finds that "There is something laughable about this" – laughable about the way the moon "dashes through the clouds that blow /Loosely as cannon-smoke." Suddenly we find the whole setting changing to something unromantic, as the comparison of the clouds blowing or floating loosely to cannon-smoke and the implied comparison of the moon dashing through the clouds to a cannon-ball shot from the cannon make it very clear. The unro-mantic self of the ageing man sees the moonlight, because it is coming down filtered through the clouds, as stone-coloured, sharpening the roofs of the houses below. In the next three lines, quoted below, we find once again ves-tiges of the romantic longings associated with the moon appearing in the per-sona, but these are negated at once:

Lozenge of love! medallion of art!
O wolves of memory! Immensements! No,

One shivers, looking up there.

The old man sees the moon as lozenge of love and medallion of art. Now a lozenge may mean a medicinal tablet (it has a nice taste), taken for sore throat or, as the dictionary says, "a charge in the shape of a solid diamond, in particular one on which the arms of an unmarried or widowed woman is displayed." And the word "medallion," again according to the dictionary, means "a piece of jewellery in the shape of a medal, worn as a pendant." These two images symbolizing the moon make it abundantly clear that the moon has in reality only a nice taste children love, or is, at best, an article of beautification and decoration. But our laughable love-longings have made disproportionately heavy investments in this satellite of waste matter orbiting the earth. Charles Dickens, the great caricaturist that he is, in his novel *Dombey and Son*, makes fun of the middle-aged spinster, Miss Tox, whom he describes as a "lady…a long, lean figure wearing such a faded air that she seemed not to have been made in what linen-drapers call 'fast colour' originally and to have, by little and little, washed out" and describes her romantic longings for the completely insensitive (insensitive to love) but immensely rich Dombey, deluding herself into believing that he loves her and will marry her now that his first wife is dead. Dickens writes thus about the lady's ridiculous longings: "At about the same period, too, she was seized with a passion for looking at the moon, of which she would take long observations from her chamber window."[3]

To the old man the preposterous investments in the moon appear now on his dimming romantic self as wolves – not a romantic image at all – of memory and also something symbolized by the improbable word "Immensements." But he immediately denies, with an emphatic end-stopped "No," such investments made in the foolishness of young age and says that one can only shiver slightly looking at the "the hardness and the brightness" of the moon. And the "plain/ Far-reaching singleness of that wide stare" is now a reminder to the persona "of the strength and pain/ Of being young." In the strength of youth boys and girls, even men and women, are filled with fervid love-longings in moonlight, and sometimes also with pain, as the lover's heart in Sidney's sonnet was, at the non-fulfilment of their love-longings. For the old man the romantic accretions to the moon are now out of bounds both because his strength has depleted and also because he has now a better perception of this barren satellite. However, the romantic perception remains "undiminished" for "others… somewhere." Now who are the "others" and where is this "somewhere?" The others are those romantic young men who are still deluded into seeing in the full moon the beautiful faces of their sweethearts. Or romantic maidens who dream of achieving, and sometimes even achieve, consummation of their sensuous love in the cool moonlight. And the "somewhere" is another world very different from the world in which the old man now finds himself. Here one is reminded of these lines in Ronald Barthes' book *S / Z*:

> The moon is the nothingness of light, of warmth reduced to its deficiency: it illuminates by mere reflection without itself being an origin, thus it becomes the luminous emblem of the castrato, a deficiency manifested by the empty glitter it borrows femininity while (an Adonis) and of which nothing remains but a leprous grey when he is old…[4]

Barthes made this observation while analyzing Balzac's novella *Sarrasine* written in 1830. Since then we have gathered more facts – very unromantic, in fact, very unpleasant truths about the moon. It is a barren lump of dead matter. There is no atmosphere and, therefore, no life on it. On its surface are many bare, high mountains, "the highest of them about a thousand feet taller than Mt Everest"; vast and arid plains, which were once mistaken for the seas; and numerous craters. Further, as *Encyclopedia Americana* tells us:

> Lacking a protective cover like the earth's, the moon is exposed to lethal radiation from the sun and incessant bombardment by meteorites. Human contact with lunar surface materials may therefore be extremely dangerous. Furthermore, heat and cold are unchecked by atmospheric insulation. Temperatures climb at about 215^0 F in the sunlight and plunge to about -250^0 in the shade.[5]

The moon has, unlike the sun, no relevance for life on earth although man has woven many superstitions around it. Edward Burnett Tylor tells us that the moon, like the sun, was a deity across cultures in the ancient world although its position was secondary to the sun. He writes: "The more usual status of the Moon in the religions of the world is, as nature suggests, that of a subordinate companion deity to the Sun, such as is acknowledged in the precedence of Sunday to Monday."[6] And *Encyclopedia Americans* tells us this:

> The moon held a commanding place in ancient pagan religion and mythology. The variety of its appearances and the unearthly quality of its light enchanted early man and he attached great significance to it. The moon was depicted in all ancient hierarchies as a goddess. The Greeks cast it as Selene, the night-riding sister of Helios, god of the sun. The Romans associated it with Diana, their chaste goddess of hunt. Superstitions about the moon abounded among farmers who planted their crops at full moon - or new moon – to assure a full harvest. In fact, research has failed to produce any definite evidence of a connection between the moon's phases and the weather.[7]

"Sad Steps" and "Solar" are not just moon and sun poems in conventional sense of the terms. Larkin's major poems have long perspectives as their essential nature. We must try to understand the two poems in these perspectives. The perception of the moon evolved even in the ancient world. Tylor discusses this evolution in his book. He says that in the ancient world "the rude savage" tribes in Brazil, Africa, Guinea and other places "recognized [the moon] as a great deity." Many of these tribes did not worship the sun. Taylor writes that even now, "In Africa moon-worship is prominent in an immense district where sun-worship is unknown or insignificant."[8]

In higher Polytheism, the sun and moon underwent evolutionary changes. Tylor writes: "In Egyptian theology, not to discuss other divine beings to whom a lunar nature has been ascribed, it is at least certain that Khonsu is the moon in absolute personal divinity. In Aryan mythology, the personal moon stands as Selene beside the more anthropomorphic forms of Hekate and Artemis, as Luna beside the less understood Lucina, and Diana with her borrowed attributes, while our Teutonic forefathers were content with his plain name of Moon." Tylor ends his section on Moon-God thus; "Thus, in tracing the development of Nature-Worship, it appears that though Fire, Air, Earth and Water are not yet among the lower races systemized into a quaternion of elements, their adoration, with that of Sun and Moon, shows already arising in primitive culture the familiar types of those great divinities, who received their further development in the higher Polytheism."[9]

The perception of the moon kept evolving with the evolution of human consciousness and in course of time the moon came to symbolize romantic love and beauty and Selene's love for Endymion became the archetype of this love and beauty. Sidney's sonnet belongs to this tradition of perception of the moon. Now we have a different (that is, true) perception of this lifeless satellite of the earth. But this perception is, unfortunately, only academic in nature because the erroneous perception, as we have seen the persona telling us about, remains undiminished for others somewhere. This is not only the case with our perception of the moon. In most cases our perception of the real reality (exceptions apart) of things is wrong, not to say pernicious. The persona in "Sad Steps", as if with "sad steps," has climbed a height of mature perception from where he sees the moon for what it is. We must shun our immaturity and embrace the truth embedded in Shakespeare's warning, "All that glitters is not gold."

Solar

"Solar" is among the most admired poems of Philip Larkin, and justly so. Seamus Heaney calls it "frankly a prayer, a hymn to the sun."[1] Andrew Swarbrick writes that "Solar" "reverently addresses a personified sun as an idealized image of self-sufficiency which yet pours 'unrecompensed' and 'gives for ever.' "[2] Sun-worship has had a long and venerable tradition across cultures. The most sacred and also the greatest hymn to the sun, known as "Ga:yatri Mantra" in the *Rg Veda*, the oldest Hindu scripture, dates back to 1500 BC. An English transliteration of the Sanskrit verse runs:

Owm
Bhu:r bhuwah swah
Tat savitur varenayam
Bhargo devasya dhimahi
Dhio yonah prachodayat.

Sir William Jones interpreted the prayer thus:

Let us adore the supremacy of that divine sun, the godhead, who illuminates all, from whom all proceed, to whom all must return, whom we invoke to direct our understandings aright in our progress towards his holy seat.[3]

S. Radhakrishnan, the noted Indian philosopher-statesman, translates the last three lines of the hymn (mantra) as follows: "We meditate on the adorable glory of the radiant sun, may he inspire our intelligence."[4] And Edward Burnett Tylor, in his book *Religion in Primitive Culture*, comments on the Ga:yatri Mantra:

Modern Hinduism is full of the ancient Sun-worship, in offerings and prostrations, in daily rites and appointed festivals, and it is Savitur the sun, who is invoked in the 'Ga:yatri,' the time-honoured formula repeated day by day since long- past ages by every Brahman; 'Tat Savitur varenayam bhargo devasya dhimahi dhio yonah prachodayat.' Let us meditate on the desirable light of the divine Sun, may he rouse our minds!

In this section of his book, Tylor traces the origin of sun-worship and its spread in different countries and the various names the sun-god acquired in them and the various attributes ascribed to him, and writes, "It is no exaggeration to say, with Sir William Jones, that one great fountain of all idolatry in the four quarters of the globe was the veneration paid by men to the sun."[5]

Sir James Frazer, in his book *The Golden Bough*, also refers to sun-worship in ancient times. He writes that the Persian deity Mithra "was regularly identified by his worshippers with the sun, the Unconquered sun, as they called him." Osiris, the famous Egyptian corn-god has, Frazer tells us, "been sometimes interpreted as sun-god." But the true Egyptian sun-god was Ra. In ancient Egypt the kings derived their titles directly from the sun-god. Frazer writes, "Whatever in fact might be asserted of the Sun-god was dogmatically predicable to the king of Egypt. His titles were directly derived from those of the Sun-god" and the Incas of Peru, who claimed themselves the sons of the Sun, "were revered like gods."[6] A similar claim was made by the dominant ruling caste in ancient India and even now many of its members, though no longer the rulers, trace their descent back to the Sun-god.

Regarding the sacrifices made to the sun-god by the ancient Mexicans, the Greeks, Spartans, Persians Messagetae, Frazer writes as follows:

> The ancient Mexicans conceived the sun as the source of all vital force, 'He by whom men live.' But if he bestowed life, he needed also to receive life from it... and as heart is the seat and symbol of life, bleeding hearts of men and animals were presented to the sun to maintain him in vigour and enable him to run his course across the sky....The constant demand for human victims to feed the solar fire was met by waging war every year in the neighbouring tribes and bringing back troops of captives to be sacrificed on the altar. Thus the ceaseless wars of the Mexicans and their cruel system of human sacrifices, the most monstrous on record....The ancient Greeks believed that the sun drove in a chariot across the sky; hence the Rhodians, who worshipped the sun as their chief deity, annually dedicated a chariot and four horses to him, and flung them into the sea for his use. Doubtless they thought that after a year's work his old horses and chariot would be worn out. From a like motive, probably, the idolatrous kings of Judah dedicated chariots and horses to the sun, and the Spartans, Persians and Messagetae sacrificed horses to him,[7]

Frazer states that, in Arctic regions when "towards the close of the Arctic winter... the sun appeared after the absence of weeks or months," the people marked it out "as the appropriate moment for a general expulsion of devils."[8] The Greek gods Helios and Hyperion too were sun-gods. The ancient Japanese were great sun- worshippers, believing that their emperors were descended "in unbroken lineage for 26 centuries from the sun-goddess Amaterasu, who aided man in his struggle for sustenance in Japan's somewhat austere climate."[9] There was a long tradition of sun-worship across cultures and countries in the ancient world. Many superstitions, to say nothing of the human sacrifice in Mexico, were associated with the worship of this deity

Philip Larkin's "Solar' can be illuminated in terms of this tradition. In fact, Larkin goes farther back – to nursery tales or rhymes in which the sun is often imaged as a lion's face suspended in the sky, or a "Single stalkless flower[sunflower]." Even in children's imagination something of the strength and mysteriousness of the sun is caught. This sun, standing still "at the centre /Of an unfurnished sky," goes on spilling light – the light that keeps life on Earth going. *Encyclopedia Americana* tells us how he does it:

> The sun's rays supply us with heat, light, food, fuel and power. During its daily apparent journey across the sky, it contributes to the growth of plant life, warms the earth, evaporates water vapour from many sources into the atmosphere, aids in the production of winds and performs a variety of other feats all of which are vital to our existence.[10]

Regarding the imperative need of the sun for maintaining all life and to keep going "every form of activity on the surface of the Earth", Fred Hoyle writes:

> Not only is the sunlight a necessity for the support of life on the Earth, but it is also the ultimate source of all energy at present used in industry. The power produced by coal and oil represents sunlight that was stored in trees and plants thousands of centuries ago. Even hydroelectric power really comes from the sun, for it is the sun's heat that sucks water from the oceans into the atmosphere...Its gravitational attraction controls the motions of the planets, and its rays supply the energy that maintains nearly every form of activity on the surface of the Earth.[11]

Larkin says that the sun stands all alone and "still" at the centre of a bare, "unfurnished" sky. But the sun is not motionless. Fred Hoyle tells us that the sun, along with its planets, moves "along a path that is roughly a circle around the centre of the galaxy with a speed that is in the neighbourhood of 1000,000 miles an hour."[12] Nor is the location of the sun the centre of the sky because the sky or cosmos, to be precise, has no centre. Then the sky, our sky in whose centre the sun seems to stand still, is unfurnished simply because between any two stars in our or any other galaxy there is a vast tract of empty, dark space which is simply frightening to look at.

The sun, "unaided" and looking like a "Single stalkless flower" – sunflower – pours light "unrecompensed." He gets nothing in return, nothing for the gradual loss of light that is his life and the source of all light on our planet. But the question that arises in our mind is: Can and should he not be recomposed for what he does for us and the Earth? The ancients thought that he should and made oblations and sacrifices to him. Larkin, too, wants us to make oblations to the sun. But how? Not by making monstrous human sacrifices, not by throwing horses and chariots into the seas, not even by strutting about, claiming our descent from him. But by utilizing his light (or energy emitted unceasingly by him) to illuminate our being and enlighten our mind in a truly philosophical-scientific sense and thereby justify the meaning and purpose of human existence, which, so far, only a microscopic minority of the humankind have done, while whole nations have lived life as vague as that of weeds.

The sun appears simplified to the eye because of its distance from the Earth. As *Encyclopedia Americana* tells us (we have quoted it above), "The distance between the centre of the sun and that of the Earth is 93 million miles. The diameter of the sun is about 110 times that of the Earth, while its volume is so large that more than a million Earths can be dropped into the space it occupies." And yet our sun is only a medium-sized yellow star. And the petal-like flares of the light-waves on its surface continuously explode and heat is the echo of the sun's gold. Stephen Hawking tells us something about what Larkin calls "petalled head of flames " continuously exploding on the surface of a star:

> A star is formed when a large amount of gas (mostly hydrogen) starts to collapse in on itself due to its gravitational attraction. As it contracts the atoms of the gas collide with each other more and more frequently and at greater and greater speeds – the gas heats up. Eventually the gas will be so hot that when the hydrogen atoms collide they no longer bounce off each other but instead coalesce to form helium. The heat released in this reaction, which is like a hydrogen bomb explosion, is what makes the stars shine.[13]

in fact, the solar flares explode in the sun's atmosphere with the energy equivalent to "millions of hydrogen bombs." It is this sun, a colossal mass of energy, to whom we are directly related in a blood relationship. As William Golding put it in his Nobel Prize acceptance speech in 1983: "Through our mother [the Earth] we are part of the solar system and part, through that, of the whole universe. In the blazing poetry of the fact we are children of the stars."[14] in fact, as Paul Amos Moody rightly observes in his book *Introduction to Evolution*, "The living processes that we combine under the term 'metabolism' require the expenditure of energy. Included among these energy-requiring processes is the manufacture of proteins and nucleic acids. What is the source of this energy? For most modern organisms the source is the sun."[15]

So without the sun the chemical processes that occur in a living organism to maintain life will not be able to take place. Philip Larkin's "Solar" is about the "blazing poetry" of this fact and something more. In a beautiful sentence, Carl Sagan tells us how the entire cycle of life on our Earth is kept alive and working by the sun: "What a marvelous cooperative arrangement – plants and animals each inhaling the other's exhalations, a kind of planet-wide mutual mouth-to-stoma resuscitation, the entire elegant cycle powered by a star 150 million km away."[16]

We have seen in the passage from Stephen Hawking, quoted above, how the stars are formed or coined. Our star (the Sun) stands openly. Nothing hides its immense burning mass. The poet says that our needs climb and return hourly like angels. Angels are invisible to mortal eyes, but they minister to the needs of God in heaven and are of heaven. Our needs may be physical as well as spiritual-transcendental. When we work, even when we breathe, we emit heat. And we absorb the heat emitted by the sun. Our spiritual aspirations are also emissions of heat-waves. And the fulfillment of these aspirations is caused by activation in us of the energy from sunlight. These invisible solar energy-currents, hourly climbing and returning, are our angels in that they not only give us life but also help us fulfil ourselves. This fulfillment is that of the godliness in us – the godliness that was fulfilled in Buddha and Christ, for example. The sun gives us light and Buddha's and Christ's kind of enlightenment for ever with open hands, if only we make use of his gifts as the very best of the humans have done.

"Solar" is a hymn to the Sun in the revered tradition of sun-worship – of the kind we find in the Vedic hymn quoted above. But it is also a post-modern poem in that it makes us see the vital relationship, at the sub-atomic level, between the vibrations of our life, our thought-processes, our feelings, our very original and self-reflecting consciousness, including our transcendental awareness, and the petal-like flares of the light-waves on the surface of the sun. The Sun, existing openly and giving light and life with open hands, is ever ready to help us to realize the how and the why of both our life and the life of the universe. Shakespeare said, "Ripeness is all." It is only the energy of the sun that can help us attain this ripeness.

"Solar" is a hymn to the Sun, but it is something more. It is about perceiving things as they are. This perception is of transcendental kind. It is this kind of perception of phenomena that can redeem human culture, an imperative need of human civilization today. In nursery tales and in superstitions, not to say abominations, associated with sun- worship in primitive culture something of the life-giving strength of the sun was no doubt recognized, but scientifically and philosophically correct perception of the value of the sun for all life here has come to man only now although something of this perception was glimpsed in the Ga:yatri mantra. Larkin's fine poetic creativity seized on this perception and has given it a transcendental dimension in his "Solar."

Vers de Societe`

As its title indicates, "Vers de Societe" is a poem about our social life in a kind of society that is degenerate and the pity or tragedy is that there seems to be no way to regenerate it.

Dear Warlock- Williams invites the persona to a party at his house. The persona, in a bitterly satirical mood, tells us in his own words what the invitation really means:

> My wife and I have asked a crowd of craps
> To waste their time and ours. Perhaps
> You'd care to join us?

The phrase "a crowd of craps" speaks volumes about the kind of people – the middle class – that constitute the main (that is, influential) social class in a country like England. They are no better than a crowd of craps, a far cry from being people with worthwhile ideas about life, its meaning and value. So the persona's reaction, though unexpressed to the host, is this short, terse sentence: "In a pig's arse, friend." Nobody will ever like to spend their evening in a pig's arse; the very thought of it is abhorrent in the extreme. But this is the objective-correlative of the abomination that the social life of these people, behind which lies a very degenerate perception of life, has become.

But, says the persona, "Day comes to an end." At the close of the day, "gas fire burns" inside the room and outside, in the darkness, "the trees are darkly swayed." At such moments, the persona says to Dear Warlock Williams, supposedly present before him, "I'm afraid." But why should he be afraid? The answer is simple: Man today has become so empty of his inner – spiritual, transcendental – resources that whenever the persona is alone, he feels afraid because he is faced with spiritual deficiency. So he tells us that it is funny "how hard it is to be alone." One should be alone at least for some time every day in order to take stock of his life, his activities, and meditate on the nature of life in general, its value and uses and so on. Instead, the persona tells us, it would be far easier for him to spend half his evenings thus:

> ' I could spend half my evenings, if I wanted,
> Holding a glass of sherry, canted
> Over to catch the drivel of some bitch
> Who's read nothing but *Which.*

Lest we should doubt the veracity of Larkin's assertion that his "bitch" has read nothing but *Which* (by Rider Haggasrd) we are reminded of what the eminent biologist G. G. Simpson says about the cultural achievement of modern American men and women. He writes with wry humour:

> Culture is what women do or are interested in. That idea finds considerable support in a recent sample poll of supposedly cultural achievements of men and women. It was found that a major cultural achievement of women, but not of men, was to have read a book all the way through. Just half the women, but many fewer men, had accomplished that feat at one time or another in their lives. Since many people outside the colleges do not distinguish between books and magazines, it is probable that the "books" that so many women had read all the way through (including, no doubt, advertisements) were movie fan magazines.[1]

The persona has spent some of his evenings (though not half his evenings) attending such parties as Mr Warlock-Williams is going to give and so he says:

> Just think of all the spare time that has flown
> Straight into nothingness by being filled
> With forks and faces.

But this kind of degenerate social life and entertainment is what most people of his class live and enjoy of an evening. And they do not regret doing this as the persona does. He regrets that all his spare time, instead of having been

repaid
Under a lamp, hearing the noise of wind,
And looking out to see the moon thinned
To an air-sharpened blade,

should have flown straight into nothingness by being filled with forks and faces, between which there is little difference, so far as intelligence and sensitivity of life in these people is concerned.

The two settings presented in close juxtaposition here stand in sharp contrast to each other. In the first setting we find the spare time completely wasted, in fact, doing harm to the person concerned, while in the second setting, it is "repaid." Repaid because it is spent watching all alone natural phenomena in action, which fills the persona at spiritual level with joy in close proximity with them.

Our spare time should be spent in meditation that the Buddha discovered – the " 'meditation' known as *vipassana*… 'Insight' into the nature of things, leading to the realization of Ultimate Truth, Nirvana. This is essentially Buddhist 'meditation', Buddhist mental culture. It is an analytical method based on mindfulness, awareness, vigilance, and observation."[2] Whether one is Buddhist or not, he must spend his spare time that can gradually lead to deeper and deeper insights into the nature of things, leading to the realization of Ultimate Truth.

Larkin's concept of meditation is that our spare time would be best repaid if of an evening we spend it as he wants us to do in the lines quoted above.

What exactly would be the repayment if we meditated as Larkin would have us meditate? We humans do not exist in isolation. We are part of nature, we are a phenomenon as so many other phenomena of nature are, and we finally merge with nature. It is by meditating on our relationship with nature that we shall realize ourselves. This will be the real life – Larkin says, "A life." "And yet," Larkin adds, "how sternly it is instilled/ *All solitude is selfish*," so much so that our deeper life capable of serious thinking and fruitful meditation has been knocked out of existence and we look like crowds of craps, we waste our spare time in pig's arse at such parties where there appears no difference between forks and faces, where a man, holding a glass of washing sherry, cants to catch the drivel of a bitch who has read nothing but *Which*. This kind of social life will lead to catastrophe, that is, atrophy of human culture.

In olden times there used to be hermits. They, with their gown and dish, would talk to God. But now both hermits and God are gone. Hermits lived a life of contemplation and meditation and gained valuable spiritual insights, claiming them to be divinely inspired. We quote below the following lines from Rumi, a great hermit,

> Make real the sublime words of the Prophet:
> "We are the last and the foremost."
> The fresh and perfect fruit is the last thing to come into existence
> For although the fruit is the last thing to come into existence
> It is, in fact, the first, for it was the goal.[3]

But do our craps and our bitches have any idea that we are the last and the foremost? G. G. Simpson, too, is of the opinion that, judged by a majority of the criteria of progress, "'Man has risen, not fallen." But, he adds, "He can choose to develop his capacities as the highest animal and to try to rise still farther, or he can choose otherwise. The choice is his responsibility, and his alone….Evolution has no purpose, man must supply this for himself." He ends his book *Biology and Man* thus:

Finally, after writing at such great length I find that Mark Twain said much of this in a more succinct way:

> "'Man is the only animal that blushes. Or needs to.'"[4]

We need to blush at the kind of life that we have been living; we seem to have forfeited the claim of us being the perfect fruit and pinnacle of evolutionary progress.

Today, Larkin says, virtue has become social. Now, there should be nothing wrong about it. Virtuous social life could regulate and guide our existence. But the problem is that it has degenerated into "routines", this "Playing at goodness," and so Larkin asks, "like going to church?" and adds, "Something that bores us, something we don't do well."

Once upon a time people going to church used to have in their hearts the imprint of the emotional grandeur and vision of Christ preaching his Sermon on the Mount. But now going to church bores us and we do not do it well. Then we find this line within brackets: "Asking that ass about his fool research." This is a serious matter. Research is a serious and creative undertaking aimed at finding out something true, something of value in a particular field of knowledge. But the researcher is now, more often than not, an ass and his research is just fooling around a particular subject in the kind of society in which crowds of craps and bitches often meet at parties in pig's arse. Playing at goodness, like going to church, is now something that bores us, something we do not do well, but we try to feel, however crudely, that it is something that should be worthwhile. But such feeling is "Too subtle" and "too decent, too" and we are neither subtle nor decent. So the persona says in disgust, "Oh hell" and adds, "Only the young can be alone freely." He does not tell us whether the young spend their spare hours in serious contemplation and meditation simply because he already knows that they don't. This is a pity because young people's spiritual life is less sullied than that of not-so- young people, among whom the persona is one. So, speaking of himself, he says

> , The time is shorter now for company,
> And sitting by a lamp more often brings
> Not peace, but other things.

His predicament is unenviable. He does not have much time for company because it fills him with disgust when he is among craps and has to cant to catch the drivel of some empty-headed young thing, and also because when, after being in such company, he takes stock of his actions, desires, failures and the time wasted in it, his inner life feels disturbed. But sitting alone by a lamp only brings him "Not peace, but other things." These other things, standing just beyond the lamp's light, are like the Furies that stood just outside Apollo's temple to pounce upon and destroy Orestes. Our failures are too many. But why do the failures occur? The reasons are also too many. So when we are sincere to ourselves, as the persona seems to be to his self, we take stock of our failures and are filled with remorse.

Here it will be in place to quote this sentence from Khalil Gibran: "Solitude is an ally of sorrow as well as a companion of spiritual exaltation."[5] This exaltation is attained by those who have, inside the phenomenon of their Being, tasted the ripe and sweet kernel of the essence of that Being, that is, who have realized the essence of their Being. Jean-Paul Sartre rightly says, "Things in general 'are,' but their being consists in manifesting their essence."[6] Rumi, whom we have quoted above, tells us this about the greatness of a human being, but who allows 'veils' and 'obfuscations' to keep his greatness hidden in darkness:

> A human being is a great thing: everything is inscribed within him, but "veils" and "obfuscations" prevent him from reading the knowledge he has within himself. The "veils" and "ob-fuscations" are various pre-occupations, worldly stratagems, and desires.[7]

The persona in Philip Larkin's poem, sitting all alone by a lamp in his room of an evening, experiences not peace and serenity, but "failure and re-morse." Spiritual exaltation eludes him because the essence of his being was not allowed to blossom into "a million-petalled flower of being here" in the kind of society in which he was born and has been condemned to live. He feels afraid of facing his true self and so his soul whispers, *"Dear Warlock-Williams: Why, of course –* " What does this whispering signify? In the first stanza we saw that he imagined telling this gentleman that he felt afraid when he sat alone in his room in the evening with gas fire "breathing" and the trees swaying "darkly" outside. He then felt afraid of meeting his true self, that is, the essence of his being. He finds himself in the same situation now also. This is a pity.

The Explosion

John Cary holds the view that Larkin possessed two voices, a male and a female voice. The male voice is, John Cary says, "the offensive Larkin who infuriates critics like Tom Paulin with his right-wing, racist views." Continuing, he writes: "This is the Larkin who sneers at Arts Council subsidies, at students, at the working class." But Larkin has another, the female voice – "the sensitive, educated, 'It deepens like a coastal shelf' voice" that "goes on alternating with the first voice throughout Larkin's life and writing." He refers to two stanzas in Larkin's letter of May1976 to Robert Conquest in which he wrote that he wanted the "so-called working class to starve;" their "wages weekly halved;" and their "women to [stew] grass" – verses which, John Cary says, "Larkin's admirers would be glad to forget." Then he writes:

What those stanzas demand comparison with, in respect to their attitude to the working class, is surely his poem 'The Explosion', one of his greatest works. it seems to me that this poem, too, was written by only half of Larkin – but this time it was the other half…the half that is concerned with human love and procreation.[1]

The excellence of the poem lies in both its technical brilliance and the depths of the common man's feelings and faiths which it fathoms with a unique empathy. The poem is about a major explosion in a coalmine and the setting is a coal mining district around the time D. H. Lawrence wrote *Sons and Lovers* (1911). John Wain, referring to the moleskin jackets the miners in the poem are seen wearing while going to the pit early in the morning, says that such jackets were worn by men in the early years of the twentieth century.

To understand this poem it is only proper to place it in its socio-economic perspective and that perspective is provided by George Orwell in his first-hand account of the hellish conditions in which coalminers lived and worked in the England of the 1930s. In his *Road to Wigan Pier* (1937), he gives this description in graphic detail and it is authentic in the sense that Orwell himself went into the pits and saw in them what he has described in his book. In the following passage, Orwell tells us that the pit is virtual hell on any working day:

The time to go there is when the machines are roaring and the air is black with coal dust, and when you actually see what the miners have to do. At those times, the place is like hell, or at any rate like my own mental picture of hell. Most of the things one imagines in hell are there – heat, noise, confusion, darkness, foul air and, above all, unbearably cramped space.[2]

In another passage, Orwell tells us how the miners, who work in hell all the time, keep our civilization going without bearing any ill-will towards us, who batten on their labour:

Watching coal-miners at work, you realize momentarily what different universes different people inhabit. Down there where coal is dug it is a sort of world apart which one can quite easily go through life without ever hearing about. Probably a majority of people would even prefer not to hear about it. Yet it is the absolute necessary counterpart of our world above. Practically everything we do, from eating an ice-cream to crossing the Atlantic, and from baking a loaf to writing a novel, involves the use of coal, directly or indirectly… In order that Hitler may march the goose-step, that the Pope may denounce Bolshevism, that the cricket crowds may assemble at Lord's, that the Nancy poets may scratch each other's backs, coal has to be forthcoming.[3]

Then we must know that coal mining is a hazardous job. Orwell writes: "The rate of accidents among the miners is so high, compared with that in other trades, that casualties are taken for granted almost as they would be in a minor war."[4] The most catastrophic casualties happen due to explosions in the pit. Orwell tells us this about these catastrophes:

The most obviously understandable cause of accidents is explosions of gas, which is always more or less present in the atmosphere of the pits. There is a special lamp to test the air for gas…it is, nevertheless, difficult to detect, because it does not distribute itself evenly throughout the atmosphere but hangs about in cracks and crevices. Before starting work a miner often tests for gas by poking his lamp into all the corners. The gas may be touched off by a spark during blasting operations, or by a pick striking a spark from a stone, or by 'gob fires' – spontaneously generated fires which smoulder in the coal dust and are very hard to put out. The great mining disasters which happen from time to time in which several hundred men are killed, are usually caused by explosions.[5]

Then Orwell gives a detailed account of the low wages the miners are paid and tells us that the compensations/ pensions in the case of disabling physical injuries/ death are a mere pittance. And as regards the residential facility made available to them, it used to be simply appalling: "As you walk through the industrial towns you lose yourself in labyrinths of little brick houses blacked by smoke, festering in planless chaos round miry alleys and little cindered yards where there are stinking dust-bins and lines of grimy washings and half-ruinous w.c.'s."[6] And if, at this point, one remembers the life of coalminers, as described in Emile Zola's *Germinal*, one's heart is filled with horror.

What Orwell has written about the miners' life is a sociological account which Larkin seems to use as the raw material for his fine poem. But the poem is a work of art, which has, as its essential beauty, the distillation from the truth of lived life.

"On the day of the explosion" we see a group of miners going to the pit to sweat it out there. They are not sullen or complaining about the conditions of their work and life. On the contrary, Larkin says,

> Down the lane came men in pitboots
> Coughing oath-edged talk and pipe-smoke,
> Shouldering off the freshened silence.

The "freshened silence" brings out the very freshness of morning's silence in a semi-urban setting. The miners shoulder off this silence – how? – "Coughing their oath-edged talk and pipe-smoke." The miners are not romanticized or idealized; they are presented simply as humans in organic relationship with organic nature in all its freshness and livingness. The miners' talk is laced with oaths as the talk of the people of this class often is. But the poet is uniquely successful in allowing the oath-edged talk (an organic happening) shoulder off the freshened silence (fresh state of organic nature in the morning) as man and nature are organically interrelated parts of the web of life. This presentation of a slice of organic, living life in the freshness and silence of morning will add to the pathos and poignancy of the tragedy that is going to happen.

The next stanza is equally remarkable. One of the miners chases "after rabbits," but rabbits run faster than men and so he is not able to catch them. Then he takes a whole nest of lark's eggs, shows it to his friends and puts it back in its place in the grass without causing damage to any of the eggs. Again, the miners are seen as naturally humans, neither upraised nor downgraded in the scale of human feelings. They are also shown in the same relationship with other forms of life in nature in their adult life as they used to be in their boyhood. They do not idealize nature nor are they aware of the transcendental relationship between their and other forms of life in nature, but they have been close to them since the beginning of their kind of life, driven by the zest of life working in them and all other forms of life operating at the physiological level. Additionally, the poet does value-addition to the act of the miner who brings the nest of lark's eggs, which provides what E. M. Forster calls Rhythm in a work of art. We shall soon see how this rhythm works in the poem.

In the equally remarkable next (4th) stanza, the miners are identified as "Fathers, brothers, nicknames, laughter" and are seen "in beards and moleskin." We are first given the familial identities (fathers, brothers) of the miners and then their personal hallmarks – nicknames, laughter. Nicknames symbolize endearment and laughter is the expression of effusion of heartiness of and zest for life. Larkin uses throughout this poem Hopkins's 'inscape' and 'instress' with the maximum poetic effect. It is these all too human miners, with their humanity, their zest for life (even their crudities, as expressed in their oath-edged talk), their identities in terms of familial relationships or their individual hallmarks fully instressed in organic terms, who "passed...Through the tall gates standing open."

Then comes stanza 5, which is of crucial significance. It is here that we are informed of the explosion in which the miners we saw in the morning and many more are killed. The stanza is masterly in its use of the meter and the broken structure of the sentence that are the exact objective correlative of the catastrophe that has taken place, as the poet does not make any direct mention of it. John Cary writes: "The meter which has been emphatically trochaic up to now suddenly alters, becoming iambic." Continuing, he writes: "Until this stanza, the lines have been mostly the end-stopped, the sense breaking at the line-ending. Now there is a slippage, a fissure. The first line breaks after 'tremor'; the next after 'second.' it's like a crack, spidering down, through geological strata."[7]

The slippage, the fissure, the spidering-down crack produce a tremendous effect on the scene around the coal mine: a tremor that sends chill down one's spine is heard; cows stop chewing cud and experience on the web of their nerves tragic sensation "for a second" without being conscious of the real nature of the tragedy; and the sun, "Scarfed in a heat-blaze," dims. Even the sun seems to be saddened at the human tragedy. Why? Because, as we are told in Wilfred Owen's great poem "Futility," it is the sun that has, through aeons of assiduous efforts, created man.

The sixth stanza is a quotation from the memorial service in the local church and the words are those spoken by the priest conducting the service.

The dead, the priest tells the people (mostly wives and relations of those killed in the explosion) attending the service, go before us and sit in comfort in God's house and when we die we shall meet them face to face. This was said "plain as lettering in the chapel" and the wives of the killed miners believed what the priest said. But did the poet believe it, and those of us who agree with him believe it? The answer is an emphatic No. But the wives believed the priest. This kind of belief of the common people is the mainstay of their exploited and poverty-stricken lives. They have no other spiritual sustenance. The wives uncritically believed in what the priest said. Not only that, they also saw "for a moment...men of the explosion/ Larger in life than they managed." Although in real life the miners worked and lived in hellish conditions, the wives have this vision, a vision that cannot but touch the hearts of those who know what deprivation is. John Wain's comment on this part of the poem is illuminating:

> The sense of a historical setting is conveyed not only by surface details (modern working men don't wear moleskins; in 1900-14 they were conventional), but also by an interior illumination, a light switched on inside the object; the women hear the words of the memorial sermon 'plain as lettering in the chapels' – the inscriptions in nonconformist chapels, mostly gold on dark wood...Larkin picks out and focuses this kind of detail because he is imagining the situation intensely and identifying with these obsolete working-class women, not patronizing them or using them as a text for a sociological sermon.[8]

Not only do the wives see their husbands larger than in life they managed, they also see them as "gold as on a coin." That is, the miners appear beatified to them. The poor wives, if they are deprived of this consolation, will have nothing to lean on in their misery. So what the priest says is a sort of placebo. Larkin, a confirmed atheist, does well to empathize with the wives in their belief in what the priest says. The most touching part of this is that the wives see their dead husbands "walking/Somehow from the sun towards them." It is not in the darkness of the underworld that the wives see them, because the priest told them that their husbands are sitting in comfort in the house of God. The wives see them in all their yearnings – their husbands coming towards them to embrace them and be embraced by them. They seem to see themselves in all the conjugal bliss which they perhaps never have had in the oppressive, deprived kind of their life. It is the hallmark of great art that it enters the very depths of the feelings and emotions of common people and gives them tragic sublimity as, for example Thomas Hardy did in his great novels: *The Mayor of Casterbridge, The Woodlanders, Tess of the D'Urbervilles,* and *Jude the Obscure.*

And then we have the final line of the poem standing separately from the rest of it, as in several of Larkin's other poems: "I Remember, I Remember," "The Building," and "The Card-Players." These last lines seem to have a special significance in the thematic structure of the poems. In the present poem, we saw earlier one miner bring to his colleagues a nest of lark's eggs. And now one of the dead miners is seen walking towards the wives with an egg in his hand. The context is that the wives are imagining the enjoyment of a kind of bliss – the bliss of conjugal consummation with their husbands coming straight from the house of God. This is an illusion for the poet and the rest of us, but for the wives it is not an illusion, it is actually what they see and yearn for – their yearning is that with their beatified husbands they should have consummation that may produce an egg. And in such kind of consummation and procreation they will be fulfilled.

Now a word to those Larkin critics to whom Larkin seems to think only in negatives. A poet who has written such great poems as "The Whitsun Weddings" and "The Explosion," not counting poems like "The Wedding Wind" and "Deceptions," has his creative self suffused with love for the common man. As a consummate artistic creation "The Explosion" is comparable to D. H. Lawrence's "The Odour of Chrysanthemums."

Chapter Six
Conclusion

Poet: What is poetry?
Daughter [Daughter of Indra, the Vedic deity]: Not reality,
but more than reality.
Not dreams, but waking dreams.
                                    Strindberg: *A Dream Play*.

In his play *Three Sisters*, Anton Chekhov writes these lines about the sorry existential condition of man:

> :Why do we become so dull and commonplace and uninteresting almost before we've begun to live? Why do we get lazy, indifferent, useless and unhappy? This town's been in existence for two hundred years; a hundred thousand people live in it, but there's not one who's any different from all the others! There's never been a scholar or an artist or a saint in this place, never a single man sufficiently outstanding to make you feel passionately that you wanted to emulate him. People here do nothing but eat, drink and sleep....Then they die and some more take their places, they eat, drink and sleep too – and just to introduce a bit of variety into their lives, so as to avoid getting completely stupid with boredom, they indulge in their disgusting gossip and vodka and gambling and law suits....And all this overwhelming vulgarity and pettiness crushes the children and puts out any spark they might have in them, so they, too, become miserable, half-dead creatures, just like one another and just like their parents![1]

If this poor crop of human race is all that our earth continues to yield from generation to generation, the earth's soil will become so barren that in not very distant future it will not yield any human crop at all. This is the remorse-less law of evolution. No wonder Philip Larkin laments that whole nations live a life as vague as that of weeds and, in another poem, raising a finger of warn-ing, says to the younger generation of today:

> They fuck you up, your mum and dad.
> They don't mean to, but they do.
> They fill you with the faults they had
> And add some extra, just for you.

The fucking up of the cognitive. Intellectual, spiritual, transcendental growth, in fact, all kinds of positive growth of the psyche of growing chil-dren has been going on for a long time now so that man's misery has, Lar-kin says, deepened "like a coastal shelf." In the circumstances, Larkin's advice to these children (or adolescents) is: "Get out as early as you can,/ And don't have any children yourselves." Larkin here sounds pessimistic but we must not, before we blame him on this score, forget the cruel words of Hamlet to Ophelia when he asks her to go to a nunnery and not be a begetter of sinners.

But Hamlet is not a pessimist, nor is Philip Larkin one. Some of his finest poems – "The Wedding Wind," "Here," "Mr Bleaney," "The Whitsun Wed-dings," "Faith Healing," "Show Saturday," "The Explosion," for example – are suffused with empathy for the common man. But all is not well with the world in which the common man lives. A creative artist worth his salt has to jolt us into a new kind of awareness of the realities (as opposed to those which are not realities) of the so-called waking world. But when he tries to uncover the ugly face of this world, in which "Nothing, like something, happens any-where," we start calling him names, such as pessimist, provincial, misogynist, kid Sophocles and what not. Those who abuse Sophocles – for to call So-phocles, one of the greatest creative writers the world has produced so far, a pessimist is nothing but heaping abuse on him – should take the trouble of just reading Herodotus' monumental work *Histories* in which he tells us of the "divine truth" Solon had declared, "no man can be called happy until he was dead"(p.40). A remarkable short poem entitled "Zola" by the American poet Edwin Arlington Robinson begins with these lines:

Because he puts the compromising chart
Of hell before your eyes, you are afraid;
Because he counts the price you have paid
For innocence, and counts it from the start,
You loathe him.[2]

In the world in which we live, our new-born lambs, from the very beginning ("first sight") of their perception of the world around them, are not allowed to see things as they are, so that they find the world "a wretched width
of cold" and are never told that there lies "Hidden around them, waiting too"
something "Utterly unlike the snow." It is a world in which we have been so
crippled (metaphorically speaking) that we "know nothing," are never sure "Of
what is true or right or real." In this world we

spend all our life on imprecisions,
That when we start to die
Have no idea why.

It is a world in which "the unfailing sense of being young/ Spread out like
a spring-woken tree, wherein [lies] / That hidden freshness" that wants fruition
and fulfillment in love – a love that solves and satisfies and sets life "unchange-
ably in order" – is never fructified. It is a world in which we find that even in
ugly, elderly women "a kind of dumb / And idiot child … still survives / To re-
awake at kindness" so that, while in the so-called "warm spring of rain of loving
care" (of the jet-set American faith-healer) lasting "some twenty seconds," they
think that at last a voice "calls them alone, that hands have come/ To lift and
lighten" and so they experience "such Joy" that "Their thick tongues blort,
their eyes squeeze grief, a crowd/ Of huge unheard answers jam and rejoice."
But the faith healer does not lift and lighten. It is a cruel world in which "the
hail / Of occurrence clobber(s) life out/ To a shape" that hardly anyone can
understand what life is or should be and even an earnest person, let us say, like
Larkin the poet, spends "youth, /Tracing the trite untransferable/ Truss-ad-
vertisement, truth." It is a vulgar and cruel world in which giant hoardings
"Screen graves with custard, cover slums with praise of motor-oil and cuts of
salmon," and show "High above the gutter/ A silver knife [sink] into the golden
butter." These monstrously vulgar hoardings have the brazenness to tell us
through "these pictured groves/ Of how life should be." But, truth to say, they

"rise / Serenely to proclaim pure crust, pure foam,/Pure coldness to our live imperfect eyes/ That stare beyond this world." Among these hoardings can be seen one in which a sexually alluring girl is seen luring men to smoke which leads to their death by cancer. It is a world in which vile commercialism exploits the overt sexual appeal of a girl "on the poster" to attract tourists to a hotel at a sea-coast:

> *Come to Sunny Prestatyn*
> Laughed the girl on the poster,
> ....
> Behind her, a hunk of coast, a
> Hotel with palms
> Seemed to expand from her thighs and
> Spread breast-lifting arms.

No wonder the poster is equally obscenely vandalized.

It is a world in which a study of the reading habits of those who read books tells us something very unflattering about the readers as well as the books they read. The typical book-reader in Larkin's poem tells us:

> It was worth ruining my eyes
> To know I could still keep cool,
> And deal out the old right hook
> To dirty dogs twice my size.

The books the persona read were a too ridiculously small hook, metaphorically speaking, to catch "dirty dogs"(again metaphorically speaking) twice his size. They also lulled him into complacency so that, even though his eyes were ruined reading them, he "could still keep cool." However, he kept reading them, though now "with inch-thick specs;" but now, he says to us, "Evil was my lark<," so that he and his "cloak and fangs/ Had ripping times in the dark," that is, he "clubbed" women with sex" and "broke them up like meringues." So Larkin's judicious advice to us in the matter of reading books is

> Get stewed:
> Books are a load of crap.

What Larkin says of books and book-readers is true of most books and most book-readers, which is a pity, considering the urgent need for both of them to change the sorry condition of the world. These books, "a load of crap," are not pulp writing, as some would have us believe. They are touted to be serious books in many fields of knowledge, but which dispense only untruths and half-truths, obfuscating realities which are more than realities.

It is a world in which lovers lying together in bed – an emblem of two people being honest to each other – should find it easiest to talk to each other, particularly as they are, in bed, at a "unique distance from isolation," that is, from "the wind's complete unrest" outside that "Builds and disperses clouds about the sky" as well as from "dark towns" that seem to be heaped up "on the horizon," none of which cares for them. "Yet," the poet tells us, " more and more of time [of the lovers in bed] passes silently" so that he wonders why at this unique distance from isolation

It becomes still more difficult to find
Words at once true or kind,
Or not untrue and not unkind.

It is a world in which the big-wigs of our business world and their ladies – "a cast of crooks and tarts" – have produced such a "thick-strewn" heap of "greeds and garbage" that it cannot "be swept up now." It is a world in which characters like Jan van Hogspew, Dirk Dogstoerd and Old Prijck – abominations of human existence – live such a degrading kind of life in a cave-like room that the poet shouts a Lear-like imprecation:

Rain wind and fire! The secret, bestial peace!

It is a world in which "the old fools," even though "crouching below/ Extinction's alp" never perceive how near it is, what is dragging them and how it will it end because "throughout...[their] whole hideous inverted childhood" they were never told the truth about life and death – that life meant bringing to bloom "the million-petalled flower of being here" and "at death, you break up: the bits [cells, molecules, atoms, sub-atomic particles] that were you/ Start speeding away from each other for ever/ With no one to see."

It is a world in which parties given by middle-class people are attended by crowds of "craps...In a pig's arse." One can attend such parties, spend half his evenings at them, "Holding a glass of washing sherry" and canting

> Over to catch the drivel of some bitch
> Who's read nothing but *Which*

At such parties one can clearly see how his "spare time" has "flown/ Straight into nothingness by being filled /With forks and faces." But cutting such parties and sitting alone in one's room of an evening does not seem to be an option either because, when "Day comes to an end" and "The gas fire breathes" and " the trees are darkly swayed," one feels afraid. Afraid because

> sitting by a lamp more often brings
> Not peace, but other things.
> Beyond the light stand failure and remorse.

And our supposed superiors in knowledge and wisdom – the dons of Cambridge/ Oxford universities – instead of dispensing and disseminating light to us, talk, at the dining table, rubbish and indulge in obscenities like discussion of the female external genitals.

But what about man's life in his recorded history, to say nothing of his pre-historical existence in trees and caves and forests? One has only to go to "An Arundel Tomb" – one of Philip Larkin's best poems – to see what the ruling elite if medieval England – barons, earls, dukes and their ilk – were: they were ignorant, nasty, vainglorious oppressors. Their period is now seen only as a "scrap" of history" and "Time has transfigured them into / Untruth."

But Larkin does not adopt a holier-than-thou attitude *vis-à-vis* Mr Bleaney; or the newly-married couples on the train one Whitsun afternoon; or the cut-price crowd, urban yet simple, in a department store; or the factory workers "Who leave at dawn low terraced houses" and sometimes come to a large cool store and stand fantasizing before "the stands of Modes for Night:/ Machine-embroidered, thin as blouses,/ Lemon, sapphire, moss-green, rose/ Bri-Nylon Baby-Dolls and Sorties" and how in their "young unreal wishes" women "Seem to be: synthetic, new/ And natureless in ecstasies." His authorized biographer, Jake Balokovsky, says some very unflattering things about him. He calls him an "old fart" and 'bastard" and says that the research he is carrying on for writing the biography is "stinking dead." In reply to a query by his companion what kind of a person the subject of his research (i.e. Philip Larkin) is, Jake Balokovsky replies:

> Oh, you know the thing
> That crummy textbook stuff from Freshman Psych,
> Not out for kicks or something happening –
> One of those old- type *natural* fouled-up guys.

But Philip Larkin is a post-modern British poet with a deep concern for the health of human civilization. A post-modern poet has a difficult task or duty to perform. The American poet Wallace Stevens tells us in his poem "Modern Poetry" that a modern poem is a "poem of the mind in the act of finding/ What will suffice." He adds:

> It has not always had
> To find: the scene was set; it repeated what
> Was in the script.

But now the "theatre" has changed "To something else" and "Its past is… a souvenir." Modern poetry

> has to be living, to learn the speech of the place
> It has to face the men of the time and to meet
> The women of the time.

To perform this onerous task "It has/ To construct a new stage." And from this stage modern poetry, "like an insatiable actor," has to speak

> slowly and
> With meditation…words that in the ear,
> In the delicate ear of the mind, repeat,
> Exactly, that which it wants to hear, at the sound
> Of which an invisible audience listens,
> Not to the play, but to itself, expressed
> In an emotion as of two people, as of two
> Emotions becoming one.

It is a very difficult task that modern poetry sets itself, but it has a duty to do by man. To do this duty creditably "the actor (that is, modern poetry) must be a "metaphysician." We have seen above what Sartre says about metaphysics and what true metaphysics does (We repeat Sartre's words and beg to be excused for this – metaphysics "is not a sterile discussion about abstract notions which have nothing to do with experience. It is a living effort to embrace from within the human condition in its totality.") According to Wallace Stevens, modern poetry is

> A metaphysician in the dark, twanging
> An instrument, twanging a wiry instrument that gives
> Sounds passing through sudden rightness, wholly
> Beyond which it has no will to rise.[3]

Philip Larkin's poetry is very much concerned with the metaphysics of man's existence in the cosmic-inorganic-cum-organic-biological-cum-psycho-social perspectives. In our analysis of poems like "Here," "Water," "Days," "The Whitsun Weddings," "First Sight," "High Windows," "Solar," "Sympathy in White Major," "Forget What Did" we have tried to show how Larkin sees and evaluates the human condition in these perspectives – what he calls "the long perspectives." He says that "our element is time" – the time that came into existence some 14 billion years ago, which continues to exist in us and which may continue to exist for another 14 billion years for all we know. The word "element" here ("basic constituent part," the dictionary meaning) is important. Without this element we do not exist at all. Julian Huxley tells us very clearly about our relationship with "the long perspectives" in these words: "…the present is the first period in which we have been able to grasp that the universe is a process in time and to get a first glimpse of our true relation with it. We can see ourselves as history, and can see that history in its proper relation with the history of the universe as a whole."[4] If man could relate his existence to these vast perspectives he would understand the value of his life better. But, unfortunately, "We are not suited to the long perspectives" although they "open at each instant of our lives." These perspectives "link us to losses." What losses? We have lost the real perspective on our lives, a perspective in which inhered an immense capacity to sublimate our lives to heavenly heights and irradiate our terrestrial existence so that truth and reality, not untruth and unreality (or untruths and unrealities) guided our lives. To understand what this immense capacity or light means it may be worthwhile to go to two beautiful short poems – "Considering the Snail" by Thom Gunn and "The Striders" by the Indian poet A. K. Ramanujan.

Thom Gunn's snail in its passage in the dark underneath the rain-drenched grass has left a trail of its slow movement – the poet calls it "the bright path" and adds that he (the snail) makes it "where rain/ has darkened the earth's dark." The poet uses the pronoun "he" for the snail, which is significant in that he sees similarities between man and the snail. Both are made from the same "simple matter" and in both there is light, the light emanating from the complex structures composed of organic constituents. In man the range and depth of this light is immensely greater than in the snail and it is also multi-dimensional; it is a different matter what use man makes or does not make of this light. But the snail does although its quota of the selfsame light is minuscule. The poet considers the snail making the optimal use of whatever light it is blest with. The trail or the path the snail makes is the outcome of the use of the light or energy inhering in his make. Not only that; he "moves in a wood of desire,/ pale antlers barely stirring/ as he hunts." The poet does not know, he does not have the real metaphysical eye to perceive this light in action, split second by split second, impelled by the "wood of desire." So the poet says

> I cannot tell
> what power is at work, drenched there
> with purpose, knowing nothing.

But he says that if he "parted the blades above/ the tunnel and saw the thin/ train of broken white/ across litter" he

> would never have
> imagined the slow passion
> to that deliberate progress.[5]

The snail stands on a pretty low rung on the long ladder of life; its quota of the light of life is very meager and yet it has a direction and purpose and he "moves in a wood of desire." The grass is heavy with water and the "rain/ has darkened the earth's dark," and yet the light in him has acquired properties such as direction, purpose and desire, though the desire is only a tangled wood in which paths are not clear. This light makes him move purposefully in a particular direction along a dark and difficult path in search of food and this movement makes a "bright path." The light of life has left a bright trail in the darkness of the world of the snail's existence. When shall we learn to leave a bright trail along the path that we tread in our life?

A.K. Ramanujan's "The Striders" is an equally enlightening poem. Striders, the poet tells us, are microscopic water bugs with capillary legs. They are seen in the New England region of the USA. They sit on the surface of water and look at it. The surface of water is the world – a world that has evolved from cosmic matter and is the source of all life on our planet – of their existence. They look at it with whatever perceptive sense they have. Which means that the light or energy which is manifested in or through their organic structures tries to bring itself to bear on the world of their existence, that is, water. It is an effort on the part of life to understand the world of objective realities. The vision is microscopic, but it is still vision or light of life. Ramanujan writes:[6]

> And search
> for certain thin-
> stemmed, bubble-eyed water bugs,
> see them perch
> on dry capillary legs
> weightless
> on the ripple skin
> of a stream.
>
> No, not only prophets
> walk on water. This bug sits
> on a landslide of lights
> and drowns eye-
> deep
> into its tiny strip
> of sky.

The poet evaluates this light – and in this he is only performing his duty as a poet – and says that, qualitatively speaking, it is the same light that prophets have had, the prophets who, blest with it in the form of their transcendental perceptions, walked on water, as the Buddha and Christ are said to have done.

What the above two poets have done in their poems is of tremendous significance for man. The snail and the strider, with their miniscule lights – and life is light, the same light that the stars have – fulfill themselves to the extent that is possible with the gift life has given them. Man's light, because of the immeasurably greater complexity of his make than that of the snail and the strider, has such range, profundity and sublimity that, on the one hand, it brings to bear itself on cosmic space and time and, on the other, it sees itself mirrored in all the constituent elements of his body (elementary particles, atoms, molecules, cells, muscles) seething with the purpose that the light of life grants them. It is this light that manifests itself in his consciousness that in its sublime manifestations creates great works of art, makes great scientific discoveries and inventions, builds great philosophical systems, makes the noble acts of social reformers, saints and prophets happen. This life is productive in the unpolluted mind of the common man – the vast majority of the humankind – so that we have crops and fruits and vegetables as well as many industrial productions that keep our body and mind in good condition. This light has been manifesting itself in the rise of great civilizations in the various parts of the world. And it is this light, this light alone – man's sole asset – that can show man the path of his future progress.

But it is easier said than done. There are ugly spots, patches of darkness, abominable, poison-secreting toads in the metaphysical make of man that have been doing their damnedest to pervert man's conscience and have succeeded in making his world "Darkness Visible." The reason for this sorry existential condition of man is given in the following lines in a poem by E.E.Cummings:

so many selves (so many fiends and gods
each greedier than every) is a man
(so easily one in another hides;
yet man can, being all, escape from none)[7]

These lines do not give a deterministic view of man's life. They only give us a realistic picture of the metaphysics of his being. It is not that man cannot subdue, if not kill, a majority of the fiends infesting his soul.

Philip Larkin has faith in the common man and his mentor in this regard is Thomas Hardy. His best poems are about the common man. The common man in his poetry is represented by such characters as the bride in "The Wedding Wind;" the not-so-ignorant church goer, at whose lower social status we like to sneer; the inarticulate newly-wedded couples on the train one Whitsun afternoon; the Mr Bleaneys of our acquaintance; the cut-price crowd, simple but urban, and "grim head-scarved wives;" the ugly and poor women whose spiritual selves, for lack of love, have become rigid; the all-too-human miners who die in the coal-mine explosion and their wives who believe that their love for their dead husbands, beatified in heaven, will have consummation of a heavenly kind.

Philip Larkin's poetry, with true metaphysics as its underpinning, is intended to wake up the common man into a new awareness of the vast perspectives in which they are brought into being. If this awakening materializes man will try to live up to his greatness and much of the ills and corruptions of the world will die, will be eliminated. But, as he points out in "Sympathy in White Major" and "Nothing to be Said," this awakening is a difficult, though not an impossible task, even though we cannot afford to forget the following words of a historian we quoted above which says that man has "the dubious distinction of being the deadliest species in the annals of biology." We would like to conclude this chapter and our work with the following lines from Walt Whitman's poem "We Two, How Long We Were Fool'd:"

> We are Nature, long have we been absent, but now we return
> We become plants, trunks, foliage, roots, bark,
> We are bedded in the ground, we are rocks,
> We are oaks...
> We browse, we are two among the wild herds spontaneous as any,
> We are two fishes swimming in the sea together,
> ...   ...
> We are also the coarse smut of beasts, vegetables, minerals,
> We are two predatory hawks, we soar above and look down,
> We are two resplendent suns, we it is who balance ourselves
> orbic and stellar, we are as two comets,
> We prowl fang'd and four-footed in the woods, we spring on prey,
> We are seas mingling, we are two of those cheerful waves rol-
> ling over each other and intertwining each other,
> ...   ...
> We are snow, rain, cold, darkness, we are each product and
> influence of the globe,
> We have circled and circled till we have arrived home again,
> We have voided all but freedom and all but our own joy.[8]

NOTES AND REFERENCES

CHAPTER I

1. Saul Bellow, *Humboldt's* Gift (New York: Avon Books, 1973; rpt. 1976), p. 255.
2. Graham Greene, *The Comedians* (Penguin Books 1966; rpt. 1967), p. 54.
3. William Golding, *Lord of the Flies* (Penguin Books,1954; rpt. 1967), p. 5.
4. _____, "Fable," *The Hot Gates* (London: Faber & Faber, 1965; rpt. 1974), p. 87.
5. Albert Camus, "Nobel Prize Acceptance Speech," *Nobel Prize Library:* Published under the sponsorship of Nobel Foundation & The Swedish Academy (New York & California: C. R. M. Publishing,1971), p. 9.
6. Samuel Beckett, *Waiting for Godot*, (London: Faber & Faber, 1956; rpt. Dorling Kindersley India Pvt. Ltd., 2006), p. 5.
7. Ibid. p. 72.
8. Albert Camus, *The Myth of Sisyphus*, Trans. Justin O'Brien (Penguin Books, 1955; rpt. 2000), pp. 112-113.
9. Franz Kafka, *The Trial*, Trans. Willa & Edwin Muir (London: Vintage Classics, 1925; rpt. 1999), p. 211.
10. T. S. Eliot, "Love Song of Alfred J. Prufrock," *Anthology of American Literature* vol. II (General ed.) George Michael (New York: Macmillan Publishing Co. 1074; rpt. 1985), pp. 1168-1171.
11. Anthony Huxley, *Plant and Planet* (Penguin Books, 1974; rpt. 1978), p. 11.

12. J. B. S. Haldane, *Causes of Evolution*, (Princeton, New Jersey: Princeton University Press, 1932, rpt. 1993) p.90.

13. Sigmund Freud, *The Future of an Illusion*, Trans. James Strachey (New York: W. W. Norton & Co. 1961), p. 7.

14. Saul Bellow, *Herzog*, (Penguin Books, 1964; rpt. 1976), p. 28.

15. Sir James Frazer, *The Golden Bough* (author's own abridgement of the book in 12 vols., Wordsworth Editions Ltd. 1993), p. 325.

16. William Golding, "The Scorpion God," *Three Short Novels* (London: Faber & Faber,1971; rpt. 1973), p. 42.

17. J. K. Huysmans, *Against Nature*, Trans. Robert Baldick (Penguin Books, 1884; rpt. 1959), p. 219.

18. Scott Fitzerald, *This Side of Paradise* (Penguin Books, 1920; rpt. 1963), p 220.

19. William Golding, *Darkness Visible* (London: Faber & Faber, 1979; rpt.1983), p. 206.

20. Saul Bellow, *Herzog*, p. 50.

21. Ibid. p. 320.

22. Joseph Conrad, "The Shadow-Line," *Three Sea Stories*, (Wordsworth Classics, 1998), p. 174.

23. Steven Weinberg, *The First Three Minutes* (New York: Basic Books A Member of the Perseus Books Group, 1977; rpt. 1993), pp. 154-155.

24. Ibid. p.154.

25. M. R. Cohen, Quoted by G. G. Simpson as Epigraph to Part I of his *The Meaning of Evolution* (1949; Yale University Press: Indian Publication: Oxford & I. B. H. Publication, Calcutta,1965), p. 9.

26. Carl Sagan, *Cosmos* (London: Abacus, 1980; rpt. 1995), p.20.

27. Martin Heidegger, *Existence and Being*, Trans. Werner Brock (London: WI Vision Press Ltd.), p. 357.

28. Julian Huxley, *Evolution in Action* (London: Chatto & Windus, 1953), p. 11.

29. Henri Bergson, *Creative Evolution* Trans. Arthur Mitchell (New York: Dover Publications, 1911; rpt. 1998), p. 78.

30. Naguib Mahfouz, *The Cairo Trilogy* Trans. William Maynard Hutchins, et. al (Cairo: American University in Cairo Press, 2001), p. 895.

31. Steven Weinberg, op. cit. p. 5.

32. Ibid. p. 5.

33. Ibid. p. 6.

34. Ibid. pp. 7-8.

35. Ibid. p. 8.

36. Ibid. p. 8.

37. Carl Sagan, op. cit. p. 21.

38. Ibid. p. 21.

39. Steven Weinberg, op. cit. p. 182.

40. Carl Sagan, op.cit. p. 23.

41. Stephen Hawking, *A Brief History of Time* (London: Bantam Books published by Transworld Publishers, 1988; rpt. 1989), p. 123.

42. Steven Weinberg,,op. cit. pp16-17.

43. Stephen Hawking, op. cit. p. 13.

44. Carl Sagan, op. cit. p. 32.

45. Werner Heisenberg, *Physics and Philosophy* (Penguin Books, 1958; rpt. 2000), p. 28.

46. Ibid. p. 29.

47. Ibid. p. 37.

48. Ibid. p. 106.

49. Ibid. p. 107.

50. Ibid. p 107.

51. Ibid.5i. Julian Huxley, op. cit. p 12.

52. Stephen Hawking, op. cit. pp. 12-13.

53. A. I. Oparin, *Genesis and Evolutionary Development of Life*, Trans. From Russian by Eleanor Mass (New York & London: Academic Press, 1968), pp.46-47.

54. Ibid. p. 41.

55. Stephen Hawking, op. cit. p. 131.

56. A. I. Oparin, op. cit. p. 58.

57. G. Brent Dalrymple, *The Age of the Earth*, (Stanford, California: Stanford University Press,1991; rpt. 2001), pp. 399 & 400.

58. Julian Huxley, op. cit. p. 12.

59. Ibid. pp. 12-13.

60. Ibid. p. 13.

61. Ibid. pp. 13-14.

62-64.. Ibid. p. 14

65. G. G. Simpson, *Biology and Man* (New York: Harcourt Brace, 1964; rpt.1969), p. 45.

66. Ibid. p. 7.

67. Fritjof Capra, *The Web of Life*, (London: Flamingo, 1970), pp. 254-255.

68. John Peter, "The Fables of William Golding," *Kenyon Review*, vol. XIX (1957), pp. 577-592.

69. Erwin Schrodinger, *What is Life* with *Mind and Matter?* (Cambridge: Cambridge University Press, 1958, rpt. 2010), p. 130.

70. G. G. Simpson, op. cit. p. 69.

71. Carl Sagan, op. cit. pp. 303-304.

72. Ibid. p. 305.

73. Julian Huxley, op.cit. p. 68.

74. J.B.S. Haldane, op. cit. p. 83.

75. Julian Huxley, *Evolution: The Modern Synthesis* (London: George Allen & Unwin, 1942, rpt. 1974), p. 574..

76. Carl Sagan, op. cit. p. 374.

CHAPTER THREE

1. *The Less* Deceived : *Philip Larkin Collected Poems*, (ed.) Anthony Thwaite (London: Faber & Faber, 1988; ebook edition,2014). "Church Going"

2. Simon Petch, *The Art of Philip Larkin*, (Sydney: Sydney University Press, 1981), p. 55.

3. David Lodge, "Philip Larkin: The Metonymic Muse," in Dale Salwak (ed.), *Philip Larkin: The Man and his Work* (Basingstoke: The Macmillan Press, 1989), p. 125.

4. Ian Hamilton, "Four Conversations," *London Magazine* IV (Nov. 1964), pp.71-82.

5. John Wain, "The Importance of Philip Larkin," *The American Scholar*, vol. 55, no. 3 (1986), pp. 349-364.

6. Keith Sagar, "Philip Larkin," in Maurice Hussey (ed.) *Criticism in Action* (London: Longmans, 1969), pp. 117-126.

7. David Lodge, op. cit. p. 126.

8. George Santayana, "Ideal Immortality," in Daniel J Bronstein & Harold M Schulweis (eds.) *Approaches to the Philosophy of Religion* (Englewood Ciiffs NJ: Prentice Hall Inc. 1954; rpt. 1960), pp.507-518.

9. Anthony F. C. Wallace, *Religion: An Anthropological View* (New York: Random House, 1966), p.vi (Preface).

10. Ibid. p.127.

11. Ibid.

12. Keith Sagar, op. cit. p. 123.

13. William James , *Varieties of Religious Experience* (New York: The Modern Library, 2002), p. 552.

14. Leo Tolstoy, "A Reply to the Synod's Edict on Excommunication," *Religion from Tolstoy to Camus* (ed.) Walter Kaufmann (New Brunswick, U.S.A. 1961, rpt 1994), pp.131-132.

15. Terry Whalen, *Philip Larkin and English Poetry* (Hong Kong: Macmillan, 1986), p. 17.

II. "Deceptions"

1. Janice Rossen, *Philip Larkin: His Life's Work* (Hertfordshire: Harvester Wheatsheaf, 1989), P. 88.

2. Khalil Gibran, "Martha," *Nymphs of the Valley, The Greatest Works of Khalil Gibran* (Mumbai: Jaico Publishing House, 7th Jaico Impression, 1999), pp.19-20.

3. *Quoted in J. Goode*, "The More Deceived: A Reading of 'Deceptions,'" (ed.) George Hartley , *Philip Larkin (1922-1985): A Tribute* (London: The Marvell Press, 1988), pp. 126-134.

4. *Philip* Larkin, Quoted by Andrew Swarbrick, *Out of Reach: The Poetry of Philip Larkin (London:* Macmillan,*1995)*, pp. 43-44.

5. John Betjeman, "Slough," *The Nation's Twentieth Century Favourite Poems*, (ed) Rhys Jones (London: BBC Co.,1999), p. 90.

6. Fyodor Dostoevsky, *The Karamazov Brothers*, Trans. Constance Garnett (Wordsworth Classics, 2010), p. 160.

7. Ibid. p. 261.

8. Geoffrey Leech, *A Linguistic Guide to English Poetry* (London:L Longman, 1969), p. 158.
9. Jean-Paul Sartre, *Being and* Nothingness, Trans. Hazel E Barnes (New York: Wahington Square Press, 1943, rpt.1992), p. 154.
10. Walpola Sir Rahula, "Buddha's Fire Sermon," *What the Buddha Taught* (Oxford: One World Publications, 1959, rpt. 2007), pp. 95-97.

"I Remember, I Remember"

1. Philip Larkin, "Not the Place's Fault," *An Enormous Yes* (ed.) Harry Chambers (Peterloo Poets, 1986), pp. 48-53.
2. Gary A Davis, "Training Creativity in Adolescence," *Studies in Adolescence* (ed.) Robert E Grinder (London: The Macmillan Co. 1963, rpt. 1970), pp.538-545.
3. "Adolescence," *Encyclopedia of Psychology vol. I.* (Editor in chief) Alan E Kazdin, American Psychological Association (New York: O. U. P. 2000), pp, 39-59.
4. *Palgrave's Golden Treasury* (London; O. U. P. 1897, rpt 1966), pp. 223-224.
5. Matthew Arnold, "The Function of Criticism," *The Norton Anthology of English Literature Fifth Edition: The Major Authors* (General Editor) M. H. Abrams (New York: W. W. Norton & Co. 1962, rpt. 1986), P. 2159.

CHAPTER IV

The Whitsun Weddings: Philip Larkin Collected Poems

I. "Here"

1. Simon Petch, The *Art of Philip Larkin*, (Sydney: Sydney University Press, 1981), p. 79.
2. Andrew Swarbrick, *The Whitsun Weddings* and *The Less Deceived* (Basingstoke: Palgrave Macmillan, 1986), p. 39

3. Jean Hartley, *Philip Larkin's Hull and East Yorkshire* (Hull: The Philip Larkin Society, 1995; rpt. 2005), pp. 17 &48.
4. Donald Davie, *Thomas Hardy and British Poetry* (London: Routledge & Kegan Paul 1970; rpt 1979), pp.6-7.
5. Ibid.
6. Julian Huxley, *The Uniqueness of Man* (London: Chatto & windus,1941), pp. 260-261.
7. Barbara Everett, "Larkin and Dockery: The Limits of the Social," *Philip Larkin (1922-1985): A Tribute* (ed.) George Hartley (London: The Marvell Press, 1988), pp. 140-152.
8. H. G. Widdowson, "Here," *The Edinburgh Course in Applied Linguistics*, Vol.3 (eds.) J. P. B Allen & S. Pit Corder (London: O.U.P. 1974), pp.214-219.
9. David Trotter, *The Making of the Reader* (London & Basingstoke: Macmillan, 1984), p.179.
10. H. G. Wtddowson, op. cit.

II."Mr Bleaney"

1. Luigi Pirandello, *Six Characters in Search of an* Author, Trans. Anthony Mortimer (Oxford: Oxford University Press, 2014), p.10.
2. Philip Larkin, quoted by Andrew Swarbrick, *Out of Reach: The Poetry of Philip Larkin* (London: Macmillan Press Ltd. 1995), p.97.
3. Jean-Paul Sartre, *What is Literature?*, Trans. Bernard Frechtman (London: Routledge,1948; rpt. 1993), p.219.
4. D. H. Lawrence, *Women in Love* (London: Heinemann 1921; rpt. 1950), p. 470.
5. H. G. Widdowson, "The Conditional Presence of Mr Bleaney," *Language and Literature*(ed.) Donald Carter (London: George Allen &Unwin, 1982), pp. 19-25.

III. "Nothing to be Said,"

1. Homer W. Smith, *From Fish to Philosopher* (Boston; Little, Brown & Co., 1953), p.184.
2. Saul Bellow, *Mr Sammler's Planet* (Delhi: Universal Book Stall, 1969; rpt. 1970), p.89.
3. ————————-, *Henderson the Rain King*, (Penguin Books,1959; rpt. 1975), p. 124.
4. Julian Huxley, *Evolution: The Modern Synthesis*, pp.577-578.
5. Carl Sagan, op. cit. p. 358.

IV. "Naturally the Foundation will Bear Your Expenses"

1. Ian Hamilton, "Four Conversations," *London Magazine*, IV,6 (Nov. 1964), pp.71-82.
2. Emile Durkheim, *Elementary Forms of Religious Life*, Tr. Joseph Ward Swain, (London: George Allen &Unwin, 1915), p. 27.
3. Samuel Butler, *The Way of All Flesh*, (Wordsworth Classics, rpt. 1994), p.304.
4. Jean-Paul Sartre, *Being and Nothingness*, Trans. Hazel E. Barnes (New York: Washington Square Press, 1943; rpt. 1992), pp. 87 &89.
5. Simon Petch *The Art of Philip Larkin* (Sydney: Sydney University Press, 1981), pp. 63-64.
6. John Wain, "Engagement or Withdrawal?: Notes on the Work of Philip Larkin," *Critical Quarterly*, vol. 6, No. 2 (Summer 1964), pp.167-178

V. "Home is so Sad"

1. Andrew Motion, *Philip Larkin: A Writer's Life* (London: Faber & Faber, 1993; rpt. 1994), p.290
2. Saul Bellow, *Mr Sammler's Planet* (Delhi; Universal Book Stall, 1967; rpt. 1970), p. 135.

3. Martin Heidegger, "Building Dwelling Thinking," *Poetry, Language, Thought* Tr. Albert Hofstadter (New York; Harper & Row, Publishers, 1971), p. 145.
4. Ibid. p. 147.
5. Ibid., 147.
6. Ibid., 148-149.
7. Richard Carrington, *A Million Years of Man* (London: Weidenfeld & Nicolson, 1963), Plate opposite p. 81.
8. Ibid., p. 104.
9. Ibid., p. 154.
10. Ibid., p. 151.
11. Ibid., P.169.

VI &VII. "Toads" and "Toads Revisited"

1. Khalil Gibran, *The Greatest Works of Khalil Gibran* (Mumbai: Jaico Publishing House rpt. 1999), p.35.
2. D. H. Lawrence, "Work," *Modern Poems* (ed.) Michael Thorpe (London: Oxford University Press, 1963; rpt. 1969), pp.42-43.
3. M. L. Rosenthal, "Philip Larkin," *The New Poets: American and British Poetry since World War I* (New York; O. U. P. 1967; rpt.1970), pp. 233-234.
4. John Wain, "The Poetry Of Philip Larkin," *Professing Poetry* (London: Macmillan, 1977), pp.161-180.
5. Eugene O'Neill, *The Hairy Ape* in *Five Plays* (Penguin Books, rpt. 1970), Scene Five *(Stage Direction)*, p. 165.
6. George Orwell, *Keep the Aspidistra Flying* (London: Martin Secker & Warburg Ltd. 1936; rpt. 1973), p. 287.
7. John Skinner, "Philip Larkin by Philip Larkin," *Ariel, vol. 20* (January, 1989), pp.77-95.
8. R. P.. King, "Without Illusion: The Poetry of Philip Larkin," *Nine Contemporary Poets* (London: Methuen, 1979), pp. 1-43.
9. W. H. Auden, "Address to the Beasts," *W. H. Auden* Poems selected by John Fuller (London: Faber & Faber, 2005), p. 95.

10. John Skinner, op. cit.

11. Colvin Bedient, "Philip Larkin," *Eight Contemporary Poets* (London: O. U. P., 1974; rpt.1975), pp. 69-97.

XIII. "Water"

1. George Bernard Shaw, *Major Barbara*, Act III, *The Norton Anthology of English Literature*, vol.2, (General ed.) M. H. Abrams (New York: W. W. Norton & Co. 1962; rpt. 1974), p.1819.

2. William James, The Principles of Psychology,p.189..

3. Thomas Mann, *The Magic Mountain*, Trans. H. T. Lowe-Porter (Penguin Books, 1924; rpt. 1971), p. 266.

4. Werner Heisenberg, *Physics and Philosophy* (Penguin Books: 1958; rpt.2000), p. 20.

5. William Golding, *Darkness Visible*, (London: Faber & Faber, 1979; rpt.1983), p.222.

6. Julian Huxley, *Religion Without Revelation* (London: Max Parish, 1936; rpt. 1957), p.1.

7. Matthew Arnold, "The Study of Poetry," *The Norton Anthology of English Literature*, vol. 2., pp. 1424-1425.

8. Erwin Schrodinger, *What is Life? with Mind and Matter*, (Cambridge: Cambridge University Press, 1967), pp. 6-7.

9. Julian Huxley, *Evolution in Action*, (London: Chatto & Windus, 1953), p. 15.

10. Fritjof Capra, *The Web of Life* (London: Flamingo, An imprint of Harper Collins, 1970), p. 82.

11. Julian Huxley, *Religion Without Revelation*, p. 21.

12. _____, *Evolution: The Modern Synthesis* (London: George Allen & Unwin,1942 rpt. 1974), p. 574.

IX. "The Whitsun Weddings"

1. Donald Davie, "Landscapes of Larkin," *Thomas Hardy and British Poetry*, (London: Routledge & Kegan Paul, 1972; rpt. 1979), pp. 63-82.

2. A. T. Tolley, *My Proper Ground: A Study of the Work of Philip Larkin*, (Edinburgh: Edinburgh University Press, 1991), p. 95.

3. Philip Larkin, Quoted in Andrew Motion, *Philip Larkin: A Writer's Life* (London: Faber & Faber, 1993; rpt. 1994), pp.287-288.

4. Philip Larkin, Quoted in Harry Chambers (ed.) *An Enormous Yes* (Peterloo Press, 1986), p. 56

5. James Naremore "Philip Larkin's Lost World," *Contemporary Literature*, vol. 15 (1974), pp.331-343.

6. Barbara Everett, "Larkin's Eden," English, vol.32 (1982), pp.41-53.

7. Donald Davie, op. cit., pp64-65.

8. Colvin Bedient, *Eight Contemporary Poets*, (London: Oxford University Press, 1974; rpt. 1975) p. 93.

9. Barbara Everett, op. cit.

10. Nicholas Marsh, *Philip Larkin: The Poems* (Basingstoke & New York: Palgrave Macmillan, 2007), p. 73.

11. John Dewey, *Art as Experience* (London: George Allen & Unwin, 1934), p. 25.

12. John Wain "Engagement or Withdrawal? Some Notes on the Work of Philip Larkin," *Critical Quarterly*, vol. 6. No. 2 (1964), pp. 167-178.

X. "Days"

1. Martin Heidegger, Quoted by Sartre, *Being and Nothingness*, Tr. Hazel E. Barnes (New York: Washington Square Press,1943; rpt. 1992), p. 50.

2. George Bernard Shaw, *John Bull's Other Island*, Act IV (Penguin Books, 1907; rpt. 1984), p. 140.

3. George Santayana, "Ideal Immortality," *Approaches to the Philosophy of Religion*, (eds.) Daniel J. Bronstein and Harold M. Schulweis (N. J.: Prentice Hall, Inc. Englewood Cliffs, 1954; rpt. 1960), pp. 507-518.

4. George Bernard Shaw, *The Doctor's Dilemma*, Act V.

5, Virginia Woolf, *The Years* (Wordsworth Classics, 2012), p. 264.

6. Erwin Schrodinger, op. cit. pp.119-120.

7. Leo Tolstoy, "Did Jesus Believe in Immortality?", *Approaches to the Philosophy of Religion*, pp. 458-464.

8. A. J. Ayer, "Is Religious Knowledge Possible?" *Approaches to the Philosophy of Religion*, pp.110-116.

9. A. N. Whitehead, "Religion in the Making," *Approaches to the Philosophy of Religion*, pp. 64-67.

10. G. G. Simpson, *Biology and Man*, (New York: Harcourt Brace, Ivanovich, 1964; rpt. 1969), p.49.

11. Albert Camus, the Myth of Sisyphus Tr. Justin O Brien (Penguin Books,1955; rpt. 2000), p.13.

XI." Ambulances"

1. A Greek adage, quoted by Will Durant, *The Story of Philosophy (New York; Pocket Books, 1926, rpt. 2006), p. 67..*

2. Doris Lessing, *The Grass is Singing* (London: Fourth Estate, 1950, rpt. 2017), pp. 194-195.

XII. "First Sight"

1. Kingsley Amis, "Farewell to a Friend," (ed.) Dale Salwak, *Philip Larkin: The Man and his Work* (Basingstoke and London: Macmillan, 1989), p. 5.

2. John Press, "Philip Larkin." *Rule and Energy,*(London: Oxford University Press, 1963), p. 105.

3. J. McH. Sinclair, "Taking a Poem to Pieces," (ed.) Roger Fowler, *Essays in Style and Language* (London: Routledge & Kegan Paul, 1966; rpt. 1970), pp.68-81.

4. Albert Camus, *The Myth of Sisyphus*, p. 114.

5. Julian Huxley, *Religion Without Revelation* (London: Ernest Benn Ltd. 1927), p. 277.

6. Ibid., pp. 276-277.

7. Stephen Hawking, *A Brief History of Time*, p.1.

8. Carl Sagan, "Foreword," *A Brief History of Time*, p.ix.

9. Bertolt Brecht, *Mother Courage and Her Children*, Trans. Eric Bentley

(New Delhi: Oxford University Press, rpt. 1999), pp. 69-71 & p. 71.

10. Edward Bond, *Bingo* (London and New York; Methuen, 1974; rpt. 1979) p. 26.

11. _____, Ibid., page not numbered.

12. Naguib Mahfouz, *The Cairo Trilogy* (Cairo: The American University in Cairo Press, 2001), p. 915.

13. William Golding, "The Writer in his Age," Quoted as a preface/an epigraph in *The Art of William Golding* by Bernard S Oldsey & Stanley Weintraub (New York: Harcourt, Brace Inc. 1965).

14. Harold Pinter, *The Homecoming*, (London: Methuen, 1965; rpt. 1976), pp61-62.

15. Mikhail Sholokhov, *And* Quiet *Flows the Don*, Trans. Stephen Garry (Moscow: Progress Publishers,1959; rpt. 1974), vol. II, p. 107.

16. Samuel Butler, *The Way of All Flesh*, (Hertfordshire: Wordsworth Editions Ltd., 1994), pp. 221-222.

17. Ashley Montague, *Man in Progress*, (New York: A Mentor Book, 1962), p. 76.

XIII. "Dockery and Son"

1. Charles Dickens, *Dombey and Son*, (Wordsworth Classics, 1995), p.6.

2. Andrew Motion, *Philip Larkin: A Writer's Life* (London: Faber & Faber, 1993, rpt 1994), p. 333.

3. Kingsley Amis, "Oxford and After," (ed.) Anthony Thwaite, *Larkin at Sixty*, (London: Faber & Faber,1982), p. 26.

4. Barbara Everett, "Larkin's Edens," *English*, vol. 31 (1982), pp41-53.

5. F. Nietzsche, *Birth of Tragedy*, Trans Shaun Whiteside (Penguin Books 1993,rpt. 2003), pp.13 &41.

6. Blake Morrison, *The Movement* (Oxford: Oxford University Press, 1980), p.142.

7. Bertrand Russell, *History of Western Philosophy* (New York: Routledge, 1946; rpt. 2002), p. 138.

8. Blake Morrison, *op. cit.* p. 142.

9. Erwin Schrodinger, *What is Life* with *Mind and Matter?* p. 31.

10. Ibid. p. 41.

11. Samuel Butler, *The Way of All Flesh*, p. 229.

12. John Wain, "The Importance of Philip Larkin," *The American Scholar*, vol. 55, No. 3 (1986), 346-364.

13. Charles Dickens, *Dombey and Son* (Wordsworth Classics, 2002), p. 441.

XIV. "Essential Beauty"

1. Plato, *Symposium, The Dialogues of Plato*, vol. 2, Trans. Benjamin Jowett (London: Sphere Books Ltd. 1970), p. 225.

2. Katherine Anne Porter, "Pale Horse, Pale Rider," *Norton Anthology of World Masterpieces*, vol. II (New York: W. W. Norton & Co., 1956; rpt. 1979), p.1645.

3. Thomas Osborne, "Polarities of Englishness: Larkin, Hughes and national culture," *Critical Quarterly*, vol. 48, no. 1, (2006), pp. 42-65.

4. Martin Bruce, Philip *Larkin*, (Boston: Twyane Publishers, 1978), p. 50.

5. D. H. Lawrence, "How Beastly the Bourgeois Is," *The Norton Anthology of English Literature*, (General ed.) M. H. Abrams (New York: W. W. Norton & Co. 1962; rpt. 1987), PP. 2496-2497.

XV. "An Arundel Tomb"

1. James Booth, *Philip Larkin Writer*, (Hertfordshire : Harvester/ Wheatsheaf, 1992), pp. 146-147.

2. Charles Dickens, *Dombey and Son* (Wordsworth Classics, 2002), p. 359.

3. Albert Camus, *Caligula* and *Cross Purpose*, Trans. Stuart Gilbert (Penguin Books, 1965), pp.162-162.

4. Christopher Ricks, "Lies," *The Force of Poetry* (New York: O. U. P. 1984), p. 380.

5. James Booth, *Philip Larkin: The Poet's Plight* (Basingstoke: Palgrave Macmillan, 2005),p. 118.

6Samuel Richardson, *Pamela* in two vols., vol. I (London: Everyman's Library, rpt. 1986), pp. 402-403.

7. G. M. Trevelyan, *A Shortened History of England* (Pelican edn. 1959), p. 196.
8. *Encyclopedia of Psychology vol.5.* American Psychological Association, Washington (New York: Oxford University Press, 2000), pp.82-87.
9. Christopher Ricks, "Philip Larkin," op. cit. pp 274-284.
10. John Dewey, *Art as Experience* (London; George Allen & Unwin, 1934), p, 34.
11. Will Durant, *The Story of Philosophy (New York: Pocket Books, 1927, rpt. 2006), p. 653.*
12. Ibid. p. 436.

Chapter V: High Windows: Collected Poems

I. "Sympathy in White Major"

1. Barbara Everett, "Philip Larkin: After Symbolism," *Essays in Criticism*, 30 (1980), pp. 227-242.
2. George Hartley, "Nothing is to be Said," *Philip Larkin (1922-1985): A Tribute* (ed.) George Hartley (London: The Marvell Press, 1988), pp. 298-308.
3. Anthony F. C. Wallace, *Religion: An Anthropological View* (New York: Random House, 1966), p. 236.
4. Julian Huxley, *Evolution: The Modern Synthesis* (London: George Allen & Unwin, 1942; rpt. 1974), pp. 575-576.
5. Khalil Gibran, "Song of Man," *The Greatest Works of Khalil Gibran* (Mumbai: Jaico Publishing House, 7th Jaico Impression, 1999), PP. 56-57.
6. Thomas Mann, *The Magic Mountain*, Trans. H. T Lowe-Porter (Penguin Books, 1924, rpt 1971).
7. Ibid.,
8. Julian Huxley, op. cit. p. 575.
9. Fyodor Dostoevsky, *The Karamazov Brothers*, Trans. Constance Garnett (Wordsworth Classics,2010), p. 340.

10. Ibid., p.334.
11. George Hartley, op. cit.

II. "The Trees"

1. Naguib Mahfouz, *The Cairo Trilogy*, Tr. William Maynard Hutchins, et al (Cairo: The American University in Cairo Press, 2001), p. 894.
2. Carl Sagan, *Cosmos*, (London: Futura, Macdonald & Co. 1980; rpt. 1983), p. 49.
3. Henri Bergson, *Creative Evolution*, Tr. Arthur Mitchell (New York: Dover Publications Inc. 1911; rpt. 1998), p. 112.
4. Carl Sagan, *Cosmos*, p.52.
5. Naguib Mahfouz, *The Cairo Trilogy*, p. 1130.
6. Anthony Huxley, *Plant and Planet* (Penguin Books, 1974; rpt. 1978), p. 12.
7. Carl Sagan, *Cosmos*, p. 48.
8-9. Henri Bergson, op. cit. p.106 & pp.105-106.
10. Anthony Huxley, op. cit. p. 77.
11. D. H. Lawrence, *Sons and Lovers* (Delhi: Sahni Publications, 2008), pp. 141-142.
12-13. Anthony Huxley, op. cit. p. 113 & p.105.
14. Quoted In Agnes Arber, *The Natural Philosophy of Plant Form* (London: Cambridge University Press, 1950), p. 158.
15. Agnes Arber, op. cit. p. 200.
16. Anthony Huxley, op. cit. p. 125.
17. Agnes Arber, op. cit. p. 77.
18. Julian Huxley, *Evolution in Action* (London: Chatto & Windus,1953), p. 103.
19. Erwin Schrodinger, *What is Life? with Mind and Matter*, (Cambridge: Cambridge University Press 1944; rpt. 2010), p. 99.
20. William Golding, *Darkness Visible* (London: Faber & Faber, 1979; rpt. 1983), p. 185.
21. Orhan Pamuk, *Snow*, Tr. Maureen Freely (London: Faber & Faber, 2004; rpt. 2005), p. 138.
22. Anthony Huxley, op. cit. p. 59.

23. Fritjof Capra, *The Web of Life*, (London: Flamingo, An Imprint of Harper Collins Publishers, 1997), pp208-209.

24-25. Naguib Mahfouz, op. cit. pp. 950 & 1310.

26. Agnes Arber, op. cit. pp. 158-159.

27. Ibid., pp. 199-200.

28. Agnes Arber, op. cit. p. 203.

29. Anthony Huxley, op. cit. p. 1.

30. F. Nietzsche, *Thus Spoke Zarathustra*, Tr. Walter Kaufmann (London: Penguin Books, 1892; rpt. 1978), p. 17.

31. Samuel Beckett, *Waiting For Godot*, (London: Faber & Faber, 1956; rpt.2006), p. 1.

III. "Livings"

1. Richard Hoggart, "Contemporary Critical Studies," *Contemporary Criticism* (eds.) Malcolm Bradbury and David Palmer (London: Edward Arnold,1970; rpt. 1979), p. 163.

2. H. G. Wells, *A Short History of the World* (London & Glasgow; Collins, 1922; rpt. 1965), pp.316-317 & p. 318.

3. Barbara Everett, "Philip Larkin: After Symbolism," *Essays in Criticism*, vol. 30 (1980), pp.227-242.

4. Geoffrey leech, *A Linguistic Guide to English Poetry* (London; Longman, 1969), p. 186.

5. John Wain , "The Importance of Philip Larkin," *The American Scholar*, vol. 55 No. 3 (1986), pp.. 349-364.

6. *The New Caxton Encyclopedia*, (London: The Caxton Publishing Co., 1977), p.1234.

7. Thomas Mann, *The Magic Mountain*, Trans. H. T. Lowe-Porter (Penguin Books 1924; rpt. 1971), pp. 369-370.

IV. "Forget What Did"

1. W. H. Auden, *Poems* selected by Roy Fuller (London: Faber & Faber, 2000; rpt. 2005), p. 92.

2. Francois Mauriac, "A Man of Letters," Tr. Huntley Patterson, *Great Short Stories by Nobel Prize Winners* (eds.) Leo Hamalian and Emond L. Volpe (New Delhi: Rupa Publications, 1950; rpt. 2012), p. 308.
3. Anthony Huxley, *Plant and Planet*, p.102.
4. Walpola Sir Rahula, *What the Buddha Taught*, p. 25.
5. William Faulkner, *The Town* (London: Chatto & Windus, 1957; rpt. 1979), p.80.

VI. "High Windows"

1. Barbara Everett, "Philip Larkin: After Symbolism," *Philip Larkin* (ed.) Stephen Regan (Basingstoke & London: Macmillan, 1997), pp. 55-70.
2. Ibid.
3. Ibid.
4. William Golding, *Darkness Visible* (London: Faber & Faber, 1979; rpt. 1983), pp136-138.
5. D. H. Lawrence, *Sons and Lovers* (Delhi: Sahni Publications, 2008), p.323.
6. Henry James, *The Europeans* (Penguin Modern Classics, 1878; rpt.1964), p. 154.
7. Stephen Hawking, *A Brief History of Time*, p. 9.
8. Ibid., p. 134.
9. Ibid., pp. 38-39.
10. Ibid., p. 39.
11. Ibid., p. 43.
12. D. H. Lawrence, *Women In Love* (London: Heinemann, 1921; rpt. 1966), p.469.
13. Jean-Paul Sartre, *What is Literature?* (London: Routledge, 1950; rpt. 1993), p. 171.
14. G. G. Simpson, *Biology and Man*, p. 45.
15. Sir James Frazer, *The Golden Bough* (Hertfordshire: Wordsworth Editions Ltd.,1993), p.362- 63
16. William James, *The Principles of Psychology* (Encyclopaedia Britannica Inc. 1890; rpt. 1977), p.189.

17. Ibid., p. 191.

18. D. H. Lawrence, *Lady Chatterley's Lover* (New York: Signet Classic, New American Library, 1962), p. 259.

VII. "The Old Fools"

1. Samuel Beckett, *Waiting for* Godot, p. 73.
2. Erwin Schrodinger, op. cit. p. 136.
3. Dylan Thomas, "Do Not Go Gentle into That Good Night," *The Norton Anthology of English 3iterature*, vol. 2. III edition, (Gen. ed.) M. H. Abrams (New York: W. W. Norton Co. Inc.,1962;rpt. 1974), pp. 2368-2369.
4. Hall Summers, "My Old Cat," *The Nation's Favourite Twentieth Century Poems* (ed.) Rhys Jones (London: B. B. C. Worldwide, 1999), p. 34.
5. John Wain, *Professing Poetry*, p. 162.

VII. "The Card-Players"

1. Julian Huxley, *Religion Without Revelation* (London: Ernest Benn Ltd., 1927), pp. 354-356
2. _____, *The Uniqueness of Man* (London: Chatto & Windus, 1941), p. 8.
3. Jean-Paul Sartre, *Nausea*, Trans. Robert Baldick (Penguin Books, 1938, rpt. 1967), pp. 35-36.
4. Bharata, *Natyasastra*, Trans. Adya Rangacharya (New Delhi: Munshi-ram Manoharlal, 1084, rpt.2019), pp. 55 &61.

VIII. "The Building"

1. Erwin Schrodinger, *What is Life* with *Mind and Matter?*, p. 129.

IX. "Sad Steps"

1. Seamus Heaney, "The Main of Light," *Larkin at Sixty*, (ed.) Anthony Thwaite (London; Faber & Faber, 1983), pp. 132-133.
2. Ibid. p.133.
3. Charles Dickens, *Dombey and Son*, Wordsworth Edition, 2002), pp. 10 & 86.
4. Ronald Barthes, *S / Z*, Trans. Richard Micler (London: Jonathan Cape, 1970, rpt. 1975), p. 24.
5. Encyclopedia Americana, vol. (New York: Americana Corpn, 1829, rpt. 1966).
6. Edward Burnett Tylor, Religion in Primitive Culture, vol. II (New York: Harper & Brothers, 1958), p. 386.
7. Ibid. p. 385. 8. Ibid. p. 388. 9. Ibid.P. 389.

X. "Solar"

1. Seamus Heaney, "The Main Of Light," *Larkin as Sixty*, p. 133.
2. Andrew Swarbrick, *Out of Reach: The Poetry of Philip Larkin* (London; Macmillan, 1995), p. 146.
3. Quoted by Ralph T. H. Griffith, *Hymns of the Rig Veda* Vol. I The Chowkhamba Sanskrit Series: Varanasi, 4th edition, 1963, p. 390.
4. S. Radhakrishnan, *The Principal Upanishads* (New Delhi: Harper Collins, 1944, rpt. 2000), p. 299.
5. Edward Burnett Tylor, *Religion in Primitive Culture*, Vol. II. pp. 378-379.
6. Sir James Frazer, *The Golden Bough* (author's own abridgement of the original book in 12 vols. Wordsworth Editions Ltd. 1993), pp.358, 384, 105 and 104.
7. Ibid. p.79. 8.Ibid. p. 551.
8. *Encyclopedia Americana*, vol. 26 (New York: Americana Corpn. 1829, rpt. 1966), p. 29.
9. *Ibid.* p. 29.
10. Fred Hoyle, *The Nature of the Universe*. (New York: New American

Library, 1950, rpt. 1960), pp. 32-33.

11. Ibid. p. 55.

12. Stephen Hawking, *A Brief History of Time* (London: Bantam Books, 1988), pp. 86-87.

13. William Golding, *A Moving Target* (London: Faber& Faber, 1984), p. 213.

14. Paul Amos Moody, *Introduction to Evolution* (New York : Harper & Row, 1953, rpt. 1970) pp. 116-117.

15. Carl Sagan, *Cosmos* (London: Macdonald & Co. 1981, rpt. 1983), pp. 48-49.

XI. "Vers de Societe"

1. G. G. Simpson, *Biology and Man*, pp. 60-61.
2. Rev. Walpola Sri Rahula, *What the Buddha Taught*, p. 69.
3. Jalaluddin B. Rumi, *The Essential Rumi*, Trans. Coleman Barks (Penguin Classics, rpt. 2006).
4. G. G. Simpson, op. cit. p. 148.
5. Khalil Gibran, op. cit. p. 349.
6. Jean-Paul Sartre, *Being and Nothingness*, p. 45.
7. Rumi, op. cit.

XII. "The Explosion"

1. John Cary, "The Two Philip larkins," (ed.) James Booth, *New Larkins for Old* (Basingstoke: Palgrave, 2001), pp.57-58.
2. John Wain, "The Poetry of Philip Larkin," *Professing Poetry* (London: Macmillan, 1977), pp. 167 & 168.
3. George Orwell, *The Road to Wigan Pier* (London: Secker & Warburg, 1937, rpt. 1973), p. 34.
4. Ibid. p. 34. 5. Ibid. p. 45. 6. Ibid. p. 46. 7. Ibid. p. 48.
5. John Cary, op. cit. p. 58.
6. John Wain, op. cit. p. 168

CHAPTER VI CONCLUSION

1. Anton Chekhov, *Three Sisters, Modern Drama* (ed.) Anthony Caputi (New York: W. W. Norton & Inc., 1966), pp.121-122.

2. Herodotus, *Histories,*

3. Erwin Arlington Robinson, "Zola," *Anthology of Modern American Literature II. Realism to the Present,* (ed.) George Mc Michael (New York: Macmillan Publishing Co., 1974; rpt. 1985), 975.

4. Wallace Stevens, "Of Modern Poetry," *Anthology of American Literature II. Realism to the Present,* pp. 1262-1263.

5. Julian Huxley, *Evolution in Action,* p.14.

6. Thom Gunn, "Considering the Snail," *The Faber Book Of Modern Verse,* (ed.) Michael Roberts (London; Faber & Faber, 1936; rpt. 1979), pp. 395-396.

7. A. K. Ramanujan, "The Striders," *Selected Poems* (Delhi: Oxford University Press, 1976; rpt. 1983), p.1.

8. E. E. Cummings, ["so many selves (so many fiends and gods)"], *Anthology of American Literature Ii. Realism to the Present,* p. 1222.

9. Walt Whitman, "We Two, How Long We Were Fool'd," *Leaves of Grass* (New York: Bantam Classic, 2004), p. 92.

BIBLIOGRAPHY

Abbreviations: 1. (TNotU): *The Nature of the Universe* 2. (TMoE): *The Meaning of Evolution* 3. (AMYoM) *A Million Years of Man* 4. (MohN): *Man on his Nature* 5. (TI) *The inheritors* 6. (RW) *Required Writing*

A Greek adage, quoted by Will Durant, *The Story of Philosophy* (New York: Pocket Books, 1926, rpt, 2006).

Amis, Kingsley, "Oxford and After"(ed.) Anthony Thwaite, *Larkin at Sixty* (London: Faber & Faber, 1962).

_____, "Farewell to a Friend" (ed.) Dale Salwak, *Philip Larkin: The Man and his Work* (Basingstoke: & London: Macmillan 1989).

Anne, Katherine Porter, "Pale Horse, Pale Rider," *Norton Anthology of World Masterpieces*, II (New York: W. W. Norton & Co. 1956, rpt. 1979).

Arber, Agnes, *The Natural Philosophy of Plant Form* (London: Cambridge University Press, 1950).

Arnold, Matthew, "The Function of Criticism," T*he Norton Anthology of English Literature. 5th edition: The Major Authors* (General ed.) M. H. Abrams (New York: W. W. Norton & Co. 1986).

_____, "The Study of Poetry," *The Norton Anthology of English Literature*, vol. Ii. (General ed.) M.H. Abrams (New York; W.W. Norton & Co., 1962,rpt. 1974).

Auden, W. H. "Address to the Beasts," *W. H. Auden Poems selected by John Fuller* (London: Faber& Faber, 2000, rpt. 2005).

Ayer, A. J. , "Is Religious Knowledge Possible?'*Approaches to the Philosophy of Religion*, (eds) J Bronstein and Harold M Schulweis (Englewood Cliffs NJ: Prentice Hall Inc. 1954, rpt. 1960).

Barthes, Ronald, *S/Z*, Trans. Richard Micler (London: Jonathan Cape,1970 rpt.1975)

Beckett, Samuel, *Waiting for Godot* (London, Faber 1956; rpt Dorling Kindersley India Pvt. Ltd. 2006).

Bedient, Colvin, "Philip Larkin," *Eight Contemporary Poets* (London: O.U.P. 1974, rpt. 1975),

Bellow, Saul, *Humboldt's Gift* (New York: Avon Books 1973; rpt 1976).

_____, *Herzog* (Penguin Books, 1964, rpt 1976).

_____, *Mr Sammler's Planet* (Delhi: Universal Book Stall, 1969, rpt. 1970)

_____, *Henderson the Rain King* (Penguin Books, 1959, rpt.1975).

Bergson, Henri, *Creative Evolution*, Trans. Arthur Mitchell (New York: Dover Publications, 1911, rpt. 1998).

Betjeman, John, "Slough," (ed.) Rhys Jones, *The Nation's Twentieth Century Favourite Poems* (London: BBC & Co. 1999).

Bharata, *Natyasastra*, Trans. Adya Rangacharya (New Delhi: Munshiram Manoharlal, 1984, rpt. 2019)

Bond, Edward, *Bingo* (London & New York: Methuen 1974; rpt. 1979).

Booth, James, *Philip Larkin Writer* (Hertfordshire: Harvester/ Wheatsheaf 1992).

_____, *Philip Larkin: The Poet's* Plight (Basingstoke: Palgrave Macmillam, 2005).

Brecht, Bertolt, *Mother Courage and her Children*, Trans Eric Bentley (Delhi: O.U.P.rpt 1999)

Bruce, Martin, *Philip Larkin* (Boston: Twyane Publishers, 1978).

Camus, Albert, "Nobel Prize Acceptance Speech," *Nobel Prize Library: Published under the sponsorship of Nobel Foudation & Swedish Academy* (New York & California: C. R. M. Publishing).

_____, *The Myth of Sisyphus*, Trans. Justin O'Brien (Penguin Books, 1955, rpt. 2000).

_____, *Caligula and Cross Purpose*, Trans. Stuart Gilbert (Penguin

Books, 1965).

Capra, Fritjof, *The Web of Life* (London: Flamingo, 1970)

Chekhov, Anton, *Three Sisters, Modern Drama* (ed.) Anthony Caputi (New York: W. W. Norton Inc. 1966)

Cohen, M. R., Quoted by G. G. Simpson as epigraph to Part I of his *Meaning of Evolution*

Conrad, Joseph, "The Shadow-Line," *Three Sea Stories* (Wordsworth Classics, 1998)..

Cummings, E. E. , ["so many selves (so many fiends and gods)"], *Anthology of American Literature vol. Ii Realism to the Present* (ed.) George Mc Michael (New York: Macmillan Publishing Co. 1974, rpt. 1985)

Dalrymple, G Brent, *The Age of the Earth* (Stanford, California: Stanford University Press, 1991, rpt.2001).

Davie, Donald, *Thomas Hardy and British Poetry* (London: Routledge & Kegan Paul 1970, rpt 1979)

Davis, Gary A, "Training Creativity in Adolescents<" *Studies in Adolescence*, (ed.) Robert E Grinder (London: The Macmillan Co. 1963, rpt.1970

Dewey, John, *Art as Experience* (London: George Allen & Unwin, 1934).

Dickens, Charles, *Dombey and Son*, (Wordsworth Classics, 1995).

Dostoevsky, Fyodor, *The Karamazov Brothers* trans Constance Garnett (Wordsworth Classics, 2010)

Durant Will, *The Story of Philosophy* (New York: Pocket Books, 1927, rpt 2006).

Durkheim, Emile, *Elementary Forms of Religious Life* Trans. Joseph Ward Swain (London: George Allen & Unwin, 1915).

Eliot, T. S. "Love Song of J. Alfred Prufrock," *Anthology of American Literature*, vol.Ii (General ed.) George Michael (New York: Macmillan Publishing,1974 rpy. 1985).

Encyclopedia of Psychology, vol.I (Editor-in-chief) Alan E Kazdin, American Psychological Association (New York: O.U.P. 2000).

Everett, Barbara, "Larkin and Dockery: Limits of the Social," *Philip Larkin (1922-1985); A Tribute,*(ed.) George Hartley London: The Marvell Press, 1988).

_____, "Larkin's Eden," *English*, vol. 32 (1982).

_____, Philip Larkin: After Symbolism," *Essays in Criticism*, 30 (1980).

Faulkner, William, *The Town* (London: Chatto& Windus, 1957, rpt. 1970).

Fitzerald, Scott, *This Side of Paradise* (Penguin Books, 1920, rpt. 1963).

Frazer, Sir James *The Golden Bough* (Hertfordshire: Wordsworth Editions Ltd. 1993).

Freud, Sigmund, *The Future of an Illusion*, Trans. James Strachey (New York; W. W. Norton & Co. 1961)

Gibran, Khalil, *The Greatest Works of Khalil Gibran* (Mumbai: Jaico Publishing, 7ᵗʰ Jaico Impression, 1999).

Golding, William, *Darkness Visible* (London: Faber & Faber, 1979, rpt.1983).

_____, *A Moving Target* (London, Faber & Faber,1984}.

_____, "Fable," *The Hot Gates* (London: Faber & Faber,1965, rpt. 1974).

_____, *Lord of the Flies* (Penguin Books, 1954, rpt. 1967).

_____, *The Inheritors* (London: Faber & Faber, 1955).

_____, "The Scorpion God," *Three Short Novels* (London: Faber & Faber,1971, rpt. 1973).

_____, "The Writer in his Age," Quoted in Bernard S Oldsey & Stanley Weintraub, *The Art of William Golding* (New York: Harcourt Brace Inc. 1965).

Goode, J. "The More Deceived: A Reading of 'Deceptions'" *Philip Larkin(1922-1985): A Tribute*, (ed.) George Hartley.

Greene , Graham, *The Comedians* (Penguin Books, 1966, rpt. 1967).

Gunn, Thom, "Considering the Snail," *The Faber Book of Modern Verse* (ed.) Michael Roberts (London: Faber & Faber, 1936, rpt. 1979).

Haldane, J. B. S. *Causes of Evolution* (Princeton: Princeton University Press, 1932, rpt. 1993).

Hamilton, Ian, "Four Coversations," *London Magazine* IV (Nov.1964).

Hartley, Jean, *Philip Larkin's Hull and East Yorkshire* (Hull: The Philip Larkin Society, 1995, rpt. 2005)

Harari, Yuval Noah, *Sapiens: A Brief Hiatory of Humankind* (Penguin Books 2014;rpt. 2015).

Hawking, Stephen, *A Brief History of Time* (London: Bantam Books, 1988, rpt. 1989).

Heaney, Seamus, "The Main of Light," *Larkin at Sixty* (ed.) Anthony Thwaite London: Faber & Faber, 1982).

Heidegger, Martin, *Existence and Being*, Trans. Werner Brock (London: WI Vision Press Ltd.)

——————, *Poetry, Language, Thought*, Trans. Albert Hofstadter (New York: Harper Row Publishers, 1971).

Heisenberg, Werner, *Physics and Philosophy* (Penguin Books, 1958; rpt. 2000).

Hoggart, Richard, "Contemporary Critical Studies," *Contemporary Criticism* (eds.) Malcolm Bradbury and

Donald Palmer (London: Edward Arnold, 1970 rpt. 1979).

Herodotus, *Th Histiries*

Hoyle, Fred, *The Nature of the Universe*, A Mentor Book (New York: The New York American Library, 1955, rpt 1960).

Huxley, Anthony , *Plant and Planet* (Penguin Books, 1974,rpt. 1978).

Huxley, Julian, *Evolution in Action* (London: Chatto & Windus, 1953).

——————, *Evolution: The Modern Synthesis* (London: George Allen & Unwin, 1942, rpt. 1974).

——————, *Religion Without Revelation* (London: Max Parish, 1936, rpt 1957).

——————, *The Uniqueness of Man* (London: Chatto & Windus, 1941).

Huysmans, J. K. *Against Nature*, Trans. Robert Baldick (Penguin Books, 1884, rpt. 1959).

James, Henry, *The Europeans* (Penguin Modern Classics, 1878, rpt. 1964).

James, William, *The Principles of Psychology* (Encyclopaedia Britannica Inc., 1890, rpy. 1977).

——————, *Varieties of Religious Experience* (New York: The Modern Library,2002).

Kafka, Franz, *The Trial*, Trans. Willa and Edwin Muir (London: Vintage Classics, 1925, rpt b1999).

King, R. P. "Without Illusion: The Poetry of Philip Larkin,' *Nine Contemporary Poets* (London: Methuen, 1979).

Larkin, Philip, "Not the Place's Fault," *An Enormous Yes*, (ed.) Harry Chambers (Peterloo Press, 1986).

_____, *Required Writing* (London: Faber& Faber, 1983, rpt. 1984).

_____, *The Less Deceived, Collected Poems*, (ed.) Anthony Thwaite (London: Faber & Faber,1988, ebook edition, 2014).

_____, *The Whitsun Weddings* (London; Faber& Faber, 1964, rpt. 1979).

_____, *High Windows* (London: Faber & Faber 1974, rpt. 1988)

Lawrence, D. H. "How Beastly the Bourgeois Is," *The Norton Anthology of English Literature* (General ed.) M. H. Abrams (New York; W. W. Norton & Co. 1962, rpt. 1987).

_____,*Lady Chatterley's Lover* (New York: Signet Classics, New American Library, 1962).

_____, *Sons and Lovers* (Delhi: Sahni Publications, 2008).

_____, *Women in Love* (London: Heinemann, 1921, rpt. 1966).

_____, "Work," *Modern Poems*, (ed.) Michael Thorpe (London: O. U. P. 1963, rpt.1969).

Leech, Geoffrey, *A Linguistic Guide to English Poetry* (London: Longman, 1969).

Lessing Doris, *The Grass is Singing* (London: Fourth Estate, 1950, rpt. 2017).

Lodge, David, "Philip Larkin; The Metonymic Muse," (ed.) Dale Salwak, *Philip Larkin: The Man and His Work* (Basingstoke: The Macmillan Press, 1989).

"Love," *Encyclopedia of Psychology* vol. 5. American Psychological Association (New York: O.U.P., 2000).

Mahfouz, Naguib, *The Cairo Trilogy*, Trans. William Maynard Hutchins et al (Cairo: American University in Cairp Press, 2001).

Mann, Thomas, *Magic Mountain* , Trans. H. T. Lowe-Porter (Penguin Books, 1924, rpt. 1971).

Marsh, Nicholas, *Philip Larkin: The Poems* (Basingstoke & New York: Palgrave Macmillan, 2007)

Mauriac, Francois, "A Man of Letters," Trans. Huntley Patterson. *Great Short Stories by Nobel Prize Winners* (eds.) Leo Hamalian and Emond

L Volpe (New Dehi: Rupa Publications, 1950, rpt.2012).

Montague, Ashley, *Man in Progress* (New York: A Mentor Book, 1962).

Moody, Paul Amos, *Introduction to Evolution* (New York: Harper & Row, 1953, rpt. 1970)

Morrison, Blake, *The Movement* (Oxford: O.U.P. 1980).

Motion, Andrew, *Philip Larkin: A Writer's Life* (London: Faber & Faber,1993,rpt. 1994).

Naremore, James, "Philip Larkin's Lost World<" *Contemporary Literature*, vol. XV (1974).

Nietzsche, Friedrich, *Birth of Tragedy*, Trans. Shaun Whiteside (Penguin Books, 1993).

_____, *Thus Spoke Zarathustra* Trans. Walter Kaufmann (Penguin Books, 1892, rpt.1978)

O'Neill, Eugene, *The Hairy Ape* in *Five Plays* (Penguin Books, 1970).

Oparin, A. I., *Genesis and Evolutionary Development of Life*, Trans. Eleanor Mass (New York & London: Academic Press, 1968).

Orwell, George, *Keep the Aspidistra Flying* (London: Martin Secker & Warburg, 1936,rpt. 1973).

_____, *The Road to Wigan Pier* (London: Secker & Warburg,1937, rpt. 1973).

Osborne, Thomas, " Polarities of Englishness :Larkin, Hughes and national culture," *Critical Quarterly* vol. 48, no, I (2006).

Palgrave's Golden Treasury (London: O.U.P. 1897, rpt 1966).

Pamuk Orhan , *Snow*, Trans. Maureen Freely (London: Faber & Faber, 2004, rpt. 2005).

Petch, Simon, *The Art of Philip Larkin* (Sydney: Sydney University Press, 1981).

Peter, John, "The Fables of Philip Larkin," *Kenyon Review*, vol. XIV (1957).

Pinter, Harold, *Homecoming* (London: Methuen, 1965,rpt. 1976).

Pirandello, Luigi, *Six Characters in Search of an Author*, Trans. Anthony Mortimer (Oxford: O.U.P.,2014).

Plato, *Symposium, The Dialogues of Plato*, vol. 2. Trans. Benjamin Jowett (London: Sphere Books Ltd.,1970),

Press, John, "Philip Larkin," *Rule and Energy* (London; O.U.P.,1963).

Radhakrishnan, S. .*The Principal Upanisads* (New Delhi: Harper Collinc, 1944, rpt. 2000).

Rahula, Walpola Sir, *What the Buddha Taught* (Oxford: One World Publications, 1959, rpt. 2007).

Ramanujan, A. K. "The Striders," *Selected Poems* (Delhi: Oxford: University Press, 1976, rpt. 1983).

Richardson, Samuel, *Pamela*, vol.1 (London; Everyman's Library, 1986).

Ricks, Christopher, *The Force of Poetry* (New York: O.U.P. 1984).

Robinson, Edwin Arlington, "Zola," *Anthology of American Literature, vol. Ii Realism to the Present*

Rosenthal, M. L. , *The New Poets; American and British Poets since World War I* (New York: O.U.P, 1967,rpt. 1970).

Rossen, Janice, *Philip Larkin: His Life's Work* (Hertfordshire; Wheatsheaf Harvester, 1989).

Rumi, Jalaluddin B, *The Essential Rumi*, Trans. Coleman Barks (Penguin Classics, rpt. 2006).

Russell, Bertrand, *History of Western Philosophy* (New York: Routledge, 1046,rpt. 2002).

Sagan, Carl, *Cosmos* (London; Abascus, 1980, rpt. 1995).

_____, "Foreword," *A Brief History of Time*.

Sagar, Keith, "Philip Larkin," *Criticism in Action*, (ed.) Maurice Hussey (London; Longman, 1969).

Santayana, George, "Ideal Immortality," Daniel J Bronstein & Harold M Schulweis (eds.), *Approaches to the Philosophy of Religion*.

Sartre, Jean-Paul, *Being and Nothingness*, Trans. Hazel E Barnes, (New York: Washington Square Press, 1942, rpt. 1992).

_____, *What Is Literature?* Trans. Brenard Fretchman (London: Routledge,1948, rpt. 1995).

_____, *Nausea*, Trans. Robert Baldick (Penguin Books, 1935, rpt.1967).

Schrodinger, Erwin, *What Ia Life? with Mind and Matter* (Cambridge: Cambridge University Press, 1958, rpt. 2010).

Shaw, G.B. *The Doctor's Dilemma*, Act V.

_____, *John Bull's Other Island*, (Penguin Books,1907, rpt. 1984).

_____, *Major Barbara*, The Norton Anthology of English literature, vol.2 (General ed.) M. H. Abrams (New York: W. W. Norton & Co. 1962; rpt. 1974).

Sherrington, Sir Charles, *Man on his Nature* (Cambridge: At the University Press, 1963).

Sholokhov, Mikhail, *And Quiet Flows the Don*, vol.II. Trans. Stephen Garry (Moscow: Progress Publishers, 1959,rpt. 1974).

Simpson, G. G. , *The Meaning of Evolution* (1949, Yale University Press; Indian Publication: Oxford & I.B.H. Publication, Calcutta, 1965).

_____, *Biology and Man* (New York: Harcourt Brace 1964; rpt. 1969).

Sinclair, J. McH, "Taking a Poem to Pieces," *Essays in Style and language* (ed.) Roger Fowler (London: Routledge & Kegan Paul, 1966, rpt. 1970).

Skinner, John, "Philip Larkin by Philip Larkin," *Ariel*, vol. 20 (Jan 1989).

Smith, Homer W,, *From Fish to Philosopher* (Boston: Little, Brown & Co. 1953).

Stevens, Wallace, "Of Modern Poetry," *Anthology of American Literature, vol. II, Realism to the Present*

Swarbrick, Andrew, *The Whitsun Weddings and The Less Deceived* (Basingstoke: Palgrave Macmillan, 1986).

_____, *Out of Reach: The Poetry of Philip Larkin* (London: Macmillan, 1995).

The New Caxton Encyclopedia (London; The Caxton Publishing Co. 1977).

Thomas, Dylan, "Do Not Go Gentle into That Good Night," *The Norton Anthology of English Literature*, vol.2.

Tolley, A. T. , *My Proper Ground: A Study of the Work of Philip Larkin* (Edinburgh: Edinburgh University Press, 1991).

Tolstoy, Leo, "Did Jesus Believe in Immortality," *Approaches to the Philosophy of Religion.*

_____,"A Reply to the Synod's Edict of Excommunication," *Religion from Tolstoy to Camus* (ed.) Walter Kaufmann (New Brunswick, U.S.A. :1961, rpt. 1994), pp131-132.

Trelyan, G. M., *A Shortened History of England* (Pelican edn., 1959).

Trotter, David, *The Making of the Reader* (London & Basingstoke: Macmillan, 1984).

Tylor, Edward Burnett, *Religion in Primitive Culture* (New York: Harper & Brothers, 1958).

Wain, John, "The Importance Of Philip Larkin<' *The American Scholar*, vol. 55, no.3 (1986).

_____, "Engagement or Withdrawal? Notes on the Work of Philip Larkin," *Critical Quarterly*, Vol.6, no.2 (1964).

_____, "The Poetry of Philip Larkin," *Professing Poetry* (London: Macmillan , 1977).

Wallace, Anthony F. C., *Religion: An Anthropological View* (New York: Random House, 1966).

Weinberg, Stephen, *The First Three Minutes* (New York: Basic Books, A Member of the Perseus Books Group, 1977, rpt 1993).

Wells, H. G. *A Short History of the World* (London & Glasgow: Collins, 1922, rpt. 1965).

Whalen, Terry, *Philip Larkin and English Poetry* (Hongkong: Macmillan, 1986).

Whitehead, A. N., "Religion in the Making," *Approaches to the Philosophy of Religion.*

Whitman, Walt, "We Two, How Long We Were Fool'd," *Leaves of Grass* (New York; Bantam Classics, 2004).

Widdowson, H. G. "Here," *The Edinburgh Course in Linguistics, vol.3* (eds.) J.P.B. Aiien & S. Pit Corder (London: O.U.P., 1974).

_____, "The Conditional Presence of Mr Bleaney," *Language and literature* (ed.) Donald Carter (London: George Allen & Unwin, 1982).

Woolf, Virginia, *The Years* (Wordsworth Classics, 2012).

THE END